OTHER BOOKS
BY MADHU BAZAZ WANGU

Fiction

The Other Shore:
Ordinary People Grappling with
Extraordinary Challenges

The Last Suttee

The Immigrant Wife:
Her Spiritual Journey

Chance Meetings:
Cross-Cultural Karmic Collisions
and Compassion

Non-Fiction

Images of Indian Goddesses

A Goddess is Born

Hinduism

Buddhism

Unblock YOUR CREATIVE FLOW

12 Months of Mindfulness for Writers and Artists

MADHU BAZAZ WANGU

Year of the Book
135 Glen Avenue
Glen Rock, Pennsylvania

ISBN: 978-1-64649-320-3 (paperback)
ISBN: 978-1-64649-317-3 (hardback)
ISBN: 978-1-64649-322-7 (e-book)

Library of Congress Cataloging Number: 2023903961

❧ CONTENTS ☙

BLOSSOMING

ᝌ Introduction ᝍ

Innumerable individuals desire to create. They begin a project with gusto, but when the initial enthusiasm dissipates, they find it difficult to continue and they give up. Most never go back to the project that they had intended to complete. This book is for those who want to create, to begin writing, painting, or making art, but have stopped because their desire to do so was doused or discouraged for some reason. It is also for those who occasionally write or make art but need daily motivation and encouragement, or those who cannot focus or who feel blocked. And last but not least, it is for those who write or paint occasionally but dream of publishing a book or having a one-person show and blossoming as an author or an artist.

For the sake of clarity, I have used the words "writer" and "writing," but if you have passion to paint, sing, play a musical instrument and so on, you could replace those words with any creative activity.

In this volume I will introduce you to the braided practices of meditation, journaling, writing, reading, and walking in nature which I call Writing Meditation Practice (WMP). You may follow WMP any day of the year to get inspired to realize your dream of seeing your ideas, thoughts, and feelings gather shape into a story, essay, poem, or book. The art of writing is a rational, logical process that adheres to certain rules. But it is also an intuitive act that progresses nonlinearly as the work-in-progress unfolds. WMP will hone the fluidity of creativity as much as refine the logical side of writing.

Coaxing the muse to arrive is not easy. But with WMP you can write for hours at a time without censoring or curtailing what needs to be said. For this you need courage, determination, and patience. Otherwise, the initial enthusiasm may fizzle out. With practice, your mindset will change.

When we are born, we are given a body that breathes, a heart that feels, and a mind that thinks. Together they make up a unique person—our whole self. We are typically taught to pay attention to what is outside us, the practical and concrete. We take our intuitive abilities and gut feelings for granted and ignore their inner whispers. They atrophy by the time we become adults. The cohesion of senses, thoughts, and feelings with which we are born goes dormant. However, WMP activates the dormant self that requires waking up. Why? Because our integrated inner self – our Authentic Self – is the source of creativity and spirituality.

WMP can also help you to cultivate mindfulness and live a peaceful life. Mindfulness can be discovered in the same way Isaac Newton discovered gravity. Gravity was there all along, but Newton brought it to our attention. His insight enriched our view of the world. Similarly, mindfulness makes us aware of the wholeness of our body, heart, and mind. Integrated together, these awaken our Authentic Self.

Like gravity, your Authentic Self is always with you, but you are not aware of it. You need to pay attention to it, experience it. Once you are linked with it, the magic begins! Your Authentic Self helps you elevate your creative skills and ennobles your life. Each morning, as you open this book, a breathing exercise and an inspiration will greet you, followed by a prompt that will motivate you to journal. At the end of the year you will be surprised to see that you have learned to meditate. At the end of this volume are suggested links to meditations for writers. Each meditation invites you to go within, to breathe slowly and deeply and feel invigorated and spirited for the rest of the day. Together these disciplines will cultivate and hone mindfulness within you and around you.

HOW IT ALL BEGAN

The seed of Writing Meditation Practice was sown in the early 1990s, when I taught *Symbolism in Buddhist and Hindu Art* to college students in Massachusetts and Pennsylvania. In class, I used images of the Buddha meditating in different postures and at different life events. My curiosity about meditation practice led me to research the practice further (more about this in Month 3). My husband and I enjoyed walking in nature, and I journaled occasionally. But by 2000, my daily routine combined meditation, journaling, and walking. Practicing them together had a magical effect on my writing and living. My attention span lengthened, my word-count increased, and my ideas and insights about the work in progress upsurged. Relationships with family and friends that were previously genuine and warm developed a depth that was new to me. Some relationships that had not felt authentic became diluted and ultimately fizzled out. I learned to let go of unnecessary burdens, both material and mental. I stopped focusing my energy on the things that did not matter or were not meaningful to me. This decreased mental static brought clarity to my writing voice and authenticity to day-to-day living.

At writing conferences and workshops, I met novice as well as professional writers. Most of them were facing impediments in their writing lives. They said how new ideas floated in their heads, but they did not have time to sit still and turn them into words. Some had family obligations. As caregivers, whatever little time they had left after a full-time job was taken by those responsibilities. A few advanced writers shared stories about incomplete drafts or completed ones waiting on a shelf to be revised and readied as final manuscripts. It seemed that life's hindrances, writer's block and, most commonly, the inability to find a chunk of time to write daily, was keeping them from changing their dream into reality. The scenario compelled me to share my routine of meditation, journaling, and walking (which I had not yet formalized as a practice) with whoever was craving to write but was unable to do so for some reason or other.

Daily discipline is fundamental. We can't wait for the time to come to us; we must make time. We can't wait to be in a good or right mood to begin writing. When our body and mind function harmoniously, we can find time (whether 30 minutes or several hours) even when distractions surround us. We must learn to change our frame of mind and just begin. As Pearl S. Buck once said, "I don't wait for moods. You accomplish nothing if you do that. Your mind must know it has to get down to work."

MEDITATION AND MINDFULNESS

I moved to Pittsburgh with my husband and our older daughter in 1974. I was working as a professional artist. In our adopted city I continued to have yearly one-person shows, yet I was unfulfilled. I felt I was unable to express all what I was feeling through the medium of painting.

One of Paul Gauguin's paintings entitled, "Where do we come from? What are we? Where are we going?" particularly resonated with me. To these questions I added some of my own – why do humans have an urge to create? Why was the subject matter of world art primarily religious until the twentieth century? Could I understand art that depicted themes from other religions without knowing anything about those religions? The recurring questions motivated me to pursue a doctoral degree in the Phenomenology of Religion.

Through my doctoral studies I learned that world religious arts and literature have a rich symbolic language. What lay women and men see in sacred images, seers, sages, and yogis experience these symbols in the inner silence of meditation. My master's thesis (*Symbolism in Visual Arts*) helped me understand that the unknown can become known through symbols. Teaching *Visual Arts and Asian Religions* made me realize that the two have one thing in common. They both are human attempts to know what cannot be known by ordinary language. Symbolic language has the power to convey the unknown. It has the ability to answer the fundamental questions that Gauguin asked – the miracle of birth, the agony of human suffering, the magic of love, and the mystery of death. These are ultimate truths that cannot be understood intellectually but experienced viscerally with the body, heart, and mind. Symbols link the unknown with the known.

The deeper I delved into research, the more I became aware of my own self as a woman searching for answers in an alien country. I was a stranger to my inside as much as to the outside. The art images of the Goddesses of India drew me in. I researched their symbols and myths and in understanding them I began to become aware of myself. My doctoral dissertation was published as *Images of Indian Goddesses: Myths, Meanings, and Models.*

After completing my doctoral degree, I taught courses in Buddhist and Hindu art at the University of Pittsburgh in Pennsylvania, and later at

Rhode Island College and Wheaton College in Massachusetts. One of my favorite classes to teach was *Buddhism and Buddhist Art*, which focused on meditating images of the Buddha. In paintings and sculpture, the Buddha is depicted in various meditative postures. As I looked deeper into the subject of meditation, I wondered about the practice of meditation: Why did the Buddha meditate? Why was it mandatory for the monks to meditate and why was meditation highly recommended for the lay community? What happens when one sits still in silence and solitude?

I resolved to sit and meditate for five to ten minutes each day no matter what. For months, after my husband and our two daughters left home for work and school, I would sit still quietly in the meditative posture the way I had taught myself from books. I focused on my breath and tried to be present in the moment. I earnestly focused on my respiration. Within the first minute, that felt like an hour, thoughts wandered in freely: the day's lecture, a tiff with my husband, worry about children's school projects, a household chore that needed to be done, and so on. This frustrated me. I could do complicated tasks with comparative ease. Why couldn't I do a simple thing like concentrate on my breathing? It was literally under my nose! Analyzing, interpreting, judging, and criticizing random thoughts impeded the practice. By the time I remembered the intent of my sitting, minutes had passed. As soon as I remembered, I'd bring my attention back to my breath. Slowly but surely, when I brought my attention back to my breath, my body relaxed a bit more, which in turn settled my mind and brought it back to the present moment. In a few seconds, again my mind wandered. On and on it went. I don't know what kept me from giving up. Motivation provided by the books I had read? The compassionate and vulnerable quality of Buddha's meditating images? My age?

I learned that bringing the wandering mind back to the present was like repetitions in exercise. It strengthened the mental muscles. Meditation is like a gymnasium for the mind. The same way I train my body to acquire increased stamina and strong muscle tone, in meditation I train my mind to acquire present-moment awareness, mental plasticity, one-pointed attention, and a sharp working memory. The ultimate purpose is to link to the Authentic Self, the source of creativity and spirituality that lies at the core of each one of us.

A year passed since I first started meditating. I could count to ten before random thoughts robbed me of my focus. With patience I succeeded in following the breath for ten cycles counting one to ten—most of the time. My attention would wander, but I had developed the ability to bring it back to the breath. My thought process went like this:

> Wherever I go, my breath is with me. It is my anchor. In and out. In and out. In and out. What it does is vital; it keeps me alive. I must not forget... the moment I was born, the breath was with me and the moment it leaves me, I'll die. I need not speed it up, force it, grasp it, push it away, or control it. It is perfect the way it is. I simply must pay attention to its natural rhythm, to simply let it continue its work, without making a big deal out of it.

I prepared a corner in my bedroom that felt cozy and comfortable. On a glass shelf I placed a candle, a prayer bell, and a bud vase. In spring and summer, I put a flower in the vase. This became my meditating corner, my creative/spiritual power spot.

MINDFULNESS AND JOURNALING

In 1997, my older daughter gifted me with three life-changing books: Julia Cameron's *The Artist's Way*, Natalie Goldberg's *Writing Down the Bones,* and Anne Lamott's *Bird by Bird*. These books showed me how meditation and creativity are intertwined. They also inspired me to keep a journal.

When I started pouring my heart out in a notebook, it was not easy. I was afraid to write my most intimate thoughts and feelings unhesitatingly and freely. What if someone read it? At the time I was obsessed with reading Virginia Woolf's writings – novels, short stories, essays, biographies, anything I could find. She believed that for a writer, journaling freely was a necessity. Her writings persuaded me to journal without restrictions or inhibitions. Hesitatingly at first, but eventually, I poured out my own feelings and thoughts as Woolf had recommended, journaling as if "an inkpot was turned over the page."

In my journal I revisited my childhood and youth, reexperiencing the emotions I had felt as I overcame obstacles and struggles. The first half of my life came alive. I had confronted and resolved most of the issues when they happened, yet some loose ends remained. Remembering and staying with them alleviated many of the painful memories. The attention I gave them by writing them down helped me dissolve them. This opened up space for new insights and ideas to surface. Returning daily to my creative/spiritual power spot for meditation and to my pages for mental cleansing tested my determination and patience. The practice helped me eliminate unwholesome memories that were replaced by new ones that until then had remained dormant. Most importantly, my attention span and memory increased, and I was writing anecdotes from my life that were meaningful.

Journaling opened something inside me. I kept at it. I filled notebook after notebook, and at the end of five years I shredded what I had written (and some of my ego with it). But before shredding them, I read them. Mostly they were, and continue to be, a mix of emotions – humbling, surprising, exhilarating. At times certain memories provided insight that helped me know myself better. I used some of them as fuel for my formal writing, such as fictional characters and settings.

I charted a practice for myself: Meditation first thing in the morning, followed by journaling, and then writing for several hours. Sometime in the day I also walked in the park or around my neighborhood. This soon became my routine. But at some point, I felt a need to meet other writers or, even better, to write with them. My desire led me to Pennwriters, a statewide writer's organization of which I became a member in 2005.

By 2007 the practices of meditation, journaling, and walking had been so beneficial that I decided to teach what I practiced at Northland Library in Wexford, Pennsylvania. I had not named my daily routine yet, but the titles of the workshops were related to it: "What Has Writing to Do with Meditation?" and "Writing as a Spiritual Journey."

After following the method of Writing Meditation Practice for a decade and then teaching at the library, I felt that I had found the key to overcoming writers' lack of motivation, time, obstacles, and fear of failure. I believed the practice would help writers who craved to write but faced personal, familial, or professional roadblocks to overcome self-resistance. The mere thought of sharing the practice with others energized me.

One day at the library I noticed a copy of L. Frank Baum's *Wizard of Oz* on display. I reread the book and realized that the three characters skipping on the yellow brick road were fragmented selves of Dorothy. She wanted to go "home" but could not until she became aware that she already possessed a brain, a heart, and courage. In her dream she was lost in a tornado, hunted by a witch, and helped by a fairy. Upon waking she was integrated, whole, and happy. Like art and religion, dreams, too, speak in symbols.

Before Writing Meditation Practice, I, like Dorothy, lived a fragmented life. My body was at one place, the mind some other, and the heart somewhere else. All along I had access to the parts of which I was unaware. Yet through attention and emerging awareness, I was able to find and integrate them. I had experienced how, when separate, body, heart, and mind are a mess. But as an integrated whole, I was able to connect with my Authentic Self which is a goldmine waiting to be discovered. AS became my inner guide and teacher. My resolve to keep practicing WMP strengthened.

WMP taught me how to live consciously and purposefully. Henry David Thoreau spent two years and two months at Walden Pond living "deliberately," meditating, walking in nature, writing, and reading, and was awakened to deeper realities. Using all his senses, he reveled in the wonder and simplicity of the present moment. "Only that day dawns to which we are awake." He had found his true self.

When at age fifty-three I decided to venture on the path to full-time writing, I did not have to leave home and live on the banks of a pond. My calling was not for adventuring to the lengths and breadths of the world or wilderness. My calling was to venture within. My journey was to simultaneously practice WMP and live a full life. By doing so I discovered my writer's voice *and* an exuberant life. Are you ready to go on this inner journey with me?

The lingering inner stillness following meditation, journaling, walking (and writing and reading) motivates and inspires. Whether I am writing the first draft of a book, an essay, or a story, or revising it, my concentration is pointed. I may delete or rewrite one sentence five times, but the mind is attentive and inwardly aware.

Prior to my daily WMP, I mistakenly believed if I wanted to better my life, my outer circumstances must change. I focused outside myself and made attempts to change what I felt was uncreative, unpleasant, and unproductive. This did somewhat improve my circumstances but did not make much difference to my inner life. However, once WMP became a daily habit, I became sensitive to my Authentic Self's inner whispers. Instead of pushing them away, I listened. I felt my AS had important things to say and teach. It taught me to pause and think before automatically responding to people and situations. It nudged me to reevaluate my priorities. It made me realize that every moment I had a choice to make. I could say no to people and events that were not in synch with my life's plan. Fearlessly, I followed my inklings. Courage to say no and a sense of discrimination made me feel confident and secure. My outer world shifted. I felt grounded in my AS, and my writing flow and productivity increased.

TEACHING

The presentations at Northland Library encouraged me to offer Writing Meditation Practice workshops at writers' conferences, art groups, and local museums. By 2010, I was fortunate to have met award-winning and bestselling authors, some of whom became good friends. Through the Pennwriters Newsletter, I invited writers of all levels to join me to meditate, journal, and write as a group. The following year, the idea became a reality. On the first Wednesday of March 2011, interested Pennwriters met at a restaurant in Wexford, Pennsylvania, for the first meeting of our Mindful Writers Group. I had written three meditations that focused on awareness of body, heart, and mind. At each weekly session, I narrated a different fifteen-minute meditation. This was followed by fifteen minutes of journaling and then several hours of writing.

We found a few guidelines useful to follow during the weekly writing sessions that are still in place for any Mindful Writers gathering. First and foremost, no distinction is made between novice and professional writers – all Mindful Writers are equal. The focus is on meditation, journaling, and writing. Occasionally, at the beginning and end of the sessions, we talk about the craft of writing, and ways to remove obstacles and unravel minor knots. But we do not discuss the business of writing. We avoid talking about agents, publishers, paths to publication, failures and successes, or a fellow writer's successful sales or award status. "Writing for the sake of writing" is our motto. Experienced writers listen to problems or issues novice writers may have. They help them any way they can, and at the Mindful Writers Retreats (which were started several years after the Mindful Writers Weekly groups became popular), they demonstrate how to get motivated and feel inspired. Humility, simplicity, and productivity are our guiding principles. Such mindful and peaceful culture deepens the creative process, increases productivity, and has become fertile ground for Mindful Writers' support system, fellowship, even close friendships. We know jealousy blocks imagination and creativity.

Within months of the beginning of the first Mindful Writers Group, attendees raved about how much they accomplished. They declared that the meetings helped them quiet their agitated minds, let go of mental clutter, and energized them to write more than they had ever written before. By the end of the year, the weekly practice sessions had not only led them to contemplate their lives but also opened new possibilities for their works-in-progress.

Word of the Mindful Writers Group spread. More writers began to join. One even drove from Ohio for forty-five minutes to be with us. I suggested she start her own group closer to where she lived to save the driving time, yet she preferred driving. After several months, she stopped attending. But the idea of having another group stayed with me. Since then, the Mindful Writers Group has had so many requests to join that four groups were started at various locations in and around Pittsburgh. For those who did not live close enough to attend in person, I started the Online Mindful Writers Group that I continue to manage but is now led by hosts of Mindful Writers. The members persuaded me to record the meditations I had been reciting so that I could also join them in meditation. I recorded *Meditation for Mindful Writers: Body, Heart, Mind* in September 2011. In 2017, I released *Meditations for Mindful Writers II: Sensations, Thoughts, Feelings*. The third CD, *Meditation for Mindful Writers III: Generosity, Gratitude, and Forgiveness* was released in 2019.

However, meditation by itself is not as effective as Writing Meditation Practice, which includes other disciplines. Fifteen minutes of cozy meditation will not transform you. When the mind is made conscious of physical sensations, heartfelt feelings, and thoughts, it grows powerful. True experience of WMP takes place within full view of the whole truth of our life, with all its challenges, difficulties, and rewards.

Only each practitioner alone can extract the nuggets of authenticity and originality from their heart-mind, called *Buddhachitta* in Buddhism.

Once we are fully linked with our Authentic Self, it is easier to connect with others, especially fellow writers, and reap the benefits of the five disciplines together including meditation, journaling, walking in nature, writing, and reading. The sociologist Emile Durkheim called the feeling you get when connected with like-minded people "Collective Effervescence." When we write with a shared purpose, something magical and momentous happens. You are linked to your imagination. This cannot be described in words.

When you write with others, your mind clears with comparative calm. Words pour out from your whole self. The practice brings you not only closer to yourself and your work-in-progress but connects you with others for hours. The collective energy, simultaneously potent and buoyant, circulates in the space.

The most important travel in your life is neither around the world nor to outer space. The most adventurous journey is to go within, to get introduced to your Authentic Self, your guide and mentor for life. Once you know what it means to go within, you write with an uninterrupted flow. Your mental disposition is the same as that of a dancer dancing, an athlete playing, a mountaineer climbing. You will experience something like a runner's high, an artist's euphoria, a poet's muse. The divide between outer and inner space dissolves, and you, the writer, become one with the writing. The feelings of fear and doubt are replaced by courage, trust, and self-worth.

In the thirty to forty minutes that you spend meditating and journaling, your mind changes from blank to brimming with ideas and insights about the work-in-progress. You feel motivated. No desire to read email, surf the web, or make a quick call. You simply do not want to extract yourself from that euphoric zone. You're hooked.

When I am one with my Authentic Self, I am one with the sense of attention and awareness that moves my body, heart, and mind forward in unison. I feel motivated and determined to write. Writing Meditation Practice allows me to be exactly where I am in the present moment. It helps me move beyond conceptual thought. Each time I write following WMP, irrespective of whether it is the first or final draft, I refine it repeatedly. I write it segment by segment of 500 or 1,000 words. I nurture each segment until the whole document is ready to leave home. But before all this can happen, I wake up the inner resources that are latent within me so that I can put them to good use. And that is done by the practice of WMP.

At the end of this book, I have included links to the meditations that I wrote, narrated, and recorded. The ten-to-fifteen-minute meditations are excellent tools for you to ready yourself for focused writing or other creative work for hours. I use these for the groups, classes, and workshops I lead.

These meditations are meant to be listened to repeatedly. The first time, you may not hear what each one points toward. The more you listen, the deeper you will go and the more you will understand how meditation and creativity strengthen one another. Follow the meditation of your choice before you sit to make something. Each session holds the promise of a new experience and makes you aware of something fresh and surprising.

12 MONTHS, 12 TOPICS

Writing Meditation Practice includes five disciplines: meditation, journaling, writing, reading, and walking in nature (you may replace walking with any non-verbal activity of your choice such as painting, dancing, playing a musical instrument, gardening, knitting and so on). If you practice each one of these diligently, by the end of the year, you'll surprise yourself with the skills you have cultivated, progress made, and confidence achieved.

Writing Meditation Practice will not only enhance your skills and strengthen the tools of the craft, but also it will also make you self-introspect and contemplate the ups and downs and learn how to balance daily life and ground yourself firmly as a creative, authentic, kind, compassionate, and content person. For such conditions to develop, I have added other necessary disciplines such as Stillness, Silence, and Solitude; Writing with Others; Writing Poetry; Traveling Mindfully; Awe, Wonder and Delight; and paying attention to primordial questions such as What is the purpose of my life? How can I align my daily routine and yearly goals to this pursuit? Each day begins with a short practice, inspiration and a prompt. Each week covers a topic that continues for a month.

This book is very personal to me. For the first time, all my work as a writer, artist, and teacher of Asian arts and religions has come together. This book draws from my non-fiction, novels, meditations for writers, and my artwork. It is the culmination of everything I've learned and taught over the past three decades. I'm very excited to be able to weave it all into a truly comprehensive book to share with fellow writers and others who might be interested in this subject. I have included insights that I have gleaned from my life experiences, what these mean to me, and why I considered it important to share them with writers of all levels worldwide.

This guidebook not only instructs and informs but also entertains with poems, humorous anecdotes, and tales from my life. It is an invaluable resource for any writer looking to increase productivity, deepen thought and emotion, and increase concentration that leads to a completed manuscript and a vital life.

Dear reader, this book is the most important thing I have ever written. There is joy and fear in my heart – an anticipation, an excitement, and a hope that this adventure will be as exciting for you as it has been for me. I leave this in your hands with the hope that the experience of reading and practicing Writing Meditation Practice will be pleasurable and transformative for you. I hope reading this work mindfully will conjure up new worlds for you and compel you to become aware of your innate intuitive beauty, your true voice, and your Authentic Self.

With love,
Madhu Bazaz Wangu
April 2023

SOWING

"The cave you fear to enter
may hold the light you seek."
—Rumi

Month 1

Mindfulness and Journaling

Suggested Readings

Opening Up by Writing It Down:
How Expressive Writing Improves Health and Eases Emotional Pain
James W. Pennebaker and Joshua M. Smyth, 2016.

Heal Your Self with Writing
Catherine Ann Jones, 2013.

The Automatic Writing Experience (AWE):
How to Turn Your Journaling into Channeling to Get Unstuck,
Find Direction, and Live your Greatest Life!
Michael Sandler, 2021.

Big Magic: Creative Living Beyond Fear
Elizabeth Gilbert, 2015.

✎ *Day 1* ✎

TODAY'S PRACTICE

Welcome to the first day of your journey toward honing your writing skills and enriching your life! Keep in mind that a daily routine builds the foundation for a creative and purposeful life.

To begin, you have three tasks: carve out time in your day, select a space in your home that feels safe and secure, and find a simple notebook to jot down your reflections. Tomorrow at the time and space which you have designated for yourself, we will begin practicing Writing Meditation.

INSPIRATION

"Last night I begged the Wise One to tell me the secret of the world.
Gently, gently, he whispered, 'Be quiet, the secret cannot be spoken,
it is wrapped in silence.'" —Rumi

This month we will focus on writing in a notebook, also called journaling. In your journal you reflect and clarify your daily intention that leads to the monthly goal. Sincere intentions turn from doing to being. Visualize them, keep working at them, and watch them become your reality. At times you may not have time to write in your notebook, but always keep your intentions and the month's goal at the back of your mind.

The place you select for your daily reflection and journaling will become your Sacred Power Spot. It is the coziest and safest place in the world. Keep returning to it daily. Here is where you mobilize your wildest dreams, your innermost thoughts and feelings, as you journal. You have been given the boon of 365 days, four seasons. The winter months are the time for slowing down, reflection, introspection, and learning to be patient. "Self-reflection results in wisdom. Early in the morning plan your day, and at bedtime spend a few minutes introspecting it; take this habit to your deathbed," my father used to say.

JOURNAL PROMPT

Make this your year of introspection, self-discovery, and self-understanding. Transform your life for happier and healthier years ahead. Pause. Notice what is present in your surroundings. What do you like and what can you change? Ask yourself: *What small habits can I alter to make my day better? What is missing from my daily routine? What do I have that I love and cherish? How can I deepen it? What will help me learn and grow?*

♒ *Day 2* ♒

TODAY'S PRACTICE

Welcome to your Sacred Power Spot. Be seated comfortably. With your eyes closed, sit in silence for 2–3 minutes with focus on your breath. Read today's inspiration and prompt. Reflect upon what you have read. Then jot down your thoughts and feelings in your notebook.

INSPIRATION

We are familiar with nine human emotions: happiness, sadness, surprise, anger, hatred, horror, love, jealousy, and peacefulness. In addition, there are many subtle or fine emotions such as awe or tenderness that you will learn about in Month 3.

When you sat in silence for those few minutes, did thoughts and memories float around between your two ears? Was your focus distracted by a single thought? If it is still lingering in your head, it is the time to pour out your feelings into your notebook. You'll be amazed to see how much journaling about what is going on in your head works like a silent friend or a therapist. It leaves you clear-headed, ready for the day.

JOURNAL PROMPT

Write about your new journaling practice. Your daily journaling will pay high dividends, I promise. Just keep practicing. You don't have to tell anyone your most intimate feelings except your dear journal.

✌ Day 3 ✌

TODAY'S PRACTICE

Sit at your Sacred Power Spot. This is your personal sacred space. Begin with a short time sitting in silence, focusing on inhalation and exhalation. Then read the inspiration and prompt. Reflect on the thoughts and feelings that arise. Note them in your journal.

INSPIRATION

When you shine the light of awareness on yourself with journaling, you spotlight your thoughts, actions, and speech. Even nonaction such as rest time gains meaning. You begin to awaken to an authentic life.

Journaling is uninhibited writing in a notebook. In writing freely, you encircle an emotion, whether joyful or distressing. You neither let it pass nor suppress it, especially if it is filled with pain. Such emotion can overtake your life, running through your mind like a broken record. It takes possession of your precious time. Therefore pen it down and feel it fully. Let the emotion gain significance and eventually fizzle out right on the pages. And leave the notebook behind with lightened heart and clear mind.

I'm neither a psychologist nor psychiatrist. Serious traumatic events must be treated by professionals. But if you are trying to heal from a social event that keeps circling in your mind, place the bitterness on the pages by writing with your hand. Such planting will transmute the angry or sorrowful feelings that the emotion has triggered. Let them root in your writing and grow into an herb to heal your pain. Reread it the next day and chew the leaves of words and feel the pain leaving you. Thus you will transform a negative emotion into a healing potion.

Journaling daily can help you work through the severe physical or mental illness of a family member or caring for elderly parents. So go ahead, pour your heart out in that notebook and watch what grows and cures you.

JOURNAL PROMPT

If you have never journaled freely before today, give it a try. Write your first entry. For experienced journal writers, free-write about a distressing or positive emotion that you often feel. Share it without any inhibition in your notebook. Would you share what you just did with anyone else?

⋟ *Day 4* ⋞

TODAY'S PRACTICE

Sit in the comfort of your Sacred Power Spot, your personal sacred space. Close your eyes and practice the silent sitting with your focus on inhalation and exhalation. Read the inspiration and prompt. Reflect upon them. Jot down everything and anything that is stirred in your heart and mind.

INSPIRATION

When you are distressed, your creative flow gets restricted. Even if you want to, you are unable to break through the emotional block of personal limitations. Freely journaling 2-3 pages about whatever is making you feel miserable is the best remedy to clear the gunk that has plugged the faucet.

In 1990, renowned psychologist Dr. James W. Pennebaker used journaling as a treatment for his patients suffering depression and anxiety. His findings show that we pay a hidden price for remaining silent about our negative emotions and keeping secrets. His extensive research proved that self-disclosure in a notebook is not only good for emotional and physical health (reduced blood pressure and anxiety) but also spiritual well-being. He called it "expressive writing."

So, what are you waiting for? Get ready with a notebook and a free-flowing pen. Your journal is neither going to be a literary work nor draft of a genre novel. Just write whatever comes to your mind. Nothing is too humdrum or out of line. The only skill you need for journaling is to pour out your heart in words – not worrying about punctuation, grammar, or spelling. That's why it is called unprepared, uninhibited "expressive writing." You will be surprised to find out how what you begin as mere jottings end up as advice, suggestions, or revelations about yourself. Just aim for 2-3 pages or 500-750 words (or more if you want). You will feel free and light afterward.

It is not magic. It is a scientifically proven fact.

JOURNAL PROMPT
Write about how journaling in the morning affects the rest of your day.

ᨳ *Day 5* ᨳ

TODAY'S PRACTICE
Make yourself comfortable at your Sacred Power Spot, either on the floor sitting cross legged or on a chair with your feet firm on the ground. Close your eyes and practice silent breathing, deep and slow. Read the inspiration and prompt. Reflect on the thoughts they discuss. Write them in your notebook.

INSPIRATION
Your inner world reflects your outer world, but the outside world is easier to maneuver. Family affairs, jobs, and household chores have maps and signposts. Events are planned and mostly completed. The inner world has no such demarcation or destination. The ethereal keeps accumulating into some dark, nebulous mental mess. Yet it is possible to declutter, bring peace, and work toward true pleasure through the practice of journaling. I say this because my mind was also confused, restless, and scattered. After I started Writing Meditation Practice that included journaling, meditation, deep reading, walking in nature, and of course writing for several hours, things began to change.

My journaling practice was fueled by Julia Cameron's book, *The Artist's Way* (1992), in which she explains the reason for writing three "Morning Pages." Having received bad reviews for a film, she began having self-doubt about her abilities. She felt blocked and needed a way to get her creative magic back. Journaling turned out to be it. Morning Pages allowed her to discard the mental clutter, "the most anxious, angry, petty, self-critical, and otherwise unflattering parts of myself," she writes. Having journaled for some time, she began to feel clear-headed and ready to tackle new projects. Once she got the confusing thoughts on the page, she could face her day with more clarity. When we journal she says, "We are more honest with ourselves, more centered, and more spiritually at ease." Journaling gave her fresh insights into herself and empowered her to make changes in her life.

Once you get hooked on journaling, you will crave it for freely expressing experiences that you cannot share with anyone else. As you write, you watch your petty or vindictive thoughts, careless actions, or unnecessary words get soaked up by the page. You find clarity about what you have done and said and what you can now do moving forward. You become your own witness.

JOURNAL PROMPT

Try journaling three Morning Pages, allowing yourself to write about all your frustrations and confusion as well as the good things that are happening.

✌ *Day 6* ✌

TODAY'S PRACTICE

Your sacred space awaits you. Make yourself comfortable either on the floor or on a chair. Close your eyes and begin with 2-3 minutes of silence, focused on the breath.

INSPIRATION

In your daily journal, you scream silently, jot down your frustrations, and scribble the things that destiny has sent your way – things you are ashamed of, that embarrass you, that are too painful to talk about. When you pen the bubbling thoughts of your sorrow, fear, anger, resentment, jealousy, desire, or doubt on blank pages, you feel healed – physically and emotionally. You are ready to face the world for the day.

Do not disregard the things you are grateful for, are proud of, or dream about. Express the ecstasy and delight you feel from small gestures (a genuine kiss, a heartfelt hug, a compliment from a friend or coworker) or a big prize (a draft completed, a book published, an award won).

Underlining the positives is as important, if not more so, than discarding the negatives.

During my early years of journaling, I saved my notebooks. I would read the pages I had written on the exact date the previous year. I noted the changes I had made or needed to make. Many entries dismayed me. *"What a muddy, miserable, maddening mess!"* And then I'd write, *"What did you expect? The pages are messy because you have poured out on them the mess you create daily and the accumulated mess you carry around. These pages reflect your chaos. Keep pouring it out. Your vessel is clearing day-by-day and eventually it would be crystal clear."* How true it felt!

Journaling turns the invisible rubbish inside your head into visible words, easier to discard. Reading the previous year's entries helped me see the progress I had made in my writing skill and daily living. If I had not wholeheartedly journaled about how much our daughters needed me, how I had not professionally accomplished what I wanted to, when my husband and I were struggling financially, if I had not poured out those emotions and thoughts onto the reams and reams of paper, what would have become of that negativity? I shudder to think about that. It would have ended in bitter silence and secrets, revealing themselves as stress, anxiety, and distress. Instead of a nebulous mess floating around in my mind, I released it. Each time I did this I felt unburdened and free.

When you are comfortable with daily journaling, the notebook turns into a most intimate silent friend, your best therapist. At the end of each journal entry, it replies to you, telling you things even you didn't know about yourself. *Who is this who knows me so well*, you wonder. *Who is it that gives me wise counsel or reprimands me?* In the daily routine of journaling, you discover a wise teacher within.

Some keep a journal in middle school and some in college, some like me when they are in late middle age. Some buy a notebook from the dollar store, and some have a diary with a lock and key. Even when journals contain no secrets, their owners feel these keepsakes to be fantastically private. When such beginnings are too small to hold all your thoughts, dreams, and goals, you can acquire more journals.

Your thoughts and emotions are private. Writing them in the journal softens the edges within you, but you could also use these in your fiction. Transform personal experiences into universal ones so that someday your words will influence and inspire your readers.

JOURNAL PROMPT

How did you feel yesterday after journaling? Be kind to yourself today as you spend 15-20 minutes writing in your notebook. Journal about what is topmost in your mind. You will be surprised at what you discover.

ஜ *Day 7* ౼

TODAY'S PRACTICE

Are you ready to extend your sitting in silence to 3-5 minutes? What about 5 minutes twice a day, just after waking up and before going to sleep? In the morning, practice as you sit at your Sacred Power Spot, and at night as you lay in the bed.

Relax. Sit in a comfortable position. Focus on inhalations and exhalations with your eyes closed. Read the inspiration and prompt, then reflect upon them and journal.

INSPIRATION

So, what do you do with all the notebooks on which you have dumped your mental mess? These heaps of word-ash await your decision. Store them for one, two, five years, or as long as you live. You might even save them to write a memoir.

Don't be in a hurry to destroy them. Go back and read those sections of your journal where you felt the heat of passion intensely. When you were overtaken by some fiery emotion. When the emotional verve you felt was as deep as you feel when you are one with your creative flow. The heaps of ash hide embers of raw feelings, great insights like gold nuggets still smoldering.

Search through the detritus and find part of a dialogue, a character detail, some feature that still carries the same intensity as when you poured it out from your heart. Use these elements in your story, essay, or poem. Use these gems, the byproduct of your potent experiences.

All the embers that glimmer in the piles of ash are not necessarily negative. Some are fulfilling, like joy, delight, and ecstasy that you are grateful for. They spark dynamic energy for wellbeing and wholesomeness. The reason so many people keep gratitude journals is to recall and reflect what has been good in their lives.

In addition to using words, you may doodle or draw in your journal or paste cutout images, photos, clippings, drawings, or even fortune cookie slips. When you read these the following year, you will remember where you were and with whom. This may prompt a new story or an essay. Your journal should bring you peace, make you happy, and nourish your spirit.

More than thirty years ago, after the death of my youngest brother, I made two collages. I now realize they were picture-journals. I made them when my mother and then my father passed away within eighteen months of his death. The collages helped me come out of my grief and brought much solace.

JOURNAL PROMPT

How has journaling helped you in an area of life that seemed impossible to deal with before you began this journey?

ℒ *Day 8* ℳ

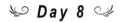

TODAY'S PRACTICE

Sit comfortably and quietly at your Sacred Power Spot. When you feel settled in your favorite posture, close your eyes and focus on the inhalations and exhalations. Now read and reflect on today's inspiration and prompt. Pour out your heart and mind onto the pages of your journal.

INSPIRATION

The picture-journals or collages I created after family deaths helped me come out of my grief and brought much peace. Over and over, perhaps 99 times and without reserve, I wrote how their passing had shocked me, numbed me, crushed my creativity. My sketches and journals held me tight, keeping me grounded as I braved the eye of the storm. I poured out the thunder, the lightning, the gushing wind that passed through my head and heart on the lined pages.

The more I emptied, the more there was to empty – a bottomless pit of sorrowful thoughts and compelling emotions. Then at some point – I don't remember when, maybe when I wrote the hundredth time – the dark clouds parted and gave a glimpse of sunshine hiding behind them. I had forgotten that the orb of dazzling sun is always present, the way my true inner self, my Authentic Self is always listening, ready to protect and guide me.

The reason I linked and continue to be linked to my AS is because I follow the practices of journaling, meditation, walking in nature, and other allied disciplines. No matter how tumultuous the storm, it passes slowly but surely. What helps you heal is witnessing yourself with words, and sitting with them in silence and solitude. What eventually emerges is the eternal wisdom of the Self. It awakens you to the fullness of life and nudges you to live mindfully and meaningfully.

JOURNAL PROMPT

The same way you observe physical hygiene for cleanliness, you must cultivate emotional hygiene for mental clarity. What practices do you follow to cleanse your mind?

ꙮ *Day 9* ꙮ

TODAY'S PRACTICE

Practice 5 minutes of a breath exercise by counting to 10 as you inhale and exhale. When thoughts carry you away, bring your attention back to the breath. Repeat. Follow the quiet sitting with reading and reflecting on today's inspiration and prompt. Then journal to your heart's desire.

INSPIRATION

When I am emotionally disturbed or intellectually challenged, I confront myself on the pages of my notebook. In my journal I'm the villain, the judge, and the jury. I realize while the notebook and the pen are the outer tools, my inner implements are honesty, sincerity, and integrity, with which I deliberate my case. A good journaling session is a mix of humility, surprise, exhilaration, and release.

Today I'd like to share with you a spiritual revelation that journaling disclosed to me. Prior to getting my books about goddesses published, my knowledge about them was scholarly and academic. I was an art historian, not a goddess devotee. But once the books were released, they left me with a question that gnawed at the back of my mind: *How did so many years of research and writing about the Buddhist and Hindu goddesses and the knowledge thus gained inform my life? What was the point?* In other words, "So what?" I continued to ask that question in my journal off and on. But no answers emerged. Only more questions.

A whole year passed. One night I had a vivid dream. I felt my body was inhabited by the goddesses I had studied. Each enshrined in that part of my body which it symbolized: Sarasvati, the goddess of arts and intellect was enshrined in my head; Laxmi, the goddess of abundance and well-being in my heart; Durga, the exquisite warrior goddess in my arms, and so on. My whole body felt replete with the goddess essence.

The dream was so energizing that it woke me. My body was invigorated. I journaled nonstop, page after page. By the fifth page I remember writing, "Whether you are a devotee of the goddesses or not is not the point. Understand that they are not mere abstractions. They are powerful feminine energies. They don't dwell in the paintings and sculptures. Their images are created to animate and vitalize the creative spirit in the onlooker, the devotee, the academic researcher. In the dream they responded to your body by activating it." Then I wrote this note to myself, "These sacred feminine essences are dormant within you. Practice awakening them!"

Eventually it was the sitting, the jotting down, the walking, and reflection that helped me understand and internalize the goddess teachings that, up until then, were nothing but intellectual understanding. The wonder of journaling awed me.

JOURNAL PROMPT

Conversing intimately with yourself is a spiritual thing. You make an attempt to undertake yourself deliberately by writing freely in your notebook. Journaling reveals possible solutions to problems, heals emotional wounds, and lends an ear when you need it. But dreams hint at solutions. Enter your dreams in the journal as well. You may or may not understand them. But writing them down can reveal a bit more. It may take a few weeks, even months, to unravel the answers, but eventually you'll get it. So what problem is on your mind, what hurts, what is knotting your belly today?

℘ *Day 10* ℘

TODAY'S PRACTICE

Practice 5 minutes of a breath exercise by counting to 10 as you inhale and exhale. When thoughts carry you away, bring your attention back to the breath. Repeat. Follow the quiet sitting with reading and reflecting on today's inspiration. Jot your thoughts about the inspiration and prompt.

INSPIRATION

So many writers began journaling after joining the Online Mindful Writers Group. They may have been novice journal writers but they reaped the benefit of the practice right away. If they lacked trust in the early stage, the demon of self-doubt took its insidious hold.

You know what that feels like. You have experienced negative thinking that threatens to choke. Journaling replaces self-doubt with self-confidence. Your honest outpouring has power. Once it is on the pages it takes over. By the time you are almost done with the free flow of writing, it may reprimand you for comparing yourself with others or not having enough courage. You can't believe the process unless you try it yourself.

Dump your emotions in the journal and watch how you come up with doable daily intentions, resolutions for the month, and gratifying aha moments. You regain peace after the anger or fear is released, a question answered, or a problem solved.

JOURNAL PROMPT

What happened the last time you doubted yourself? Did the self-doubt keep you from accepting a challenge or make you miss out on an opportunity?

❦ *Day 11* ❦

TODAY'S PRACTICE

Settle in and close your eyes. Notice the sensation of breath underneath your nostrils and over your upper lip as you breathe in and breathe out. Feel the air moving in and out of your body as your chest slightly rises and falls. The abdomen slightly expands and contracts. Take long and deep inhalations and exhalations. Watch how your thoughts settle down.

Read today's inspiration and prompt. Reflect upon them for a couple of minutes and write freely in your journal.

INSPIRATION

While growing up, were you told not to cry but to smile while your heart was hurting, mind buzzing? Irrespective of the intensity of disappointment or feeling of a raw deal, were you asked to do the opposite of what you really felt like doing?

Dr. James Pennebaker writes that keeping secrets, suffering in silence, and not fully expressing negative emotions – swallowing or pushing them down – affects your heart, mind, and body for the rest of your life.

Girls and young women especially are taught to behave. By the time they are grown women, they succeed in hiding their fears, anger, and hurt from the world. In doing so, they hide from themselves.

It is an arduous task to replace the mask of "goodness" and niceness with authenticity. What has become part of you is hard to purge. It takes time. First you must recognize the anger, hurt, and fear buried deep inside, followed by the acceptance of these negative emotions. Some require therapy and hypnosis to cleanse the system, but most of us can do this by writing in various forms.

You may write a letter to yourself, to the one who hurt you, or to the one who was responsible for creating negative feelings in you. You may or may not deliver the letter. What matters is the pouring out, the purging of sly emotions. How do you do that?

Through journaling. In the notebook you work through the feelings and bring yourself back to the present moment. You know all that happened in the past, and the present is safe and secure. Journaling relieves the past suffering and keeps the present pain at a distance.

JOURNAL PROMPT

Journal about an event that left you with strong feelings that you never got a chance to purge. Now is the time to do so again and again.

∿ *Day 12* ∿

TODAY'S PRACTICE

Welcome back to your seat! Make yourself comfortable and practice the short breathing session. Watch your breath going in and coming out. Keep in mind that you are not making yourself breathe. It is happening by itself. The more you watch it, the more the mental chatter will settle down and the clearer your mind will become.

Read today's post, then reflect and write in the notebook.

INSPIRATION

You may have asked yourself what mindfulness has to do with journaling. You may not have associated the two practices yet. But I see them as yin and yang of imagination and creativity. While mindfulness is being attentive at the present moment, journaling is the free, uninhibited, and spontaneous outpouring of feelings and thoughts.

You have been practicing taking long and deep inhalations and exhalations and returning your mind to where you are seated. This breathing exercise makes you mindful. Focusing on your breath is one of the best habits you can cultivate. In time, the awareness of breathing becomes second nature.

You are so busy moving through the hectic days that you have forgotten how to live mindfully. When was the last time you were mindful of the tiny miracles around you – fingers writing, feet walking, sunrays greeting you with a new day, dusk bidding goodbye with the promise of another day, the dark sky studded with stars, or a full moonlit night? Last but not least, the faces of your spouse or children or a good friend?

Enjoy the life of which you are becoming aware. Enjoy yourself whom you are beginning to know and discover!

JOURNAL PROMPT

Go for a walk surrounded by trees and water. Be attentive to what you see and hear and smell. Then write a poem about how it feels to be mindful of the sights, sounds, and smells.

୬ Day 13 ୬

TODAY'S PRACTICE

After settling at your cozy corner, focus on your breathing. Start with paying attention to the air near your nostrils, followed by the chest and then the abdomen. Breathe slowly at each area. Where does it feel the most comfortable? Continue to breathe slowly at the place of your ease.

Most people's breath is unnaturally shallow. For whatever reason, in present times speed and stress have accelerated the number of in-breaths and out-breaths per minute. The slower you breathe, the more you will become aware of your inhalation and exhalation, and the more its natural depth will reestablish itself.

After the breathing practice, jot down your thoughts on today's inspiration and prompt.

INSPIRATION

Journaling makes you witness yourself, makes you watch what you do right and what you do wrong. The practice reinforces your strengths and mends your mistakes so you become closer to your true self. When you journal honestly and repeatedly, you value yourself more. You become conscious of your own positive qualities.

What qualities in you are you proud of? Are you generous, a go-getter, kind, gracious? Does your vocation reinforce your strengths? I learned generosity and kindness from my mother, reason and discipline from my father. Much later in life I realized that between the two of them, they had taught me to think with my heart.

Before the regular practice of Writing Meditation Practice, when someone said something negative about me, I'd mull over it for hours if not days... but when someone complimented me, I would let it slip. In my journal I began asking, "Why is this so?" I jotted down positives about myself. The more I wrote good things about my strengths, positive attitude, and kind behavior, the more confident I became. I extended affection, kindness, and compliments to myself. No one else needed to know.

Being generous, kind, and caring to others is good, but there are times when I do not extend the same caring to myself. Intellectually I understand that I deserve as much kindness and love as I offer to others. But there are times when only I know the hurt I feel. Journaling comes to the rescue. If I don't listen gently and lovingly to myself, then who will?

JOURNAL PROMPT

Write a dialogue between you and your inner critic. Let your inner ally surface and join the conversation.

✌ *Day 14* ↩

TODAY'S PRACTICE

At your personal sacred space, you are determined and energized, yet sitting still in silence and solitude. That is being grounded, being balanced. In this state, practice slow and deep breathing. Continue as long as you can. Then read the inspiration and prompt. With your eyes closed, reflect on thoughts that stir. Jot them in your notebook.

INSPIRATION

Are you a people pleaser? Do you pretend to be what others expect of you? Are you different depending on where you are or who you are with? Do you "change colors" to match your environment like a chameleon?

To be subtly different at different places and with different people is only natural. You can't be exactly the same in professional circumstances as when you are at home with your spouse or children, but there certainly should run a common thread of your Authentic Self of which you are always aware.

Who are you when you are by yourself, breathing deliberately, journaling, warming shoulders in the late morning sunshine, cooking, gardening? When you are laughing aloud, or when you are watching a movie that moistens your eyes? When listening to a song and you get a lump in your throat or your heart swells with pride? Who are you then? Many things touch you that may not touch the person sitting next to you. That is who you are. Begin to be more like that true Self and feel connected to it. That is not who you think you are but who you feel yourself to be.

JOURNAL PROMPT

What brings you genuine delight? What makes you feel fuzzy all over? Journal about a person, place, or thing that fills you with love and joy.

ꙮ *Day 15* ꙮ

TODAY'S PRACTICE

Welcome to your personal sacred space! Practice what you have learned so far. Slow, deep and steady breathing. With your eyes closed, reflect on the thoughts the inspiration and prompt stir. Then write them freely in the journal.

INSPIRATION

The difference between journaling and writing is the way your mind works. In journaling you pour out raw feelings and unchecked thoughts that surface and clutter your mind. Once you clear that away, deeper thoughts emerge.

The difference between passing and deeper thoughts was brought home to me in art college by seeing an artwork and "looking" at it. The first time you look at a painting, your own emotions are reflected back to you. But upon "looking," with mindful analysis and interpretation, you see what it truly means. This enriches the onlooker's enjoyment.

For example, the first time I saw Domenico Ghirlandaio's painting, *An Old Man and his Grandson* (circa 1490), I did not notice the unique realism, but felt that the nose of the old man was marred with large pimples. I did not see the emotional poignancy in the manner in which the little boy's chubby hand rested on the grandfather's chest. I did not take in the contrast between the man's weathered and wise face and gray hair, and the child's delicate profile and golden curls.

Beauty in this painting is not so much in the deformity of the old man but the total compositional color effect and play of the light it has on a mindful onlooker. Once my mind was cleared of the static of personal feelings and thoughts, I began to observe the skill of the artist in delineating forms and coloring shapes. Only through complete attention and awareness was I able to appreciate that "beautiful" is a combination of mindfulness and intellectual understanding. The same principle applies to music, dance, mathematics, or computer systems.

Journaling gets the personal feelings and thoughts out of your way. In no way are they petty or without use. They surface no matter what you do, but to clear them by writing them in your notebook leads to better, more relevant thoughts about the story of your day, your life.

JOURNAL PROMPT
Beauty is all around you. Journal about how to appreciate and enjoy it. Write about a time when "beautiful" was suddenly revealed to you.

◟ *Day 16* ◞

TODAY'S PRACTICE
It has been two weeks since you began your practice of settling at your Sacred Power Spot and doing breathing exercises. Once again, begin with focus on your in-breath and out-breath up to 5 minutes. Then read the inspiration and prompt. With your eyes closed, reflect on both. Then pour your heart out in your journal.

INSPIRATION

It feels so good to empty all that anguish in your trustworthy friend, your journal. You won't be declared crazy and no one can overhear what is hurting, annoying, or frustrating you. This writing exercise has two advantages. One, it lightens your heart and clears your mind. Two, when you read it after one year or five years it feels different. It has either decomposed into manure or is saved as energetic embers of ideas for you to use.

What you pour on the blank pages of your journal can be compared with a landfill, "the mountain of the dump" of your mental trash – it is all biodegradable and turns into fertilizer for new writing pieces. It often happens that upon rereading your journal you gain greater insight into the things that had happened in the previous year or many years before. Personal events gather universal significance.

When I reread old journal entries, I am amazed by how much I've forgotten. Memories flood in, accompanied by tender and potent emotional states. This practice reinforces my belief about how important it is to leave the daily clutter on the pages of my notebook and move on. At times it surprises me what a long way my daily journaling has led me.

JOURNAL PROMPT

Journal about something that felt negative and useless when you wrote about it but turned out to be wonderful for your future self, so much so that you thanked your past for that happening.

ॐ *Day 17* ॐ

TODAY'S PRACTICE

Sit comfortably on your chair or mat. Bring your heart and mind to where your body is seated. Become conscious of your breath. Feel the present moments one at a time. Let the thoughts pass by, eventually settling down. If you like, conjure up the image of your favorite mountain, a flowing river, or a path through lush trees. Stay with it for a few moments as you slowly and deeply breathe in and breathe out.

Follow the breathing exercise with reading the inspiration and prompt, reflecting upon them. Then write your heart out in the notebook.

INSPIRATION

When I don't journal for a while, a restlessness gnaws at me. My mind feels muddled and overwhelmed with a mosaic of petty thoughts and feelings. And when I do journal, it helps heal my wounds, clear my mind, and affects the rest of my day with peace.

If for some reason you stop pouring out your heart on the pages, you won't know the cause of your irritability. But when journaling becomes a daily habit, it turns into an internal alarm; it becomes an intrinsic part of your day. The desire to write stirs from inside. It can only be relieved by writing every day.

Read recommended books about journaling to digest the neuroscience that confirms the value of this discipline. Only personal experience will solidify your belief in its benefits and reaching the depths of your being.

It needs repeating that journaling can lead to the writing of essays, stories, and poems. One word of caution: Daily journaling for long hours does not make you a writer. That would be like an artist sketching for long hours but not creating a painting or sculpture. Journaling will certainly unburden you, honing your writing skills, and clearing your mind, but it won't make you a writer.

It will, however, certainly purge negative feelings and petty thoughts, and make you emotionally healthier.

JOURNAL PROMPT

Write a letter of gratitude to your journal. Tell it how it has healed your wounds, accepted your petty sentiments, and in the process improved your writing skill.

✌ *Day 18* ↩

TODAY'S PRACTICE

You may be wondering about the benefits of settling and repeating the same breathing exercises. Do these 5-10 minutes of pause and attention to your body and mind calm you down? Do you feel connected to something inside of you?

Read today's inspiration and prompt, then close your eyes and reflect upon them. Journaling time!

INSPIRATION

Self-doubt is one of the major emotions creative people go through, especially those who do not have regular nine-to-five jobs. There are days when you feel overwhelmed or sluggish without any tangible reason.

What can you do? Let a rainstorm of words from the heavy dark clouds fall on the pages of your notebook. Trust that by the end of three pages it will shed light on things you were only partly aware of, and it will present possible solutions.

Trust is the antithesis of doubt. Did you trust your diary in high school? If someone read your diary as a young person and broke your trust, it left an emotional wound. Did you courageously pull yourself out of it by journaling again? Good for you!

I started doing serious journaling in my fifties after I changed professions from teaching college to becoming an independent writer. It felt so good, I wondered why I had not started journaling sooner. Not only was I able to free my mind and lighten my heart, but my brain was primed for writing the work-in-progress in a seamless flow. I never stopped.

Writing spontaneously, without worrying about spelling or grammar, is a potent salve for emotional suffering and physical pain. It heals deeply. Writing by hand, creating collages, and making pencil or digital drawings all are good. The kind of tool you use is not as important as the process of spurting what is happening in your heart-mind.

JOURNAL PROMPT

Journal about the lightness you feel after dropping your emotional burden onto the page. Write out the sensations of lightness to savor them for a moment longer.

∾ *Day 19* ∾

TODAY'S PRACTICE

Make yourself comfortable at your safe, secure, and sacred space. Do a breathing exercise, then read, reflect, and journal.

INSPIRATION

What is one thing you dream about? What is your deep, driving desire that you want to take to the limit? Whatever it is, begin bit by bit, in short increments, enjoying it daily. Begin with almost every day, then every day... a nudge to take the first step is enough.

If you want to be a writer but don't know where to start, begin with a few pages of journaling – healing, helpful, building hope. You don't have to think of "writing" as only a book, story, or essay, but rather helpfulness and hopefulness of befriending your Authentic Self via dialogue. No grand literary reward is necessary... just an honest confession. That's all!

And watch where the practice takes you! Nudge by nudge. Five minutes of breathing. Just breathing in and breathing out. Fifteen minutes of journaling. Twenty minutes of stretching, walking, or biking.

JOURNAL PROMPT

What project did you begin, using small steps then later taking it to the limit? Journal about the experience. Give yourself full credit for making it happen. Be proud of yourself!

✌ *Day 20* ✌

TODAY'S PRACTICE

Our daily routine is precious. How long do you spend at your creative/spiritual space? The breathing exercise, reading, reflection, and writing should not take more than 30 minutes. Have you carved out that much time for yourself? You certainly deserve it!

INSPIRATION

What stimulates you to do things you have been thinking of doing but haven't started yet? Keep repeating your dream or desire in your journal until it begins to gel into action, motivates you to take the first step, galvanizes you to act. What you think turns into words and becomes your action.

You write it down. You say it aloud. You visualize it and suddenly you feel motivated to move boldly in the right direction. Once you visualize yourself doing something you have imagined, your mind begins to work toward that action and your heart cooperates. You feel you have already done it once.

When passion stirs, you have already mentally practiced what you want to do in the future. You develop a positive image of yourself like a powerful pep talk.

Trust you can do it. Believe in yourself. Let me ask you... where are you now? For the last three weeks how much have you practiced and learned?

Why not celebrate what you have achieved so far? Acknowledge what you have accomplished already. You begin your morning with a healthy new routine that turns the rest of your ordinary day into an extraordinary day. You are providing a shield of resilience during good as well as bad times. You recognize your positive qualities. This is no ordinary feat. Keep in mind all the good things you are doing for yourself. Don't ruminate on things that did not go right.

Notice all the baby steps you are taking. By the end of the month those accumulated steps will look like a refreshing walk. Just keep at it. Don't let anyone or anything spoil your day. Let the positive and good vibes come to the surface.

When are you at your best? When are you your complete, authentic, natural self? Make a list of five times.

⚝ *Day 21* ⚝

TODAY'S PRACTICE

Here you are! I admire your determination and punctuality! Settle down at your designated seat in a comfortable posture. Gently bring your mind and heart to your body. Practice inhaling and exhaling as you have been doing. Read the inspiration and prompt. Close your eyes for several minutes as you reflect, and then write in your notebook.

INSPIRATION

Do you send feelings of gratitude to your muse? Do you wholeheartedly appreciate when the muse visits you?

As a verb, the word *muse* means to consider something thoughtfully or deeply. When you give deep thought to something, you're musing. You can't muse for a minute. It may take years to muse on certain ideas as I mused before writing this book.

As a noun, *muse* means someone who inspires creativity and is herself or himself a source of inspiration. In plural, *the Muses* refer to nine Greek goddesses of the various arts and sciences including poetry, music, and dance.

Muses visit you as inspiration or motivation. They begin at a creative point and ascend into larger circles until you end up with several pages of writing or painting. When nothing to write comes to mind, use your drawing journal. Sketch or make a collage of cut-out pictures? Go ahead and scribble something, anything that your heart desires, and find yourself in the next ascending circlet. The more attempts you make at your craft, the more you feed your imagination.

When you sit at your personal place, a calm comes over you. At the same time, an energy vibrates throughout your body when you are your most creative self. An idea has turned into something concrete. Your muses are witnessing your silent joy. They love to spend time with you when you are absorbed within. Watch them dance in your heart.

JOURNAL PROMPT

Write a letter to your muse telling her how grateful you are for visiting you. Share how much you appreciate her company.

༄ *Day 22* ༄

TODAY'S PRACTICE

Breathing exercises sharpen your senses and enrich the moments of your day. You may discover that, up until these exercises, you had not fully enjoyed all the beauty and love and kindness that surround you. Do you feel this way?

In each of the remaining days this month, continue the practice of breathing, reading, reflecting, and journaling.

INSPIRATION

The first, second, or even third drafts of my writing projects are rough and clumsy. It would be an embarrassment if someone read them. This is after having written ten fiction and nonfiction books and hundreds of essays and stories. The final manuscript is always something to be proud of, but at the beginning stages, it is not good enough to see the light of the day.

Yet I keep working at it, as I imagine you must do as well. A trick I use to keep going is to come up with a tentative cover design. I keep that cover alongside an image of my completed manuscript in my heart as I work, thanking my muse for sending small accidents, ideas, insights, and blessings my way.

If I let my "shitty" first drafts and ambiguities close my mind, then I get paralyzed. Instead I let go of the brick wall of expectations that my inner critic builds. If that doesn't work (and here's where my journal comes to my rescue), I ask, "What should I do? Where should I go?" I vent my grievances and complaints. I don't carry them around. I may disclose them to a trusted family member or close friend but no one is as intimate as my journal.

As you may have experienced by now, when you purge the obstacles or conundrum in your notebook at the end of the session, you receive answers. You get some inclination where you are and where you may go next. Possibilities open. It never fails to lead you to clarity.

Journaling daily for a decade, and then on and off for two more decades, has made my little world ridiculously positive. However, there are still days when I'm surrounded by negative thoughts. Journaling keeps me from drowning in that whirlpool of ordinary worries and anxieties.

JOURNAL PROMPT
What gnarl, protuberance, or negative knot has emerged in your day? Journal about it and let it move from your heart-mind onto the pages. To maintain your inner peace, try not to miss journaling the way you choose not to skip exercising to maintain your vigor.

ꙮ *Day 23* ꙮ

TODAY'S PRACTICE
Breathe, read, reflect, journal.

INSPIRATION
"The starting point of discovering who you are,
your gifts, your talents, your dreams,
is being comfortable with yourself.
Spend time alone. Write in a journal."
—Robin Sharma

If journaling has not become a habit yet, for the rest of this month, push yourself to write half a page or a page about whatever comes to mind. One day at a time. Doing something repeatedly changes your attitude. After one week you will want to extend to two and then three weeks. Why 21 days? Deepak Chopra assures us that doing something for three weeks turns it into a habit. When you succeed in journaling continuously, reward yourself. Celebrate! Rewards help you stick to the new routine.

Journaling requires belief in yourself and believing that this practice has inherent merit. You may stumble, you may fall, but stumbling and falling are not *failing*. Each day, return to your notebook the way you return to your power spot, to your breathing exercises.

Try to journal 2-3 pages. By the time you are on the third page the reason for your discomfort and imbalance will reveal itself. That reason may be as mundane as needing a full night's sleep. But day by day and page by page you will discover what else is going on within you. Your journaling will reveal how and why you feel stifled or bored or empty or rushed. You will look at your familial, professional, social, and spiritual life with new eyes. You will realize some of what is really going on inside you that you were not even aware of.

JOURNAL PROMPT
What is the most difficult part of your personal routine these days? If a close friend of yours was having similar difficulties, what would you say to encourage this person?

ꝏ *Day 24* ꝏ

TODAY'S PRACTICE
Breathe, read, reflect, journal.

INSPIRATION

"A sheltered life can be a daring life as well.
For all serious daring starts from within."
—Eudora Welty

I didn't read poetry until 2005. Then I received a gift of two books: Edward Hirsch's *How to Read a Poem and Fall in Love with Poetry,* and Molly Peacock's *How to Read a Poem and Start a Poetry Circle.* I enjoyed reading both. Then years went by without my reading a poem.

Between 2007-2011 I wrote commentaries about four of my favorite scriptures from world religions: *Tao Te Ching, Dhammapada, Bhagavad Gita,* and *Devi Gita.* I titled them "As I Understand It." Once a week, I'd copy a chapter and write a short commentary about the lesson I learned. Having completed the self-assigned task, I realized that through reading and copying hundreds of verses I had unwittingly learned to appreciate and get a feel for poetic form. More poetry books and several years later, I made my first attempts at poetry writing. I began jotting verses in my journal. Almost all of them were about journaling, writing, and meditation.

This is what I came up with:

> Scrapings of my pen on a blank page whisper
> The murmuring of voices from the depth of my being.
> They speak of patience when fuzziness distorts.
> They speak of courage when obstacles interfere.
> They speak of going within with words,
> Of revealing suffering, distress, adversity, hope.
> The words take me to the depths of my being,
> Insights emerge and surprise me.

By 2005, my journal had become my confidante, as it will become yours and surprise you with what you hear. It'll drone and prod, nudge you, give you clues and cues. It may compel, demand, even reprimand. If you're fortunate and hear murmurs from the unknown, pay close attention to them.

JOURNAL PROMPT
When an idea strikes you and wakes you up, write it in your journal. Rewrite it as verse. Keep revising it until it reads like a poem.

❧ *Day 25* ❧

TODAY'S PRACTICE
Breathe, read, reflect, journal.

INSPIRATION

When I turn a brand-new page of my notebook I eagerly begin writing whatever flows from my pen. This is the favorite part of my day. It wasn't so many years ago when I felt intimidated by a blank page. Slowly I realized how this simple exercise relieves stress and anxiety.

My earliest attempts of journal keeping started during a time of extreme trauma, transition, and transformation. Within the span of eighteen months, my youngest brother was killed in an automobile accident, my mother passed away, and my father followed her within a few months. It was the time when I also gave birth to my second daughter. That baby kept me sane and brought me back to my senses. Those days of journaling was a source of emotional relief and good therapy.

Unlike many journal keepers, I had no secrets to hide. I simply and freely poured out my distress, my pain, my sadness. It didn't matter what I wrote, but the very process of journaling helped keep me calm every single day.

It doesn't matter what you write about, only that you do. When you continue the journey for days and months in your journal, you uncover secrets – secrets even you didn't realize you held.

JOURNAL PROMPT

Did you ever keep a diary? What lessons did you learn that help you now? If you didn't keep a diary, write about an event or incident that taught you something that is useful even now.

∾ *Day 26* ∾

TODAY'S PRACTICE

Breathe, read, reflect, journal.

INSPIRATION

Your notebook is the space for your mind to wander and release whatever is floating or rushing through. Go out on a date with yourself to buy a notebook. It could be the one with a fancy cover, or a calendar journal with pockets and ribbons, or the one that has a memorable quote at the top for inspiration.

You can also create a journaling file on your computer. You could write a disguised title or simply write, "My Journal." The type of notebook doesn't matter. What is important is what goes into it.

It does help to organize your day, your month, your year, to record your intentions and reach your goals. You may have more than one journal. When you are ready, choose the one that you feel most motivated to write in. Scribble in it the things you have "zipped your lips" or "held your tongue" about. Don't let the beautiful appearance take over or lead you away from being sincere and bold about your thoughts.

You don't need to write in fancy journals to reach your goal. A spiral notebook from the drugstore or dollar store will work equally well. The important thing is to keep the habit of free writing, to keep your thoughts and words flowing.

JOURNAL PROMPT

How do you journal? On your computer or in a notebook? What kind of notebook do you like? One with a whimsical or fancy cover, or plain? Do you like journals with 400 pages so there are enough leaves for the whole year, or several with 100-150 pages? Play with words as you journal about your favorite kind of notebooks that invite you to write in them every day.

෴ *Day 27* ෴

TODAY'S PRACTICE
Breathe, read, reflect, journal.

INSPIRATION
Reflecting daily on the blank page is a good practice. How your day unfolds is unpredictable, but the one thing you can count on and control is putting pen to paper. First, breathing exercises followed by journaling unfurls the rest of your day soothingly. But what about your nights?

Have you considered a dream journal? Keep one easily available, especially if you have vivid dreams and can remember them. Such a notebook will collect your personal symbolic and magical elements which you can introduce in your stories.

Keep your dream journal next to your bed and let it stay there until you have a vivid dream that is worth recording. To not disturb a loved one sleeping next to you, invest in a pen with a light. They are inexpensive and available online.

When you reread your dream journal, you'll be surprised by sentences and ideas that you don't remember having written. Some images will take you deeper into the meaning of the dream to better understand the situations you face during the days.

JOURNAL PROMPT
Do you have certain dreams that recur over weeks, months, or years? What elements of these dreams do you recognize? Once you journal about them, are you able to draw any symbolic connections between things in your dreams and your real life?

৬৹ *Day 28* ৫৶

TODAY'S PRACTICE
Breathe, read, reflect, journal.

INSPIRATION
At the tail end of our Semester-at-Sea voyage, we were driving back to our ship after sunset in Lantau Island, Hong Kong. In the windowpane over my own reflection reeled the images of various religious monuments we had visited – Hindu and Buddhist temples, mosques, churches, synagogues.

Lantau Island features a monumental statue of the Buddha on a mountain peak, symbolizing the harmonious relationship between man and nature. Seated next to me was our day guide, a young local woman. She broke the silence by asking, "Which religions do you belong to?"

The question was abrupt. I had never before reflected upon such a thought. Although born in a Hindu family with a humanist father and a pious mother, I was not particularly religious. I was an admirer of religious art, however. That whole day my heart had softened with the joy of observing the vulnerability and compassion reflected in images of the Buddha.

I smiled. I paused. Then from somewhere inside me came this response: "I do not belong to any religion. All religions belong to me." My heart-mind surprised me. I accepted this answer right away.

Now, 26 years later, those spontaneous words have sunk deep within. They are ingrained in my heart and often echo in my mind. I felt gratified when I found similar sentiments validated by one of my favorite poets and mystics, Rumi. "I looked in temples, churches and mosques. But I found the Divine within my heart."

JOURNAL PROMPT
Have you had a sudden flash of insight, or even a dream, in which you found an answer to a problem you were having?

✣ *Day 29* ✣

TODAY'S PRACTICE
Breathe, read, reflect, journal.

INSPIRATION
It's good to pour out your thoughts and feelings each day, some raw and bitter while others are full of joy and rewards. Such writing helps you to release intense emotions. It is a way of calming down.

Mindful Writer Audrey Snyder started to keep a diary at age four after her mother died. She saved them all, and years later when she reread them, she realized that her younger self had a lot to teach her current self. She turned the content into a memoir, *Worth the Climb*, a compilation of things she wanted to share with her mother. "Although I hoped it would help my mother to know me, it also allowed me to know myself better. My children and grandchildren have read my memoir, which gave them a deeper appreciation for the path I chose and why. It helped them understand the lessons I have tried to instill in them, and gave them something to pass on to their children. Today, though, I am grateful for the vehicle of journaling that allows me to feel happy and confident."

"We all want to make the most of our lives…
to become the highest expressions of ourselves.
There's no better way to find that aha! than by keeping a diary."
—Oprah Winfrey

JOURNAL PROMPT

What's jumbled in your life today? What can you do to unjumble things? What steps will you take today to start the process?

✒ *Day 30* ✒

TODAY'S PRACTICE

I have included 30 days in each month, irrespective of how many days it has in a calendar year. The reason is that it allows you to start Writing Meditation Practice in any month, and it also gives you a free day in case you miss one.

On this last day of the month, practice your breathing exercise with your eyes closed for 5-10 minutes. You will continue to do this in the coming weeks until you can sit with your breath for 15-20 minutes. This, if not more, is certainly possible by the end of the year. Next comes reading, reflection, and journaling.

INSPIRATION

I used to write in my notebook before my breathing exercise. Later I discovered journaling afterward made the entries more focused; I felt more present and the voice of my inner self was clearer.

Before we begin the next month about "Mindfulness, Attention, and Awareness," think of what your intention was to complete this month. Have you made progress with the task you intended to finish? Were there unforeseen snags? Did you miss several days?

You have helped yourself replace negative energy with positive energy by extracting your inner turmoil into your journal. It is helping you to observe what you think and feel. This exercise creates distance from your intense emotions and passing thoughts. You witness them as an outsider and deal with them objectively. This is good for your mental hygiene.

The daily sitting, breathing, and journaling ritual has begun to ground you. Make this ritual an integral part of your day. It will create a new foundation for your writing time. You are planting seeds for hours of creativity and productivity. You are also sowing a seed for meditation which we'll refine in Month 3. Trust these seeds will eventually sprout and blossom.

END OF MONTH PROMPT

Reflect on your month. What gains did you make? Where did you feel blocked? What did you discover about yourself? What appropriate action are you going to take? What would you like to add to your current practice? How does it relate with your yearly purpose? When your intentions come deep from your heart-mind, they become a reality.

Month 2

Mindfulness, Attention, and Awareness

Suggested Readings

*Conquest of Mind: Take Charge of Your Thoughts
and Reshape Your Life Through Meditation*
Eknath Easwaran, 2019.

*The Mind Illuminated:
A Complete Meditation Guide Integrating Buddhist Wisdom
and Brain Science for Greater Mindfulness*
Culadasa (John Yates), 2017.

*Peak Mind:
Find Your Focus, Own Your Attention, Invest 12 Minutes a Day*
Amishi P. Jha, 2022.

A New Earth: Awakening to Your Life's Purpose
Eckhart Tolle, 2008.

ᜃ *Day 31* ᜂ

TODAY'S PRACTICE

Welcome back! I'm delighted that you've returned to your personal sacred space. This month you are going to learn a lot about attention and awareness. These mental qualities are a must for each of us, but especially for those who want to find a writer's voice and unfurl the day with confidence.

You will not only practice to be attentive and aware of what is going on around you but also within you. This month:

…Settle down comfortably.

…Continue to do a breathing exercise for as long as you do it with ease.

…Read the day's inspiration and prompt. Reflect upon them for some time.

…Write in your journal.

INSPIRATION

The word "meditation" is often confused with "mindfulness" or the other way round. Meditation is the discipline of sitting still in a particular posture in silence and solitude with focus on the breath. (You will learn more about it in Month 3.) Mindfulness is a state of total awareness of the mind that results from the daily practice of meditation.

You often pay attention to a task at hand. However, you may not be aware of what is happening around you and within you. In meditation you learn to combine the power of attention and awareness, deepening your consciousness.

You have practiced focusing your attention on your breath. In so doing, you watch your own mind. You witness yourself as an "outsider." This is similar to looking at your own reflection in a life-size mirror. The way you study your face, your torso, the whole body is not different from witnessing your passing thoughts and body sensations, to determine how they make you feel. But you are watching these as if from a distance.

Such self-awareness is essential to your creative and spiritual growth.

When something agitates or upsets you, thoughts rush through your mind. Sitting in silence, asking yourself, *Why did that thought cross my mind? Why did I act the way I did? Why did I say what I said?* and watching your mind until the body calms down is of great benefit. This habit makes you your own judge and jury. You can't cheat, lie, or ignore the truth deep within that you are witnessing.

JOURNAL PROMPT

Journal about how you understand awareness. What is the difference between being aware around you and within you?

⤷ *Day 32* ↺

TODAY'S PRACTICE

Settle in, breathe, read, reflect, and journal.

INSPIRATION

To clarify the difference between attention, awareness, and mindfulness, let's go deeper. Attention and awareness are basic faculties used in our breathing exercises and meditation practices. When combined, they result in mindfulness. Read more about them below to know how you can strengthen these faculties.

Attention

We are born with limited conscious power but we can expand and strengthen it. The good news is that you can do this through the practices of journaling and breathing exercises (that eventually lead to meditation). The job of attention is to focus on one object at a time outside of the general field of consciousness. It is encrgized by your conscious power. For instance, as you breathe, you pay attention to the sensations of air going in and out of the nostrils; as you journal, you pay attention to the words you are writing; in a walking meditation, you pay attention to the movement of your feet and legs.

Awareness

Like attention, awareness also gets its energy from conscious power. As you pay attention to the breath in the exercises, you also become aware of thoughts circulating in your mind, or the sound of a distant car, or the smell of a scented candle in the room. In journaling, your attention is on the words pouring out of your pen, but you are also aware of your thoughts and feelings and the warmth in the room. While walking, you pay attention to the movements, but you are also aware of birds chirping and leaves swishing.

Do you see the difference? Attention is self-absorbed focus. Awareness puts the focus of your attention within the context of whatever you are experiencing. Although your five senses and mind take in data all the time, awareness filters out unimportant information that is not relevant to you.

When there is optimum interaction between attention and awareness, there is mindfulness. The more you practice breathing and journaling, the more you train your attention and awareness to work together. These two disciplines expand and strengthen mindfulness.

JOURNAL PROMPT

Which activities do you engage in where your attention and awareness are functioning fully?

ꙮ *Day 33* ꙮ

TODAY'S PRACTICE

Settle in, breathe, read, reflect, and journal.

INSPIRATION

We are not naturally mindful. But mindfulness can be cultivated and developed through the deliberate use of attention and awareness. Eventually with practice, the two faculties merge to become one. This results in an expansion and strengthening of your conscious power. In summary: Attention + Awareness = Mindfulness = Stronger Conscious Power.

Increasing your conscious power is like body building or weight training. You simply do your daily physical exercises and over time reap the benefits. Similarly, you practice mental exercises routinely and watch yourself become less stressed, calmer, kinder, and more importantly more mindful during the whole day.

With this ritual of daily sitting and breathing and writing, you are training your mind to pay attention to one thing as well as to "stand back" and become aware of it. When this happens, it changes everything about the way you think, feel, and speak.

You get glimpses of strong mindfulness when you are in the creative "zone" or when your artistic "flow" is effortless. You may have felt this way during journaling, writing, walking in nature, or similar nonverbal activities. When this happens, time slows. You become attuned to every detail, senses turn vivid, and you may even feel you are witnessing an event unfold. This is one of the most pleasurable experiences attentive and aware minds can have.

JOURNAL PROMPT
Write about an activity where you combine attention and awareness. What happens when you are mindless? What do you lose in the process?

ஃ *Day 34* ﻌ

TODAY'S PRACTICE
Settle in, breathe, read, reflect, and journal.

INSPIRATION
Have you understood how mindfulness develops and is strengthened? Let's dig deeper. When you sit still to focus on your breath, keep in mind that whereas attention is under your conscious control, awareness is not. Whereas you can train attention, you cannot train awareness. Awareness arises automatically in response to your attention on external

sensory data and internal stimuli such as sensations, feelings, and thoughts.

Although you are taught to pay attention, no one teaches you to be aware of what is in your mind and heart. Awareness of your surroundings is ignored and self-awareness gets stunted. Fortunately, what you are practicing now – a focus on the breath and journaling – cultivates and nourishes awareness. You will be healthier, happier, and at ease with yourself because of sharpened attention and awareness which will result in your being mindful.

JOURNAL PROMPT

How attentive and aware are you? How mindful are you about what is happening within and around you? Have you ever thought people were criticizing you behind your back, only to later discover they were trying to arrange a surprise party for you? Journal about a similar event or misunderstanding you have experienced.

◟ *Day 35* ◞

TODAY'S PRACTICE
Settle in, breathe, read, reflect, and journal.

INSPIRATION
The practice of mindfulness connects our conscious ego self with our boundless Authentic Self within. In the beginning stages, the practice is not different from learning to ride a bike. Typically you don't learn on the first try. You fear. You doubt. You fall. But in doing so, you learn. You keep practicing until you feel the pleasure of going downhill against the breeze.

I have jotted simple steps that happen when you are in tune with the universe:

1. You feel grounded, aligned with the universe.

2. You feel ready and aware. When an idea flashes, when opportunity knocks, you accept the challenge.

3. Having accepted the challenge, you trust it completely and are confident that where your passion is leading you will reveal your talent and hone your creative skills.

4. Problems may arise, anxiety may take over, and you may even begin to doubt. Friends and family may douse your passion. But you will have faith in yourself – one day at a time.

5. You develop complete faith in yourself, resulting in self-confidence. You come to know your gifts and skills more intimately. You have listened to the call of the universe. Now be careful and turn inward. Try not to confide your nascent dream with anyone. Quietly carry it to initial success.

JOURNAL PROMPT

The creative process cannot be restricted. We must let it flow. Creativity and imagination have a life of their own. They thrive in unpredictability. Journal about a time when you strictly followed an outline to write a story or an essay but ended up aborting the project even before you reached the end.

≈ *Day 36* ≈

TODAY'S PRACTICE

Settle in, breathe, read, reflect, and journal.

INSPIRATION

Feeling inadequate for the work you are "called" to do is a prerequisite for creative individuals. Yet, when you immerse yourself in the work, your true inner self (as well as the universe) awakens to help you.

Any creative work is a collaboration between you, your inner mentor, and the universe. When you begin writing a book or creating an artwork or any project, you know only half of the story. You discover the rest of it as you write or paint and astonish yourself every few steps when it unfolds in a way you did not intend. This happens all the way until "The End" is reached, a painting is completed, or a project is finished.

When your passion is alive, why not respond to the little calls that you hear? Such calls assist the life's Big Calling. Each of us has unique skills which make certain outcomes possible. So, when something feels right to your thinking-heart you must give it everything you've got.

When your attention and awareness are combined and you are fully mindful, you've awakened your true inner mentor I call Authentic Self, the most energetic and awakened part of your being. Strengthen your connection to it within the silence and solitude of your daily sitting in silence.

JOURNAL PROMPT

Today when you sit comfortably at your sacred space, turn off the logical part of your brain and turn up your imagination. Play with free association. Connect with something you once thought was unconnectable. What did you come up with?

ೊ *Day 37* ೨

TODAY'S PRACTICE

Settle in, breathe, read, reflect, and journal.

INSPIRATION

Do you sometimes ponder, *Whatever thought I come up with, or whatever story I write, it has already been written by someone in some language at some corner of the world? Why bother trying to write something "new"?*

If so, this is what I say to you: What you can write, no one else can. What is "new" is you – your singular way of observing the world and expressing it in words. When you pour out your heart and mind, your unique personality and authenticity shine through. Your readers reverberate with your original writer's voice. Just like your face, your voice is one of a kind.

The secret of success is in trusting the path that you have chosen to walk, trusting the calling that has been bestowed on you. Let that path lead you wherever it may. Your only job is to work wholeheartedly and know that there is no one else in the world who could or would complete it the way you would. When you selflessly do a job without desire for fame or riches, your work will shine with its own light and provide immense contentment.

JOURNAL PROMPT

Journal about what you can do the next time you're faced with doubt about a project you're working on.

৩ *Day 38* ৩

TODAY'S PRACTICE

Settle in, breathe, read, reflect, and journal.

INSPIRATION

Sitting still in silence and solitude and paying attention to your breathing is also called meditation. Meditation has many forms. While sitting and lying meditations focus on breathing, walking meditation focuses on the movement of feet. Each is geared toward increasing awareness and gaining deeper insight into yourself.

Making yourself the center of attention is not an admirable trait, but if your upbringing has cautioned you against focusing on yourself, try to forget that warning. By practicing inner and outer awareness, you are learning to be mindful. Mindfulness teaches you to focus on something that is greater within you. But that inner awareness remains dormant unless you stir it with Writing Meditation Practice.

With mindfulness you will also pay attention to your outer self: your physical appearance, original works, and their successes. And you'll make attempts to know yourself better. Mindfulness will help you slow the rushed life so you can enjoy living in the present more. You will find clarity of mind. Unhurried days will unfurl when you interact with others with thoughtfulness and kindness.

The only way to improve yourself and understand and appreciate the values you want to live by is through attention and self-awareness.

JOURNAL PROMPT

Which of your values and daily practices are leading you to become your best self?

⊱ *Day 39* ⊰

TODAY'S PRACTICE

Practice 5 minutes of a breath exercise by counting to 10 as you inhale and exhale. When thoughts carry you away, bring your attention back to the breath. Repeat. Follow the quiet sitting with reading and reflecting on today's inspiration and prompt. Jot down your thoughts in your journal.

INSPIRATION

Perhaps the word "awareness" is still eluding you. Remember how you prevailed after facing a problem, struggled to solve it, and succeeded (or not), then took a different turn.

When a problem begets another question instead of letting you solve it, such a turn somehow jump-starts your inner journey. Going within leads you to a better understanding of yourself because it makes you aware of your inner landscape.

Usually you have such an experience between the ages of forty to sixty. Before the so-called middle age, you pay attention to only your outer appearance, what you see reflected in the mirror. Your awareness is directed outward upon things, people, and places.

In midlife your body is changing. In addition, with the passing of one or both parents – when the impermanence of life registers and comes alive – you hear primordial questions being whispered from inside. "Is that all there is?" "What is authentic about my life, what is permanent, what is it that will truly make me happy?"

Each of us defines happiness differently. Physical health, joy, and contentment that has resulted from years of Writing Meditation Practice make me happy. What makes you happy?

JOURNAL PROMPT

In which area of your life do you need to develop more self-awareness? Is it physical, emotional, professional, or creative/spiritual?

⤷ *Day 40* ⤶

TODAY'S PRACTICE

Settle in, breathe, read, reflect, and journal.

INSPIRATION

The year I started the Mindful Poets Group with poet Gail Oare as its leader, I purchased *The Complete Poems of Emily Dickinson*, edited by Thomas H. Johnson, and made it part of my morning reading.

Dickinson's biography was inspiring, her poems powerful, unassuming and quiet. Every day I read aloud several poems until one reverberated with my heart. I would copy it in a notebook meant especially for this exercise. This I followed by reflecting upon it. It took me one year to read aloud all 1775 poems and copy my favorite ones. By the end of that project, I had 220 of my favorite Dickinson poems copied.

This exercise not only deepened my prose but also inspired a few poems of my own. It enhanced my love of nature and life, helping me accept my status of being an unknown female minority author in the United States, and giving credibility to the quiet life I prefer to live.

Dickinson's poems underline the significance of looking inward, to be in tune with the inner self, and to pay heed to inner whispers. In short, being mindful. Mindfulness, you will know by the end of this book, can by cultivated through journaling and sitting in silence with focus on the breath which is the beginning of meditation. With this practice, the mind calms down and you are able to go into deeper levels of consciousness. The deeper you go, the darker it is. You find yourself in stark darkness but your inner mentor, the Authentic Self, is there to guide you. In Dickinson's words, "I am out with lantern, looking for myself." Your lantern is your AS.

JOURNAL PROMPT

Which writer speaks to you? How has he or she influenced your writing? Your way of living?

⊱ *Day 41* ⊰

TODAY'S PRACTICE

Make yourself comfortable at your Sacred Power Spot. Settle in the posture you usually sit in. Close your eyes and for the next 5 minutes notice the sensation of breath as you breathe in and breathe out. Feel the air moving in and out of your body as your chest and abdomen slightly expand and contract with each inhalation and exhalation. Watch how your thoughts settle down in your mind as the breath takes the space of succession of thoughts that pass by one after the other.

Then read today's inspiration and prompt. Reflect for a couple of minutes before you journal about them.

INSPIRATION

Growing up I was taught to take the smallest piece when sweetmeats were passed around. I was taught never to praise myself, even when I had something great to share. And I was taught to offer the best I had. In short, being humble was one of the greatest virtues my young mind was taught to cultivate.

I learned to be humble, all right. But its side effects meant being compliant, unassuming, doubtful. Being the youngest of nine siblings increased my meekness. I was loved and cared for by my older siblings so it never occurred to me that "humility" needed to be balanced with confidence. Confidence comes from self-knowing. And self-knowing and understanding come from going within. No wonder I was seeking my Self in my middle years!

Finding who you truly are means knowing when you should be humble and when you should be courageous, bold, and proud. Later in life, the practice of meditation and journaling sharpened my self-awareness. I realized that humility goes well with confidence. It carries respect and kindness for others. Awareness of Self with confidence is the essence of humility.

JOURNAL PROMPT

How do you see yourself in relationship to some of your close family members and inner circle of friends?

✒ *Day 42* ✒

TODAY'S PRACTICE

Welcome back to your seat! Make yourself comfortable. Practice your usual breathing session. Watch your breath going in and coming out. Keep in mind you are not making yourself breathe. It is happening by itself. The more you watch this, the clearer your mind will become and help the chatter in your mind to settle.

Read, reflect, and write whatever today's inspiration and prompt inspire.

INSPIRATION

The more you pay attention to one thing and become aware of it within its context, the more attentive you will be. You not only become mindful of things around you but also within you. The small changes you make in your daily habits will slowly accumulate toward positivity.

When mindfulness seeps into your consciousness, you begin to identify the genuine person you are and want to be. As you journal about self-awareness, you will feel clear-headed. The topics of interest that you have pondered, or a concept that has lingered in the shadows of your mind for years, will surface. When you recognize them, you are in charge of starting or stopping them. You will make changes in your daily routine. Small steps. One step at a time. Making progress. A good way to begin the journey.

After Writing Meditation Practice you may walk into the kitchen, click on the television or turn on the radio, fill the kettle for tea or start the coffee maker, and staring at you are yesterday's unwashed dishes. You decide that the new you won't leave the kitchen at night before cleaning the dishes. That will make your mornings more pleasant. Now you have a few extra minutes to walk outside and to say hello to birds on the lush tree, or be greeted by shimmering snow on the ground. You breathe in the smell of coffee or brewing tea leaves before taking a sip and savoring the moment as you begin your day.

JOURNAL PROMPT

What small steps in your daily life can you take? What changes can you make so that your tomorrow is better?

℘ *Day 43* ℘

TODAY'S PRACTICE

After settling at your cozy corner, focus on your breathing. Start by paying attention to the air near your nostrils, followed by the chest, and finally the abdomen. Pause at each area and take a few slow and deep breaths. At which place does breathing feel the most comfortable: nose, chest, or abdomen? Continue to breathe at the place that feels most satisfying.

After the sitting practice, jot down your thoughts on today's inspiration and prompt.

INSPIRATION

Mindfulness (outer and inner awareness) not only makes you feel alive but also keeps you energetic and joyful for the rest of the day. You are kinder to yourself and the people you come in touch with. You smile more often. You are not restless when you have to wait or are asked to be patient. Mindfulness brings contentment into your day.

But it doesn't happen automatically.

You have to cultivate it by not missing the Practice. Then for the rest of the day, you pay attention to the task at hand and keep your senses of sight and hearing alert. The senses of smell, taste, and touch will come alive when needed, such as when walking or relishing a meal.

Push yourself outside your comfort zone. If something painful or hard needs to be done, do it. That is a mindful thing to do and will deepen your self-awareness. As a creative person, you do this all the time. You work hard at using your imagination to write, to create. Build new stories, develop new characters, plot novels, and find exotic settings. Use this talent in other areas of your life as well.

JOURNAL PROMPT

What hurdles did you cross to declare yourself a writer? What challenges you as you write? What actions do you need to be mindful about so you may strengthen your craft and "grow" as a writer?

✎ *Day 44* ✎

TODAY'S PRACTICE

You look great, sitting with ease at your Sacred Power Spot, determined and energized. Close your eyes. Feel the air moving in and out of your body as your chest and abdomen slightly expand and contract with each inhalation and exhalation. Watch how your thoughts settle down in your mind as the breath takes the space of a succession of thoughts that pass by one after the other.

Then read today's inspiration and prompt. Reflect for a couple of minutes before you journal about them.

INSPIRATION

Attention and self-awareness that lead to mindfulness are not easy to cultivate. Without a regular practice, especially in the beginning stage, they can easily slip away.

Practice sitting in silence with your focus on the breath. Think of positive, good, wise thoughts and write them in your journal along with today's reflections. Some keep a separate gratitude journal and write in it often.

It took me many years to develop the discipline of sitting in silence and solitude into a daily habit. The journey was not easy either. As I was unsure of what lie ahead, my self-confidence began to fizzle. Blinded by feeling as if I was doing nothing, a "nobody," I forgot I had voluntarily chosen to practice *and* that I had a loving, caring family.

My mind would focus only on my shortcomings. I thought the worst of myself. I pretended to smile to show I was fine, but inside I counted and repeated my own failings.

I know now that I was not unique in thinking in this manner. So many of us fall into this trap. Today I neither self-doubt nor self-criticize. If my mind brings a shortcoming to the surface, I deal with it right away. Unravel the knot by becoming aware of why it is happening. Pay attention to it, and you're certain to arrive at the reason of its appearance when you pour out your insights in your notebook. I have learned that nature does not bestow mindfulness upon you. You must cultivate it with practice.

JOURNAL PROMPT

What are your positive character traits? Write in detail. If shortcomings surface while you are writing your good traits, jot them down on the last page of your notebook. Plan how to deal with them. Act upon this plan, then tear out the page.

ᘓ *Day 45* ᘔ

TODAY'S PRACTICE

Settle in, breathe, read, reflect, and journal.

INSPIRATION

Mindfulness can be cultivated using various disciplines and tools. However sometimes a family member, friend, or even a stranger may help you discover your inner Self.

My mother-in-law was a pious woman, not an easy person to live with. Her neighbors and disciples adored and respected her. But to me she would say things that emotionally hurt me. For nine years she lived with us half of the year, and then during the last four years of her life she lived with us year round. What was I to do? I decided to make a list of the things she said or did. If I lived to be in my late eighties or nineties, I promised myself I would not say those things or act in that manner to my children. I took it as an opportunity to refocus the negativity I felt into positive lessons.

That experience was immersive. It would not have been possible if I had not already had a regular Writing Meditation Practice. I read a lot of material that brought hope and ushered solace into many unhappy days. One of the teachings by Martin Luther King, Jr. stuck: "We must develop and maintain the capacity of forgiveness. He who is devoid of the power to forgive is devoid of the power to love. *There is something good in the worst of us and some evil in the best of us.* When we discover this, we are less prone to hate our enemies."

My M-I-L was certainly not an enemy. During my younger days, when I lived with my husband's family for three years, I watched how she was lovingly devoted to her family. Most importantly she had birthed and brought up my husband who is kind, wise, giving, and loving.

It is amazing how much we can learn about ourselves by keenly observing others with whom we live. Learning about yourself fosters self-understanding, and self-understanding leads to self-awareness. I tell myself there is "some evil in the best of us."

JOURNAL PROMPT

Write a letter to your future self about what you hope to achieve through Writing Meditation Practice. Write the letter on paper or print it out and seal it in an envelope. Open it at the end of the year after you have finished reading this guidebook.

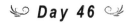

☙ *Day 46* ❧

TODAY'S PRACTICE

It has been two weeks since you began your practice of settling at your creative power spot and doing breathing exercises, and six weeks since you began to freely pour out things into your journal that you were bursting to share with someone whom you could completely trust. How are the two exercises coming along?

Sit in silence. Make yourself comfortable. Practice your breathing as long as you want, focusing on your in-breath and out-breath. Read the inspiration and the prompt and write in your journal anything that is on the top of your mind.

INSPIRATION

Are you a full-time writer but feel inferior for not having a job with a salary? Does that shake your self-confidence? I trust you have a "steady income and a room of your own," as Virginia Wolfe recommended. So why not honestly believe that your current vocation is meaningful?

The path you have chosen tells me that you are a unique human being. You were never meant to be like anyone else. You are meant to stand out. Stop beating yourself up for your shortcomings. Instead pat yourself on the back for your strengths.

When you shift away from negative self-talk, it opens space for positive thinking and self-awareness. It empowers you.

Say and do what you truly believe in. At the same time, be attentive. Be aware, outside and inside. Mindfulness is a great companion and friend. It brings you closer to your inner self, your Authentic Self. The closer you are to your AS, the more mindful you become. As long as you are honest with yourself and have no agenda with others, your day will unfurl and surprise you with peace. You will be admired and awarded for your authenticity.

JOURNAL PROMPT

What is important to you in terms of home life, friends, and your career? List one or two items from each of these areas in your journal and refer to this list when making important decisions.

❧ *Day 47* ❧

TODAY'S PRACTICE

Sit comfortably on your chair or mat. Bring your heart and mind to where your body is seated. Become conscious of your breathing. Feel the present moments passing as you breathe in and breathe out. Let the thoughts pass by.

When you are ready, conjure up an image, a mountain peak, a flowing river, a path through lush trees. Stay with it as you do your breathing exercise. Follow the exercise with reading the inspiration and prompt, reflecting upon them. Then pour out your feelings and thoughts in your notebook.

INSPIRATION

In *The Happiness Project: Why I Spent a Year Trying to Sing in the Morning, Clean My Closets, Fight Right, Read Aristotle, and Generally Have More Fun*, bestselling author Gretchen Rubin writes that she had an epiphany one rainy afternoon in the unlikeliest of places – a city bus. "The days are long, but the years are short," she thought. "Time is passing, and I'm not focusing enough on the things that really matter." In that moment, she decided to dedicate a year to her own happiness.

Reading her musings, I remembered how many decades ago it occurred to me that I could not change the world but I could change myself. But how? I reread the world wisdom books, researched new scientific literature on mindfulness and meditation, and read literature about the meaning of kindness, wisdom, and contentment. I discovered that a day practicing proven disciplines is a productive day. Combined with loving family relationships, good friends, a concern for others, and yearly travels with my husband, it enhanced my life and became a powerful source of happiness.

While daily discipline and order enhances inner peace, helping those in need – even strangers and visiting unknown places – makes a big difference toward the betterment of life.

When you are attentive and self-aware, you have stronger relationships, are more creative, confident, and a better communicator. You don't go into the nitty-gritty of why things happen, but rather you focus on what you can do about them. You act. You commit to developing focus and awareness.

JOURNAL PROMPT

Write 5 things in your journal that make you happy.

ᒷᓬ *Day 48* ᒷᓬ

TODAY'S PRACTICE

You may be wondering about the benefit of sitting at your Sacred Power Spot day in and day out. Repeating the same breathing exercises in silence, the statement comes to your mind, "*I could use these 30 minutes doing other things that I need to do.*" I hear you! Because that's what I asked myself at the beginning of my meditation practice. It took me months (if not a whole year) to realize that what I was doing was a potion for my soul the same way Tylenol or Advil are medications for pain.

These precious minutes of journaling, deliberate breathing, and self-contemplation are usually the first to go in a speedy and noisy world. While living in that world, you don't realize the qualities of calm and joy when your body, heart, and mind are integrated, when your conscious self is linked to your Self within. Now, let's practice our daily routine.

INSPIRATION

You are learning to cultivate mindfulness. Mindfulness is beneficial and positive. Yet to learn this discipline is challenging. Your natural tendency is to stray toward negative self-talk. Why not journal about it today and then read it back to yourself? Ask yourself if you would be that unkind to any person you know. Then why would you say such a thing about yourself? Being kind to yourself is not encouraged in our families or society. The reason is because it takes effort for you to do so.

Your breathing exercises will warm you up for meditation practice next month, helping you to be kinder and gentler toward yourself and others. It will lead you to wisdom. After a few months of the combined practice of journaling, mindfulness, and meditation, you will have a lingering feeling of goodness. This reaction may dissipate soon after. However, when meditation becomes a habit, the feeling of joy stays with you for the rest of the day. Similarly, people around you notice your positive attitude and instead of reacting, they interact with you.

In your day-to-day interactions, decide not to get pulled into negativity. Remember to interact and not react to other people's actions even when you feel tempted. Mindfulness will teach you to pause and *interact*.

JOURNAL PROMPT

Journal about yourself from the point of view of a loved one or friend. How would that person describe you to someone else?

ᕙ *Day 49* ᕗ

TODAY'S PRACTICE

Make yourself comfortable at your safe, secure, and sacred space. Do a breathing exercise, then read, reflect, and journal.

INSPIRATION

What brings you true happiness comes from inside you. The more attention you pay to inner things, the more they multiply and intensify. Such moments take root in the dark soil within. Their light reflects on your face and in your luminous attitude.

Keep in mind that suffering is never too far from joy. While creating moments of joy or excavating happy memories, you may come across past instances of doubt, shame, guilt, abuse. You may feel hurt because of a sickness or emotional wound that someone may have provoked or society may have ignited. Don't shove away the painful sensations and negative feelings. Stay with the hurt until it dissipates. Journal or talk to a close friend about it. When the pain subsides, you will discover that hidden deep beneath is the everlasting source of joy. It is beyond fleeting pain and pleasure. This delight is the presence of your inner friend, Authentic Self.

Unwanted suffering is beyond your control, but whatever it is, it passes. Be with it as you must. Stay with it as if you both were at a transit station waiting to go back to your home. Painful events, both physical and emotional, can become portals through which you enter the inner source of joy.

Let your wounds and hurts become doors to your inner wisdom. Everyone experiences suffering at some point. No one is exempt. I could not have appreciated my life as much as I do if I had not encountered the tragic deaths of some of my close family members and experienced anguish. Such sad events made me aware of my own mortality and deepened my appreciation of the blessings of life.

JOURNAL PROMPT

Journal about physical sickness or emotional pain that you may have experienced or are experiencing. What has it taught you? Let your notebook be the mirror of your mind. Make your words alleviate your physical and mental anguish. Let your journal help you better understand the gift of life you have been given.

⤳ *Day 50* ⤳

TODAY'S PRACTICE

Let's begin our precious routine. How long do you spend here at your creative/spiritual space? With 5-10 minutes of a breathing exercise, reading, reflection, and journaling, this time of "Sowing" good seeds should not take more than 30 minutes.

INSPIRATION

In the process of learning and developing my attention and awareness on a project, I "forget" my own self – body and mind. This is so because I have merged with the task at hand.

Any new thing I create, story I write, book I read, or painting I make, unknown to myself I bring along my whole self, memories, experiences, thinking, and emotions.

Whatever project I'm in the process of creating has my voice, my signature and style. In return it helps me develop my beliefs and values further. Therefore, I try to be mindful of what I think, say, or do.

Being attentive and aware has reduced the instances of my mindlessness. Mindfulness has helped me get better at it. What about you? Are you seeing any difference in your behavior and how you see the world?

JOURNAL PROMPT

In your journal, jot down your intention, whether you plan to practice Writing Meditation Practice for a year, a decade, or a lifetime.

✌ *Day 51* ✌

TODAY'S PRACTICE

Here you are back at your sacred space. I admire your determination and punctuality!

Sit comfortably in your favorite posture. Bring your mind and heart, your thoughts and feelings, to where you are seated. Practice inhaling and exhaling for as long as you want. Read the inspiration and prompt. Pause for several minutes to reflect, and then write what you are bursting to pour out.

INSPIRATION

I try to keep attentive and aware from the time I leave my personal power spot, through the day and until I go to bed. But you know what? Sometimes I forget. Then I remember and return to the task at hand the same way I return to my breath during my breathing exercises. That happens because haste, noise, and petty feelings, and passing thoughts hijack my attention. With the practice of mindfulness, my attention and awareness have improved.

Naturally, the mindfulness has also affected my writing voice and my attitude during the day. I wish I had been as mindful as I feel now when I wrote my first book. Recently, I reread it and shuddered.

Is your life fragmented? Are you facing a stumbling block that keeps you from writing or creating what you intended? Why not hunker down now? Let the daily practice of journaling and breathing begin your day. Jot down freely what it is that is keeping you from grounding yourself, settling at your personal spot. If this is wintertime, these months are great for productivity. If it is any other season of the year, sitting in the silence and solitude with your body, heart, and mind at one place will start your day in a positive routine. For the rest of the day, you will feel balanced. Just remain mindful of who you are and what you intend to write or create. Be aware of your attitude throughout the day. Make sure it is going in the right direction. Follow the joy you have begun to derive from your daily practice and soon the joy will start following you!

JOURNAL PROMPT

Since the beginning of this practice, how much time have you spent on sitting in silence and solitude and journaling? If you had to change one thing in your day, what would that be? Jot down as many things as come to your mind, then select one that seems most important and change it to something productive that feels better.

◡ *Day 52* ◡

TODAY'S PRACTICE

Sit comfortably at your Sacred Power Spot. Breathe, read, reflect, then write. You're ready for the day!

INSPIRATION

Your days consist of family obligations and things you desire to do for yourself. How do you balance these obligations with your own goals? In order to feel like a creative person and view the world as a writer, you must activate your mindfulness. Braid your day with obligations as well as personal objectives. The two cannot follow separate paths.

My day is a weave of journaling, meditation, deep reading, writing the work-in-progress, physical exercise, cooking, cleaning, and so on. Yet there are days when as I'm going through this routine (which I thoroughly enjoy), there comes a stumbling block, either physical or emotional, sometimes both. When the obstacle is major, my routine takes a secondary position until the problem is solved. More often the problem is smaller. It takes away my focus. I pay attention to it until it is done. That is life, a combination of calm and chaotic. But the duration of calm and peace increases with a disciplined practice. Your routine braids with whatever life brings your way. My husband and I are retired. Therefore following Writing Meditation Practice daily is easier for us.

But if you have a full-time job and young children, most likely you won't be able to fit hours of writing into one day. Never miss the time at your Sacred Power Spot. Be creative about weaving a half-hour or hour of writing time before anyone wakes up or after everyone goes to sleep.

On the days when you can't write, don't regret. Let that not discourage you. Just keep the subject matter of your writing at the back of your mind. Let it grow and deepen there. Next time when you get an hour to write, precise words and stunning sentences will flow on paper and surprise you.

JOURNAL PROMPT

How do you deal with the story or essay you want to write or are currently writing when you have no time to write?

ꙮ *Day 53* ꙮ

TODAY'S PRACTICE

With your eyes closed, practice the breathing exercise for 5-12 minutes with an awesome image playing on your eyelids as the screen. Read and reflect, then journal.

INSPIRATION

One of the greatest enemies in a writer's life is self-doubt. Whenever you don't write, you say, "I can't write." And when you do write, you say, "I suck! What a fool I am that I dream of writing." In his poem "Berryman," U.S. Poet Laureate W. S. Merwin (1999-2000 & 2010-2011) says:

I had hardly begun to read
I asked how can you ever be sure
that what you write is really
any good at all and he said you can't

you can't you can never be sure
you die without knowing
whether anything you wrote was any good
if you have to be sure don't write

The poem says it all. The only thing that keeps us from writing is sneaky self-doubt. The way you can erase doubt is by challenging it with daily sitting and journaling and accumulating heaps of words. When you reread that pouring from your heart, you may stumble on a story of your own.

Writing or typing fingers release a flurry of words that fill pages, which may turn into a story or an essay. You need not even question whether it's possible. It happens! Just practice!

JOURNAL PROMPT

In which ways does self-doubt crop up for you? Does it happen only in writing or in other parts of your life as well? Think how the Attention + Awareness = Mindfulness formula helps you release the voices that hinder your desire to create.

❧ *Day 54* ☙

TODAY'S PRACTICE

Sit still in silence and solitude. Breathe, read, reflect, then journal.

INSPIRATION

Did you wake up with a smile, thinking of a good day ahead? If not, think of the story, essay, or poem you are writing. Does it make your heart sing? Does it stir a feeling of warm satisfaction?

You may have already written or be in the process of writing something that not only gives you deep satisfaction but will outlive you and educate, inform, and transform future generations of readers.

Beginning your morning with Writing Meditation Practice can fill your day with mindfulness that in turn makes your heart sing. On a day when you feel lost, as soon as you wake up or sometime later, find time to do something creative – write a journal entry, prepare a dish for your family, make a drawing or painting. For me the simple act of cooking a dish, journaling, or walking outdoors changes my mood. I am ready to write.

Use any of the tools you have learned so far to enter through the doorway of your imagination. A new world opens up and unclogs your creativity so your writing flow streams forth.

Put you pencil to the page and see what comes... words or pictures. Journal or draw freely and see in which direction your hand takes you.

ॐ *Day 55* ॐ

TODAY'S PRACTICE

If mornings are almost impossible for you to sit at your Sacred Power Spot, then carve out a half-hour any time of the day when you can. The routine stays the same.

With your eyes closed, practice the breathing exercise, then read, reflect, and journal.

INSPIRATION

Exercise. Yes, exercise is important for physical health, but it also improves mental health and acuity. It's a vital part of creativity. It's practically a miracle drug.

I'm a lifelong exerciser – workout machines, weights, TRX, and walking. Body movement never fails to lift my spirit. Sixty to eighty minutes, four to five times a week maintains my vigor. I can't imagine life without it. And as I age, I realize even more how important exercise is. Which types of exercise have you incorporated in your life?

Perhaps you are thinking of adding walking (we'll talk about this more in Month 7), running or yoga into your day, but a small voice in your mind suggests it is best to avoid that thought. I understand the reluctance. Even after decades of exercising, there are quite a few days when I don't want to move. At that point I recall how I feel after I have finished exercising. I think of the pleasure of adrenaline running through my body, the pat on my shoulder my inner Self gives me, and the fact that my energetic body makes my mind vital, igniting endorphins.

If you are physically limited in how much and where you can safely move, consider small movements that don't involve risk. Fluid movements induce creative thinking which further helps hone your writing skills. Research has shown that even writing by hand and coloring or tracing shapes can prompt creative thinking. So invite some type of fluid movement into your life. Slowly and gently, try to ease past resistance, and mindfully explore exercise as something that would energize you physically and artistically.

JOURNAL PROMPT

If you have some sort of physical movement as part of your routine, kudos to you. But if not, what about making a list of exercises you would do if you could? How does walking in nature sound? What about roller skating outdoors during warm days and yoga stretching indoors during cold months sound?

১ত *Day 56* ৩৶

TODAY'S PRACTICE

Breathe, read, reflect, and journal.

INSPIRATION

Ahh, the comforting sensations of rest – soft, warm, quiet! Blissful reprieve! Restful pauses throughout the day are as important as body movement. Rest results from self-awareness which wakes you up to self-caring. I let my work match the rhythm of my breathing – inhale and exhale, writing for hours and taking restful pauses.

We often expect ourselves to work until we drop. But wisdom lies in taking time throughout the day to read, to nap, to daydream, to garden, to knit, or to cook. The reason that two out of the five disciplines of Writing Meditation Practice focus on rest – nonverbal activities and reading – is because rest inspires and bestows energy. Pauses are as important as the mad rush to write or revise. Rest heals.

Rest is a vital part of creativity. If you ignore periods of rest, your imaginative mind will suffer. When do you pause? Now as you have carved 30 minutes for yourself, do you reflect how you have been squeezing your writing in between your day job and parenting or caregiving? How you try to write in segments whenever you get an opportunity? But please do not neglect yourself by failing to stop and take a few breaths. Make sure you take 10-15 minute pauses sometime during the day. Those are as important as your writing. Not only will your ideas revitalize at this time but also fresh ideas will float up. A joy arises that refreshes and gratifies.

Your time at your sacred spot is your healing space. Visit it often and sit for a few minutes. You will discover how relaxation helps increase productivity, pumps energy, sharpens ideas, and makes a better life.

Embrace your restful time at your sacred space. Add one or two more pauses to your day.

JOURNAL PROMPT
Write how your day used to go without a restful pause. Has the half-hour of daily practice changed the day for the better? How would another short pause or a short nap affect your day? Your writing time?

✒ *Day 57* ✒

TODAY'S PRACTICE
Settle in, breathe, read, reflect, and journal.

INSPIRATION
Just as a plant has the capacity to bring scented flowers to life, as black rock can crystalize into a glittering diamond, and as an egg can grow to become a captivating dancing peacock, you too can transcend into an authentic human being. When you are fully present in the now, when you are embodied, whole and grounded, you are at your truest self. Let the intelligence of your body with its sensations, intuitive sense, and energy inform you, awaken you, and guide you through life.

Instead of being lost in thinking – with petty thoughts circulating around and around, and getting distressed by sentiments and emotions that disconnect you from your body – you would be present in the moment with your senses alert, with awareness of the significance of your daily life. You would feel animated and energized.

How can we learn this? How can we become our true, Authentic Self? How do you learn to embody yourself?

Be present in your body by becoming aware of your physical sensations, by practicing meditation, staying with your inhalations and exhalations, and being attentive and aware. These are the most essential skills you are learning on your creative and spiritual journey.

Within you there is a bud ready to sprout, like a rock that has the potential to transform into a crystal or an egg with the magnificence of a peacock.

Getting from where you are now to reaching your full potential is a matter of self-discipline, daily practice, and an intent and determination to become who you want to become. So what are you waiting for?

JOURNAL PROMPT

Out of health, relationships, professional work, and spirituality, which area in your life most needs attention? Jot down what changes you are making to help that happen. Whenever you come across a surprise or a meaningful observation, collect it in your journal like a jewel in your jewelry box.

ᕉ *Day 58* ᕈ

TODAY'S PRACTICE
Settle in, breathe, read, reflect, and journal.

INSPIRATION

The breathing exercises you have been practicing for almost two months have gelled by now. Are you silently counting your in-breaths and out-breaths? "One" as you inhale and "two" as you exhale? The counting works as a tool to assist your mind when it gets lost in thoughts. It is a valuable device to bring your mind and heart home. If you go beyond your count of 10 or so, the counting gently reminds you to begin again.

Let's do something new today. Let me guide your breathing exercise. Please follow along upon my prompting. Sit comfortably in an upright position. Relax your shoulders. Place your hands one over the other, resting in your lap with thumbs touching... Your feet are firm on the ground, or you are sitting on the floor with your legs crossed... Close your eyes... Sense the space that surrounds you... Feel any sensations arising within... Let your thoughts settle... Let's begin...

Count quietly with each inhalation and exhalation. Count to twenty and begin again with one.

Breathe in – *count one*	Breathe out – *count six*
Breathe out – *count two*	Breathe in – *count seven*
Breathe in – *count three*	Breathe out – *count eight*
Breathe out – *count four*	Breathe in – *count nine*
Breathe in – *count five*	Breathe out – *count ten...*

Continue counting to twenty or begin another cycle of ten. Keep counting and breathing up to 12 minutes.

As you try to focus on your breath and count, your mind will begin to wander. But as your practice hones, it will jolt you back into breathing when you hit 10 or 20, depending on which number you intend to stop at. Then start again. Simply note whatever thought passes by or any physical sensations you may feel. Be gentle with yourself. There is no bad breathing exercise or good breathing exercise. It is a beginner's practice. Once you learn to become absorbed in your breath, you are meditating. That is the discipline we will refine next month.

JOURNAL PROMPT
Write a one-line mantra that is meaningful to you. "Revise Your Day," "I Am Thou," or "A Yearlong Journey for Betterment of Life" comes to mind. Begin by jotting down whatever thought you feel about creating your own mantra. Keep revising it until it feels right.

✌ *Day 59* ✍

TODAY'S PRACTICE

Did you come up with your personal mantra? How does it sound when you say it aloud? How does your mantra feel when you silently utter it with your eyes closed? Does it need further polishing? If you are satisfied, repeat it in your mind as you practice your breathing exercise. Then read, reflect, and journal.

INSPIRATION

Have you ever consciously thought about your physical self, the body? We don't normally pay attention to our self until pain disrupts the flow of time. You push the disruption aside and if the pain is intolerable you take medication. It dissipates and once again you forget that you have a physical self.

When discomfort keeps you from functioning at your usual levels, you see a doctor.

Your body is your life. Without this sophisticated finely tuned miraculous machine, we do not exist. In fact, the seed pod we are sowing the first three months is only possible because we have our physical self. You could neither journal nor think about mindfulness nor meditate if you didn't have a human body.

The body communicates through sensations. If you are in tune with your body, do not pooh-pooh its signals when something is not right. If the sensations are acute, seek medical help. Don't wait for a physical hinderance to stop you from functioning normally.

JOURNAL PROMPT

What were your thoughts about the body before starting this journey? Did you ever think that your body was the most precious gift you have been given? Journal about what you think or what has changed your thinking about your body.

❧ *Day 60* ☙

TODAY'S PRACTICE

With your eyes closed, silently repeat your chosen mantra as you practice your breathing exercise. Read, reflect, and journal.

INSPIRATION

Today ends the month you devoted to understanding how attention and awareness result in mindfulness. When you cultivate the quality of mindfulness, it strengthens your consciousness and enriches your life.

Meditation is yet another practice which we do with our body. Journaling uses our hands, mindfulness our body, heart, and mind... as does meditation. With the practice of meditation, you will come to experience the connection between body and mind. Tomorrow I will introduce you to something which I have been practicing for three decades, sowing a seed pod that is nurtured over time by sun and rain, resulting in healthy sprouting. Its use will ultimately blossom into a lush tree of Writing Meditation Practice. Once sown with your intentions and yearly goal, your practice will sprout buds, and they will blossom with your life's purpose.

END OF MONTH PROMPT

What gains did you make during this month? Recall the benefits of journaling and reflect upon how your mindfulness practice feels so far.

Month 3

Mindfulness and Meditation

Suggested Readings

Mindfulness for Beginners:
Reclaiming the Present Moment and Your Life
Jon Kabat-Zinn, 2016.

Flow: The Psychology of Optimal Experience
Mihaly Csikszentmihalyi, 2008.

Tracking Wonder: Reclaiming a Life of Meaning and Possibility
in a World Obsessed with Productivity
Jeffrey Davis, 2021.

Focus: The Hidden Driver of Excellence
Daniel Goleman, 2015.

✌ *Day 61* ✌

TODAY'S PRACTICE

I am excited to introduce you to guided meditations, specifically those written and narrated by me. Links to the meditations are provided (directly in the ebook, and at the Resource page in the back of the print book). You may listen on the device of your choice, from YouTube, my website, or even Spotify.

Now to the practice. Make yourself comfortable in your favorite posture at your special place. Settle with a feeling of joy. With your eyes closed, you may either practice the daily breathing exercise (5-12 minutes) then follow it with the guided meditation, or practice only the guided meditation.

Meditation: "Body Meditation" (see Guided Meditations List on page 432)

Further reflect on the significance of your body awareness and importance of attention to your physical self. Read and reflect upon today's inspiration and prompt, then conclude the session with writing in your journal.

INSPIRATION

During the first month, you may have simply poured out heaps of words on blank pages of your notebook. You may have named your so-called diary or didn't care who you were talking to. Are you saying things to it that are filled with anguish, resentment, and anger? Has it helped you lighten your mind, calmed you down, helped you make a sacred space in your heart that reflects a personal place outside you? Have you realized that in your journal you are conversing with yourself? But this inner Self knows you better. It never fails to lend its ear, and is always kind and wise. It is your Authentic Self, your personal therapist – the best in the world!

That was the summation of the first month.

The second month was about how attention and awareness can be cultivated.

This month we will use guided meditations as a continuation of the breathing exercises you have been doing.

The sacred space within you that is currently developing will take time to form, perhaps the whole year. This place, within and without, will evolve into a significant space in your own particular world. This is because you are embarking on the most precious and personal voyage of your life. This travel is neither through the country nor around the world, or even to outer space. This journey is to plant the seed pod and witness its growth. By the end of the year, you will get to know your Authentic Self, your companion and guide for life. This daily reflection and meditation will familiarize you with it.

If you are unable to keep a daily schedule, don't fret. Once you have established the practice, missing a session once in a while will not stop the intuitive moments and serendipity that the practice brings.

JOURNAL PROMPT

In your notebook answer the following questions: *What is the purpose of your year-long journey? What is your intention? Are these intentions connected to your purpose?*

ꕥ *Day 62* ꕥ

TODAY'S PRACTICE

Settle with a feeling of joy. Close your eyes and breathe.

Meditation: "Body"   Read, reflect, and journal.

INSPIRATION

If you have never meditated, let's begin with your sitting posture and focus on the breath. It is the same as you have been practicing for the last two months. Whether you sit in a chair or on the floor to meditate, make yourself as comfortable as you can. Having thus settled, review your posture. Close your eyes and make sure your head, back, and neck are aligned. Sit with the shoulders even, your hands placed one over the other resting on your lap and thumbs touching. If you prefer to keep your eyes slightly open, direct your gaze at the floor in front of you. Lips can gently touch, teeth slightly apart, with the tip of the tongue at the back of your upper teeth.

Slowly scan your body from the top of your head all the way to the soles of your feet. If some part is tense, relax it. When you focus on your inhaling and exhaling you are engaged in mental exercise. It is the stuff of the mind. A relaxed mind results in a relaxed body.

Sit with an attitude of dignity. Imagine your body is a mountain and your head its peak. Now breathe through the nose naturally without any control or force. Observe the rise and fall of the abdomen, the expansion and contraction of the chest, and finally the sensation of the air moving in and out of the nostrils across the tip of your nose and upper lip. This focus makes you aware of the present moment.

The focus on your breath with attention and awareness of your inner self is the beginning of the practice of mindfulness, the result of your posture and breathing. Your breath is always with you. Observe it any time you feel anxious, nervous, or fearful. It will calm you and make you realize that there is nothing to worry about at the present moment. In 21 days, such daily practice turns into a habit. This practice has already begun to grow and is working at maintaining your physical, emotional, and spiritual well-being.

JOURNAL PROMPT

Journal about your body. Practice focusing on your breath for several minutes, then write in your notebook. After the breathing exercise and meditation, write again about how your body feels. Do you feel any difference in the content of your two entries?

Reflect on these questions: *What do I think about my body? What does the body sense when I think about it?* Journaling about your body and practicing breathing exercises are two of the ways to take care of your physical self. Your body carries a personal, unrecognized rudimentary pattern of your desires and dreams that is potent. Pay attention!

ೞ *Day 63* ೞ

TODAY'S PRACTICE

Meditation: "Body"   Read, reflect, and journal.

INSPIRATION

Your Sacred Power Spot will develop a character that reflects your temperament and personality. If you like, and in addition to your current sacred space, you may choose an outdoor spot for spring and summer months.

Yet, the deeper you get into daily practice, the less it will matter where you sit. Once you uncover which space feels most conducive to quiet reflection, that's where you will be able to focus and do your creative work for longer hours.

During fall and winter months, I practice in my study but during spring and summer, the change and growth outdoors entice me. I carry my notebook and laptop and sit on the back porch overlooking the little patch of garden where hellebore is flowering and tiarella and lamium are ready to sprout. When summer arrives, hosta, hydrangea, and anemone bloom while I work.

My Mindful Writer friend Kathleen Shoop walks outdoors in deep winter to reflect upon the writing project she is working on. The freeze of winter season inspires her. Another Mindful Writer friend, the late Ramona Long, loved practicing on a hammock in her garden. That was her favorite contemplative place. She'd lie under the shade of a tree and look up at the sky and focus on her breath. In this suspended posture, when her body was not touching the ground, she imagined negative energy and bad vibes leaving her body, evaporating toward the sky above and into the earth below. The experience soothed and healed her.

The spaces where we practice may be different for each of us. Yet all of us want to arrive at the space, inside and out, where we feel inspired and experience creativity, contentment, and ultimately joy. And this, my dear reader, you too will eventually feel with the daily practice.

JOURNAL PROMPT

What do you imagine your perfect outdoor Creative and Spiritual Power Spot to be like? Journal about a space where you'd be undisturbed and feel comfortable and secure.

ᨠ *Day 64* ᨢ

TODAY'S PRACTICE

Meditation: "Body"   Read, reflect, and journal.

INSPIRATION

With the combined disciplines of daily reading and reflection, journaling, and meditation, you clear your mind, open your heart, and make yourself more mindful of who you are.

No pretense. No mask. Authenticity gradually unplugs the debris clogging the creative flow. Your ego self will be introduced to your inner self. Steadily your productivity will increase and intuitive ideas about your current creative project proliferate.

When you get closer to your Authentic Self, it awakens from its dormant state. You are able to hear its whispers of wisdom which always point toward beneficence. Your inner self slowly aligns with the universe. You discover the solutions and answers from the universe were always available... but they had passed by you when you weren't paying attention. Your inner antennae was not yet linked.

Your intentions and goals will never get fulfilled by external events or forces. Only inner resolve will bring about the changes you seek. You possess inner resources, skills, undiscovered knowledge, and strength to bring about transformation. However, more often than not, these inner resources get buried beneath household chores, financial burdens, and lack of time. The feelings of turmoil and anguish create waves of stress.

The more you focus on daily meditation and journaling about daily happenings, the more you will come to know what is keeping you back. You will be able to discern which external forces affect you even when you don't have anything directly to do with them. You'll learn how to reduce their influence.

Be in charge of your body and thoughts, understanding there are things you can choose to do and not do. How you feel in your body and mind affects your outer circumstances in important ways. When you realize that you are the protagonist of your own life story, you get jolted out of the slumbering way in which you have been living. Learn to perform only those actions that you must, and intend to move forward with patience.

JOURNAL PROMPT

Who are the individuals you consider significant shapers of your life? Trace back some of their beliefs and values that influence your current life and why.

✌ *Day 65* ✌

TODAY'S PRACTICE

Meditation: "Body"   Read, reflect, and journal.

INSPIRATION

As you settle at your Sacred Power Spot today, notice while you are seated that your mind is elsewhere and heart someplace else. Attend to your whole body first, then gently bring your mind to the present moment and to the rhythm of your breath. Then return the things of the heart to the present moment. In a minute or two of such attention on your mind and heart, your fragmented self integrates. You align your whole self with the larger circles surrounding you and ultimately with the universe.

The thought that your year-long journey will reveal to you the hidden aptitudes and possibilities thrills me. Bringing your body, mind, and heart together each day as you sit will connect you with something bigger than your mere ego self. Practicing in this manner is key to your journey.

The trinity of physical care is exercise, nutritious food, and restful sleep. And the trinity of emotional care is meditation, journaling, and creativity. Sitting at your Sacred Power Spot is as important as keeping your doctor's and dentist's appointments. Spend time with yourself in silence and solitude, reflecting on your thoughts and feelings. You will feel whole and holy.

JOURNAL PROMPT

How do you pay attention to your body? What feelings emerge when you think of your physical self? Besides practicing here, what do you do to take care of your body, mind, and heart?

❧ *Day 66* ❧

TODAY'S PRACTICE

Meditation: "Body"   Read, reflect, and journal.

INSPIRATION

"At the core of human personality, hidden in the very depths of our consciousness, there is a divine spark that nothing can extinguish." To Eknath Easwaran's observation I must add that this spark is the source from which you draw everything and anything. This is your Authentic Self.

You have a whole bountiful year of inspiring mornings and peaceful nights ahead of you. Your goals will not get fulfilled by external events or forces. Only your inner resolve will bring about the changes you intend.

As you set your daily goal of practicing meditation, journaling, reading, and reflecting, keep in mind that major changes occur over time. What you intend to do may not happen exactly the way you visualize. But one thing is certain: At the end of the year, Writing Meditation Practice will fulfill you emotionally, hone your skill, and help you grow kinder and wiser. Instead of letting the ego control your day-to-day decisions, you will listen to inner clues and cues.

What has being linked to your Authentic Self to do with being a good writer? Everything! Authentic Self is the source of all. It has power to infuse your artistic voice with your writing skill, thus making your craft stronger and more meaningful – both to you and your readers.

What feelings emerge when you think of the goal you want to accomplish this year? Does the project feel daunting? Do you feel fearful or doubtful? Remember, you are practicing just one day at a time. That is manageable, isn't it? In your notebook tell yourself that your journey has just begun. There is no reason to feel discouraged.

ᝍ *Day 67* ᝍ

TODAY'S PRACTICE
Meditation: "Body"   Read, reflect, and journal.

INSPIRATION

There is great power in beginning the day with a focus on your breath, silently scanning your body and then journaling about intentions that relate to your year's purpose. It is also practical to make a mental note of the work you did or did not do.

"All our lives we are taught to look outwards," says the Vipassana Meditation teacher S. N. Goenka. "We get accustomed to looking that way. But the only way to experience the ultimate truth is to look within." Humanity, creativity, and spirituality are experienced simply by observing your own self. Paying attention to physical sensations, focusing on the knots in the belly, passing negative thoughts, letting them go, and finally connecting with the creative source within are a few of the outcomes of meditation which you are learning to practice this month.

Attend to the breath with complete attention. While scanning your body, attend to any and all sensations. Then become aware of sensory data in your peripheral awareness. Gradually bring this awareness to the mind. Watch the passing thoughts sail by. If a feeling is taking your attention away, make a mental note of it and let it pass.

My introduction to meditation was in 1989 when my family moved from Pittsburgh to Massachusetts for four years. I was home alone, lonely, and restless. Fortunately, having taught Buddhism and Buddhist art for a decade, I knew meditation had the power to turn loneliness into solitude and calm the mind, yet I had never practiced it.

After my husband and daughters left home for the day, I tried to sit still, quietly copying the meditative posture of the Buddha unsuccessfully. In my art history classes, I had shown the slides of the Buddha standing, lying, seated, and walking. I had interpreted and analyzed them a million times. But I had never experienced the message those images conveyed.

I decided to teach myself how to meditate. I focused on my breath and tried to be present in the moment. Within the first few seconds, my mind wandered somewhere else. By the time I remembered to return to my breath, minutes had passed. Slowly but certainly, when I brought my attention back to my breath, over and over again, my body relaxed a bit, which in turn settled my mind and brought it back to the present moment. But after only a few such moments, my mind would wander again. On and on it went. I don't know what kept me from giving up. Perhaps because the practice promised serenity, peace, tranquility, and well-being. Over the years I have realized it is better to begin with a guided meditation.

And now thirty-plus years later, I meditate daily for more than an hour. I journal for 15-20 minutes and find my mental chatter subsides, the static gone. I am at peace. My writing flow is smoother and faster. Combined with walking and reading, nothing else provides me as much comfort, calm, and confidence as the morning practice of Writing Meditation Practice.

JOURNAL PROMPT

You have established your Sacred Power Spot and set a schedule for your practice. What about your daily intention and yearly goal? In your journal, write about one professional goal and one spiritual aspiration.

～ *Day 68* ～

TODAY'S PRACTICE	
Meditation: "Body"	Read, reflect, and journal.

INSPIRATION

Sitting still in silence and solitude in a comfortable posture to focus on your breath is called meditating. It is a simple practice, but as you know by now it is not easy.

You learn what it is to be mindful, what it means to be integrated and aligned, after you have practiced sitting over a long period of time. The practice results in calm replacing restlessness, it clears the foggy mind, and the heart can turn from indifferent or cold to loving and kind. The attitude of mindfulness flows into your daily life even after you leave the meditation cushion.

Within you dwells a spirit of adventure. Call forth this wondering and wandering spirit. This inner voice, as gentle as air and as strong as a swan's feather, does not reveal itself easily. Use the time with yourself to dig deeper and excavate. Listen attentively. Feel strongly. Connect and strengthen this currently fragile bond.

On rare occasions, you may feel uneasy and dejected, thinking, *I'm capable of so much more than what I am right now.* Such feelings emerge when your body, heart, and mind are not integrated... when you are disconnected from the sacred space within. But there is a desire to unite with what is "more than" you. Perhaps at the end of the last year you had no clue how to do so. Unknown to you, the Self waited patiently. But now you have embarked on a practice that will make this possible.

Writing Meditation Practice gives you a special ability to shrink the gap between the small ego self and the Authentic Self. So learn to listen to your gut feelings and whispers from your AS.

The discipline of meditation is subtle. You need to be patient. Learning to meditate is like learning to write. You begin with the alphabet, then words, sentences, grammar, and it goes on and on. Then one day it clicks... *I can write! I can meditate.* Give yourself time and consistency.

JOURNAL PROMPT

Have you begun to acquire a certain degree of mental readiness? When you decide to do something, does your gut nudge you to do something else? Do you listen to it?

৬৹ *Day 69* ৬৺

TODAY'S PRACTICE

Meditation: "Body"   Read, reflect, and journal.

INSPIRATION

Things to ponder:

Each day you may face a minor new challenge or confront a major one. Don't go around it. Go through it. Make your best effort to solve the problem. Make sure you change the question mark into a full stop and move on. It will test and teach you.

Problems only go away when you find solutions. But for some questions, some challenges, you may not have an answer or a solution. Yet if you pay attention, any challenge reveals something you did not know before; most of all it reflects your vulnerability. Questions such as: "Where do I come from?" "Where do I go?" and "What is the true purpose of my life?" not only make you conscious of human vulnerability but also aware of the fundamental need for love, kindness, companionship, and relationships.

By meditating and writing with a friend or a group, you can generate strong fellowship. You may share and discuss questions and problems. What would alleviate the fear or sadness caused by these unanswerables? Meditation and journaling help. They soften your heart and sharpen your mind about self and others.

With your practice gelling slowly, always keep this thought at the back of your mind: *Something wonderful is going to happen!* Your telephone may ring, an email may arrive, the front doorbell may chime and surprise you. Pay attention to even little surprises and small things that occur; find meaning in them. By the end of the year, you will have "ten thousand things" that made you happy. They will categorize themselves into four areas: health, relationships, creativity (work), and spirituality (authentic life). Which area do you feel you need to pay attention to?

JOURNAL PROMPT

What small thing do you intend to do today to improve the rest of the days that will follow? When you have a revelation or get a surprise, do you collect it in your journal like a new gem in your jewelry box?

❦ *Day 70* ❧

TODAY'S PRACTICE

Meditation: "Body"   Read, reflect, and journal.

INSPIRATION

After you settle in the meditation posture and feel comfortable, try breathing from the heart center. Inhaling with care at your chest makes you tender, kind. Take 5-10 long and deep breaths. If breathing from the heart center feels good, continue with this exercise for the rest of this meditation session.

Mindfulness leads you to profound adventures of self-discovery and mental cultivation. You will learn to use your mind with proficiency and attend to your inner silent nudges, urges, and commands. Life-changing insights may be rare but paying heed to gentle whispers helps you take bold turns, make right decisions, and move in better directions.

As children, we were innocent, open, and whole. Once again, you may regain and cultivate that childlike innocence. The seed of unconditional love is dormant deep in your heart, waiting for you to connect not only with loved ones but also with others. Let go of past regrets and resentments, let tension evaporate, and let loving kindness flow outward from your heart.

The childlike unconditional and boundless love is latent in all of us. Breathing in from the heart center and breathing out from the nose gives you courage to love yourself and also fearlessly connect with people you normally see no reason to.

JOURNAL PROMPT

Journal about how you met an individual who ended up becoming your best friend. What surface qualities attracted you to the stranger first? What resisted you? Later, what inner strengths turned a stranger into a friend?

ᘓ *Day 71* ᘒ

TODAY'S PRACTICE

Meditation: "Mindful"   Read, reflect, and journal.

INSPIRATION

I have been practicing meditation for decades, but only achieved deeper focus twelve years ago when I began the Mindful Writers Group (2011) and paid attention to whispers of wisdom within. Sometimes I trusted it and sometimes I didn't. Finally in late 2017, something happened that made me forever stop doubting the voice of my Authentic Self. I heard this voice encourage me to establish and grow an online group for Mindful Writers. *Post something once a week*, it suggested. I did it for a year. When it nudged me to post something meaningful every morning instead of once a week, I followed the direction. But it was too much work. I couldn't imagine continuing this and wished the voice would cease. I was simultaneously thrilled and nervous but reluctant to enter unknown territory.

Here's how the soundless conversation went: "What am I going to write about every day?" *Something will emerge*, the voice answered. "365 posts and prompts? Where will I find the ideas?" *Believe in yourself! Take the leap of faith. The universe will come to help. Trust yourself and trust the universe.*

The voice was crystal clear, insistent but calm. I accepted the challenge. Would I be able to execute it? Did I have the talent, time, or capability to accomplish it? I did not know. Yet the calling emboldened me. I decided to use my knowledge, skill, and experience to compose the posts. As soon as I made the whole-hearted commitment, my intention slowly started to turn into action. The first year of daily posts was so much work that I told myself I had to shut it down. But then once again a conversation ensued. *Take a break! Invite authors you respect to post occasionally.* So that's what I did.

The following year I wrote posts the first week of each month and invited guest-hosts for the following three weeks. And what a beautiful experience that was! It thrived. Yet the need for inviting, organizing, and administrating infringed on my writing hours.

I transferred the work of daily posts for the Online Mindful Writers Group to its dedicated followers at the end of 2021. The site had been a beacon during the pandemic years 2020 and 2021, with unique guest-host voices from various writing genres. Those who felt inspired generously agreed to continue the work. From 2023 onward, the OMWG has been led by volunteer guest hosts. Each one is a Mindful Writer.

I faced obstacles, frustrations, and struggles within, and trials and tribulations without. But support and help came from wise Mindful Writers, women and men. The universe came to my rescue in the person of those esteemed guest-hosts. They became my creative collaborators.

The wisdom within you always points the way when you feel a deep driving desire to do something.

JOURNAL PROMPT

Has there been a time when you delegated a daunting task to a group of friends or colleagues? Was your fearlessness in doing so rewarded by the universe in a way that surprised you?

✌ *Day 72* ✌

TODAY'S PRACTICE
Meditation: "Mindful"   Read, reflect, and journal.

INSPIRATION

The Sanskrit word *prana* means both breath and life. The moment you were born, the breath was with you, and the moment it leaves, you die. If you can breathe, you can meditate. Wherever you go, your breath is with you. It is your anchor. In and out. In and out. In and out. The breath is perfect the way it is. You need not speed it up, force it, grasp it, push it away, or control it. You simply must pay attention to its natural rhythm, letting the breath continue its work without making a big deal out of it.

You have been paying attention to the movement of breath around the nose and growing aware of the physical sensations. You are also keeping track of sensory data coming from outside. Now is the time to move your peripheral awareness within the mind. Observe the memories, thoughts, and ideas that float up while inhaling and exhaling. Don't dwell on what is emerging. Just notice it, let it go, and return to the breath. If something important emerges, simply take mental note of it.

Breathing mindfully is the basic tool of meditation. Though its practice is a great deal of work inside you, its spirit arises in the way your writing voice emerges and develops. The more you practice, the more benefits you gain. It is like adding coins to a spiritual piggybank; the benefits keep accumulating.

A half-century of neuroscientific research has concluded that meditation is as important to mental well-being as exercise is to physical health. If you exercise regularly, you build stronger muscles, denser bones, and increased stamina. If you meditate daily, your attention span, memory, and patience increase. You become more insightful, intuitive, and can manage negative situations more efficiently. Sitting in silence strengthens resilience, calm, and a sense of connection to others.

JOURNAL PROMPT
You are as much the author of your own life as you are the writer of your story. Do you "live deliberately" as Henry David Thoreau advised? Do your personal aspirations and

needs harmonize with your daily routine, or do you adhere to someone else's notion of how to live?

ᴄᴼ *Day 73* ᴄᵕ

TODAY'S PRACTICE

Meditation: "Mindful"   Read, reflect, and journal.

INSPIRATION

No one knows how long you will live, But know this: It is not going to be forever. This fact should coax you to live each day as if it were the last. Live productively, positively, and passionately. Savor each minute like a sip of fresh spring water, the first taste of morning coffee or tea, or a glass of wine with your loved one.

Here is one of my favorite parables about the daily gift each of us receives:

Every morning a mendicant stood in front of the door of a wealthy merchant. The merchant gave him alms and in return the mendicant gifted the man a piece of fruit. The man accepted the unimpressive gift and as soon as the mendicant turned around, he tossed the trifle over the trellised window into the grass growing behind his mansion.

One year passed. On the first morning of the new year the mendicant arrived. As always, he handed the gift of fruit to the merchant. No sooner had he left than the wealthy man's pet monkey came jumping through the doorway and leaped upon his shoulder. The man playfully handed the fruit over to the monkey. The monkey took several bites of the fruit. To the man's surprise a jewel dropped out and rolled across the floor. The man's eyes grew wide. He hurried to the ground behind his house where the grass had grown tall and dense over the fruit he had discarded. There on the ground lay a mass of rotten fruit in various stages of decay and amidst the debris a heap of 365 priceless jewels lay waiting to be collected.

The parable reflects what you may be doing with your days. The fruit the mendicant gifted the wealthy man represents each new day you are freely given. How you spend it and the benefits you accumulate are revealed only at the end of the year, or several years later. If you live each day mindfully instead of carelessly tossing it away, the gifts will be yours forever.

With your daily Writing Meditation Practice there is a good possibility that at the end of each day you will collect gems and put them in your "piggybank." Through the year, the merits and benefits keep accumulating and in time reveal the goldmine within. Each day is a treasure; let's treat it thus.

JOURNAL PROMPT

What is it that you find extraordinary in your ordinary day? Is it different each day, such as finding fresh, juicy sweet peaches at the grocery, or completing 15 minutes of meditation, or writing 3-5 pages of your manuscript?

✿ *Day 74* ✿

TODAY'S PRACTICE

Meditation: "Mindful"   Read, reflect, and journal.

INSPIRATION

As children, we were introduced to characters and symbols in fairytales such as dragons and ogres, witches and warlocks, wisemen and wise-women, serpents, a frog near a well, talking trees or a talking cat, a ten-headed serpent and so on. As adults, you may meet them again in your dreams or nightmares. But imagine if you relook and examine them as a basket of creative ideas.

Both fairytales and dreams have one common purpose. They bring images and uncanny symbols of your dark unconscious into the daylight. You may or may not understand or like them, but they are the sparks and seedbeds of your potential stories. In them lay your imagination and creative power.

You can carry them wherever you go, the way you carry your unconscious mind. These are the rejected, unadmitted, unrecognized, unknown, undeveloped facets and factors of your daily life. Whereas in meditation you connect with that component of the unconscious that radiates the power of calm, kindness, and serenity, the same mind also hoards the potent ambiguous dark symbols.

Your mindful meditation and journaling practice make it easier to unravel problems you have tended to avoid. Keeping silent about your secrets – the experiences you can't share with anyone else – ends up residing permanently in the unconscious. Pouring them out on the pages of your journal or watching them pass by like clouds in your meditation empties the conscious mind and clears your thinking.

With daily practice you are able to assimilate, solve, and dissolve the crinkles and wrinkles. In doing so you churn up gems for new writing pieces. The sparks and seedbeds of creative possibilities await. In meditation you fertilize a seed and cultivate it to maturity as a full-fledged story or essay.

JOURNAL PROMPT
Have you used images and symbols from favorite fairytales in your own stories? Do some of those symbols reflect any of your life experiences?

✆ *Day 75* ✆

TODAY'S PRACTICE
Meditation: "Mindful"   Read, reflect, and journal.

INSPIRATION
Flow and *in the zone* are words creative individuals use to describe the ideal state of mind during their best output. When you are fully committed to an activity and wholeheartedly attentive, the work feels almost effortless. It is one of the most pleasurable and valuable

experiences a person can have but requires efficiency and clarity of purpose.[1]

As novices, we experience what is quite opposite of the flow. In the early stages of meditation when we sit with eyes closed, the thoughts and images we face are chaotic, negative, and petty. We can't stand our own mind and complain, "Why do I confront such junky thoughts?" It is so because we have accumulated these thoughts for years without any attempt to clear our minds the way we clean our homes.

You must understand this: What is coming out of the mind is what you have been putting into it... your thoughts, actions, and words. What you feed your mind is dormant until a memory or feeling triggers its returns. You may succeed in keeping it at bay consciously, but you can't cheat the unconscious. Your own negative stuff floats up. This you don't want to accept. If instead you feed your mind nourishing thoughts of goodwill and kindness, truth and wisdom, then that's what will surface. The practice simply makes you aware of what you mentally ingest. Fortunately, it also lets you know what you ought to stay away from. Guard your mind like a sentry!

Learn to accept the reality of petty thoughts and intend to get rid of them. In silent meditation, witness your mind. Watch what it is thinking without analyzing, criticizing, or commenting. Let it pass by, repeatedly. Eventually minor thoughts will leave, while major thoughts that have affected you deeply will return. Keep letting them go, forgiving... forgetting... Eventually the layer of junky froth will disperse, creating space for original and intuitive ideas. By the end of the year, this practice will help clear the mental cobwebs and cleanse your mind. Feeling the experience of flow or being in the zone is more accessible only after such cleansing is complete.

JOURNAL PROMPT

Journal about the cobwebs of troubling thoughts you confront repeatedly. Freely write about a positive experience for which you are grateful.

---

[1] For more on this topic, read Mihaly Csikszentmihalyi's *Flow: The Psychology of Optimal Experience.*

✒ *Day 76* ✒

TODAY'S PRACTICE
Meditation: "Mindful"   Read, reflect, and journal.

INSPIRATION

"Be Human and Lift Yourself Up" was the caption of a captivating watercolor landscape that hung in my father's study. It depicted a figure carrying a load on its back while walking up a hill to reach a silver peak against the crystal blue sky. Each time I entered the study, it attracted my attention. Over the years its meaning kept changing as it embedded into my unconscious and nourished me. It continued to intrigue me, giving me hope, and now inspires me to fulfill my bundle of responsibilities as I ascend toward my goals. I feel blessed with loving confidence to continue my ascending journey. The image has affected my lifestyle and my worldview. It helps me regain momentum when I must stop to make a choice or when I have a setback. Then I keep ascending as I try to make each new day better than my yesterday.

Daily meditation has made me kinder and more selfless. Sitting mindfully is the mightiest tool for becoming thoughtful and kind. It refines the way you speak, act, think, and live. That is the mighty power of meditation – it helps you become more and more like the reflection of your Authentic Self.

Do you remember an image, a song, a movie, or words of wisdom from your childhood that left a lingering effect on you? Does it continue to guide you? There may be several such remembrances but only some stick with us. "Be Human and Lift Yourself Up," has elevated my life to a higher level of self-understanding and self-compassion.

JOURNAL PROMPT
Journal about a movie, excerpt from a book, a poem, or a thought from a family member or friend or stranger that refined a habit, changed an attitude, or taught an attainable lesson while you were in your impressionable years. Why do a few of these inspire you? How do you decide which ones to let go and which ones to keep?

⸎ *Day 77* ⸎

TODAY'S PRACTICE	
Meditation: "Heartful"	Read, reflect, and journal.

INSPIRATION

I have been meditating first thing in the morning for more than three decades. I also have read hundreds of books on meditation and mindfulness, both time-honored texts and those based on recent scientific research. The tremendous benefits of the practice can only be experienced, not verbalized. This is the reason I keep nudging you to begin meditating if you haven't already.

I honestly want you to taste what happens once meditation becomes your daily habit. It is in the calm that self-revelations and understanding and kindness emerge. When combined with the other disciplines of Writing Meditation Practice, it feels magical. The skills you acquire from successfully practicing on a regular basis are plentiful. You learn to sit daily at a designated place and time you have allotted for yourself. You keep full attention on the voice of a guided meditation, an image, or an object, and become gently aware of your surroundings. Such sitting results in sharp mindfulness.

Most things that make you happy are beyond your control, but the things that bring you peace and joy are inside you. This means they are within your power to achieve. However, if you are experiencing painful emotions or physical pain, you must feel it before you can reach the source that is eternally joyous. All pain is real. Don't shove it away. Learn to tolerate it. It is meant to teach you something. Stay with it until it dissipates. At the same time, keep in mind that at a deeper awareness of being, peace awaits you. It is here that wounds and hurts may become portals to wisdom.

JOURNAL PROMPT

What has a personal sickness or death of a loved one taught you? How did you overcome it? Let your journal be the mirror of your heart-mind. Let your writing hold your hand and listen to you. Then, let it lead you to a better understanding of the gift of life.

৺ *Day 78* ৺

TODAY'S PRACTICE

Meditation: "Heartful"   Read, reflect, and journal.

INSPIRATION

Like fairytales, ancient stories contain characters replete with symbolic meaning. They come alive while you read them, and after they end, they stimulate introspection. You don't read simply for entertainment but for their thought-provoking and transformative qualities. You mull over the content and try to untangle the meaning. Such are the stories from *The Arabian Nights*. One such tale is "Abu Kasem's Slippers" from *The King & The Corpse* by Heinrich Zimmer.

Abu Kasem was a wealthy merchant of *attar* – perfume from the essence of roses. Yet his tattered slippers were a visible sign of his greed. Even a beggar would have been ashamed to be caught in those slippers. Kasem wore them so the townspeople's attention would get diverted from his prosperity.

One day after making a successful business deal, he went to the public bath to celebrate. He left his clothes and slippers in the changing room where he met a friend who told him with great concern that he had become a laughingstock. "Can't a clever and rich businessman like you afford a pair of decent new slippers?" he said. Kasem ignored him.

While the miser was enjoying his bath, the judge of Baghdad also arrived to bathe. Kasem returned to the changing room. Next to the place where he had left his slippers, he saw a beautiful shiny jeweled pair. He thought a jokester had replaced his slippers. Without searching, Kasem slipped on the new shoes. As he walked home, he reflected that this would save him the trouble of bargaining and buying a new pair.

When the judge returned, he found a disgusting pair of slippers in place of his own, which everyone recognized as Abu Kasem's footwear. The judge sent for the culprit, locked him behind bars, and returned the old slippers.

Sad and sorry, Kasem went home and, in a fit of anger, threw the old slippers out the window. With a splash they fell in the Tigris River that rushed muddily past his house. A few days later a fisherman thought he had caught a particularly heavy fish but when he hauled it in, what did he see? The celebrated slippers! He hurled the soggy and soiled objects through Kasem's open window. They landed on his table next to uncapped crystal perfume bottles of *attar* with a crash.

"Those wretched slippers," Kasem cried. "They dare not do me any further harm." He went to his garden, dug a hole, and quickly buried the things. Kasem's neighbor watched. He thought, *What a miserable miser! He has servants but he is digging a hole himself. Why? He must be burying a treasure.* Thinking thus, the neighbor went to the governor's palace and informed him about what Kasem had done.

The governor summoned Kasem and asked him the reason for digging the hole. Kasem explained that he had dug a hole in the earth to bury his old pair of slippers. Upon hearing this, everybody in the court laughed uproariously. The more Kasem insisted about his plight, the guiltier he seemed. He was thunderstruck when he was told the amount of the fine he was to pay.

How was he to get rid of those filthy slippers? *To be continued tomorrow.*

JOURNAL PROMPT
Like Abu Kasem, are you holding on to something for no good reason, even after you have thought of getting rid of it, or after a friend has suggested it?

ꙮ *Day 79* ꙮ

TODAY'S PRACTICE
Meditation: "Heartful"   Read, reflect, and journal.

INSPIRATION

So, how was Abu Kasem to get rid of his slippers?

Kasem went far away, deep in the country, and dropped his slippers into a pond. The pond was a reservoir that fed the town's water supply. The slippers swirled to the mouth of the pipe and blocked it. The governor's repairman fixed the damage and found the notorious slippers. The shoes were recognized. Kasem was reported to the governor for polluting the reservoir. Once again, Kasem sat in jail. This time he was fined far more.

What was he to do with the slippers that had returned to him over and over? He decided to burn them, but they were still wet so he put them out on the balcony to dry. The dog next door became interested. He jumped over to Kasem's balcony and snatched a slipper. As he was playing, the shoe, heavy with water, fell to the street below. The wretched thing spun through the air and landed on the head of a passing pregnant woman. The sudden shock to her head resulted in a miscarriage. Her husband complained. The judge demanded damages from the rich old miser.

Kasem was out of his mind, but forced to pay the fine. Now a broken man and not so wealthy, he tottered from his home to the court where he raised his unlucky slipper aloft. Earnestly he cried to the judge, "My lord, these slippers are the fateful cause of all my suffering. They have reduced me to beggary. Please command that no longer should I be held responsible for the evils they will most certainly continue to bring upon me."

The judge could not reject this crying plea that came from Kasem's heart and seemed true. The indestructible slippers had cost Abu Kasem many times their value. They were worth nothing in themselves, yet they drained him of his fortune.

How do we interpret such a potent symbol? Abu Kasem's relationship to his slippers was dark, fateful, even mysterious. But what do they say about destiny and our role in creating our own? *To be continued tomorrow.*

JOURNAL PROMPT

Kasem's destiny spun out of a series of chance activities. Separately, each situation was possible, but all in a series for the same individual? How can one avoid such a fate?

◡ *Day 80* ◠

TODAY'S PRACTICE

Meditation: "Heartful"   Read, reflect, and journal.

INSPIRATION

I re-read the tale of Abu Kasem's slippers every year to remind myself that a major part of my fate is in my hands, under my control. Kasem's slippers represent his vice – avarice. If he had relinquished those slippers when his concerned friend suggested it, he would have gotten rid of them along with his vice. Instead, he deluded himself by thinking, *Why waste money on a new pair of shoes? Who is going to look at my feet?* So, by the time Kasem left the bathhouse his greed had turned him into a thief. The tattered slippers came to symbolize his self-destructive avarice. With each event, his negative trait magnified and wove his miserable destiny.

In your own life, if you are unable to overcome negative characteristics, they keep returning in different forms. You may refuse to recognize the effects, even when they keep snowballing. You may ignore this while it intensifies, goes unnoticed, and plays tricks on you. Slowly the accumulated "fateful" events get deeper and deeper. You can no longer get rid of them. They turn into your "destiny."

Meditation would have helped Abu Kasem to become mindful. Mindfulness would have helped him to grow attentive and aware. It would have:

- Allowed him to recognize his options.

- Nudged him to listen to his concerned friend and make a right choice.

- Helped him change past conditioning before his total self-destruction.

- Helped him to hear the whispers of his Authentic Self, leading him to self-understanding and wisdom.

JOURNAL PROMPT

What lesson did you glean from the story? Out of the three cravings – wanting to become wealthy, dreaming of fame and power, and desiring admiration and praise – which of these brings you down?

ᕳ *Day 81* ᕲ

TODAY'S PRACTICE

Meditation: "Body"   Read, reflect, and journal.

INSPIRATION

Your position and possessions do not provide an insurance against loneliness, boredom, distress, or purposelessness. If you depend completely on success and accomplishments to make you happy, you are setting yourself up for emotional anguish. Irrespective of how much you have achieved professionally or how famous you have been or continue to be, the time comes when you are no longer what you were. This is when you must search for someone you can believe in, trust, and from whom you can hear what is true. This may be a mentor, a teacher or professor, or a trusted friend. However, such a guide already dwells within – but it takes many years of attending to, observing, receiving, and accepting its whispers. Meditation introduces and connects you with this inner friend. So, begin connecting with it in meditation. If not now, then when?

If you start your career at age 21 or 31, the trajectory of that work life ends in 35 or 45 years. In our seventies we naturally slow and can no longer keep pace with long working hours. Contemplating life brings satisfaction and joy. But it is also when a fear of death emerges and is magnified.

The desire to keep busy, working even after retirement, is rooted in the fear of death. Instead of pretending that mortality does not exist, we may alleviate the fear through Writing Meditation Practice. WMP combines the practices of meditation, journaling, deep reading, walking in nature, and other artistic pursuits. These have brought me a long way from obsessing over mortality to the peaceful and joyous frame of mind that recharges me daily.

Accepting the truth of your own mortality aids you to go deep within, getting closer to your Authentic Self, the source of all there is, and drawing upon its wisdom. Creative pursuits such as writing, painting, music, and spiritual ideals like authenticity, selfless love, and kindness strengthen your inner power and decrease the fear, anxiety, guilt, jealousy, and other self-destructive emotions.

JOURNAL PROMPT

Which friend, mentor, or teacher do you remember who imbued a love of creativity and wisdom? Why did this person leave such an indelible impression?

ꙮ *Day 82* ꙮ

TODAY'S PRACTICE

Meditation: "Body"   Read, reflect, and journal.

INSPIRATION

While learning to meditate, cultivate the habit of paying attention to your breath, even when you are not meditating. This will deepen your sitting practice. When you do sit to meditate, keep track of any thought that inspires. "We become what we meditate on," writes Eknath Easwaran. The thought you focus on turns into a helpful tool for the rest of the day.

Don't undo the energy you gain during meditation by getting involved with negative emotions. In the early stages of meditation, you may have a hundred little imps of distraction dancing in your head. Confront them during meditation. The fewer distractions you have during the day, the fewer disturbances you'll face in the quiet of sitting. Most problems do not come from outside but are caused by your own cravings, greed, fears, resentments, or guilt. They claim power over your attention. The fewer preoccupations with yourself, the clearer your mind.

Be aware of the needs of those around you. This will also deepen your meditation. Face the rough moments of the day the same way you accept the smooth moments. Laugh them off. Give your best and watch how distractions lessen day by day. As you move into deeper levels of awareness, only few distractions remain: anger, greed, jealousy, fear. These are sturdy, and you know them well. But you can train yourself to deal with them.

Distractions originate in the mind and express themselves in words and actions. You have to learn not to act upon them. You cannot let them win. In meditation, pay attention to whatever emotion emerges. Don't push it away. Mull it over. Think how you can praise the person you envy, how you can pretend to love the person you hate, and confront the fear that gnaws at you. As the days pass, your behavior will become more kind and helpful. No human is born bad. We turn into villains and monsters when emotionally or physically wounded. By first healing our own wounds, we are able to recognize the suffering of others and help them so they too may heal.

JOURNAL PROMPT

Journal about what makes you furious or fearful. Write whatever is churning in you. The first step to clear your mind and open your heart is not to suppress your own grief and pain, but to honor it. Only when you tenderly care and have compassion for your own sensations and feelings can you care for and have compassion for others.

❧ *Day 83* ❧

TODAY'S PRACTICE
Meditation: "Body"   Read, reflect, and journal.

INSPIRATION

The practice of daily meditation subtly shifts your consciousness. Mindfully observed things seem to behave differently from those unobserved. You get your best thoughts in the silence of meditation. In stillness, vivid images and ideas that are uniquely yours present themselves effortlessly. More importantly, meditation nudges you to observe yourself. Self-witnessing results in insights that hone you into a better writer and more caring individual. Mindfulness, creativity, and spirituality are inextricably linked.

But the mind wants to wander, to think this and that, not meditate. Your attempts to make it sit as you sit will likely fail. The mind keeps running away. You bring it back. It runs away. You bring it back again. This is difficult but essential work. Because, gradually, the mind quiets. You ask it to focus on one positive thought, a poem or a quote, and the mind learns to settle. Because it has something to do. It stays quiet for a minute or several minutes, but those are important moments. All kinds of mental and physical healing takes place during that time. Those few minutes become possible only when you have trained the mind to quiet or reflect. Progress is slow but definitely happening.

Time in solitude, withdrawing from the outer world, creates a condition of intuitiveness. You experience a state that is dull to the outer world but vividly alive to inner imagination and creativity. You are in the writer's creative zone. The combination of stillness, silence, and solitude is creative magic, a portal to the true secret of an artistic mind. This may not happen every single day but often enough. Those who follow WMP attest to the mood this practice creates.

JOURNAL PROMPT

In the silence of meditation, when you have nowhere to hide, what disguise do negative thoughts appear in: self-doubt, jealousy, anger, resentment, hate, guilt, fear, other? Journal about one incident when the ego in the guise of an emotion came in the way of your creative flow. Did it command you to do things that your Authentic Self warned you against?

ᘳ Day 84 ᘰ

TODAY'S PRACTICE

Meditation: "Body"   Read, reflect, and journal.

INSPIRATION

The path of creativity and spirituality that you have embarked upon is a spiral within you. Its center can only be reached unhurriedly, mindfully, and authentically. You can't rush it. Besides, there is no haste. You have nine more months to sit in silence and solitude in your Spiritual and Creative Power Spot.

To ground in your practice during meditation and for the rest of the day, here is a list of Twin Spiritual Skills. Read them to anchor you before you sit. By the end of the year, not only will they dwell permanently in your mind but also within your heart.

1. Attention on breath and body
2. Intention and courage
3. Silence and solitude
4. Simplicity and authenticity
5. Patience and persistence
6. Gratitude and generosity

To further refine your practice, hone these Four Fine Feelings:

- Tenderness from kindness
- Awe and wonder stirred by walks in nature
- Inspiration for imagination
- Delight and joy caused by practice

JOURNAL PROMPT

Journal about three values that are integral to your day-to-day living. Why are these values important to you?

✌ *Day 85* ✌

TODAY'S PRACTICE	
Meditation: "Body"	Read, reflect, and journal.

INSPIRATION

Why are artistic individuals and creative greatness associated with wild behavior? No such link exists. Yet many of us continue to believe that creative people are eccentric. Here are a few observations I have gleaned from the lives of writer and artist friends and my own life.

First, creative people constantly challenge the status quo and think beyond the box. They refuse to accept social norms if they doubt their validity. A society at large may accept discriminatory treatment of gender, race, and religious biases even when these harm people. Artistic individuals rebel against such norms.

Second, creative people innovate, experiment, and continually demonstrate that there are worlds beyond the material universe and worlds deeper within. They have awakened the source of creativity and spirituality from which they draw novel ideas and liberation.

Third, the source within is dormant unless activated by artistic and spiritual practice. During the creative process, these individuals are in the "zone." They feel the "flow," the aesthetic joy explored by Mihaly Csikszentmihalyi. In that ecstatic dimension, they cease to be mere mortals; they become Godlike, albeit temporarily. Having experienced the ecstasy, they find the material world juiceless – perhaps the reason for their erratic behavior.

Fourth, the reason societies have labeled creative minds as "nuts" or "not quite right in there" is because no matter how talented or successful creative individuals are, they suffer from self-distrust. Even if they have several good works under the belt, even when their fans want more, they continue to remain uncertain about their abilities and skills, unsure if they can repeat previous successes.

Fifth, there is no need to link passion and overwhelming emotions of creative minds with madness. When emotions and ideas overflow, they develop into great books, or gel into phenomenal musical compositions, masterpieces of visual arts, profound philosophical insights, and amazing scientific theories.

To label the behavior of creative minds as eccentric is a mindless accusation. The creative process is beyond the creator's conscious reach. When they are in the "zone" or experiencing the "flow," they are working beyond their conscious level. They may be using their intellectual and technical abilities, but the actual creative process is full of surprises. It is only when heart-mind is one with the work in hand that ego transcends and art is born.

JOURNAL PROMPT

Is there a moment after you have completed a book, a painting, or a musical composition when you feel you can't create another one? Are you fearful of being called an eccentric? At the time when your confidence and self-esteem is not at its best, journal your heart out.

ꥠ *Day 86* ꥟

TODAY'S PRACTICE

Meditation: "Body"   Read, reflect, and journal.

INSPIRATION

The practice of guided and silent meditation changes you for the better, and in the process surprises you in more than one way. Inner changes occur in micro boosts. You may not notice them, but change is taking place. This happens because you have begun to replace stressing-about-things-not-under-your-control to focusing on body sensations and the resultant feelings.

You began the practice to energize your body, to become more aware, to deepen your imagination, and to receive original ideas for writing projects or other artistic pursuits. Are you eager and ready to keep going, or has some fear percolated which is making you doubt yourself? Are you having second thoughts about a project, wondering if you are up to the challenge? Starting a piece of writing or any other creative project and then taking it all the way to the finish line is a perilous task. You feel vulnerable.

Write down what you intend to achieve by dividing the work into daily segments. If you have a writing project, then 1000-1500 words, even 500 words a day will do. If at the end of the day you have done the work, reward yourself with something nice. Little successes are worth celebrating. If you miss one day, don't feel guilty. You are human. We all stumble at times. Next day, do the segment you missed and then some more. But keep going. At the end of the year your daily work will multiply into the draft of a book. Next year revise it into the final manuscript.

In the company of Robert Frost, choose the road not yet taken and experience all the difference it will make. Glance at your list of intentions and goals. You may have slacked a few days due to circumstances beyond your control but don't let that stop or freeze you with fear or lethargy. Keep walking fearlessly and be ready to confront whatever unknown entities may block your way. We are in this together. The energy and the intuitive ideas will continue to flow in and amaze you on this journey.

JOURNAL PROMPT

Write a letter to your future self. Talk about your greatest achievement and about the wildest thing you have done. Then write about the things you wished you had done but either didn't or couldn't.

৩ *Day 87* ৩

TODAY'S PRACTICE

Meditation: "Mindful"   Read, reflect, and journal.

INSPIRATION

Think of one thing you are most passionate about. Sit with that intention in your mind. Attend to it with the inbreath and outbreath – 5, 10, or 15 minutes, as long as you can focus. Feel the body become still and the static in your mind calm down.

At first with your eyes closed, you see nothing but darkness. You may not want to sit because too many things are rushing to your mind. But the practice is to keep paying attention to your breath. It is your only guide within. The moment you realize that you have likely become lost in the crowd of strangers – fleeting thoughts, unwholesome memories, images, future worries – spot your guide and begin again. Then again. And again. Bring your attention back to the breath and to the present moment.

The act of getting lost, recognizing and beginning again and again, is essential to the practice of meditation. You need an inner light to recognize ideas and insights. Your daily practice helps you discover, cultivate, and sustain such ephemeral impressions and keeps you connected to their source, your Authentic Self.

In her book, *Real Happiness: The Power of Meditation*, Sharon Salzberg compares meditation practice with chopping down a tree. She writes that when we chop down the trunk of a tree, we need each and every stroke. The falling of the tree is the result of every single attempt we make before we succeed. What makes that final cut possible is our willingness to keep going.

"Keeping at it" is also true with meditation practice. Even when you are sleepy, bored, restless, or anxious, your practice is deepening. Your patience and persistence, your effort and hard work, your attitude toward the possibility of learning all that is required for becoming mindful of the Self and aware of the surroundings will eventually coalesce.

Over time the physical discomfort, the mental exertion, and other *negative experiences* will move you toward self-transformation. "Ninety-nine times you hit a tree trunk with an axe, and nothing happens. On the hundredth stroke it splits," continues Salzberg. That doesn't mean that during the first 99 repetitions nothing was happening. No, it means the results were accumulating and came to fruition the final time.

Whenever you feel "nothing" is happening in your meditation sessions, remind yourself of Salzberg's wise words, that the hundredth stroke is "what splits open the wood, and the world."

JOURNAL PROMPT

Do you record the days when you meditate and when you skip? It's okay to skip but when you do, be conscious of the fact that you missed. Accepting it keeps you connected with your inner Self. You may sit quietly any other time of the day for 5-10 minutes. This keeps the seed of your practice watered and fertilized.

⤷ *Day 88* ↩

TODAY'S PRACTICE

Meditation: "Mindful"   Read, reflect, and journal.

INSPIRATION

A gift! These words rarely come to mind when we wake to a brand new day. Instead, our mind is already occupied with memories and anticipations. The blank page of the day stands waiting to be filled with feelings of comfort, joy, and moments that are uniquely ours. But we are not present for it.

I've learned my lesson through the years. When I open my eyes in the morning, I have a habit of saying, "Thank you!" I wash my face, brush my teeth, drink a glass of water, and sit at my Sacred Power Spot to meditate. Then comes deep reading – a poem or short chapter from a collection or anthology which is meaningful to me. This is followed by journaling. By this time, my mind has been enriched with benevolence and peace. The compass of my mind points to the day's tasks yet to be accomplished with positive energy.

For you it has been almost a month of practicing meditation, journaling, and walking. Consider which body of water you feel like when you sit in the silence of your Sacred Power Spot. Is it a waterfall, river, lake, or a combination of these?

Waterfall

As novices and intermediate meditators, the mind is like a waterfall. It thunders with torrents of thoughts and feelings, and you are oblivious to physical sensations. Even when torrents tighten your muscles, you are clueless. You don't know you are tense.

Focus on your breath and try to get in touch with your physical sensations. Sit for 15 minutes and then move on to journaling. Your awareness of what you are doing and who you are is a powerful grounding tool at this stage.

Pour out the excess emotions and fleeting thoughts into your notebook. Journaling will absorb the gushing overflow. Your writing may catch some drips from the spill, but the body and the breath will anchor you.

River

An intermediate practitioner's mind grows from the torrential waterfall to a flowing river. You attend to the body sensations and observe your feelings and thoughts as a continuous flow. The river's flow does not feel as overwhelming as the gushing of the waterfall. It is slower and gentler. Self-doubt and negative thoughts loosen their grip. You are not as impulsive as you used to be. You pause and mull over things if they disturb you. People no longer seem to disturb your mental peace. If they need responding, you respond. Otherwise, you let go of their opinions and arguments.

Lake

Finally, as a skilled meditator you are calm. Your flow is smooth, vast, and open like the surface of a lake without ripples. Your practice is a continuous state of meditative awareness. When you experience intense emotions, positive or negative, you do not get overexcited or agitated. Instead, you transcend them and use them in your writing to turn them into art.

Above and beyond these three categories is the adept or master meditator. This level of expertise in meditation is not necessary unless you want to move from being a writer to a spiritual teacher. For an adept meditator, the balance shifts from creativity to deep spirituality. Such persons experience constant meditative joy and are one with their authentic selves.

Neuroscientist Sara Lazar of Massachusetts General and Harvard Medical School has studied the stages of meditation. She observes that people who practice daily meditation have more gray matter in their frontal cortex. This part of the brain is linked to decision making and working memory. Her conclusion? While most people see their frontal cortex shrink as they age, those who meditate 15-45 minutes daily have the same amount of gray matter as those who are half their age.

JOURNAL PROMPT

Great writing demands emotional drama, suffering, pain, trauma, disease, death. What sort of pain do you feel deep down in your bowels that writing demands? Which of your passions do you share with your readers?

༄ *Day 89* ༅

TODAY'S PRACTICE

Meditation: "Mindful"   Read, reflect, and journal.

INSPIRATION

What does it mean to live in the present moment? It means becoming absorbed in whatever you are doing, free from past and future thinking, training your mind to return to the task at hand, the way you return to the breath in meditation. People are not in the habit of taking in what is right in front of them. They want to move on to the next thing and the next. This attitude keeps you in an endless cycle of wanting.

The present moment is the only *living* moment you have. Even when you are going through a painful or difficult time, it is better to work through the pain, moment by moment, until it alleviates or dissipates. And it is equally beneficial to delight in good times and enjoy pleasurable moments. The person who lives in the present is truly alive. Once this way of working becomes a habit, life seems to flow effortlessly.

Living in the present moment does not mean that your past and future are unimportant. They are significant but only when relevant to the present. Bring them up when needed. No insights or intuitive ideas emerge when regretting the past or fearing the future. Living in the present brings inner quiet and deepens your focus and imagination.

In meditation you train your mind to live in the present, to focus on inhaling and exhaling, and to witness your thoughts. Guide your own mind. Let it know who is the boss. Instead of the mind directing you, you direct it. Say, "No, thank you," to things that make you sad and lonely. When negative thoughts appear, bring the mind back to the breath and body sensations. This shifts your attention to the present moment. With self-awareness you come closer to your breath and your Self. Don't believe the mind's dark chatter. With meditation practice train your mind to act the way that is in accordance with your deepest values, not what it randomly thinks.

JOURNAL PROMPT

How familiar is this scenario? An idea strikes. You write several pages. They feel pretty good. The muse has arrived. Then monkey-mind butts in. *"You are making no progress!"* or *"You are not such a good writer as you think you are!"* You stop. Again, it interjects, *"Your friend is in town. She doesn't visit often. Why don't you take her out for coffee or something?"*

Monkey-mind! What do you do? Do you get caught in the snare of your restless mind or do you refocus and continue working on your intended idea?

⤷ *Day 90* ↵

TODAY'S PRACTICE

Meditation: "Mindful"   Read, reflect, and journal.

INSPIRATION

Today ends the theme of "Meditation and Mindfulness." Now is a good time to remind yourself of the obstacles you may have faced during silent meditation. These are: numbness, drowsiness, restlessness, boredom, fear, sadness, or pain. Here are some suggestions how you may mitigate or eliminate them.

Numbness

In the early stages of the practice, only after a few minutes of sitting, some body parts may feel numb. You may feel cut off from your body. It takes time to get in touch with each body part and recognize its sensations. Make a deliberate attempt to get familiar with the physical sensations. Befriend them. Remember, they are always present whether you are aware of them or not. Only through these sensations can you feel fully and have clear thinking. Only when you can sense the body, feel deeply, and think clearly can you link to the Authentic Self.

Drowsiness

Drowsiness is one of the most common obstacles faced in silent meditation. This may happen when you are tired and simply need more sleep, or if you have a stimulated day before you sit still. The mind may think, *Time to sleep!* To avoid drowsiness, keep your eyes open. Take deeper inhales and exhales. Observe how your body senses sleepiness or what your mind does when you feel drowsy. Watch the sleepiness subside. Do not criticize yourself for feeling drowsy or judge your sleepiness. And most importantly, make sure you sleep as many hours as your body needs.

Restlessness

For a beginner practitioner, restlessness is as common as sleepiness. Physical restlessness becomes obvious when we try to sit still. Simply notice that you are experiencing it. Do the "Body Scan Meditation" and notice any areas of tightness or discomfort. Watch them and accept them as they are. Then try to be still. Avoid the tendency to criticize or judge yourself.

Boredom

When you are trying to sit still, boredom is inevitable. Don't despise or ignore it. Embrace it as part of the practice. This will give you a rare opportunity to explore your relationship with the feeling. You will understand what happens to your body when you are feeling bored. What sensations do you experience?

Fear

With closed eyes and still body, you may feel fearful. Allow it to be. Notice the fear you are feeling is not a fear in the present moment but your thoughts about having been afraid in the past or an imagined fear in the future. The imagined thoughts make you afraid in the present time. Place your hand on your heart and whisper, "I am grounded and still. There is nothing to be afraid of here now." Visualize the image of a loving and kind person. Shift your attention to the physical sensations. Soon, like the changing weather, your feeling will change, too.

Sadness

As part of the human experience, sadness arises like fear. Recognize sadness and allow tears to flow. Attend to the sensations lovingly as you do with fear. Scenes of loss may arise. Stay present. Breathe with the sadness, hold yourself with loving presence, allow the waves of grief to surface and pass. If the waves feel too strong, remember that opening your eyes and stepping back is a wise gesture of self-compassion. Do not criticize or judge yourself for being sad or afraid.

Pain

Notice areas of discomfort. Notice how your experience of pain changes constantly. Surround the painful area with your attention until it subsides. If the pain is wearing you out, direct your attention to something else and then come back to it. It is fine to slowly shift your posture. Use phrases of love and kindness. No need to "tough it out" or to "give up."

And finally, in the silence of your meditation, don't mistake the chatter of self-criticism and doubt for the whispers and voice of your Authentic Self. The whispers from AS are always helpful and benevolent. The negative chatter is an inner shadow, your shadow side. While your AS shows the path, the shadow says you can't walk on it; your AS says trust it. The shadow doubts you; your AS points to your goodness. The shadow taunts and criticizes; your AS is your best friend and the giver of joy. Its whispers *feel* right. Its gentle murmurs originate from the inner source.

JOURNAL PROMPT

Compose an email to your shadow mind telling it you will no longer tolerate the messages it has been sending you. Tell it exactly what kind of messages will be allowed inside that sacred and secret space in your heart-mind and at your Power Spot.

END OF QUARTER PROMPT

Have you completed the task you intended to finish by the end of these first three months? Were there unforeseen snags? Did you take a couple of missteps? Journal without self-criticism, trying to understand what you can do to resolve the difficulty.

SPROUTING

"Raise your words, not voice.
It is rain that grows flowers, not thunder."
—Rumi

Month 4

Mindfulness and Reading for Pleasure

Suggested Readings

The No. 1 Ladies' Detective Agency
Alexander McCall Smith, 2003.

An Unknown Woman
Alice Koller, 1981.

A House for Mr. Biswas
V. S. Naipaul, 1961.

Life of Pi
Yann Martel, 2001.

Homegoing
Yaa Gyasi, 2016.

ᘒ *Day 91* ᘓ

TODAY'S PRACTICE

This month, continue the practices of meditation, reflection, and journaling. Add time for pleasure reading.

Meditation: "Walking through the Forest"   Read, reflect, and journal.

INSPIRATION

After reading the nightmarish poem, "A Dream" by Hermann Hesse, I shuddered and wrote a short story, excerpted below:

> I walk to the monastery on the hill and enter. Its walls are lined with books from ceiling to floor. The stacked spines glitter in the morning light. I pull out the nearest book, *Meaning of My Life*. The leather cover tooled in gold promises a story still untold. What wisdom will the book reveal?

> I read the front folio aglow with words, *"Learn to see separately with two eyes and separately with two ears. You'll see sound and hear colors."* I am in paradise. All knowledge stands at my command. Volumes filled with entertaining stories, scholarship, wisdom. My thirst is finally going to be quenched. I examine the next book and the next.

> Awed and delighted, I look away to take in what I have realized and give my eyes a rest. I notice a man standing in front of the tomes. An archivist? Librarian? A monk bedazzled? I watch his slow, blue-veined frail hands intent on some task. He is holding a book and inspecting what is inside. With pallid lips he blows upon the cover. His fingers wipe across the spine, then each page inside the covers. Silently, he erases the text and replaces it. He keeps repeating this to each book he holds.

> What is he doing? Once again, I pull out *Meaning of My Life*. He has touched and blown on it, too. No longer do I see the title or the text that transported me to bliss with its wisdom. Its universe is dissolved, faded, rewritten. He has blown new inquiries, new formulas, new problems and

promises, replacing the wisdom of the ancient past. He plies his magic style on all the volumes and then disappears."

Can you imagine a world where knowledge and wisdom and insight is constantly rewritten? Who decides what information will be shared and what will be discarded? Having a library of such volumes changed is almost as horrifying as having no books at all or choosing not to read when you know how.

I'm grateful to my father for inculcating the habit of daily reading in me from an early age. Listening as he read to me, slowly graduating to read myself, escaping into absorbing new worlds... *What a blessing!* All my eight siblings read stories in English, Hindi, and Urdu, some voraciously, others not that much. But everyone read and continues to read.

There was nothing like adventuring with exciting and romantic heroes and seeing the blood and gore of the villains – terror and horror in the service of aesthetic enjoyment. Magically it all stays between the covers, waiting in that space for us where we reluctantly leave only to get back to it later.

JOURNAL PROMPT

Why are books important in a civilized society and how would it be if they disappeared from our world?

ᔆᓚ *Day 92* ᥴᵥ

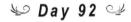

TODAY'S PRACTICE

Meditation: "Walking through the Forest"   Read, reflect, and journal.

INSPIRATION

Whether reading for pleasure or personal growth, what you enjoy depends on your interests and experiences. What are you seeking? What you choose to read is as unique as what you enjoy eating or wearing.

I read to be entertained, to learn, to adventure into unknown worlds where my heart is slashed, where my guts are punched, or a brick falls on my head. It is not what you choose to read but what happens to you when you are absorbed in a book – that pleasurable feeling of forgetting who and where you are, temporarily experiencing life through someone else's perspective.

When you find an author whose work you love, read everything by them. Notice how even a good writer's work ripens with time and practice. Early books will likely not be as good as later ones. Use this as a learning tool, allowing this knowledge to free your own mindset as a writer.

During different periods of my life, I have experienced the pleasure of reading almost everything by Virginia Woolf, Pearl S. Buck, V. S. Naipaul, Joyce Carol Oates, Hermann Hesse, Jhumpa Lahiri, Mulk Raj Anand, R. K. Narayan, Naguib Mahfouz, Jon Kabat-Zinn, and Eknath Easwaran. How they construct a reality with mere words boggles my mind.

Mindfully exploring the oeuvre of each of your favorite writers is a lesson in observing subtlety, nuance, and beauty. With each book you read, your emotional and intellectual sensibilities will emerge and deepen.

JOURNAL PROMPT

Who inspired your love of reading? What was the first book you fell in love with?

✌ *Day 93* ↩

TODAY'S PRACTICE

Meditation: "Walking through the Forest"   Read, reflect, and journal.

INSPIRATION

Do you read a different book in the morning from the one before going to sleep? I do. I'm most focused in the morning and least focused at night. So, in the morning I read things that are either difficult to comprehend, poetic, or that have lessons to teach. Like morning meditation and journaling practice, the morning deep reading calms me, ushering in joy. I feel aligned, ready to dive deeper into my writing. The thoughts therein keep me energized. Consider works like:

The Seven Storey Mountain, Thomas Merton
Coming to Our Senses, Jon Kabat-Zinn
The Power of Myth, Joseph Campbell
Man and His Symbols, Carl G. Jung
The Seeker's Guide, Elizabeth Lesser
Moon in a Dew Drop, Dogen
Odes to Common Things, Pablo Naruda
God Makes the Rivers to Flow, An Anthology of World's Sacred Poetry & Prose, Eknath Easwaran

At night I look forward to delving into a fictional world. This routine helps me slip into a restful sleep. Some of my evening reads include:

The Secret Garden, Frances Hodgson Burnett
The Poisonwood Bible, Barbara Kingsolver
The Kite Runner, Khaled Hosseini
Eat, Pray, Love, Elizabeth Gilbert
The Lowland, Jhumpa Lahiri
All the Light We Cannot See, Anthony Doerr
The Invention of Wings, Sue Monk Kidd
The Feeling Good Handbook, David D. Burns

In 2003, a group of doctors in Wales prescribed reading as a cure for patients with mild to moderate depression. This brainchild of clinical psychologist Professor Neil Frude worked so well that he named it "Book Prescription Program." His patients found themselves with a library card instead of a drug prescription.

A published study in the UK found that reading self-help books in conjunction with face-to-face support sessions helped more than 42 percent of patients find relief from depression and anxiety without the use of anti-depressants. Another study found reading reduces stress by 68 percent, more than listening to music or going for a walk. And it doesn't require hours to reap the benefits. Just 10-20 minutes of reading lowers stress levels.

JOURNAL PROMPT

Make a list of books you always wanted to read but haven't yet. What would you like to read for fun? What is your favorite time to read? Do you read more than one book at a time?

ᔰ *Day 94* ᓚ

TODAY'S PRACTICE

Meditation: "Walking through the Forest"   Read, reflect, and journal.

INSPIRATION

I love to travel with my husband, both within the country and abroad. I also love to watch award-winning American, South Asian, and foreign movies. I travel and watch movies for the awe and delight these provide me, helping me liberate from limiting beliefs and values, and exposing me to how people with different worldviews living in other cultures and believing in other religions embrace life. This improves my mental plasticity and physical agility.

However, I can't travel for more than a couple of weeks at a time or watch movies constantly. But I can read about cultures, religions, and people at any time of the day. Reading has become such an integral part of my routine that when a few days go by without my picking up a book, I hear them gently calling me. Without a book I feel off-kilter and out of sorts.

Uninterrupted reading transports me from this world to one the author has created. I feel showered with abundant pleasure. Now that's true entertainment! But entertainment for its own sake can easily become pointless. A book must also touch the heart and enlighten in some way.

As a writer, you have the power to affect people's lives. Each of us suffers in one way or another. Your writing can become a conduit for others to find light in their darkness. Truths about life's suffering are more easily understood when molded into a well-crafted, absorbing story. In real life, lessons are learned the hard way but in books bitter truths are winkled out. Instead of filling us with sorrow they shower us with learning and artistic pleasure.

JOURNAL PROMPT

Which books have given you comfort during a dark time in your life? When does an entertaining book lose its allure? At what point does an educational book turn boring?

◡◠ *Day 95* ◠◡

TODAY'S PRACTICE

Meditation: "Walking through the Forest"   Read, reflect, and journal.

INSPIRATION

Mindful Writer Denise Weaver shares:

"I've been a reader since childhood. My earliest favorite, *Bunny Hopwell's First Spring* by Jean Fritz, was a lengthy picture/storybook that I'd have my mother read over and over, then learned to read myself. My heart still flutters a little just thinking of it, and I continue these many years later to think about spring being 'just around the corner.' I moved next to stories of The Bobbsey Twins (Laura Lee Hope), Black Beauty (Anna Sewell), and on to Nancy Drew (Carolyn Keene) and The Hardy Boys (Franklin Dixon), rereading until I could acquire the next installment in the series.

Though my parents were not readers beyond newspapers and magazines, they never denied me in my reading quest, having a lovely built-in bookcase created in my bedroom, and allowing me to fill it with my books. In addition to fiction, I treasured my Childcraft and World Book Encyclopedia set along with numerous dictionaries.

Books became my friends. I grew up in a rural area and didn't have neighborhood kids to play with and didn't deem my little brother (who was five years younger) a worthy playmate. Books took me on adventures, entertained me, allowed me to escape what I viewed as my humdrum life, provided goals and interests, and led me on the path of loving and continually seeking information and knowledge." (Posted at Online Mindful Writers Group in 2021)

JOURNAL PROMPT

If you can find one or more books from your childhood or youth, reread them. What attribute or aspect of your life today correlates directly to your experiences of reading those books?

⸎ *Day 96* ⸙

TODAY'S PRACTICE

Meditation: "Walking through the Forest"   Read, reflect, and journal.

INSPIRATION

Probably your daily schedule is unlike mine. I don't have to be somewhere in the morning and stay there for 8-10 hours. I'm able to keep my weekday routine without a problem.

But you may have a stressful job with long hours and a young family to take care of. Perhaps you are squeezing in reading here and there, and don't yet have dedicated time to sit with a book and read in peace. With a situation like that it can be hard to absorb or remember what you are reading.

Would you be able to carve out 15-20 minutes a day to read, if not daily, perhaps several times a week? You can sit in your Sacred Power Spot, or in a comfortable nook, or in bed just before bedtime to make your reading time relaxing.

For a few minutes, warm up for reading as you would for the workout. Before opening the book, close your eyes and practice your breathing exercise for a minute or so. Then open your eyes and read. Don't rush; enjoy. Allow yourself to wallow in the voice of the author, loving the style and the feeling it stirs. Read for 20-30 minutes. When the reading time is about to end, close the book, close your eyes, breathe for a minute or two. Then reflect upon what you just read. Feel proud of yourself for doing this.

JOURNAL PROMPT

A good practice is to begin and end a reading session with a micro-meditation. What have you read since yesterday's practice? Journal about it. How does it feel?

✿ *Day 97* ✿

TODAY'S PRACTICE
Meditation: "Walking through the Forest"   Read, reflect, and journal.

INSPIRATION

Read and reread books until your own book is born.
Your mind-born lies dormant at the core of your heart.
Hatch it on grass, leaves, lichens of your readings.
Feed it worms of your author voice and style.

Neither being self-conscious nor contriving
manifest your book to join forces with the masters
melding their skills with your imagination.
Don't give up. Be patient.

Overcome emotional obstacles and mental boulders.
Stay focused, motivated, inspired.
Write for the readers the way the masters wrote for you.
For the benefit of all you'll prevail in your works.

Reading is the obverse side of writing. Yet, I have met aspiring writers who declare they are not readers. They say they "have neither time nor motivation to read." They only want to write. However, one of the essential ways to learn writing skills or develop a writer's voice is by reading voraciously.

Read inside and outside your genre, whatever attracts your attention. As a novice writer, this is like assembling a scaffolding around your work that keeps it steady until you develop a strong writing "backbone," refining your emerging voice and cultivating an authentic style.

Your reading speed does not matter, fast or painfully slow. All that matters is that you love what you read. You cannot transport your readers to another dimension unless you have read a book that transported you. The more you read, the better you will write.

JOURNAL PROMPT

What books have swept you away? Are there any you have read a second and third time, highlighting paragraphs, underlining sentences, filling the margins with notes? Journal about how the author was able to mesmerize you, winning you over with mere words.

✌ *Day 98* ↢

TODAY'S PRACTICE

Remember to grant yourself time for pleasure reading this month!
Meditation: "Walking through the Forest"   Read, reflect, and journal.

INSPIRATION

The first time I delve into a book is for the sheer joy of reading. But if a book enlightens me or jolts my mindset or questions my values or opposes my beliefs, I read it again and again, the second time to scrutinize it and ponder over its contents.

In my journal, I write a summary of why I value the book enough that I'm willing to spend additional time on it. What did I like and didn't like? What meaning did the book convey to me? If I have highlighted a page or a paragraph during my first reading and it still scrapes my mind or echoes in my heart, I rethink it. I also mark any paragraphs that I glazed over or skipped, or dialogue that felt unnatural or stilted or was flawless. I admire the precise words and underline unfamiliar ones to learn their meaning. If a word does not exactly convey what the author seemed to mean, I search for it. Such exercises help me hone my writing skills.

The second time I read, I know how the book ends, so I watch for clues the author strategically placed along the way. This is such a helpful tool. Mindful reading, with all my faculties alert, is a stimulating exercise.

After a few years of this practice, and to my pleasant surprise, I discovered that I had trained myself to read for recreation with an eye for meaningful learning. Some books I reread a third or even fourth time. But this is only to savor the exceptionally well-written and pleasure giving pages.

JOURNAL PROMPT
Write about a book you have read more than once that has enriched your own writing.

Day 99

TODAY'S PRACTICE
Meditation: "Walking through the Forest"   Read, reflect, and journal.

INSPIRATION
In *Reading Like a Writer*, Francine Prose emphasizes the necessity of noting clarity, grace, and sentence construction in classic literature. She says the cadence of the most celebrated passages moves her when she reads them *aloud*.

During my doctoral program, I read four Buddhist and Hindu scriptures for their lyrical style, beauty, and precision of words. Then I reread them aloud, critically and carefully, noting what deeply affected me. Sections that detailed rituals were tedious but when wisdom was revealed through symbols, similes, and metaphors, the reading was pure pleasure. Reading aloud with my senses on alert made it easier to absorb the wisdom and grasp meaning.

At the end of critical re-readings, I wrote commentaries for each scripture. This exercise introduced me to new words and vivid verbs. The preciseness of my improved vocabulary became evident not only in my nonfiction writing but also in my short stories and novels.

Read aloud from a completed draft of your own writing. Print it out. Open it in front of you. Hear yourself, sentence by sentence. Listen with complete trust, without self-judging. Listen to the words you chose, the voice with which you wrote, paragraph by paragraph, with an open mind and trusting heart. You will sense what you need to change to improve and refine your style.

Hearing your writing voice in your spoken voice transports you to the creative zone where you and your imagination existed while you were writing. You hear the whispers of your Authentic Self. With your mind present (and your thesaurus and dictionary open), your gut feelings will surprise you. Be receptive. Force nothing.

JOURNAL PROMPT
Read aloud a draft of your work in progress, trusting your gut and making changes that feel intuitively correct.

ꙮ *Day 100* ꙮ

TODAY'S PRACTICE
Today is the hundredth day of your Writing Meditation Practice. Congratulations!

Meditation, journaling, and reading for fun have become your daily habits. It feels good to do some things for yourself that make you feel good.

Let's celebrate with a new meditation: "Gratitude"

Feel grateful for following a practice that increases self-understanding and self-compassion. You are spending quality time with yourself each day. This care enables you to enhance your days in ways even you were not aware of.

Read and reflect for a few minutes upon today's inspiration and prompt, then journal.

INSPIRATION
On days when I doubt my ability to write, I shift to reading biographies of my favorite writers or a collection of their letters. Such readings inspire and encourage me. They make me realize how writing is a universal struggle. I learn how all great writers remain attentive to their

work, and what practices and methods they have used to think clearly, stay focused, and continue their dedication to their craft. Writers are thinkers. Before beginning a draft, they mull over the theme, the storyline, the plot, and the characters of what they are going to write. As they go about their daily business, occupied with wordless activities – like showering, gardening, cooking, walking – out of the blue comes a brand-new idea to feed their intention.

After returning from a transformative safari through Southern Africa, I suffered a writing setback. I was drawn to Wendy Suzuki's *Healthy Brain, Happy Life*. It persuaded me to return to my writing schedule. I joined a NaNoWriMo challenge[2] that helped me keep marching forward. By December 2018, I completed the final draft of the volume, the goal I had set for myself before I left for vacation.

Excellent books rub off their excellence on your work. When you read good stuff, you write better stuff. Eventually the practice of reading good literature pays off.

JOURNAL PROMPT

You may feel that your work does not in any way resemble that of writers you have read. No worries. Take a deep breath. The process of learning to write like the authors you admire is long and slow. It demands patience and practice. Journal about your inability, frustrations, and disappointments. Experiencing and writing about negative as well as positive emotions is solid ground for your work-in-progress. What has colored your writing style? What has created your unique voice?

⤷ *Day 101* ⤶

TODAY'S PRACTICE

Meditation: "Gratitude"   Read, reflect, and journal.

---

[2] November is National Novel Writing Month. https://nanowrimo.org/

Inspiration

Singing the praises of reading, Horace Mann advised, "Resolve to edge in a little reading every day even if but a single sentence." Erasmus wrote, "Before you sleep, read something that is exquisite and worth remembering." Reading improves vocabulary, reasoning, concentration, empathy, social perception, and emotional intelligence. "When you walk in the mist, you get wet," says the thirteenth-century Zen master Dogen. He means that you absorb the environment that surrounds you.

Reading lets you step out of your cloistered life and dwell in the midst of masters. By the process of unconscious assimilation, good books enter your mind. You learn from previous generations and transmit knowledge to future generations. Thus, a writing lineage is formed. Get influenced by writers greater than you; copy their best works. Read them aloud and prepare your "mulch." It will feed and fertilize your own sprouts.

Read new books and read old books. Read books written by living writers and those from earlier eras. Read everything you feel is relevant. Read books in English and in translation from as many other languages as interest you – even better is if you can read them in their native languages. Reading is the single most powerful thing you can do to improve your writing skills. What matters most is the miracle of your experiences getting communicated intimately to your readers. There are no wrong books. Let reading be your tool of discovery into the unknown of what to read and write next.

Journal Prompt

How do you decide what to read next: word of mouth, books recommended by friends, book reviews, books for research about what you are writing? Does the book you finish compel your next book selection? Do you pick a book randomly, or plan months ahead what you will read next?

༄ *Day 102* ༄

TODAY'S PRACTICE	
Meditation: "Gratitude"	Read, reflect, and journal.

INSPIRATION

The street on which Mindful Writer Deborah Catanese lived was to be ripped up and redone for storm water management. Soon trucks, workers, chainsaws, and jackhammers would start work Monday through Friday from 7 AM to 5 PM to take down trees, rip up cement, install new catchment basins and drains and gutter grates, and then put the street back together again with water-permeable cement. A week before the work was to begin she wrote with a positive attitude about it in a post. I was impressed and asked how she could feel that way. She said, "Learning that all sorts of events can make for a good story has made a huge difference (in my attitude)."

I agree. Channeling frustration and anger into writing fuels creativity. Journaling negative emotions can be cathartic. Beginning pages may overwhelm but when hopelessness is put on sheets, its energy transfers into inspiration that motivates one to take action, to do something about the situation. Documenting bleak situations becomes a lifeline that gets you through the defeat, despair, or helplessness.

Another way to overcome a negative mood is by reading about characters who have experienced similar emotions or worse situations. When you delve into their lives, real or imaginary, it helps restore your calm, similar to meditation or journaling.

Reading for pleasure transports you to a world of love, hope, adventure. These words have the power to please, entertain, and make you happier. That's the beauty of art, elevating ordinary experiences into extraordinary magical ones.

JOURNAL PROMPT

Journal about a time when life brought you unfortunate circumstances. Try to channel any negative energy and emotions into creating a powerful scene for the reader, full of detail and visceral action.

᭟ *Day 103* ᭠

TODAY'S PRACTICE

Meditation: "Gratitude"   Read, reflect, and journal.

INSPIRATION

I get fresh ideas from what I read in novels, short stories, poems, nonfiction, or magazine articles. In the history of literature, new works are almost always rooted in those of previous masters. Like mature fruit of a tree, these seeds get embedded in the soil and sprout new life. Powerful books seed fertile minds. It is not plagiarism because once inspired, you pour your own spirit into your work. Your unique personality transforms what you have read and write into a singular new creation.

Georgia O'Keeffe's mountainous landscapes of New Mexico influenced my own watercolors, and Henry Matisse's work motivated me to create compositions with brilliant flat surfaces. My art echoed the sensibilities of these masters until I made them my own. Being influenced by the work of genius is not new. Whole schools have been inspired by the masterworks of their predecessors. History is replete with such stories. But how can you feel inspired unless you visit art museums to look at works of art or read great books voraciously? Ravenous reading got me into writing professionally as I'm sure it did for many. If I hadn't read, ideas wouldn't have sparked, imagination wouldn't have fueled, and I wouldn't have become an author.

My parents were readers and my father was a prolific writer. Whereas he wrote and read in English, my mother read Hindi novels and magazines. I still remember them absorbed in their respective readings after lunch and before going to bed. They never asked their children to read, but we all learned by their example. It is said that if you want your children to read, read to them or read yourself.

JOURNAL PROMPT

Journal about how reading a particular author or authors has influenced your own reading habits or writing.

ᔐ *Day 104* ᙚ

TODAY'S PRACTICE

Meditation: "Gratitude"   Read, reflect, and journal.

INSPIRATION

Fiction was not regarded as legitimate literature in my family. Yet I loved novels by Premchand, Rabindranath Tagore, Mulk Raj Anand, R.K. Narayan, and others. Some were well worn by the time they got into my hands. Even now, when I am writing a scene set in India, images from these novels pass through my mind and help me create a scene that is a mix of fictional India and the India I lived in.

Reading inspires me to create stories and essays. I remember writing one short story about my mother's domestic help, Janak, and the other about her cacti garden, which was embellished with silvery black, sharp-edged rocks amidst succulents.

I must have been nine or ten then, and the help was not much older. Before dinner when my sister and I did our homework, Janak would sometimes leave the kitchen and come to where we were seated, showing us tricks using spoons, forks, rulers, pencils, and even a ladle. When he heard our mother call, he would ignore her a couple of times until she yelled. He would then return reluctantly with such a sad face that we felt bad for him and angry with her.

My story about the rocks surrounding the prickly cacti and shining like rare gems and crystals worthy of lakhs of rupees, inspired me to purge my thoughts and feelings about the situation of young men such as Janak.

Anything you experience intensely or read that strikes your sensibility can spark ideas and guide your work. You may not even realize when it is happening. Channeling real or fictional influences allows you to tap into your sense of wonderment and pleasure.

JOURNAL PROMPT

Write about a real-life incident or an element from your reading that originated from a specific moment in your life, influencing a story you wrote but only realized the inspiration after the fact.

◟ *Day 105* ◞

TODAY'S PRACTICE

Meditation: "Gratitude"   Read, reflect, and journal.

INSPIRATION

In the twenty-first century, we can read or we can listen to books. Mindful Writer Larry Ivkovich says he tried audiobooks but only "once got through the first half-hour" of a book by John Grisham. "I guess I really don't like to be read to unless it's a short passage. Listening to an entire novel while driving or doing something else has never really appealed to me. There are too many outside distractions, and I don't get that complete immersive experience that I get while sitting down and reading a physical book or e-reader," he confesses.

He goes on to say, "I know a similar argument can be made for not reading on an e-reader. Too impersonal, too techy, not having the right *feel* for a book. I understand, as I used to feel like that myself. But honestly, I just like to hold a book physically and read. The in-my-hands medium doesn't matter. I'll read cuneiform on stone tablets if need be. I read both print and ebooks now and like to consider myself a 'hybrid reader.' There are hybrid publishers, after all, so why not readers?"

However, numerous Mindful Writers love audiobooks, especially during long drives or when picking up kids from school or running errands. Audiobooks serve a demand and terrific purpose. It is not only a big market for writers but a useful choice for readers. Ancient storytelling is rooted in oral tradition and precedes the written form by several millennia. Ultimately it is the fictional dream, the words conjuring visuals in our imagination that counts the most, irrespective of how the words are conveyed to readers or listeners.

JOURNAL PROMPT

Journal about the importance of the spoken and written word and how each can affect the reader/listener in different ways.

↬ *Day 106* ↫

TODAY'S PRACTICE

Meditation: "Gratitude"   Read, reflect, and journal.

INSPIRATION

My father started reading to me when I was eight or nine years old. Not stories written in Hindi – those I could read on my own – but he read aloud English books so I would learn the language that was most used in India. He would say, "Soon you'll be speaking 'tidbit, tidbit'." It was a made-up phrase meaning that I would learn to speak English fluently.

Two of the books he read to me sentence by sentence were *Alice in Wonderland* (1865) and its sequel, *Through the Looking-Glass* (1871), by Lewis Carroll. I did not know English at all. Hearing the sounds of foreign words charmed me. I now realize it was his love and concern for me to grow up to be an educated woman that captivated me and kept me glued to him for 20-30 minutes every Sunday evening.

I reread *Alice in Wonderland* when I was in college and understood. What makes the book a great read for children is because when you are young, it is easy to overlook the deeper meaning this classic piece of literature conveys. No need to delve into questions of personal identity, fluidity, or the transition and transformation from childhood to adolescence. Alice's world is a cruel and dangerous place. But we read it just for fun. My father must have loved the book not only because of its whimsical characters with unique personalities but also for its deeper meaning. You can say listening and reading has been a constant in my life even before I learned to read in "tidbit." I started to learn English from ninth grade. In eleventh grade my father gave me *Lust for Life* (Vincent van Gogh's biography) and *The Agony and the Ecstasy* (Michelangelo's life) to read. Listening to *Alice in Wonderland* over and over again had done its trick. I was able to understand the stories of the two great artists, albeit superficially, until I reread them later in life.

JOURNAL PROMPT

Write about your favorite book when you were very young and how it prompted you to read more.

ꙮ *Day 107* ꙮ

TODAY'S PRACTICE

Meditation: "Gratitude"   Read, reflect, and journal.

INSPIRATION

When you read, words turn into images in your mind that awaken your senses, feelings, and thought process. Two-dimensional pages conjure three-dimensional realities. You become absorbed in the sensory experience of an unfamiliar world. Body forgotten, you live the protagonist's life subliminally. Events seem real as you shed tears, smile, laugh, or feel heartache. You experience pleasure or suffering, but from an artistic distance. Hours fly by.

Then suddenly a call, a noise, a smell catapults you out of your imaginary orbit and back to your armchair. How you wish that had not happened. Reading can be that fantastic. And much more. "Much more" for me is when intense reading persuades me to actualize what I have read, coaxing me to adventure into the setting of the book, with me as the protagonist.

In 2007, my husband and I did exactly that. I had read as much as I could about ancient Egypt. This persuaded me to fly to Cairo and travel the country with my husband, cruising the Nile from Luxor to Aswan.

We loved it so much that we did it again, this time including Alexandria in our itinerary.

Reading can convince you to turn literary images into reality. It happened again for me in 2019 when I read *Undaunted Courage: Meriwether Lewis, Thomas Jefferson, and the Opening of the American West.* A compilation of daily records of Lewis and Clark's journey, this journal followed no grammar, punctuation, or spelling rules, and was hard to read. Yet I could see, hear, smell, taste, and touch the era of August 1803 through September 1806 during which Lewis and Clark adventured uncharted land west of the Mississippi River. Populated with Native Indian tribes, the frontier was mostly wilderness, high mountains, vast prairies, wide rivers, and flora and fauna unknown to zoologists and botanists of the time. North America before 1803 was a mind-boggling reality.

As I read for pleasure for hours and hours, I found myself on that boat with Lewis, Clark, Sacagawea (the young Native American woman), her French husband and their baby boy, and thirty young military men, testing "our" endurance and exploring spirit. Only because of the magic of reading was I able to vicariously enjoy the company of these exemplary explorers and the brave woman, Sacagawea. The book conjured pristinely beautiful images filled with awe, allure, mystery, and romance. It wowed me with such intensity that my husband and I followed the voyage of discovery and adventure in May 2020.

JOURNAL PROMPT
Has there been a time when you read a book that called you, coaxing you to get up from your armchair and plan a trip to the place you were reading about? If not, what would you like to read about that might inspire such a trip?

❧ *Day 108* ☙

TODAY'S PRACTICE
Meditation: "Gratitude"   Read, reflect, and journal.

INSPIRATION

Reading can help you discover precious gems of information worth studding in platinum. One such jewel was the news about a monastery in Thailand. In 1957, an entire monastery was being relocated by a group of monks. One day while moving a giant clay Buddha, one of the monks noticed a large crack. On closer investigation, he saw golden light emanating. The monk used a hammer and a chisel to chip away the clay exterior until an image made of solid gold was revealed. Art historians believe that centuries earlier, monks covered the gold Buddha with clay to protect it from attack by the Burmese army.

The news fascinated me because there was a perfect metaphor hidden in its discovery. Your Authentic Self is the golden Buddha shining inside you. It is not out there somewhere, not in your spouse or children (they have their own Buddha mind to discover), or in your job, or in a new location or somewhere in the future.

Your "golden Buddha" is within you and way closer than you believe. What happens over the course of your life is that your golden Buddha gets covered in layers of clay... layers of your own doing, layers added by external conditioning from parents, teachers, society, bosses, co-workers, and the media. Eventually you are so heavily soiled that you forget this Buddha, the true self within.

The secret to find your Authentic Self, your higher purpose, lies not in the future, but in breaking your own limiting beliefs that prevent you from following your dreams and fulfilling your potential. Something occurs in life (usually a loss or tragedy of some sort) and you start chipping away at the clay to discover or rediscover your true passion.

I wouldn't have known about this news if I didn't read everything I got my hands on. Reading helps you chip away the clay.

JOURNAL PROMPT

What is your passion? Are your intentions rooted in that passion? Or have layers of "clay" blocked you from being able to see it? What tools can help you chip away the layers?

∾ *Day 109* ⌇

TODAY'S PRACTICE

Meditation: "Gratitude"   Read, reflect, and journal.

INSPIRATION

Are you a multitasker? Do you listen to music while exercising? Cook while watching the news? Walk while listening to podcasts? Such multitasking is common and not such a bad habit. But what happens when you are doing something that demands both your attention and awareness? Can you multitask while practicing meditation, journaling, reading?

Whether reading for pleasure or for growth and transformation, the activity demands your total attention. Readers are mono-taskers, as writers must be. When absorbed in reading, nothing else matters. Having the ability to concentrate is a prerequisite for being a mindful reader. For a successful Writing Meditation Practice, you must work on one discipline at a time.

As a writer, possibly you are introverted by nature. You love solitude and seek quiet spaces. In such environments you lessen mental static and clear the mind of random thoughts. Your imagination conjures up a fictional world with characters. You are used to being in that mindset for hours. When you join your non-writer family members or friends, you notice how everyone always multitasks. This behavior results in restlessness and anxiety.

During the COVID quarantine of 2020-21, it seemed my husband and I were "prisoners" in our own home. But I found the diminishing social activities and solitude soothing. With nothing else to do but focus on meditation, journaling, reading, exercise, and writing, I came closer to a blissful state. Some of my friends wrote complete book drafts during those months. Others read fifty to seventy books. The time allowed us to focus on one thing at a time and deepened our experience in all areas of life.

JOURNAL PROMPT

Reading is a mono-task discipline. Which other disciplines would you describe as mono-tasks?

❧ *Day 110* ❧

TODAY'S PRACTICE

For the rest of the month let's practice "Mountain and Lotus."

Read and reflect upon today's inspiration and prompt, then journal.

INSPIRATION

As a reader, do you wonder sometimes how writers choose a title, write the first five sentences, or the first five pages of a book? How do they choose sentence constructions? You understand how challenging it is to write those first few pages, the middle (the hardest section of any manuscript), and the ending. Between the first "shitty" draft and the final draft there may be five, ten, or more additional drafts.

Once the final version is complete, you might realize your working title no longer reflects the creation to which you just gave birth. Gestating the manuscript develops into something which no longer expresses your original story concept. You need to change the title. This is hard. How can you change the name of your mind-born that you have been cherishing since you wrote the first five pages?

Mindful Writer Meredith Cohen talks about selecting a title for her book: "I can draw three lessons from my experience. First, as with other features of your book, ultimately it is less important what you think and more important how others react to it. Second, if your child's name ever changes, you won't love that child any less. And third, as a writer, it is good, if not essential, to be flexible, open-minded, and adaptive to change. That is just a reality of this field that we have chosen."

So, how do you title your books, short stories, or poems? What comes first – the substance or the title? And if the latter, how often does the title change after the work is otherwise complete?

JOURNAL PROMPT

Choose one of your favorite novels – one you know well and have read at least a couple of times. Give it a new title! What would you name it and why?

✑ *Day 111* ✑

TODAY'S PRACTICE

Meditation: "Mountain and Lotus"   Read, reflect, and journal.

INSPIRATION

In 2022, my husband and I spent the month of March with our daughter and her husband and their two children, our adorable grandson (then 5) and granddaughter (newborn). We were exhilarated. Our days were filled with overwhelming emotions for tender new life that had overnight changed everyone's daily routine.

At the end of each day we were tired. But we were happy and slept soundly. For our daughter, however, just because the sky turned indigo the day didn't truly end. She was the most exhausted member of the family, followed by her husband. Our "perfect" routines turned topsy turvy. Yet, I didn't miss it at all. My meditation and journaling practices were put to the test as I realized how flexible the new baby had helped me become.

When I held her, I babbled to her, breathing in her fresh scent. With the warmth of her delicate body in my lap I could sit for hours while our grandson played with his Lego universe or made colored drawings. I thought, *Playfulness may belong to childhood but it is essential at every stage of life*. As he was learning about the world, about himself, and about me, I felt rejuvenated. The two little ones were helping me to relearn to play, making me think about the relationship between playfulness and creativity.

Writers need to play as much as children do. Play requires imagination, stimulates creativity, and enhances problem solving – all critical to creative minds. Play reduces stress and energizes and cues the pituitary gland to release endorphins that make you feel joyous.

Have you forgotten to play because of your "to do" list that fills your day? Do you realize how essential it is to schedule time each day to play, to create, to let joy and laughter emerge naturally? Pausing to play may save your life and increase the years you live. Set aside time for play. It will not only enhance your writing but also make your life happier and whole.

JOURNAL PROMPT

Use the time you would have taken to respond to the prompt to play instead! What about a game of cards or chess or board game with your husband, friend, or children? What about putting on some music and dancing to its tune, or drawing your favorite indoor plant and coloring it with colors your imagination sees?

⌇ *Day 112* ⌇

TODAY'S PRACTICE

Meditation: "Mountain and Lotus"   Read, reflect, and journal.

INSPIRATION

Have you focused on a work of art, a book, or a piece of music for hours, or over and over again? Read the same book repeatedly? Is there a book worn out and shelved that you once found absorbing as a young adult, in college, after having kids, or when your children left home that you may read again? So many versions of the same book! Only you have changed. What does each subsequent reading of this book teach you about your life?

I read *The Glass Bead Game* by Hermann Hesse three times and *Coming to Our Senses* by Jon Kabat-Zinn more than three times – in my fifties, sixties, and now in my seventies. The first time I read these books, what I felt was unfamiliar terrain. The pleasure was purely subliminal. I did not completely understand the stories or the thought behind the words, yet I was magnetized to the authors' voices. At the second and third readings, my attention was to comprehend how the authors had created those feelings in me. They were writing about subjects I was passionate about – spirituality, intellectualism, meditation, the interconnectedness of humans and nature. I was familiar with their specialized language. I became able to apply the lessons therein to my own writings and life.

Every year, Harvard professor and art historian Dr. Jennifer Roberts assigns her students the task of going to a museum and choosing a single work of art which they then must study uninterrupted for three hours. Even for art lovers, three hours is a long, long time to stare at a single painting or sculpture. It is painful and difficult. The point of this assignment is to teach the benefits of immersive attention, to the exclusion of everything else. Roberts describes works of art as little windows into the mind of the artist. During the exercise a student gets to spend a long while inhabiting the artist's mind, seeing what he or she must have seen, noticing details painstakingly captured. It is a worthwhile discipline for not only novice artists but also writers. Based on observations, we build fictional worlds in which we become immersed for months or even years.

This immersive exercise is similar to the meditation practice which requires you to pay attention to and become aware of breathing on a single breath, one at a time. You slow down, turn inward, and focus fully and completely to discover new worlds in darkness.

JOURNAL PROMPT

Think about any books you have read more than once. Journal about how it made you feel the first time, then the second or third time. Did you keep notes from any of your readings?

༄ *Day 113* ༄

TODAY'S PRACTICE

Meditation: "Mountain and Lotus"   Read, reflect, and journal.

INSPIRATION

Take a leisurely trip to your local library and choose books that will nourish your soul, reduce stress by distracting you from daily worries, and allow you to relax and escape to worlds far, far away.

Researchers from Yale School of Public Health showed that reading for 30 minutes a day can add two years to your life span. It keeps the brain active enough to prevent a decline in thinking and processing. Cognition associated with Alzheimer's is strengthened by reading, which builds cognitive power that can compensate for the loss of brain cells damaged by aging and disease.

Those who read consistently exhibit significantly greater memory and mental abilities at all stages of life. They are also better public speakers, thinkers, and, according to some studies, better people in general. Irrespective of what you read – a thriller, suspense, romance, or spiritually uplifting stories – opening a book before you go to bed or sleep could help combat insomnia. A research study at the University of Sussex shows that reading even for 6 minutes before falling asleep reduces stress. It is better than listening to music or drinking a warm cup of milk.

A book is not only a pleasant distraction but also actively engages and expands your imagination, thus helping you enter an altered state of consciousness. Reading clears your mind and improves the quality of your work in progress. Reading helps you to live in the present, not the time of the setting of the story, but the process that takes place between you and what you are reading.

The subject matter of a book is revealed to you linearly. In literature, places, people, and events come alive in the present moment; characters breathe in the present. The setting is vivid in the reader's mind in this moment. What is implicit in the language becomes explicit as a living thing in your mind. Like a lamp lighting another wick, the writer's voice enlightens your mind even though not present or long gone.

JOURNAL PROMPT

What books have caused you to feel most immersed in the "present moment" and why? When you do not have a book to read before falling asleep, what do you do instead? Imagine a day in your life when you do not have a book, magazine, or anything to read. How would you feel? Journal about it.

✒ *Day 114* ✒

TODAY'S PRACTICE
Meditation: "Mountain and Lotus"   Read, reflect, and journal.

INSPIRATION

Reading is to the mind what exercise is to the body. Similar to meditation, it improves attention, memory, whole brain function, and enhances neural pathways. Neuroplasticity forms and reorganizes synaptic connections in response to learning, allowing the brain to grow, expand, learn, and relearn. The science of neuroplasticity explains how the human brain can adapt, master new skills, store memories and information, and even recover after a traumatic brain injury.

Imagine not being able to read. As an infant you "read" using your senses and motor movements. As a toddler you explored and absorbed by feeling a book's texture: a smooth rabbit, crinkled paper, fuzzy lamb. But children with attention difficulties find maintaining focus challenging. For them, reading may turn into mental and physical struggle. In the absence of a quiet brain and calm body, reading is meaningless and certainly no fun.

Some older individuals in their eighties or nineties, even if they were avid readers when younger, lose their ability to recall. A short story may be easier to comprehend but reading a novel and remembering all they read until the end eludes them.

Mindful Writer Karen Fatica Geiger writes: "Research shows that along with diet and exercise, reading can stave off signs of dementia. Reading books and magazines, writing and other mentally stimulating activities, no matter your age, can help to keep memory and thinking skills intact." Also, reading aloud helps you remember the story and improves comprehension.

Karen adds, "Reading sparks the imagination, improves empathy, and stimulates the amygdala, which in turn creates memory association. In one study noted in *Psychology Today*, participants who read consistently had a 30 percent decrease in memory loss. The study also revealed, via post-mortem examination, that those patients who reported reading as an important habit, did not exhibit neural lesions or plaques commonly associated with cognitive decline." What a wonderful reason to make daily reading a habit!

JOURNAL PROMPT

What is your reading habit? Is there a reading or cognitive goal that you would like to achieve?

ʚ Day 115 ɞ

TODAY'S PRACTICE

Meditation: "Mountain and Lotus"   Read, reflect, and journal.

INSPIRATION

Three of my father's study room walls were covered with bookshelves. He shelved the books neatly but they were placed vertically as well as horizontally wherever they would fit. Reading was his portal to knowledge, entertainment, and adventure. For him it was a treasure no one could take away. He encouraged even our domestic help to read. When they left our home to work elsewhere they had gained the priceless ability to comprehend the written word.

On the first page inside the cover on the right-hand corner, my father wrote his name and the date. I remember titles in gold on burgundy, black and navy-blue spines, my fingers sliding across words that lined his bookshelves. Then there were hardcovers and newer paperbacks in Hindi. I remember books by Premchand, Rabindranath Tagore, Mulk Raj Anand, Pearl S. Buck, Eric Fromm, and Carl Jung. Ralph Waldo Emerson is believed to have wisely said, "I cannot remember the books I've read any more than the meals I have eaten; even so, they have made me."

Unbeknownst to me, my father kept track of what I was reading as well. He appreciated my interest, asked questions, initiated discussions, and if my siblings were around would involve them in a debate.

Some books had more staying power than others. *Lust for Life* hit me hard. That such a talented artist would be ignored, neglected, and die young, left a long-lasting wound in my heart.

I now have ten books from my father's collection. When I open the covers and see his faded name and the date, memories come flooding of him asking questions, discussing books, and debating with me and my siblings. I'm transported to his sunlit library facing the top-floor terrace. The smile begins on my face and spreads through my body... and I sigh. A sigh that lifts me up.

JOURNAL PROMPT

What books do you associate with specific memories? Do you reread these books? What personal memory is attached to these books?

৩০ *Day 116* ৩৶

TODAY'S PRACTICE

Meditation: "Mountain and Lotus"   Read, reflect, and journal.

INSPIRATION

> "People talk about escapism as if it's a bad thing...
> Once you've escaped, once you come back,
> the world is not the same as when you left it.
> You come back to it with skills, weapons, knowledge
> you didn't have before. Then you are better equipped
> to deal with your current reality." —Neil Gaiman

When the language, prose, and plot of a book I'm reading weave intricately into a story, I am transfixed. I may be doing other things, but at the back of my mind is the curiosity about what's next. When the time to read is over I say to myself, *Just one more page, one more chapter.* I escape into a history or future yet to come, emotionally or cognitively feeding my mind.

Do you read to escape stress, to defer your reality? Reading broadens your imagination by stimulating the right side of your brain. Losing yourself in the universe of a book enhances neural connectivity, thus improving brain function. You forget your day-to-day troubles and the fictional universe transports you to a fantasy world that becomes reality in your mind's eye. Not only does it benefit adult minds, but reading also has the power to strengthen children's ability to be empathetic.

JOURNAL PROMPT

How and when do you use reading as a form of escapism? What are you escaping from – everyday life, extra stress, writing – and what types of books are you drawn to in these circumstances?

❧ *Day 117* ❧

TODAY'S PRACTICE

Meditation: "Mountain and Lotus"   Read, reflect, and journal.

INSPIRATION

Reading is an adventure that allows you to be transported into someone else's imagination – their mind, their heart, their soul. When a story draws you helplessly into its world, you become emotionally charged and may change. In the creative zone of reading cognition, emotion, and memory, your emotions roller-coast along with those of the writer from anger to relief, from love to heartbreak, from fear to courage.

If you are a writer, you aspire to make readers feel the emotions you felt while writing the book. Your sadness, joy, and anguish morphs with the storyline, setting, and dialogue. Your feelings get disguised, transformed just like the emotions of the characters in your story. The book becomes a shared experience between author and reader.

All emotions can entertain when distanced from personal life. Universalizing emotions is one of the skills a writer must possess. Each book works as a cathartic release. The genre of a novel steers readers' emotions and has an emotional impact, often unforgettable.

The books you choose depend on your emotional state, to lift a mood or deepen thought. How do you choose a book for your reading list? Which books have had profound impact on your emotional state?

JOURNAL PROMPT

Choose up to three books which evoked strong reactions from you. How did reading them change you emotionally?

‎Day 118

TODAY'S PRACTICE

Meditation: "Mountain and Lotus"   Read, reflect, and journal.

INSPIRATION

I find reading and watching movies to be a most inspirational pastime. Whereas movies are over quickly, a book stays with me for weeks, a month, or more. I get emotionally and cognitively involved with characters and setting. By the end I'm so invested in this imaginary world that I'm sad to let go. I wish it would last longer. With a pang in my heart, I close the book's covers and shelve it. The thought that I can read it again sometime in the future pleases me.

I read to feel inspired, to enjoy the story and the language, to learn from its theme and characters. A well-written story makes me glide through the prose with ease. I want to sit in the solitude and silence of my Power Spot to become immersed and get motivated to continue working on my own manuscript.

Inspiration to write often comes to me from reading fiction or nonfiction. Classic works about honing writing skills and enriching writing practice can also motivate and inspire. Consider volumes like Natalie Goldberg's *Writing Down the Bones,* Anne Lamott's, *Bird by Bird* or Stephen King's *On Writing.* It would be difficult not to feel animated when these great writers teach their craft.

Finally, I suggest you do not always allow yourself to say, "Just one more chapter." Whether reading for entertainment or inspiration, there comes a time when you must put the book down and pick up the pen!

JOURNAL PROMPT

Do you have a genre that you gravitate to when searching for a new book? Do you write in the same genre you read?

ॐ Day 119 ॐ

TODAY'S PRACTICE

Meditation: "Mountain and Lotus"　　　　　　　　　Read, reflect, and journal.

INSPIRATION

Did you know that stress stimuli can be deflated by reading a well-written book? As a writer, you make up things all day long. Reading someone else's made-up world is a relief. And if you do not write professionally, reading offers your mind the opportunity to recreate the author's world and expand it beyond the confines of your personal imagination.

In children's literature, stories explain the world using pictures and words. I read Dr. Seuss's *The Lorax* to my five-year-old grandson. He viscerally understood the meaning of "deforestation," "sustainability," and "protecting the environment." The beloved story teaches kids to treat the planet with kindness and stand up and speak up for others. With lessons on the beauty of nature, especially Truffula Trees, it speaks of the danger of taking our earth for granted. Written fifty years ago by this visionary, the story is timely, playful, and hopeful. Its final pages teach not only children but adults that just one small seed, or one small child, can make a difference.

"Unless someone like you cares a whole awful lot,
nothing is going to get better. It's not." —Dr. Seuss

When good books are read to children they jolt them out of their comfortable routines. They boggle their minds and unnerve them. But they make the kids come alive, demanding to be read to again and again!

JOURNAL PROMPT

Which children's books do you enjoy as much as your children or grandchildren do and why?

✌ *Day 120* ✌

TODAY'S PRACTICE

Meditation: "Mountain and Lotus"   Read, reflect, and journal.

INSPIRATION

During my complete knee surgery I went through a few spurts of awakening. Spikes of wisdom might have been due to the pain pills I was prescribed for the unbearable pain of the incision and the adjustment my knee was making with the new bionic parts. I was put into a state of consciousness that was spacious, devoid of ego and grateful. Here's what I realized:

> That billions of people around the world are going about doing what they do each day – toil and struggle to make lives better for their families and themselves. Majority of the people are good.

> What we hear through media – printed, visual, verbal – about wars, diseases, sickness, terrorism, natural disasters, and other negative subjects is not normal but news. Normal is not negative. But when we are constantly fed destitution, destruction, and bitterness, they beget resentment, hatred, and deprivation.

The world is normal. So let's focus less on media and more on reading. I was in no condition to read after the surgery, no books at my bedside. But when I came home a deck of books on the bedside felt like heaven. *The Dance of the Dissident Daughter* by Sue Monk Kidd, *Why We Write*

About Ourselves by Meredith Maran, and *Circe* by Madeline Miller ushered in a feeling of joyfulness.

Three fantastic fictional dreams awaited me, inviting me to jump in their realms. And when I did, my pain seemed to subside. There were moments when I forgot myself as I got lost in the novel realms. Reading held my hand and helped me get back to my practices of meditation, journaling and reflecting. I healed faster.

END OF MONTH PROMPT

Have you completed the task you intended to finish by the end of the fourth month? Were there unforeseen snags? Did you take a couple of missteps? Journal without self-criticism, self-loathing, or discouragement you may have faced. What can you do to resolve such difficulties?

Month 5

Mindfulness and Deep Reading for Growth and Transformation

Suggested Readings

The Power of Now: A Guide to Spiritual Enlightenment
Eckhart Tolle, 1997.

The Art of Happiness
Dalai Lama and Howard C. Cutler, 1998.

The Way of Lao Tzu (Tao-te ching)
Tr. & Intro. by Wing-Tsit Chan, 1963.

Meditations of John Muir: Nature's Temple
Comp. & Ed. by Chris Highland, 2001.

The Four Agreements: A Practical Guide to Personal Freedom
Don Miguel Ruiz, 1997.

---

๒ Day 121 ๛

TODAY'S PRACTICE

Did you enjoy the month of reading for entertainment? Did you develop a reading habit? If you are already addicted to books, you will love this month of reading for growth and transformation. If you just began daily reading for fun, you are in for some surprises.

Meditation: "Animating Seven Energy Centers"

Read and reflect upon today's inspiration and prompt, then journal.

This month, build in time to read a book that offers something new for you to learn or refine. Try to read at a time when you are most alert.

INSPIRATION

The previous month awakened you to the entertaining and creative benefits of reading. Next month we focus on the pinnacle of language – poetry. But first let's spend this month to do some transformative reading that will help you grow in your writing and enrich your daily life. Such reading has the power to light the dark cave of your mind.

Did you know that people who read have more gray matter in their brains than those who don't? Readers grow and change for the better. And if you read in silence with attention, your ability to think improves.

Reading mindfully for personal growth is hard work. The focus, understanding, retention, grappling with ideas, and connecting new information to a lifetime of mental networks challenges you to grow as a person. The process of reading hard books can be like that of a "decoder," deciphering and wrestling with complex words and ideas. Reading mindfully, with attention and awareness, creates space to let in new information and allows you to relate it to what you already know.

You may need to slow down and consider each sentence and its context. When you get absorbed at this deeper level, new meanings surface that may or may not fit with what you already know, like finding a diamond where you were not looking for one.

Unearthing the jewel might take time when reading challenging texts, but like all such treasure hunts, the prize is more than worth the effort. Hopefully you'll experience this level of meaning and joy in the use of language or through enhancing your skills or understanding. Begin with books about topics that are of great interest to you. Once you make mindful reading a practice, you won't want to read any other way.

JOURNAL PROMPT
What was the last difficult, complex book you read? Were you able to find that sweet spot between mental work and mindfulness when you tackled that text?

ꙮ *Day 122* ꙮ

TODAY'S PRACTICE
Meditation: "Animating Seven Energy Centers"   Read, reflect, journal.

INSPIRATION
Although many writers have created passionate and transformative works while going through desperate conditions – poverty, homelessness, malnutrition, incarceration – for most of us, certain basic necessities must be met before we allow ourselves time to read or, for that matter, write.

Maslow's famous hierarchy chart about how basic needs must be met before we are able to make room to educate ourselves and acquire tools for personal growth lists the following necessities:

- Food, shelter, clothing, sleep
- Freedom from fear and abuse, safety
- Love and affection from family and friends
- Self-compassion, kindness, and caring for others
- Curiosity, knowledge and understanding, need for meaning
- Appreciation for artistic and natural beauty
- Self-fulfillment, personal growth and peak experiences

- Trust and belief in values that transcend the personal self, spiritual and creative

---

JOURNAL PROMPT

Think about a most difficult period in your life, a time when you felt unsafe, felt your life – or the lives of your loved ones – were in danger. Or a time when your self-esteem hit new lows, or you were unfairly criticized. Were you able to read or write during this turbulent time in your life? What did you notice once the stressors dissipated?

∽ *Day 123* ⌇

TODAY'S PRACTICE

Meditation: "Animating Seven Energy Centers" Read, reflect, journal.

INSPIRATION

Today let's move on to readings that are pleasurable as well as educational. Creative nonfiction belongs to this category. It is a form of storytelling that employs the techniques of lyrical fiction to retell a true story. Pioneered by Professor Lee Gutkind, the genre is believed to be about real life, reflection, and research.

Autobiographies and memoirs are slightly different in contexts, but both fall in the category of Creative Nonfiction. Reading them mindfully is the only way to read true stories. We can learn and grow from the experiences of other people, whether famous or ordinary. Some examples that fall in this category include *Reading Lolita in Tehran* by Azar Nafisi, *When Breath Becomes Air* by Paul Kalanithi, *Being Mortal* by Atul Gawnde, *The Immortal Life of Henrietta Lacks* by Rebecca Skloot, *Operating Instructions* by Anne Lamott, *Between the World and Me* by Ta-Nehisi Coates, *Long Quiet Highway* by Natalie Goldberg, *Dandelion Wine* by Ray Bradbury, *The Year of Magical Thinking* by Joan Didion, and *Eat, Pray, Love* by Elizabeth Gilbert.

Mindful reading of creative nonfiction can transform you emotionally and intellectually. These books overlap entertainment with self-growth and knowledge and can be read at several levels. Some such books are relaxing and informative upon first reading but others feel like work, though ultimately at the second or third reading, worth it. It's magical to get lost in foreign worlds, ancient lands, or universes beyond your own. They are peopled with characters who leap from the pages and settings that transport you as you turn them.

Carl Sagan said, "A book is made from a tree. It is an assemblage of flat, flexible parts (still called *leaves*) imprinted with dark pigmented squiggles. One glance at it and you hear the voice of another person, perhaps someone dead for thousands of years. Across the millennia, the author speaks, clearly and silently, inside your head, directly to you. Writing is perhaps the greatest of human inventions, binding together people, citizens of distant epochs, who never knew one another. Books break the shackles of time – proof that humans can work magic."

JOURNAL PROMPT

Have you read creative nonfiction before? If so, what have been some of the most powerful books for you personally?

༄ *Day 124* ༅

TODAY'S PRACTICE

Meditation: "Animating Seven Energy Centers"   Read, reflect, journal.

INSPIRATION

We bring our own unique understanding to what we read. Skillful writing utilizes literary devices that get interpreted according to the reader's upbringing and cultural, economic, and religious background. These devices take us deeper into the reading. As you plunge beneath the surface of comprehension, you see the beauty of language. Hidden literary gems reveal themselves to you.

Our psyche communicates through devices such as symbols and metaphors. When an experience is new and you have no words to convey it, the mind employs literary or visual devices. They grow from the same source as the imagination and can appear spontaneously in dreams. As a writer, you select and transform objects from nature and life into symbols to communicate an idea or feeling. Things undergo a metamorphosis. They lose their original identity and get charged with new meaning that signifies something entirely different, for example, when a lover and her beloved are compared to a scented rose and a honeybee.

There is a tendency to use the word "symbol" loosely. We say Rolls Royce is a status symbol, and smoke is a natural symbol of fire. That is not correct. But when we say ocean is the symbol of vastness and depth, that is the right use of the word "symbol." A lion symbolizes courage and a lamb meekness. Metaphors, however, compare two things that are not comparable, like someone "drowning in paperwork." The understanding of such symbols and metaphors by the reader is intuitive, spontaneous and automatic.

JOURNAL PROMPT

Do you use symbols or metaphors in your writing? If so, consider which ones recur frequently in your writing. If not, what topics would lend themselves well to the use of symbols or metaphors in your work?

⚘ *Day 125* ⚘

TODAY'S PRACTICE

Meditation: "Animating Seven Energy Centers"   Read, reflect, journal.

INSPIRATION

Would you have become a writer if you never read? Would you have written if a combination of words had not stirred your mind and made you think and feel? Would you have read if, as a child, you weren't read to or watched your parents read?

In middle school, my father took me and my sister to the American Library in New Delhi. My knowledge of English was rudimentary then. So I picked books whose illustrations mesmerized me. Words seemed dull in comparison. I responded to the images. Irrespective, my nose was always in the illustrations, so to speak. I couldn't wait for our next trip to the library, and also the pastry shop afterward, to which our father treated us. While savoring pineapple, mango, or chocolate pastry with sweet Darjeeling tea, I imagined myself alone with my books.

When I find myself inspired to write, often the impetus is from reading someone else's work that has shaken me up, swallowed and spit me out, or changed me somehow. I go back to such books over and over to understand why and how. Mindful reading leads me back to myself, again and again.

Stephen King suggests, "The real importance of reading is that it creates an ease and intimacy with the process of writing... a place where you can write eagerly and without self-consciousness."

Don't you love the times when you read a book and feel overwhelmed with an emotion? It unclogs the debris and lets your writing flow freely. Without being self-conscious, you simply pour out the percolating feelings and thoughts onto the pages of your journal or manuscript.

JOURNAL PROMPT

Which books have made you sink deeply into your favorite chair? Which books have inspired your own writing?

⟍ Day 126 ⟍

TODAY'S PRACTICE

Meditation: "Animating Seven Energy Centers"   Read, reflect, journal.

INSPIRATION

Inspirational or spiritual reading includes works written by seers, seekers, visionaries, or even ordinary individuals who are on a quest to find a deeper meaning of life.

As I mentioned earlier, I dedicated a few years to reading and commenting on selected sacred books of India and China. In recent years I have focused on poets such as Rumi who speaks to my heart,

Pablo Neruda who takes pleasure in ordinary things and the present moment, and Emily Dickinson who writes about quivers and flourishes of life, and the nature of death.

Other books have greatly affected me. They have helped me experience my Authentic Self by removing layer after layer of deluded thinking. Repeatedly, they have stirred genuine pleasure.

- *The Power of Now,* Eckhart Tolle
- *Man's Search for Meaning,* Viktor E. Frankl
- *The Alchemist,* Paulo Coelho
- *The Art of Happiness at Work,* Dalai Lama and Howard C. Cutler
- *The Essential Rumi,* Intro. & Tr. Coleman Barks
- *The Way of Lao Tzu* (Tao-te Ching), Intro. & Tr. Wing-Tsit Chan
- *Conquest of Mind: Take Charge of Your Thoughts and Reshape Your Life Through Meditation,* Eknath Easwaran
- *My First Summer in the Sierras,* John Muir
- *John Muir: Spiritual Writings: Selected with an Introduction,* Tim Flanders.
- *The Four Agreements: A Practical Guide to Personal Freedom,* Don Miguel Ruiz.

More such books by authors like Julia Cameron, Marianne Williamson, and Elizabeth Gilbert are equally transformative.

JOURNAL PROMPT
Think about a book you found unforgettable. How did that book capture and change you? Why?

ꙮ *Day 127* ꙮ

TODAY'S PRACTICE
Meditation: "Animating Seven Energy Centers"   Read, reflect, journal.

INSPIRATION
Another kind of transformative reading is where no words are involved. It involves reading *memorabilia*... like photographs, greeting cards you have received through years, or your favorite works of visual art.

After my husband and I got married, we created a photo album. At a much later age when I "read" these pictures, I asked myself: *Who was this young couple in love, full of energy, yet so naïve?* I also enjoyed the albums of our two daughters as toddlers, in middle and high school and their college years. Connected with those photos were memories that evoked intense feelings. Thoughts were absent, just feelings from the bottom of my heart so potent that I'd lost track of time... yet I was fully present in the past.

Our daughter Shonu's favorite item is a ceramic sculpture of an elderly couple which she purchased when she was ten or twelve on a Sunday flea market trip. When she appeared on the television show *Jeopardy* in April 2022, she was asked about her most treasured possession. She answered, "A porcelain music box with grandma serving tea as grandpa reads the daily paper. It plays the music of 'There's No Place Like Home.' The music box used to sit in our family room when I was a little girl. My parents gave it to me when I was first married. It always reminds me of happy days in my childhood."

I realized that she was able to "read" that musical box to inspire warm feelings of her childhood and memories of home.

JOURNAL PROMPT
What is one piece of memorabilia that triggers your memories?

❧ *Day 128* ❧

TODAY'S PRACTICE
Meditation: "Awakening the Senses"   Read, reflect, journal.

INSPIRATION
Like most writers, when I was growing up, I loved reading. But I did not know that I would be a writer. My father, a journalist and an author, was a major influence on my love of books. He immersed me in the river of deep reading by giving me biographies of Michelangelo (*The Agony and the Ecstasy*), Vincent Van Gogh (*Lust for Life*), and novels written

by Pearl S. Buck, Rabindranath Tagore, and Premchand. I vicariously learned about similes, metaphors, and symbols in the emotional layers of their stories.

By talking with him about what I read, he taught me to develop a personal point of view. Because of his guidance, I learned about the richness of language. He made me a student of literature and arts for life.

Now every time I buy a new book it is a thrill. I imagine a whole world between its covers. I have come to understand that like the onlooker of a painting, the reader of a book plays an important role. Without the audience, the story or painting remains incomplete. "Many years ago," Mindful Writer Donna Snyder-Lucas tells us, "a reader's view didn't matter." Prior to 1960, readers' views about the books they read were not considered important. Then a group of literary critics – Louise Rosenblatt, Stanley Fish, and Wolfgang Iser – argued that the reader's responses were significant to a book's value. The trinity – the author, the book, and the reader – should be celebrated, as the reader's prior knowledge, experience, and personality enriches the text they read.

As serious readers, we become not just passive but active thinkers. Donna suggests, "Non-readers misunderstand the serious work you are doing with your nose in the book. You are breathing life into it. By being a critical reader and active participant, you inhale the emotions, senses, and thoughts that author has exhaled in their work."

JOURNAL PROMPT
Jot down the types of cues and tools authors use that pull you right into a story. How might you use them in your own writing?

⫷ *Day 129* ⫸

TODAY'S PRACTICE
Meditation: "Awakening the Senses"   Read, reflect, journal.

INSPIRATION

Poet Rabindranath Tagore's collection of 103 poems, *Geetanjali: Song Offerings,* won him the Nobel Prize in Literature in 1913. Originally written in Bengali, Tagore himself translated the poems into English. One of my favorites is:

 # 50

"I had gone abegging from door to door in the village path, when thy golden chariot appeared in the distance like a gorgeous dream, and I wondered who was this King of all kings!

My hopes rose high and methought my evil days were at an end, and I stood waiting for alms to be given unasked and for wealth scattered on all sides in the dust.

The chariot stopped where I stood. Thy glance fell on me and thou cameth down with a smile. I felt that the luck of my life had come at last. Then of a sudden thou didst hold out thy right hand and say, "What hast thou to give to me?"

Ah, what a kingly jest was it to open thy palm to a beggar to beg? I was confused and stood undecided, and then from my wallet I slowly took out the least little grain of corn and gave it to thee.

But how great my surprise when at the day's end I emptied my bag on the floor to find a least little grain of gold among the poor heap. I bitterly wept and wished that I had had the heart to give thee my all."

JOURNAL PROMPT

Write a poem or journal entry suggested to you by Tagore's writing. Or choose something you love in nature and write about it.

～ *Day 130* ～

TODAY'S PRACTICE

Meditation: "Awakening the Senses"   Read, reflect, journal.

Inspiration

Sometimes health and life issues impact our ability to read, so that even what we normally consider to be pleasure reading suddenly presents challenges. For me, it happened when I switched the medium of reading from Hindi to English. The art of writing was slowly revealed to me as I learned and practiced this new language. It required patience, persistence, hard work, and encouragement, but eventually I became a full-time writer in English, albeit late in life.

I attended a Hindi medium school. The longest pieces I wrote were Hindi essays. My father read them with interest and encouraged me to keep writing. In ninth grade when instruction shifted from Hindi to English, I was traumatized. But like the rest of my classmates I accepted the "challenge" as the normal path to higher education. High school culminated with my winning a gold ribbon for the best class essay – but it was written in Hindi.

In art college, although most of my classes were painting, print making, and sketching, term papers in English were required for theory classes. They felt like impossible barriers. Masterpieces of world art stirred deep thought and emotions in me. Questions rose, ideas bubbled, but how was I to express them with my limited grasp of the language and even more limited vocabulary? This made me feel inadequate and unintelligent. I disliked English for the wrong reasons. In addition to my art history and aesthetics textbooks, I read all required and recommended books. In time, much reading improved my writing skills.

During the summer break of my senior year, one morning my father, himself a prolific writer, asked me to join him in his study. There he pulled out pages from a folder and handed them to me. Somewhat yellowed handwritten pages of my award-winning and long forgotten school essay in Hindi touched me. He said, "The language in which you write is not as important as the feelings and thoughts you pour out. Just keep practicing." The thought of him saving the pages affected me as much as his words. I knew if I learned English well, it would open portals to future possibilities. That was the summer I decided to enroll for a master's degree in Art History.

After two years it was time to defend my master's thesis. I sat facing three external examiners and thought, *If they grade me for English fluency, my academic life is over.* They didn't. They tested my knowledge of symbols, history, and aesthetics. I had "poured my heart out" and got a high pass.

JOURNAL PROMPT

Wisdom is to knowledge what meditation is to thought. Journal about a time when you tackled reading a book that felt difficult to you.

ﭏ *Day 131* ﭏ

TODAY'S PRACTICE

Meditation: "Breathing and Body Scan"   Read, reflect, journal.

INSPIRATION

Nine days after graduating from college, I got married. Three years later we moved to America with our firstborn. For all practical purposes the only language spoken, read, written, or sung was in American English. The English I had learned in India was British English. It was not easy for us to understand many phrases, especially the accent. The lingo such as "what's up," "bummer," "no kidding," "hang in there," "whatever," "he's nuts/she's bananas," and so many others sounded alien and amusing. When I listened to the music I could neither recognize the singer nor understand the lyrics. Instead, Bollywood songs echoed in my ears. I frequently hummed them while cooking and cleaning.

During the day, when my husband went to work and our daughter to school, loneliness inched into my day unawares. I wrote long letters home, both in Hindi and English. The silence and solitude that surrounded me could have easily turned to boredom and loneliness but I read and painted. I was clueless about the incomparable richness that utter silence and depth of solitude could provide. (More about this in Month #9.)

When I enrolled for the doctoral program at the University of Pittsburgh, I had no choice but to converse with other students in English which improved my conversational skill.

JOURNAL PROMPT

Journal about a book that was difficult for you, yet you managed to finish reading it because it felt right. Was it ultimately worth the effort? How did that make you feel?

☙ *Day 132* ❧

TODAY'S PRACTICE

Meditation: "Breathing and Body Scan"   Read, reflect, journal.

INSPIRATION

At the University of Pittsburgh, I attended the English Workshop that helped me with my term papers. One of the papers I submitted was the rough draft of my first essay on the tenth-century Chola-period bronze sculpture from India in the collection of the Cleveland Museum of Art.

The English professor taught me how to incorporate my research and historical jargon into the body of the essay, as well as why and how to correct the grammar and syntax. Her skillful way of teaching did not feel daunting but was encouraging. I remember asking her rather challengingly, "What is the use of the English word 'the'?" Kashmiri and Hindi do not have 'the', and neither does Sanskrit" (which I was also learning in the Classics Department). She laughed sweetly and said, "The more you write and read in English, the more you will learn how to use it." I still do not completely understand where, when, or how to use the English word "the."

In addition to reading and writing, teachers matter. That professor's thoughtful encouragement kept me going. Later when I taught at Wheaton and Wellesley Colleges in Massachusetts, and the University of Pittsburgh and Chatham College in Pennsylvania, I discovered we also learn as we teach. Teaching, speaking, and writing in the classrooms and outside eventually brought me on par with my colleagues.

JOURNAL PROMPT

Have you been a student of something which you were able to teach later and became better at it? Journal about how you found the transition.

✎ *Day 133* ✎

TODAY'S PRACTICE

Meditation: "Breathing and Body Scan"   Read, reflect, journal.

INSPIRATION

In 1997, I received an opportunity to join 700 students and 32 faculty members on a voyage around the world. For 105 days I spoke nothing but English. We visited ten countries on four continents, spending three or four days docked in a cultural city, then sailing for two nights. At the beginning and the end of each new day, I meditated upon whatever I was absorbing and learning.

I filled two journals. One entry reflected that I had not given a second thought to the Hindi language after leaving grade school. I realized that if I wanted to write in Hindi as fluently as I wrote in English, by then I would have to go through decades of training all over again. Suddenly I felt as if a loved one had died.

Traveling through disparate countries, we met people who looked different. We visited their homes, universities, monuments, museums, and places of worship. Everywhere people were good natured, friendly, and helpful. They spoke and sang in Spanish, Tamil, Swahili, Cantonese, Chinese, Japanese, Tagalog, and various versions of English. We did not understand what they were saying but our human hearts bonded us.

By the end of the voyage a voice inside me whispered, "*So what if you don't know English well? Look at the number of languages the world speaks!*" My ego was wounded. However, one thing was becoming clear – the distinction between my ego and the voice of my Authentic Self. Languages are for communicating. But beyond language there is also silence and the human vibe. We must go beyond words to understand our fellow human beings. We must learn to communicate with our thinking hearts.

JOURNAL PROMPT
Journal honestly about a time when you met someone who was unable to communicate fluently with you. How did it feel? What did you do?

❧ *Day 134* ☙

TODAY'S PRACTICE
Meditation: "Breathing and Body Scan"   Read, reflect, journal.

INSPIRATION
Learning to write, read, and speak well in English was a long and arduous path for me. But writing has given meaning to my life. This vocation makes me feel whole – intellectually, emotionally, and spiritually. It makes it possible for me to share thoughts, ideas, and emotions. Connecting with my audience – with you, my reader – is an invaluable part of my life that I cherish.

Through writing, the impossible became possible for me: I attempted writing poetry. When I shared my early attempts, Mindful Writer Kathleen Shoop insisted that I get my poems published. Recently, when one of my poems was accepted for publication, my dormant Hindi awakened and rubbed her eyes in disbelief.

For me, not reading is like ignoring a treasure hidden under the ground beneath me. My mind is thirsty each day to drink water of precise words, crisp sentences. My pen is ready to dig deeper in search of the source of water.

There was a time when I had to cajole the muse to come and write with me. Like a shy child it would hide behind the door. But it is no longer threatened. When I walk into my study, the muse is waiting for me to begin. The shy muse has turned into my writing and reading buddy, with intimations of my intentions. All this because of the Writing Meditation Practice.

I once struggled, toiled, and faced linguistic obstacles, but now the rewards are plentiful. Life is shaped by the intentions we have, the goals we work toward. Our deep driving desires have power to make us who we want to become.

JOURNAL PROMPT

Does the path you are on feel right at the core of your being? Let your journal tell you if you are gratified, neutral, or unsatisfied with what you are doing.

✤ *Day 135* ✤

TODAY'S PRACTICE

Meditation: "Breathing and Body Scan"   Read, reflect, journal.

INSPIRATION

Mindful reading with a goal, combined with thorough research, can transform your life. My own transformation from an art student to a writer of essays, stories, and poems is due to the significance of daily reading.

When I was admitted to one of the most prestigious art schools in India, I wasn't thrilled. When my father suggested it, I complied because I myself wasn't sure what I wanted to study. But being a diligent student I practiced daily – sketching, watercolors, oil painting, print making, or basic sculpture, depending on the college year. I did the reading assignments diligently and also read on my own.

What I learned during those six years opened my eyes to the world of art and aesthetics, to Western and Asian art history. I understood that the reality that each artist lets the onlooker peek into is uniquely their own and different from anyone else's.

Besides looking at the artworks and experiencing life, it took me hundreds of books to understand what it meant to be uniquely yourself. Reading always came to my rescue.

JOURNAL PROMPT

Did you know what you wanted to be when you grew up? Did you choose a path of your own choice? Journal about how that was or was not the perfect choice. If not, did you change your course partway through? Are you happy with the work you do now?

ᘛ *Day 136* ᘚ

TODAY'S PRACTICE

Meditation: "Breathing and Body Scan"   Read, reflect, journal.

INSPIRATION

As a master's student in India, I focused not on painting or print making, but studying art history. I was so enthralled by the reading and research that I did not miss doing art. I mistakenly believed that making art was not my forte. I came back to it when we immigrated to the United States, where I joined several Pittsburgh art groups and exhibited my works in one-person shows and group exhibitions. Those were happy years. But something inside me kept telling me that picking up the paint and brush meant not doing what I could do with words. How could I believe this voice?

Despite writing my master's thesis in English, I was neither fluent at speaking nor writing it. But I never stopped reading books written in English. That helped me climb the next rung of my reading ladder. What was revealed to me through books would have been unimaginable otherwise, and the love of writing grew with this deep appreciation for reading. Not only that love, but the skill and craft of great writing unfolded before me during those years.

Write about a difficult situation, stumbling block, or setback for which you had to work very hard to resolve and straighten it out despite seemingly insurmountable odds or overwhelming obstacles. How did you resolve it?

❧ *Day 137* ❧

TODAY'S PRACTICE
Meditation: "Breathing and Body Scan"   Read, reflect, journal.

INSPIRATION

I had gained intellectual knowledge. I had studied the history of Indian arts, and knew about the how, why, and what of art. Books had turned me into a dedicated devotee of the written word. But was it possible, I wondered, to find my way from academic knowledge to the creative realm that I too had tasted? There was something different about creativity, something elusive, beyond words. Reading about creative people and writing about art wasn't enough. I wanted to dig deeper, know more about it. Would it have anything to do with inner knowing, spirit, spirituality? What was it that I could not put into words, that was beyond words?

It took me seven years to earn a doctoral degree in Phenomenology of Religions combined with Art History – all gained by reading, research, and writing. This was followed by fifteen years of teaching. Again the same restlessness overcame me as I'd had as an art student and artist. What was I to do next? My husband encouraged me to leave teaching and focus the rest of my life on writing. And so I did.

What does my story about changing professions – from being an artist to art historian to professor, to a lost soul – tell you? Never ever give up! If your inner voice is coaxing you to keep moving in another direction, follow your heart. More importantly, keep reading!

If there were no books, if there were no teachers to suggest which book to read, if there were no writers who wrote those books, where would I be today? Where would you be today? I would be a frustrated artist, a bored or boring art historian, someone who had so much to tell, so much left to experience, but couldn't because I didn't pay heed to my inner friend, Authentic Self. That was precisely what I couldn't pinpoint, the thing that was elusive.

JOURNAL PROMPT

Journal about a time when you heard the voice of your inner self pointing you in the opposite direction of where you were going. What did you do?

✆ *Day 138* ✆

TODAY'S PRACTICE

Meditation: "Breathing and Body Scan"   Read, reflect, journal.

INSPIRATION

At age 53, I quit teaching and began my journey to become a full-time writer. During this between and betwixt period, I had no grounding. Although I created a schedule the same way I had for my semester courses I taught, I wasn't centered. I religiously followed my self-created timetable and within six years published four books on Buddhism, Hinduism, and Buddhist and Hindu goddesses. This was a great achievement, but the emotional release I felt in creating art was more powerful than writing.

I revisited my earlier journals from the doctoral years. They had been wonderful for purging whatever was swirling inside me. The emotions poured on those pages became the kernel for a short story. I had no intention of writing fiction... but short stories *are* fiction. One became two, then two became twenty, and my first collection of stories, *Chance Meetings,* was published in 2015.

The more fiction I wrote, the more I felt how much it had in common with my paintings. Both helped cleanse my mind and let me express thoughts and ideas that I could not do in nonfiction volumes. This was transformational for me. At the current stage in my life, I still have not given up on change, because change allows for growth, and change leads to transformation.

JOURNAL PROMPT

Did your life journey ever take a turn that transformed your life? Was it a geographical move, family shift, or career change? Or did you think your life was running okay but then you heard whispers from your inner voice that you needed a change? Did you heed this voice?

◟◞ *Day 139* ◞◟

TODAY'S PRACTICE

Meditation: "Breathing and Body Scan"   Read, reflect, journal.

INSPIRATION

Let's now think about those individuals who, for one reason or another, have difficulty reading words and understanding their meaning.

What happens when reading is difficult? Mindful Writer Jennifer D. Diamond writes: "There are many factors involved in the cognitive processes of individuals who live with reading issues. To a layperson the term dyslexia may conjure images of backward-facing letters, where in reality there is a complex and wide range of characteristics involved."

An educator who lives with dyslexia, Carolyn D. Cowen says, "Dyslexia is much more than experiencing frustration while struggling to read text … It offers about as much help as skipping a meal offers a well-nourished person insight into starvation. Fortunately there are many valid, research-based instructional methods which have proven effective in teaching individuals who have been diagnosed with dyslexia or other reading difficulties… no one should ever give up hope or say the words, *I hate reading.*"

Jennifer adds, "It can be beneficial for a person who experiences reading difficulties to try different font styles, font size, background color, and letter-spacing to find the pattern that feels most comfortable for them."

JOURNAL PROMPT

If you have experienced reading difficulties, journal about it. Otherwise, write about a time when you felt like a fish-out-of-water, perhaps socializing among people who talked in their own professional jargon or being submerged in an unfamiliar culture. How did it make you feel? How did you handle it? Did you speak up and ask questions? Or did you nod and smile?

✌ *Day 140* ↩

TODAY'S PRACTICE

Meditation: "Arriving Home" Read, reflect, journal.

INSPIRATION

When children share what is going on with their lives with Mindful Writer Jennifer D. Diamond, she says she feels privileged. They need someone to listen to them. Even saying words out loud can make them feel shameful. Below are some true stories from the children who have difficulty concentrating to read.

—A kindergartener bursts into tears. His grandma told him he was bad, so last night he moved back into his dad's apartment. This morning his dad's girlfriend put garbage bags full of his stuff in the dumpster. She called every item that belonged to him as "his" garbage.

—A sixth grader fell asleep while sitting upright in her chair. She had stayed up all night gaming online with her dad. She calls her mom the "B-word" because after a huge fight this morning, her mom made her go to school. The child doesn't understand that her mom can't afford another truancy hearing with the monetary fines that come along with it.

—A ninth grader stares blankly out the window. He hopes it keeps raining because then his mom and dad can't "go riding" on their motorcycles, leaving him to babysit his little sister. The next day he hoped he'd have an evening to simply be a kid. No luck, because they decided to drive the car to "go out," which was code for spending the night barhopping.

What happens to humans whose basic needs aren't met first? How do we understand the psychology/physiology behind our capacity for learning? A strong family foundation is a must.

"If children do not have their basic needs met," Jennifer says, "then their learning abilities will most likely function at less-than optimal levels. But I am constantly amazed at their resilience. What people endure and grow from, makes human beings amazing."

When basic physical and emotional needs are not met, the reading abilities suffer.

JOURNAL PROMPT

Have you or someone you know gone through a struggle where even basic needs were not met? How did this affect the ability to tackle tasks which required higher functioning? How was the situation ultimately resolved?

ᘯ *Day 141* ᗡᎨ

TODAY'S PRACTICE

Meditation: "Arriving Home"   Read, reflect, journal.

INSPIRATION

You tend to forget how fortunate you are to be able to pick up a book of your choice, have time to get immersed in the story, and temporarily have an out-of-body experience. You are seated here but your mind is on an adventurous journey elsewhere.

For many around the globe, the benefits of nearby bookstores and libraries aren't available. Let's be grateful for having books available to us and never ever take such opportunities and availability for granted.

Being able to immerse yourself in a book, in a world created by the author, allows you to experience how someone other than yourself might react differently than you. A reader who feels what the character feels isn't simply reading to gather information; they are also experiencing a world beyond themselves.

When it comes to reading, if a person does not have a sufficient vocabulary and hasn't yet mastered the rules of social communication, they may not be able to relate to the reactions and emotions of the people portrayed on the page.

In psychology, the terms "metacognition" and "theory of mind" are used to describe the ability to think about how we think, and to understand that other people may think differently than we do. It can be difficult to want to invest time and effort to participate in deep reading where the story on the page does not unfold in a manner which you might have chosen.

JOURNAL PROMPT

When was the last time you stopped reading a book because you just didn't like it? What was it that made you stop? Was it difficult to "get into the story"? If yes, why? How might this inform your own writing?

༄ *Day 142* ༈

TODAY'S PRACTICE

Meditation: "Arriving Home"   Read, reflect, journal.

INSPIRATION

Whether you are a voracious or an occasional reader, whether you read quickly or slowly, it is good to know how the mind of a reader works. Complex neurological processes must function simultaneously for a reader to chew, analyze, and digest what is being read. That is how knowledge works. Reading about new topics brings new vocabulary to consciousness.

As a writer, you provide stories that enhance your readers' vocabulary. The sentences you construct are not simply a string of letters, blank spaces, and punctuation marks. Your writing provides meaning for new words by connecting them to a reader's prior experiences. You create new worlds for them to immerse themselves in – or you pull them into unfamiliar worlds or show a familiar world in a new light – telling mind-expanding stories. You show readers a novel approach to your characters' problems, challenging them to take on a new viewpoint.

You, as a writer, are crucial in helping readers to draw from a collective knowledge. The more stories you write, the more things there are to read out in the world, and the more interconnected we all become.

JOURNAL PROMPT

Think about the last time you had trouble reading a book. You had to look up unfamiliar words in the dictionary. How did this impact your reading experience? Were you able to draw upon your prior knowledge and make connections? Did you feel a sense of accomplishment when you finished reading?

ꙮ *Day 143* ꙮ

TODAY'S PRACTICE

Meditation: "Arriving Home"   Read, reflect, journal.

INSPIRATION

The river of my life has changed course more than once for a deeper understanding of who I am and how to lead a purposeful life. The reason for changing course has been transformative books I have read and people I've met at pivotal crossroads on my journey. For the rest of the days this month I'll share books that have been significant to help me chip away at unnecessary baggage.

The Power of Now, Eckhart Tolle

I had read much about the importance of living in the present. I understood the words but to experience them was not easy. Then I read *The Power of Now*. It taught me how to actually practice living in the present. This simple lesson is not easy to follow as it doesn't come naturally. I have to remind myself to live in the present moment even when I am frantic, the same way I remind myself to breathe when in meditation my mind wonders.

An essential point to remember is not to confuse creative thoughts with the thinking mind. The thinking mind is your natural enemy. Attention and awareness of your breath and body brings you back to the pain-free present moment, to your creative thinking.

As I do with most of my morning deep reading, I read and reread *The Power of Now*, to learn its simple principles that can be understood but difficult to practice. Once the practice to live in the present moment is experienced, it helps discover truth and light within. It has helped me get closer to my true self, to my Authentic Self.

The arduous journey of going through this volume was spiritually gripping. It taught me how to connect to the indestructible inner essence. Tolle says that only after liberated from the thinking mind, gaining awareness of the inner essence and living in the present, is there enlightenment.

JOURNAL PROMPT

Have you been able to observe your thinking mind as petty thoughts float through it? Journal about how this mind differs from the mind that stirs creative thoughts. Practice living in the present as you meditate, then journal about it.

ஃ *Day 144* ஒ

TODAY'S PRACTICE

Meditation: "Arriving Home"   Read, reflect, journal.

INSPIRATION

The Art of Happiness, Dalai Lama & Howard C. Cutler

According to the Dalai Lama, the purpose of life is happiness. In this book, Howard Cutler travels with the Lama around the country and discusses and explores what one needs to do to find happiness.

The key word in this book is "compassion," for yourself and for others. To feel connected with your fellow beings and with the world in which you live is one of the highest virtues. I too believed in this concept, but it was not until I read this book that I learned how to experience it. The

Dalai Lama's lifestyle teaches how you too can experience compassion and kindness.

Decades of meditation and journaling practices have helped me to rise above anger, jealousy, hate, and indifference. But reading this book made me promise myself never to let any negative emotion enter my inner sanctum, even when I witness one coming during moments of lapsed attention.

The emotion of hatred was to dissipate first, then anger dissolved, next was jealousy. Indifference was hard to clear out because I'm basically an introvert. But I take interest in the people whom I come across on a daily basis, especially those who are less fortunate than myself.

My heart goes out to those who are at the circumference of our society – discriminated, disliked, discarded. My indifference has changed into curiosity, getting to know, giving and being knowledgeable about "the other." All this because reading about the Dalai Lama taught me how we can be happier helping others with kindness or cash.

Growing scientific data confirms the insight that those who are kind and compassionate are happier. Researchers on human happiness concludes that compassion and service to others are key characteristics shared by the world's happiest people.

JOURNAL PROMPT
Which book has helped you understand the meaning of compassion? Journal about your definition of love, compassion, and kindness.

༄ *Day 145* ༄

TODAY'S PRACTICE
Meditation: "Arriving Home"   Read, reflect, journal.

INSPIRATION
  The Way of Lao Tzu (Tao-te Ching), translated by Wing-tsit Chan

The teachings of Lao Tzu are thousands of years old but this book's 81 chapters contain timeless lessons. Selected verses from the 81 kernels, once sown in your mind, can grow as expansive as a banyan tree of wisdom. If you seek peace, contentment, and harmony in life, the *Tao-te Ching* is one of the resources you can use.

The chapters are often a half-page long. Lao Tzu's simple and direct words speak directly to the heart of the reader. The translation and commentary presented in this edition were done by Wing-tsit Chan, my Chinese Philosophy professor at Chatham College (now Chatham University). As he taught, he seemed to imbue the wisdom of Lao Tzu. The subject matter is Tao – the stuff the universe is made of, philosophy, politics, society, religions and relationships – but the chapters that have left a lasting impression on me are:

> 11. This speaks about nonbeing. It is not the clay pot but the space inside it that is essential; it is not the room with its walls, windows, and door but the space in it that is essential; it is not the spokes of the wheel but the hub that makes it go. The empty space, the center, are the nonbeing.

> 45. "What is most perfect seems to be incomplete… what is most full seems to be empty… what is most straight seems to be crooked… The greatest eloquence seems to stutter." The chapter points out that the person who seems poor, stupid, lowly, or weak may be a possessor of great wisdom or virtue.

> 57. ". . . The more taboos and prohibitions there are in the world, the poorer the people will be. The sharper weapons the people will have, the more troubled the state will be. The more cunning and skill a man possesses, the more vicious things will appear. The more laws and orders are made prominent, the more thieves and robbers there will be."

JOURNAL PROMPT
Which scripture or religious text presented challenging reading for you and yet made sense?

༄ *Day 146* ༄

TODAY'S PRACTICE
Meditation: "Arriving Home"   Read, reflect, journal.

INSPIRATION

The Artist's Way by Julia Cameron

While this book is geared to people in the creative field, it also talks about spirituality. The course Cameron traces unlocks your creative flow to let spiritual sentiments flow through you.

The first time I read the book, I followed everything it suggested: the 12-week course to get in deeper with my artistic side and renovate my spiritual side; the gentle affirmations, inspirational quotes, Artist's Date, writing letters to myself, and filling-in-the-blanks. In short, the book was very helpful to break through creative blocks and foster confidence. After finishing the book I made meditation, journaling, and deep reading part of my daily schedule. It has been more than three decades now since I read this book.

The Artist's Way persuaded me to embark on a creative journey after I turned fifty. It helped me find a deeper connection with the purpose in my life. It opened opportunities for self-growth and self-discovery. And it was Julia Cameron's guidance on starting a "Creative Cluster" of fellow writers that was partly responsible for me creating the first Mindful Writers Group which eventually supported my own creative endeavors.

This evolutionary program for personal renewal truly helped me get back on track after I had stopped teaching. I rediscovered my passion for art and writing, and took steps that I needed to transform my life of happiness and contentment.

JOURNAL PROMPT
You have been journaling the last four months. Write a letter to yourself, telling your younger self how much you admire that person, and are grateful and gratified as you look back and remember how she/he led the life that has made it possible for you to be who you are at your present age.

∿ *Day 147* ∿

TODAY'S PRACTICE
Meditation: "Arriving Home"   Read, reflect, journal.

INSPIRATION

The Alchemist, Paulo Coelho

I read this book because Malala Yousafzai highly recommended it. A slim volume, it tells the story of Santiago, an Andalusian shepherd boy who yearns to find worldly treasure on his travels. On his search he finds many riches because he always listens to his heart.

The essential wisdom I harvested from the book was the significance of listening to our heart and giving heed to omens and signs strewn along our path if we want to cultivate a wise mind and compassionate heart.

I have followed my heart through years as I changed careers from being an artist to enrolling as a doctoral student, from teaching at universities and colleges to deciding to become a full-time writer. Even founding Mindful Writers Groups and Retreats resulted from paying attention to and being aware of my Authentic Self.

The Alchemist teaches that to follow a purpose-driven life you must have intentions and goals, you must pay attention to the intuitive whispers and be aware of signs and signals. There will be times when you don't know where you are going, but if it feels right, go ahead. Doubt and determination go together. Similar to Santiago, do it no matter what. Completely trust yourself and never give up.

JOURNAL PROMPT
Have you learned to listen to your heart-mind, your Authentic Self? Journal about your own life's journey and the treasures you have found along the way. Were those "treasures" the same ones you set out looking for?

❧ *Day 148* ☙

TODAY'S PRACTICE	
Meditation: "Arriving Home"	Read, reflect, journal.

INSPIRATION

The Four Agreements, Don Miguel Ruiz

This insightful book teaches that self-limiting beliefs not only create needless suffering but rob you of joy. In the tradition of Carlos Castaneda's books, this text distills the essential ancient Toltec wisdom. It offers a code of conduct that can transform your life to one of true happiness, love, and freedom.

The Four Agreements is a roadmap to enlightenment. It teaches how to live as the peaceful protagonist of your own life in the twenty-first century. It will prompt you to think, encourage you to reshape your daily routine, and improve your day-to-day behavior. Small but profound changes can transform your life.

Following Ruiz's agreements I started being mindful of how I behaved and what I said to people. *How honest am I? Do I mean what I say?* If the answer was "no," I would count to three before saying or behaving disapprovingly. The words *"Be impeccable with your word (and action)"* are always at the back of my mind even though I slip now and then.

Ruiz's agreement, *"Don't take anything personally,"* was kind of an awakening. It made me realize how I *did* take things personally. That I was not the center of the world and the choices and actions of others had nothing to do with me. It was freeing to distance myself from what others said or did. The third agreement, *"Don't make assumptions"* further strengthens the second. If there is a misunderstanding, I now ask questions to clarify what the person meant whose remarks have hurt me.

Combined with other agreements, the fourth agreement, *"Always do your best,"* came alive. I had read similar advice but this time, combined with other agreements, it impacted me more. I adopted it. It confirmed the fact that when I did my best, there was no doubt in my mind about my performance and no reason to judge myself.

Being mindful of how you interact with others, not taking anything personally, not assuming anything before confirming it, and being true to yourself will improve your happiness by several notches. All just because you have read a slim volume.

JOURNAL PROMPT

Do you follow a purposeful roadmap to a meaningful life that will lead you to happiness and freedom? If so, what does this roadmap look like? What are the milestones along the way? And if not, do you see value in discovering or creating such a roadmap for yourself? Why or why not?

༄ *Day 149* ༄

TODAY'S PRACTICE

Meditation: "Arriving Home"   Read, reflect, journal.

INSPIRATION

John Muir: Spiritual Writings,
Selected with an Introduction by Tim Flanders

"Beauty surrounds us but usually we need to be walking in a garden to know it," wrote Rumi. This was the case with me when I visited national parks before I had read the works of John Muir (1848-1914) and after. His books became a garden that showed me what it is to be one with nature when I am surrounded by nature. He wrote, "Rocks and waters, etc., are words of God and so are men. We all flow from one fountain Soul."

Muir's affinity with nature was grounded in deep spirituality. Living in the wilderness, he experienced communion with the sacred. His writings taught me how to have ecstatic experiences in the wild. He gave me a new vocabulary to speak about wilderness.

From 1867-1873, Muir embarked on a six-year journey of self-discovery. It was an archetypal journey that crafted his spiritual character in the American wilderness. His encounters with the sacred during this time built his identity and sense of purpose. This echoed the feelings I had while reading Henry David Thoreau's *Walden* and Thomas Merton's *Seven Storey Mountain* – two more books that have helped my spiritual awakening.

Muir's books persuaded me to pay attention to nature's details and made me aware of the sacred quality of nature and its restorative effects on the people who live in cities and suburbs. Overly civilized people diminish human spirit, he writes. I too have experienced such sacrality when I am deep in the valley or ascending the mountains. It used to leave me after I returned home, but Writing Meditation Practice has the power to make the spirituality within permanent, irrespective of where I am.

JOURNAL PROMPT

When did you first become conscious of being part of nature? What sort of relationship do you have with the natural world? Has it developed and grown since you first noticed it?

ঙ৹ *Day 150* ৹ঔ

TODAY'S PRACTICE

Meditation: "Arriving Home"   Read, reflect, journal.

INSPIRATION

I sincerely hope by now you have some idea of the difference between light reading and reading for growth and transformation. The books that make you forget your daily stresses and anxieties, that incite playfulness and positivity, are as important in our reading practice as the books that take you deeper into yourself.

What do books that need rereading or reading without interruption in the quiet hour of the day do for you? Once comprehended, they make you excavate deeper into your mind and heart, they nudge you to look at yourself, your true self, in the mirror to discover what it is that you truly want from your life.

Are you living your life fully? Are you true to yourself, not wearing any masks or pretending to be someone you are not? What is your true driving desire? Have you journaled about it? Have you meditated over it? Have you read books about it where you are bound to find some good answers?

Be courageous and begin by making small changes in your day. Plan what you truly want to do, how you want to live. Make a goal and work toward it.

END OF MONTH PROMPT

Find out which books may contain some answers to the questions you may have about your life besides your job and family life. In other words, what is deeper within, beyond your work, that makes you money for the basic necessities of life and your family life that will make you more content and happier? Journal about it.

MONTH 6

MINDFULNESS AND WRITING POETRY

Suggested Readings

Nine Gates: Entering the Mind of Poetry
Jane Hirshfield, 1998.

Devotions: The Selected Poems of Mary Oliver
Mary Oliver, 2017.

So Far So Good
Ursula K. Le Guin, 2018.

Writing Poems (8th ed.)
Michelle Boisseau, Hadara Bar-Nadav, and Robert Wallace, 2011.

Odes to Common Things
Pablo Neruda, 1994.

ᔌ *Day 151* ᔍ

TODAY'S PRACTICE
New month, new meditation.
Meditation: "Self-Forgiveness and Compassion"   Read, reflect, and journal.

INSPIRATION

As a young college student, I admired poets and those who enjoyed reading poems, but rarely did I read poetry myself. Late in life, my younger daughter, Zoonie, gifted me Pablo Neruda's *Odes to Common Things*. I loved each of those jewels, simple yet stunning.

To understand the structure and methods of writing poetry, I read Edward Hirsch's *How to Read a Poem and Fall in Love with Poetry* and Molly Peacock's *How to Read a Poem and Start a Poetry Circle*. Several years went by without my reading another poem. Writing one had not even occurred to me.

Between 2007-2011 my website blogs were commentaries on *Tao-te Ching, Dhammapada, Bhagavad Gita,* and *Devi Gita.* Each week I wrote one chapter from one sacred book followed by a commentary and lesson learned. At the end of the blog entries I realized I had unwittingly practiced poetic forms by reading, reciting, and copying them. In appreciating the verses I not only learned spiritual lessons but also intuitively absorbed the essence of poetry.

More books and several years later I made my first attempts to write poetry, of which fifteen are included in Kathleen Shoop and Lori M. Jones's book, *Writing Inspiration Through Mindful Walking.* When the poet and Mindful Writer Gale Oare started Mindful Poets Group I began to submit poems for our monthly meet-and-critique sessions.

In the 1980s I loved watching the Chinese cooking show called *Yan Can Cook.* Host Martin Yan used to say, "Remember, if Yan can cook, so can you." To echo his encouraging remark I say to you, "Remember, if Madhu can write poetry, you can too."

Write a thought, a feeling, a belief you have about which you feel strongly. It could be four lines or four paragraphs or whatever feels comfortable. We will work with it this week.

❧ *Day 152* ❧

TODAY'S PRACTICE
Meditation: "Self-Forgiveness and Compassion"   Read, reflect, and journal.

INSPIRATION

You may not yet be interested in reading poetry, but I hope this month's inspirations change your mind. Poetry grows on you. It's enjoyable, but more importantly, it refines your writing skill. Mindful Writer Chris Weigand signed up for a poetry class to improve her writing. She didn't intend to become a poet but believes, "Poets seem to have a grasp on words and their organization that we can all profit from."

Reading poetry is a private, intimate experience. It widens your emotional space. It stirs self-examination. It helps us deal with paradoxical emotions we don't understand. Poems have messages that speak directly to the reader. When a poem syncs with your heart, it feels like the poet has shared a secret. The relationships between the poet, the poem, and the reader inspire awe and delight.

When a thought nudges me to write a poem, I jot it down and set it aside. After a day (or several) I read it aloud, ponder over it, and then revise. Then I put it away for a day or two, contemplate its content and revise again. Thoughts that felt humdrum at first begin to deepen. With precise word choices, rewritten lines clarify meaning.

Not yet satisfied, I revise once more before sharing the piece with my critique group. Others read it aloud and critique it. They may suggest changes or additions. Usually there are lots of suggestions and encouragement. On rare occasions they may say, "Wow!" then I go home to revise one final time. I also ask myself what it was that I wrote that touched the members of my poetry group the most.

Miraculous things are right in front of you. You may write down simple observations, but most of us are either too busy to notice the "ordinary things" or our sight is jaded. Through poetry we can turn even the simplest item into a thing of beauty. Try writing a poem this week while I share my process with you.

JOURNAL PROMPT

In yesterday's prompt you wrote some lines or paragraphs about an idea you are passionate about. If not, take a few minutes now to write straightforward prose about a strong emotion. Read your work aloud to yourself. Throughout this coming week, we will create a poem from these lines.

Here is what I wrote:

"Now as I've become a grandmother, I want to bequeath the jewelry box my mother gifted me to my granddaughter. How can I tell her about the other gems she owns? How do I explain to her that the jewelry box that has been passed down to her through generations is not as precious as the one the Great Mother Nature has blessed her with? Would she understand? Would she have the realization that I had in my middle years?"

ꝏ *Day 153* ꝏ

TODAY'S PRACTICE

Meditation: "Self-Forgiveness and Compassion"   Read, reflect, and journal.

INSPIRATION

When you write, paint, or create, you balance the rational and logical side of your brain with the creative and imaginative. You feel whole. Poetry expresses emotions and weaving words gives it structure. You become more acutely aware.

Deep inside your systems – circulatory, nervous, skeletal – images, symbols, and metaphors stir and wake. From the depths of your subconscious, these churn to the surface, transforming your inner happenings into words.

Writing a poem brings breath, blood, bones, and marrow together. At the same time, it illumines the path you must take and turns you must make. Reading and writing poetry combine the doing and being.

Poetry has its own way of knowing, conveying, communing with the world around and within you. It can be your companion in solitude. It helps you chip away what you don't need in your life and reveals treasures that lie at the bottom of your subliminal ocean. It improves your writing skill and encourages mindful living.

Here's how I rewrote yesterday's passage:

> "Having observed my granddaughter for years
> watching me adorn myself for family gatherings
> I said one day,
> Come my heart, choose something from the jewelry box.
> Anything! She bent to pick a jewel.
> Can I choose two?
> Her smile bewitched me.
> Should I tell her?
> No.
> I will wait for her to recognize
> the white pearls she is endowed with
> are more precious than the ones she covets."

JOURNAL PROMPT

Read aloud the prose passage you wrote yesterday. Feel it in your blood, bones, and body. Rewrite the passage, breaking phrases and sentences into verse. Take your time!

ꙮ *Day 154* ꙮ

TODAY'S PRACTICE

Meditation: "Self-Forgiveness and Compassion"   Read, reflect, and journal.

INSPIRATION

What is poetry if not of the arts – storytelling, image making, and singing – complex, lavish, and mysterious.

Poetry conveys feelings *and* thoughts. It may rhyme or have rhythm which helps to lend understanding. The sounds of the words reflect emotion as well as meaning. Their image strengthens what the words express. First read a poem and feel it at an intuitive level, then read it at an intellectual level, and finally read it aloud to bring clarity to what you understood and the emotions you experienced.

With attention and awareness, poetry teaches us to notice what is within the poet's heart-mind. It turns the mundane or meaningless into beauty and meaning. It pulls us out of boredom and sadness and restores us to normalcy, even serenity. It has the power to convey the profundity of life.

Continuing to refine my poem, the passage now reads:

> At the tenth birthday of my granddaughter
> Two treasures I want to pass on.
> One tangible she covets
> One inner she is not aware of yet.
> How do I convey
> You don't need the first
> to realize the pricelessness of the second?

JOURNAL PROMPT

Concentrate on what you have written so far. Come up with new ways to describe your original statement, using focused attention to a single thought, using fewer words, or replacing weaker words with more precise ones.

◡ *Day 155* ◡

TODAY'S PRACTICE

Meditation: "Self-Forgiveness and Compassion" Read, reflect, and journal.

INSPIRATION

I used to believe writing poems required extraordinary skill and was meant only for those who had talent and imagination as spacious as the sky. Yet I kept reading poetry. For several years, every morning I'd read one poem, first silently then aloud, and copy it into my journal. Imitating masters such as Rumi, Lalla, Emily Dickinson, Ted Kooser, and others gave me the courage to try to write my own. From the practice of copying poems, I learned that images and emotions are at the core of a poetic heart. Its meaning grows out of the emotion it conveys and the images it stirs.

My fumbling efforts led me to write and rewrite. When a poem looked finished, I'd ask myself, *Is this any good? Who would give me an honest critique?* I needed to join a poetry group. Thus, the idea to form a Mindful Poets Group was born and in 2020, with the help of Gail Oare as our leader, we began to meet monthly.

Our poetry circle is one of the most pleasurable mornings of my month. We each submit one or two poems, then recite each other's work and offer honest critique. This is the most beneficial gift a group can offer to its members.

Here's the next revision of the passage:

On my granddaughter's tenth birthday
I give her two gifts
A jewel from the chest,
And words of wisdom.
She doesn't need the first
when she is wise to the second.

JOURNAL PROMPT

From your not-yet-born poem, reduce as many words as you can. If a word still does not feel right, replace it with another. It's getting there!

⚘ *Day 156* ⚘

TODAY'S PRACTICE

Meditation: "Self-Forgiveness and Compassion"　　　　Read, reflect, and journal.

INSPIRATION

Poetry emerges like the bursting of a bud. It grows and ripens like fruit. But its craft is deliberate, attentive, and requires absolute concentration. It is simultaneously intuitive and inventive.

The relationship between poet and reader is that of an apple tree and someone eating an apple. The taste is neither in the tree nor in the taster, but in the simple act of eating. Similarly, the joy of reading poems is not in poetry or the poet, but in the act of reading, understanding, and feeling its power. Inert words come to life in the reader's imagination. Like the sublimity and majesty of nature, reading poetry inspires awe and wonder, mingled with surprise, and finally rapture.

I wrote and revised my stanzas five times before showing it to the critique group. The passage finally became one of five stanzas in a poem I titled, "Thirty-Two Pearl Necklace." You may read it under Day 180.

JOURNAL PROMPT

Once again revise the stanza you have been working on. If you belong to a poetry group, take your completed poem to be critiqued, or show it to a friend who enjoys reading poems.

⚘ *Day 157* ⚘

TODAY'S PRACTICE

Meditation: "Self-Forgiveness and Compassion"　　　　Read, reflect, and journal.

INSPIRATION

My earliest poems were about meditation. I started to meditate as a dilletante before becoming its regular practitioner. Decades of practice taught me how basic stillness, solitude, and silence were to meditation.

Occasionally, when a metaphor or simile has appeared to my mind's eye, there was invariably a natural object involved – an animal, mineral or vegetation. A bird's flight represents freedom, the sprouting of a seed is comparable to the emergence of an idea, and pouring out a long forgotten intense emotion is volcanic eruption. Such elements from nature can convey feelings and thoughts powerfully and poetically.

For the rest of the month, I encourage you to dabble in verse about topics of your choosing in your journal. Most of mine evolved from prose paragraphs, the same way we worked on one passage the previous week. Here is an example:

Sitting and Walking in Silence

No need to write or read.
No need to speak.
Just be.
Eagles fly effortlessly.
Goldfish swim effortlessly.
Peonies bloom effortlessly.

Under the expansive sky, below the lush trees
I walk effortlessly.
The air turns into my breath,
Linking birds, fish, flowers, and me
As my breath turns back into air
Leaving behind a trail of joy.

JOURNAL PROMPT

On a topic of your choosing, compose a paragraph of prose, or jump straight to verse. There are no rules. Allow yourself to experiment with whatever feels right in the moment.

✿ *Day 158* ✿

TODAY'S PRACTICE

Meditation: "Self-Forgiveness and Compassion"   Read, reflect, and journal.

INSPIRATION

At each meditation session you focus on your breath as you sit in silence to inhale and exhale. Yet there are days when thoughts continue to break your concentration. In that case repeat a mantra that inspires you. It could be a syllable or a short line.

Poetry is more than its syllables and lines, though. It is a tapestry composed of threads that work together to weave image and emotion. The first mantra I made for myself was, "Revise my day."

Revise My Day!

I weave my mantra on the loom of my mind
And let the joy and grace course through me.

I weave it under sun and under moon.
I whisper it for them to hear.
I recite it and then retain it in the lotus of my heart.

I weave it on the loom of my mind
to shape my life of hundred thousand days,
to comb the twists and knots of my ten thousand thoughts.

No more do I weave regrets and worries.
For peace has come to me by weaving—
by ceaselessly lacing the mantra on the loom of my mind.

No time is to be set, no action needed,
for weaving it.
for chanting it.

JOURNAL PROMPT

Revisit the prose or verse you began yesterday. Are there ways to tighten any of the thoughts? Can you replace weak verbs with more powerful ones? What emotion do you want to convey to the reader?

❧ *Day 159* ❧

TODAY'S PRACTICE

Meditation: "Self-Forgiveness and Compassion"   Read, reflect, and journal.

INSPIRATION

Most of the time you may not feel whole. Your thoughts carry you away. Though your body is here, you feel disintegrated. Your sensations, feelings, and thoughts are scattered in different directions. What should you do? Practice to integrate the three essential yous as you sit until they feel whole.

With closed eyes, sit in silence and focus on inhaling and exhaling the way you did several months ago. Practice breathing for 15 minutes and watch the Self within. Rumi said, "It doesn't use words" yet "listen" to it.

Breathe!

In
Out
In
Out
In
Out
In stillness, listen!
Listen to what reveals itself
Self dwells within and never ceases to be.

Listen to it with awareness and openness.
Listen to the silent voice.
Listen to the secret of what is and what is not.

Its flow never ceases.
Its trust never diminishes.
It never changes.

Most are too impatient to wait to hear its voice.
Instead of being afraid
Go within to experience the Infinite in all its wonder.

JOURNAL PROMPT

Continue what you started with the previous day's poem, or begin something new.

⥽ *Day 160* ⥼

TODAY'S PRACTICE

Meditation: "Self-Forgiveness and Compassion"　　　　Read, reflect, and journal.

INSPIRATION

What are the benefits of a regular meditation practice? It is so hard to sit still in silence, to repeat a mantra, to focus on the breath. All that you find hard currently will melt away with practice and reveal the gems hidden in the cave of your heart. Your imagination will flow like a sacred stream opening the blockages of your mind. Meditate and know thyself!

Yoking to the Flow

Sheer silence dwells in the lotus of my heart.
It brings to awareness what lies concealed inside,
stimulates scribblings that stream as words like dewdrops on petals.

The flow harnesses me to the universal consciousness
Revealing myself to me.

JOURNAL PROMPT

Allow yourself to experiment. If you have been playing with writing poetry that rhymes, try free verse, or vice versa.

༄ *Day 161* ༅

TODAY'S PRACTICE

Meditation: "Animating Seven Energy Centers"   Read, reflect, and journal.

INSPIRATION

Do you know who you are? It took me many professions and many lifetimes to understand who I am. I still don't fully know, but I have a basic idea. And because of this, I have confidence to chip away the irrelevant parts and pieces that feel like unnecessary baggage. The more I chip away, the lighter and happier I feel.

Who Am I?

Who am I? An artist, a teacher, a writer, a nobody?
A fragmented self. What should I do?
Meditate, journal, read, doodle and draw.
Boulders will move; underneath, ideas will sprout.

Sprouts whisper, *keep practicing!*
They point the way: inspiring, prompting intuitions.
Whispers turn into wisdom
They nudge to share the practice with budding minds.

From my jottings, my doodles, my rhymes
a compilation rises.
The culmination of everything
I've learned and taught,
is here!

Diving deep into the cauldron of consciousness
Body, heart, mind merge in the spaciousness of Self.
Muses arrive, imagination blooms, writing flows.
Writing Meditation Practice grows!

JOURNAL PROMPT

Many websites exist with daily writing prompts. Visit one, like:
www.pspoets.com/blog/30daypoetrychallenge.
Select a topic that speaks to you today and write for 5-10 minutes.

❧ *Day 162* ❧

TODAY'S PRACTICE

Meditation: "Animating Seven Energy Centers"   Read, reflect, and journal.

INSPIRATION

I have a fascination with what is true, permanent, and unchanging, and what is fleeting, impermanent, and temporary. Having accepted the fact of my own finite self, I often wonder what about me is worth everlasting. It always comes back to things of the heart: love, courage, generosity, fearlessness, gratitude.

What Lasts

I scanned my life of seven decades.
I winnowed what would fade
From what would last till I lay prostrate.
I boxed the stuff that would last
And let the chaff flow away.

On a winter night I searched for the box.
It was empty.
Then a voice said, *See within.*
The receptable for what lasts is in the cave of your heart.

JOURNAL PROMPT

Select a topic and set a timer for just 5 minutes. Allow words to flow to your page, unfiltered and unedited. When the timer dings, set your work aside and return to it tomorrow.

❧ *Day 163* ❧

TODAY'S PRACTICE

Meditation: "Animating Seven Energy Centers"   Read, reflect, and journal.

INSPIRATION

Journaling is one of the five disciplines of Writing Meditation Practice besides meditation, play, reading, and writing/creativity. But personally I have found the twin disciplines of meditation and journaling have immediate benefits.

Journaling

From the depths of my being, voices murmur.
Scrapings of my pen on a blank page whisper.
They speak of patience when fuzziness distorts.
They speak of courage when obstacles interfere.

They speak of going within, of silent journaling.
Of revealing ecstasy, toxicity, bliss, suffering.
They take me to the depths of my being.
Insights emerge and surprise me.

JOURNAL PROMPT

Revisit yesterday's 5-minute musings. How can you bend or shape it, mold or strengthen it?

❧ *Day 164* ❧

TODAY'S PRACTICE

Meditation: "Animating Seven Energy Centers"   Read, reflect, and journal.

INSPIRATION

The next five poems are about Nature.

SPRING

Outside my window a robin sings
I hear the song.
I smell the song.
I taste the song.
I wear the song.

My folded wings spread,
I soar the sky.

From the blue expanse
I see the oceans and the lands,
I see the earth, my home,
my womb, my tomb.

Back on the firm ground
I am a woman—a human

JOURNAL PROMPT
On a topic of your choosing, compose a paragraph of prose, or jump straight to verse. There are no rules. Allow yourself to experiment with whatever feels right in the moment.

ꙮ *Day 165* ꙯

TODAY'S PRACTICE
Meditation: "Animating Seven Energy Centers"   Read, reflect, and journal.

INSPIRATION
I must confess I don't particularly enjoy walking. And walking in winter does not sound pleasant. When the Mindful Writer Kathleen Shoop invited me to participate in the Kooser Project, where we were asked to walk outdoors during winter and write a poem about it, I was reluctant to go. But I had promised her that I would. So I went. Here's what I thought and felt during those walks. The remaining poems in this section were inspired by the Kooser project.

Walking in Winter

Should I?
I shouldn't.
Should I?
No, I shouldn't.
Should I?

I must. I must keep my word
just for twenty minutes.

I lock the front door and the cold air hits me.
First five minutes and I begin to freeze.

Without warm socks
my fingers in satiny gloves
a wide woolen headband
thick cotton pajamas
I say to a lone figure, "Colder than expected."
"I know. I had to borrow this jacket, I'm visiting."

Ten minutes and I turn a corner.
Not a soul in sight.
Not getting used to this freeze.
I see cutout "JOY" in red. What joy?
The breeze is chilly. Time to turn back.

Returning feels good.
I unlock the door and enter my happy place.
Phew, I kept my promise!
Tomorrow I'll wear a woolen cap,
woolen gloves, woolen pants and shirt and
For God's sake thick socks!

JOURNAL PROMPT

Head outside today, regardless of the weather (but wearing appropriate clothing!).
When you return home, pen your musings in verse.

✌ *Day 166* ✌

TODAY'S PRACTICE

Meditation: "Animating Seven Energy Centers"   Read, reflect, and journal.

INSPIRATION

The Kooser Project continues.

Neighborhood Walk

Pale sunrays trying to warm the windless air.

Dressed in wool from head to toe
I turn right from the front door
to walk up "Cardiac Hill" with deliberate steps.
The first thoughts:
Our physician daughter is getting immunized on Friday for COVID-19.
Grateful, grateful, grateful.

At the top of the hill in eight minutes,
then three descents, four ascents,
time to turn around.

The first thoughts have settled down, flown away.
The pale sun rays shine on the Christmas decorations
on the lawns of the quarantined.
Painted red "Joy" reflects some glee today.

JOURNAL PROMPT

Consider what brings you joy, and allow yourself to muse on it within a short (or long) poem.

✌ *Day 167* ✌

TODAY'S PRACTICE

Meditation: "Animating Seven Energy Centers"   Read, reflect, and journal.

INSPIRATION

I hesitated to leave the warmth of my home, even after walking daily for several weeks. But writing about it after returning home added charm to the experience. I kept going and writing about it afterward.

Outdoor Christmas

Why leave the warmth?
Yet I lock the door behind me
to crunch the virgin snow with my soles.

A lone bird makes waves in the sky, then warbles.
Snowflakes shower me,
My shoe makes prints on the snow.

Red and green decorations contrast the white
over streets, trees, grass, roofs.
A holiday feel.
Wonder how the "Joy" would feel today.

I turn to get back home
and see my footprints in reverse.
Not a soul in sight.

A FedEx truck comes my way.
The driver in a Santa suit, waves. I wave back.
A bird calls, a human waves, Christmas connects.

JOURNAL PROMPT

Compose a poem about one of the four seasons. It can mirror the weather outside for you today, or be set during another time of year.

✏ *Day 168* ✏

TODAY'S PRACTICE

Meditation: "Animating Seven Energy Centers"   Read, reflect, and journal.

INSPIRATION

By the time I wrote this poem, I had started to enjoy the morning walks. On and off I continued to take winter morning walks, more off than on. But now my winter walks from 2020 are written forever.

White Christmas Day

I stand outside the door
Golden bright.
A swath of white.
I edge along the street
with my hat pulled over my brows,
half of my view obscured.

Stillness heavy on distant tree limbs.
Soundless stunning snowscape.
A shrill caw.
Calm interrupted.
Clear sidewalk
I step around a white mound.
An un-shoveled part.
Old folks or those who dread cold like me?

Back home, I secure the dry jacket, hat, and gloves
with the snow boots to recover them
for tomorrow's walk.

JOURNAL PROMPT

Reflect on a time when you had to do something you didn't want to. Allow it to flow onto your pages. Are you proud of yourself for making it through? Can you, from this distance in time and space, discover a different way it could have been accomplished? Or would you do it all over again?

༄ *Day 169* ༄

TODAY'S PRACTICE

Meditation: "Animating Seven Energy Centers"   Read, reflect, and journal.

INSPIRATION

"The language of art is only spoken in silence.
When you find yourself alone remind yourself that God
has sent everyone else away so that there is only you and him."
—Rumi

The next set of poems are "Things Unseen," poems about our True Self. In this one, I try to understand and discover who is this whom I call my Self with a capital S.

Authentic Self

Follow her daily and you never stray from your path.
Hear her voice and your imagination thrives.
Heed her always and you face no obstacles on your way.

When she leads you, you're fearless.
When she entices you, you're energized.
When she courses through you, you're tireless.
When she graces you, you reach your goal.
Make this house of blood and bones her abode.

Who is She?
Your creative flow.
Your inner voice.
Your Authentic Self.

JOURNAL PROMPT
Allow the journey you have been pacing toward your Authentic Self to be the topic of your journaling today. Begin either in verse or prose, and see where it leads you.

⤸ *Day 170* ⤷

TODAY'S PRACTICE
Meditation: "Animating Seven Energy Centers"   Read, reflect, and journal.

INSPIRATION

"And you? When will you begin that long journey within yourself?"

—Rumi

True Self

Only few creative minds hear the inner voice.
Fewer still pay heed to the whispers they hear.
Fortunate are those who listen to the Self.
Rare are those who mull over what was murmured.
Blessed are those who make the Self an illumined teacher.

The intellect does only half the work.
The other half is whispered by the Self.

The Self is beyond perception,
Hidden in the lotus of your heart,
It is above pain and pleasure.
It is neither body nor heart nor mind
Three melded as One,
the source of aesthetic pleasure and abiding bliss.

The creative sits still in silence and solitude,
The Self may journey far away.
Moving into everything everywhere to bring back
pristine intents and inklings
When you connect with the Self within,
Learning changes into growth and growth to transformation.

JOURNAL PROMPT

Pull out the musings on your Authentic Self journey from yesterday. If you wrote in prose, use the process we outlined earlier in the month to shape it as a poem. If you went straight to verse, are there ways you can today elevate the emotion?

❧ *Day 171* ❧

TODAY'S PRACTICE
Meditation: "Awakening the Senses"   Read, reflect, and journal.

INSPIRATION

"Sit, be still and listen!" —Rumi

Self Within

Authentic Self is enshrined in the lotus of your heart.
Swifter than thought,
Transcending all.
One moment an abyss away,
the next moment with you.
Self within holds your universe together.

Deny knowing the Authentic Self,
remain enveloped by the darkness of your sight.
Deny knowing it, remain devoid of joy.
Know its truth by meditating, by journaling, by playfulness.
Oh writer! Stay yoked to the Self.

Practice Writing Meditation daily
Enter the realm of imagination.
Stay with the flow of creativity.
Receive insights with your eyes closed.
Cross the sea of fear.
The body turns to dust but your words are immortal.

JOURNAL PROMPT
Consider the immortality of all the words you have written. We are here in this life but a short time. What do you most wish you could tell the You of your past? What would you like to share with your future self?

༂⃝ *Day 172* ༂⃝

TODAY'S PRACTICE

Meditation: "Awakening the Senses"   Read, reflect, and journal.

INSPIRATION

"You must keep breaking your heart until it opens."
"All despair is followed by hope; all darkness is followed by sunshine."
—*Rumi*

Creativity

1.

Each wondrous sight appeared and vanished.
Each thought, each feeling rose and faded.
I drank my fill,
thought the source would never run dry.
Paintings, tutorials, stories
Gratified, pleased,
yet I remained unsatisfied
What was it that I yearned for?

I craved and I longed for
Believing myself a failure as an artist, teacher, writer
Why did I flounder so?

2.

Unfulfilled
I continued to write, to create
no more turns.
At the threshold my failures stood like sentries,
lampposts lighting the path.
nudging me to persevere
teaching me patience
whispering to go deeper where I stood.
Wonder what I would have done without my "failures."

3.

Failures. Better failures. Success.
Go deeper and see what failures look like.

They are open at the other end, leading to possibilities.
Success is a brick wall.

4.

A drop of ocean within me
where neither success nor failure matter.
The drop emerges from the ocean
and returns to the ocean.
Nothing but eternal flow.

JOURNAL PROMPT

Revisit the poems or musings you have been creating over the past month. Are there any themes that unite some of them? Could you collect any of them into a short set, as the grouping I shared above?

✅ Day 173 ✅

TODAY'S PRACTICE

Meditation: "Awakening the Senses"   Read, reflect, and journal.

INSPIRATION

There was a period in my life when I wrote only about writers and writing. The final poems this month were previously published in *Writing Inspiration Through Mindful Walking* by Kathleen Shoop and Lori Jones. The slim volume was meant for writers. You don't have to be a writer to feel inspired. Reading them will nourish any and all artistic-minded individuals.

Simply Write

Simply write!
Do not speak of your writing.
Do not speak of other people's writings.
Do not speak of the business of writing.

Sit still in silence and solitude.
When body, heart and mind are one

When your senses have moved inward
Let the stream flow.
Unravel your knots in spontaneous words.

Other writers' success or failure does not affect you.
Profit or loss does not touch you.
Praise or criticism does not ruffle you.
Derive pleasure solely from writing.
Experience bliss.

Simply write!

JOURNAL PROMPT

Today, use your poetry to offer support, guidance, or wisdom to yourself and other writers. What have you learned about the process of writing? Every insight is valuable, as we are all beginners when we come to the blank page. Write either in verse or prose, as you are comfortable.

∽ *Day 174* ∾

TODAY'S PRACTICE
Meditation: "Awakening the Senses"   Read, reflect, and journal.

INSPIRATION

My experiences with the writing life have shown that when you are determined to lead a writer's or artist's life, when you sincerely follow the daily Writing Meditation Practice, doors of opportunity will open for you. You need to be patient, dedicated, and realistic.

Door of Opportunity

A careless critique from a fellow writer?
Return hers with honest comments.

"Here," she hands you the draft, the weak parts highlighted.
Show her where her strengths lie.

He grabs the opportunity that was rightfully yours.
Congratulate him on his success.

By critiquing honestly,
By learning from your own strengths and skills,
By preparing through tough circumstances,
Attain the strength no one else can.

When you are ready
The door of opportunity opens only for you.

JOURNAL PROMPT

Have you had any experiences with critique groups? Allow today's writing to either reflect on one such meeting, or muse about the ideal group you would like to create.

ᕓ *Day 175* ᕕ

TODAY'S PRACTICE

Meditation: "Awakening the Senses"   Read, reflect, and journal.

INSPIRATION

I do my best writing in the solitude of my study with "the door closed," as Stephen King suggests. No music or white noise. I surrender to the silence that carries with it hidden potentialities and possibilities for my work-in-progress. They are not mine yet, but floating around for me to grab and use. But sensing the potential, feeling the possibility is like seizing a fish in water with my bare hands. With daily practice, catching them gets easier.

Mindful Writing

I sit still in solitude.
Same place. Same time.
A silence speaks to me.
It speaks of complete surrender
to feelings,

to thoughts,
to muses.

Feelings flow,
They shift me to my fictional dream.
I scribe in silence.

Past suffering transforms into compassion.
Past trial into today's courageous act.
Past transgression into redemption.

My poems and pieces have no second,
They're mind-born from the source within.

JOURNAL PROMPT

On a topic of your choosing, compose a paragraph of prose, or jump straight to verse. Allow yourself to include details from what is happening right now, wherever you are in your day and life.

ᘛ *Day 176* ᘚ

TODAY'S PRACTICE

Meditation: "Awakening the Senses"   Read, reflect, and journal.

INSPIRATION

I often wonder how different it is for a writer to be reading than for a non-writer engaged in the same activity. Writing anything – a poem, novel, short story, or essay – is like a protagonist's journey on a new adventure.

Reading allows you to vicariously experience the adventure as intensely as the writer felt when they wrote what you are reading. Experiencing emotions and thoughts takes you beyond the exploits of the page to an aesthetic joy of discovering the process. That's what I have tried to convey in this poem.

Writers Write! Readers Read!

Write,
Write alone!
Let the vital energy emanate from you.
Write with others,
Feel charged with the collective energy.

Write,
Go on a quest. Conquer demons. Find the elixir.
Narrate your experiences
As a gift to your readers.

Read,
Reinvigorate the energy that exudes.
Rejoice in the gift.
Connect with the writer, the giver.

Connect with the glorious energy beyond
beyond the writer,
beyond the reader,
To the timeless creative act.

JOURNAL PROMPT
Revisit any of the poetry you have crafted this month. Read it out loud as though it were the first time you have discovered something wonderful from a different writer.

ꗌ *Day 177* ꗌ

TODAY'S PRACTICE
Meditation: "Awakening the Senses"   Read, reflect, and journal.

INSPIRATION
So often it happens that after having written the first draft of a poem or a story I leave it alone. When I return to it after a few days, or a week, even a month I surprise myself. How did I come up with that idea? How did I write it? *Did I write it?* Then I realize that when I wrote it I was

not alone. My inspiration, my muse, my spirit within – whom I have been referring to as the Authentic Self – was one with me.

Writing Mindfully

Who writes the stuff to which I sign my name?
Who whispers behind the mask?
What gushes forth during moments of quietude
then sidles back swiftly wherever it comes from?

Sliding down my arm to my fingertips,
I transcribe fiery truth.
Enraptured, I write until my wrist hurts.
I stop when the whispers leave for their hidden abode.

Where does this recluse hide, whom does it abide?
It comes and returns on its free will.
It writes the word, the line, the prose, the poem.
I only attach my name to what It scribes.

JOURNAL PROMPT

Do you ever read your work later and wonder about its origins as I have? Write today (in verse or prose) about the experience of surprise when you discover something you composed that feels "other."

‿ Day 178 ‿

TODAY'S PRACTICE

Meditation: "Awakening the Senses" Read, reflect, and journal.

INSPIRATION

This is how I felt about writing a completed piece, long before I wrote a book.

Birthing

Read and reread books until your own book is born.
The unborn lies dormant at the core of your being.

Hatch it on grass, leaves, lichens of your readings.
Nurture it with imagination and inspiration.

Neither self-conscious nor contriving,
join forces
with the masters who went before you
melding their skills with your practice.
Don't give up. Be patient. Determined.

Overcome obstacles and mental boulders.
Stay focused, motivated, inspired.
Your book will benefit readers the way masterpieces benefitted you.
You'll prevail in your creations.

JOURNAL PROMPT

One day at a time, one verb or phrase or sentence at a time, you are creating words that will endure. Some days you add words. Other days you subtract. Journal about what your writing journey is leading toward. Will you submit your essay to a magazine? Or share a short story or poem with a group? Will you birth a book?

✌ *Day 179* ↻

TODAY'S PRACTICE

Meditation: "Awakening the Senses"   Read, reflect, and journal.

INSPIRATION

Relationships stir sensations, feeling, emotions, passion and ultimately rapture. These qualities saturate seeds of poetic ideas to germinate saplings of new poems. True poetry forms when these saplings bear flowers. Here is a sapling that sprouted from my thoughts about age.

Old Age

A tooth fell...
A milk tooth from a five-year-old.

A tooth cracked...
A hollow tooth from an eighty-five-year-old.

One blossoming to life,
The other withering away.

The child learning about the elements.
The elder merging back into them.

Teeth fall, dentures break but spirit remains.
Why isn't this wisdom passed down?

Something more lays beyond the falling tooth, changing dentures.
Revealed only to unhurried, contemplative.

JOURNAL PROMPT

Consider one important relationship in your life. Perhaps it is with a child, parent, or spouse. Maybe it is with a friend or coworker. Or perhaps it is the relationship to Self. What similarities and differences strike you?

ᔕ *Day 180* ᔐ

TODAY'S PRACTICE

Meditation: "Awakening the Senses"   Read, reflect, and journal.

INSPIRATION

This poem started with my prose paragraph that we developed into a poem, the exercise I shared earlier this month.

Thirty-Two Pearl Necklace

1.

My mother gifted me the trousseau with
a necklace of a hundred black pearls,
a diamond ring,
emerald earrings and gold bangles.

Nestled in a velvet-lined jewelry box.
Rarely used but covetously peeked at
when I imagined myself bejeweled.
Carried the box to family celebrations.

Once the ring went missing.
Panicked,
I searched frantically.
I can buy a new one.
But found it stuck under the fold of the velvet lining.

2.

Mother Nature gifted me with
thirty-two white pearls
two deep crystals
a pair of hearing device
a breathing instrument.
and a lip enclosed well.

Everyone has them.
They don't feel special.

3.

The day I lost one white pearl.
A shocking realization,
of its uniqueness,
singularity,
preciousness.
Couldn't leave home for weeks.
Watched the remaining thirty-one
with an eagle eye.

4.

On my granddaughter's tenth birthday
I gave her two gifts
The emerald earrings from the chest
And the wisdom of natural gems,
"cherish the gems mother nature blessed you with."

5.

Blessed with priceless treasures at my birth
Instead I coveted jewels.
The choice was wrong.
Grandmother why didn't you awaken me sooner?

END OF MONTH PROMPT

Reflect on your journey with poetry this past month. Was writing poetry new for you? Did it come easily? What revelations surprised you? What do you wish you had known sooner?

BUDDING

"Let silence take you to the core of life.
Your silence has thunder hidden inside."
—Rumi

MONTH 7

MINDFULNESS AND NONVERBAL ACTIVITIES

Suggested Readings

A Walk in the Woods:
Rediscovering America on the Appalachian Trail
Bill Bryson, 1998.

No Mud, No Lotus: The Art of Transforming Suffering
Thich Nhat Hanh, 2014.

The Hidden Life of Trees:
What They Feel, How They Communicate
(The Illustrated Edition)
Peter Wohlleben, 2018.

Barefoot Walking:
Free Your Feet to Minimize Impact, Maximize Efficiency,
and Discover the Pleasure of Getting in Touch with the Earth
Michael Sandler and Jessica Lee, 2013.

♬ *Day 181* ♬

TODAY'S PRACTICE

This month we will focus on walking and other nonverbal activities. Any one of the hobbies that do not use words is a necessary respite for those of us who breathe, think, and write words. We will also return to meditations with which we began this journey – body, heart, and mind.

Meditation: "Body"   Read, write, and journal.

INSPIRATION

Walking is the par excellence nonverbal activity that we will focus on this month, the others being cooking, gardening, painting, playing a musical instrument, traveling, dancing, and so on. Wordless hobbies give our writer's mind a break.

I cook three to four times a week throughout the year. I garden during spring and tend to the seeds I sow – the annuals that sprout and perennials that grow and flower during summer and fall. I also walk during spring, summer, and fall but when I'm challenged I even walk during deep winter. I also take pleasure in traveling, and making art.

For the next few weeks we will talk about the benefits of physical activity – mindful walking in neighborhood and in wilderness, in familiar places and foreign lands, in country and in city. Then during the remaining days of the month I'll share mouthwatering recipes which hopefully you'll relish.

So you can plan ahead, browse the entries for Day 204-210 and if there are ingredients that don't look familiar, you can buy them next time you are at the grocery store, as so many Indian spices are now widely available in the U.S. Here is the menu of dishes to tempt your tastebuds:

1. Paneer and Vegetable Pulao (Pilaf)
2. Plain/with Peas, Basmati Rice and Indian Breads (Puree)
3. Chickpeas with Tomato and Lemon
4. Chicken Drumstick and Thighs with Ginger

5. Cauliflower and Potatoes
6. Cucumber Raita
7. Mint and Walnut Chutney
8. Vermicelli with Milk
9. Sweet Brown Vermicelli

You can eat the first dish by itself but when accompanied with side dishes #6 and #7, the taste is enhanced. The rest of the dishes go well with #2 plain rice or rice with green peas or, if you prefer, Indian breads (which are rather complicated to make, so buy them from a store).

JOURNAL PROMPT
What nonverbal activities do you routinely enjoy? Make a list in your journal and consider how frequently you get a chance to do them, and also whether you would like that amount to change in the future.

๙ *Day 182* ๙

TODAY'S PRACTICE
Meditation: "Body"   Read, write, and journal.

INSPIRATION
Here's a guided walking meditation. Read it once. If you like, memorize it or record it to listen before a walk.

Walking Meditation
Before you begin, gather your awareness into your body. Take one deep mindful breath – inhale and exhale. Feel the sensation of your feet in contact with the ground. Breathe: inhale one, exhale two; inhale three, exhale four; inhale five, exhale six. Keep breathing until you count to ten.

When you feel ready, begin walking mindfully, slightly slower than your normal pace. With each step, pay attention to the sensations on the soles of your feet as each foot touches the ground. It doesn't matter whether you are wearing shoes or not. Just keep noticing the sensation as each foot meets the ground. Notice the changes in pressure and sensation, one foot after the other.

You'll need to keep enough awareness of the world so you stay safe, but the focus of attention is sensing the soles of your feet. (If you're in a small space, you can walk the length of the space, and then turn around.) Walk in rhythm with your breath: inhale one, exhale two; inhale three, exhale four; inhale five, exhale six. Keep breathing until you count to ten. Then repeat.

When the mind wanders away from the sensations in the soles and feet, gently guide the focus back to them. There is no need for any frustration or irritation if the mind wanders. We all experience this distraction. Simply bring the focus back first to your breath and then to the feet as many times as you need.

Continue walking naturally, expanding your attention to what you can see. Bring your full attention to what is in front of you and around you. Take in the various colors, the play of light and shadow, the movement and stillness. Put aside any mental commentary, no labeling or judging. Just be present with what is here now. Again, if your mind wanders, guide it back to being fully present to what you sense and see.

Now expand your attention to hearing for several minutes. Whether you're indoors or outdoors, pay attention to the sounds. Notice them without getting caught up in whether they are pleasant or unpleasant.

In the final moments of the walking meditation, bring your focus back to awareness of the physical sensations on the soles of the feet. No matter where you are, your mind may have wandered. Your job is to bring your awareness back to your breath, to your feet, to what you see, to what you hear, and back to the sensation of each foot touching the ground, one by one.

When you're ready to end the walk, pause and take one deep and slow breath. An awareness will emerge from your mindful walking. For the rest of the day, intend to take this awareness to all that you think, say, or do.

Wherever you go, you carry your Authentic Self with you. Each day you become one with it at your Sacred Power Spot. But you also take it with you when you go for a walk. Bring it to your attention before you begin and connect with it at the end of the walk. It will help you benefit from this practice.

JOURNAL PROMPT

Your true self within is wise and kind. It is always with you but comes alive when you journal, meditate, read, and practice nonverbal activities. It helps you solve problems, and when the mind clears, new ideas and insights emerge.

What does your Authentic Self feel like? What happens when you take a walk with all your senses alert?

ᘓ *Day 183* ᘒ

TODAY'S PRACTICE

Meditation: "Body"   Read, write, and journal.

INSPIRATION

Henry David Thoreau (1817-1862), one of the most famous writers who walked daily, believed that men and women should regard themselves as part and parcel of nature rather than a member of society. Whereas in nature one has absolute freedom and wildness, social freedom is merely civil and cultural.

Walking has become mainstream now, but during Thoreau's time people did not walk as a pastime or for pleasure. Only "one or two persons in the course of my life who understood the art of walking" or who had "a genius for sauntering" walked frequently. Some did not walk at all; others walked in the highways; a few walked across parking lots. He adds, "Roads and lots were made for horses and men of business." Do not walk in them. "I walk out into a nature such as the old prophets and poets, Manu, Moses, Homer, Chaucer, walked in."

If you practice the noble discipline of a daily walk, you know what requisite leisure, freedom, and independence it provides. If you don't, why not start today? Thoreau goes on to say, "Me thinks that the moment my legs begin to move, my thoughts begin to flow." Legs were not made to sit upon, he declared, but to stand or walk upon. Adventure through the woods and over the hills and fields absolutely free from worldly engagements. True sauntering takes place in the woods and meadows.

Okay, so you have walked a mile into the woods. Your body is walking but your mind may be elsewhere. "What business you have in the woods if you are thinking something out of the woods." Focus on your breath or on your moving feet. Left, right, left, right. Keep your hearing tuned in to your surroundings – flowing water or the cackling of wild geese. The air of the mountains and the woods inspires and feeds your spirit.

JOURNAL PROMPT

Take a walk today, in whatever time and space you can create. Use short walks through a parking lot or between meetings to begin your practice if needed. Focus on the breath, then the soles of your feet. Do not worry about creating the "perfect" conditions for a mindful walking meditation. Simply begin!

ᓬᓂ *Day 184* ᓂᓬ

TODAY'S PRACTICE

Meditation: "Body"   Read, write, and journal.

INSPIRATION

Henry David Thoreau was not the only thinker who walked for four or more hours a day, but through the centuries, many creative masters and geniuses used walking to stimulate and cultivate their artistic minds.

"Walk like a camel." It is said that the only beast which ruminates when walking is the camel.

The English poet William Wordsworth had a state-of-the-art library but he was spotted most days out of doors walking and contemplating.

Beethoven made a ritual of walking. During the workday, he took a short morning walking break to clear his mind, and a longer walk in the afternoon. He carried paper and a pen with him to jot down notes when inspiration struck.

Both Aristotle and Socrates, the Greek philosophers, inextricably linked thinking to walking. They also used walking as a pedagogical tool. Both conducted their lectures outdoors. Aristotle walked the grounds of the Lyceum carrying his books while his students followed, listening and learning.

Friedrich Nietzsche walked to clear his mind and stimulate it. As thoughts sprang to mind, he scribbled them down in a notebook. To him walking was not just to relax but also to work. His motto, "All truly great thoughts are conceived while walking," was born out of his own experience. When writing a book, he would walk alone for up to eight hours a day.

If you have never walked alone, give it a try for 20 minutes. Keep a topic in your mind. Contemplate it as you stay focused on your breath or movement of your feet. When back home, journal about the experience.

JOURNAL PROMPT

How long did you walk yesterday? What did you think about? Did you begin walking with a topic or an intention in your mind? Journal your responses, then take another walk today!

↢ *Day 185* ↣

TODAY'S PRACTICE
Meditation: "Body"   Read, write, and journal.

INSPIRATION

When you are by yourself, you may feel lonely. You mind yearns for human connection. You may wonder, *What is the point of solitude?* But you will feel differently when you are amidst nature. Amongst trees and streams and hills and pastures, loneliness takes on a different character. It connects you and the world around you, turning loneliness into solitude. A connection between who you think you are and who you truly are begins to emerge. A walk in nature then strengthens that connection between you and your Authentic Self. So just walk – breathe deeply, be mindful, and have an intention in mind.

When Mindful Writer Lorraine Bonzelet walks, she contemplates life's problems and creates poetry. "Walking has been a life-saving technique for my heart and soul." She once met a wheelchair-bound man who advised: "Before the tragedy [that shattered his leg bones], I loved to run, hike, and play basketball. But I took them all for granted. If I had known that would be my last walk, run, hike or basketball game, I'd have observed every movement with pleasure." What if today is your last day to walk?

Most of us are not going to lose our ability to walk, but we do take our bodies for granted. Consider what it would be like if you were not able to get out of bed and walk into the kitchen to make a cup of coffee? Unable to do the most basic activities?

Become aware of the significance of your legs – they help you walk, run, and play. Be aware of your physical self. Pay heed to your heartbeats and breath. Thank your ankles, knees, and hips for joining forces to propel you forward.

JOURNAL PROMPT

Have you ever lost the use of your foot, ankle, knee, or leg? What was that like? Do you have pain or trouble walking still? Describe how limited mobility or pain makes you feel. What if you knew today was your last day to walk? What would you do differently?

৬৩ *Day 186* ৫৬

TODAY'S PRACTICE

Meditation: "Body"   Read, write, and journal.

INSPIRATION

When you walk through a forested park, the wild woods, or on the shore of a lake or a river, do you use your senses of sight, hearing, smelling, and touch? Do you observe what passes by you? Do you carry a notebook to jot down an idea that pops or an insight that is stimulated? Do these the next time you go for a walk.

Take a peek above you. Look at the color of the sky, the movement and sound of the swaying trees. Do you hear birds chirp? Touch the ferns, wildflowers, and grasses that reach your ankles or knees.

Observe as the green ground passes under your feet. Think of the life under the ground. There is a web, a network of roots that communicates, exchanges nutrients, sends warning signals, and even sabotages unwelcome intruders. Trees have their own language and the sensations they feel are shared with us at some level.

Why pay attention to the underground? Because in knowing how plant life communicates and exchanges information, it may open your understanding of the world at large – at the level of animal, plant, mineral. Greater understanding may lead you to know how everything in the world is connected. The forester and ecologist Peter Wohlleben calls this underground connection "Wood Wide Web." He stunningly portrays the phenomenon in his documentaries such as *Fantastic Fungi* and *The Hidden Life of Trees: What They Feel, How They Communicate*.

JOURNAL PROMPT

Sit on the forest floor. Imagine the intelligence of the complex root system of the forest (trees and mushrooms) flowing underneath. How does it make you feel?

ᘛ *Day 187* ᘚ

TODAY'S PRACTICE

Meditation: "Body"   Read, write, and journal.

INSPIRATION

Most of us walk early in the morning or in the evenings. Have you walked at night when the sky is India Ink black-blue, when stars are twinkling brightly or when the moon is full? If you have, you will know how night walks heighten your senses of hearing and smell. They titillate your body and mind.

When you walk in the dark, the sight diminishes and hearing takes over. If you focus on your breath, the inner stillness feels stronger in darkness than in daylight. Slow your pace. When it is safe, tilt your head upward, and gaze in wonderment at the expanse of stars.

You have to walk under the majesty of the night sky to feel its serenity and magical spell. It clears your mind, calms you, even makes you forget petty problems that had made you anxious. The coolness of the night, the tranquility of the silver moon, or the light of the full moon not only frees you from stress but also surprises you by resolving a problem or two that were floating in your mind.

I remember the night we spent at the Safari Lodge in Tsavo National Park in Kenya. Under the night sky the tables were set for dinner on the bank of a lake that reflected two blazing bonfires that provided light as we ate. When I looked up, the firmament, immense and dark, twinkled with billions of stars. They seemed so close to earth that I stood up from where I was sitting to touch the sky – that's how close it felt to me... like if I tried, I could pluck a twinkling star from the depths of darkness.

A 15-20 minute stroll in your neighborhood after dinner can help aid digestion and help lose belly fat, and to top it all, you will sleep better.

JOURNAL PROMPT
After dinner this evening, make time for a short walk under the night sky. Practice your breathing and shift your focus alternately from sights to sounds.

✦ *Day 188* ✦

TODAY'S PRACTICE
Meditation: "Body"   Read, write, and journal.

INSPIRATION
In my back garden, two ground coverings called Mother of Thyme and Wooly Thyme spread like green snow from early spring to summer months. From early April they slowly turn green, then lush green, and by the end of June sprout into tiny mauve blossoms like a developing

photograph. In May the ground covering is dewy. In June and July it is cool to the touch, and in fall months moist. As the colors and texture of the ground change, it is tempting to walk on it, a space of fifteen steps. And I do. Walking barefoot on the ground is called "earthing" or "grounding," and when you do it mindfully, you feel intimately connected with Mother Earth. As I walk, I pay attention to the feel of the soles touching the spread and imagine the energy of the earth rising upward through my legs and torso, through my spinal cord, and finally to my head.

Some studies have shown walking barefoot on the ground allows you to absorb the earth's energy, stabilize your daily cortisol rhythm, and transmit neural messages from your feet to your brain, thereby heightening your spatial awareness. It also reduces stress and improves blood cell function for a healthier heart.

While growing up in India, walking barefoot was not uncommon. We not only walked that way on grassy parts of our front lawn but also inside our home. Footwear would be left on the side of the grass or, when visiting a friend, outside their front door. Why don't you try it yourself? Sometimes it is a good thing not to follow the norms. They sharpen your senses.

JOURNAL PROMPT

Go "Earthing" or "Grounding." Walk barefoot mindfully, even if just in your backyard. Then journal about your experience.

ᨏ *Day 189* ᨏ

TODAY'S PRACTICE

Meditation: "Body"   Read, write, and journal.

INSPIRATION

Walking through a well-maintained cemetery is a unique experience. Observing the headstones and monuments of those who have gone before us not only grounds us but also there is a feeling of serenity that stirs contemplation.

During my doctoral study, I walked through New England cemeteries to do my research project. I didn't find these resting places of long-gone ancestors morbid or depressing. On the contrary they were calming and tranquil. After drawing and making rubbings of headstones, I was inspired to take longer walks on the pathways that webbed the greenery.

My fascination with the inevitability of death motivated me to start writing my novel, tentatively titled *Meaning of My Life*. The moment we're born, we begin our journey toward death. Each human life's path might be vastly different, but it ends the same way.

Whenever you get a chance, walk peacefully through a cemetery and observe the resting places of those who have passed on. Contemplate your own death – not in a morbid way but to mull over how you can make your life even better than it already is. There is something about such a contemplative walk that gives courage to face your own mortality. You feel heightened appreciation for each new day, and a deeper connection with your loved ones... and even strangers who lived once but have now left this world. With such an attitude, you live more fully and make stronger connection into your Authentic Self, who you truly are. And not who you pretend to be.

JOURNAL PROMPT

Are you afraid of death? What do you want family and friends to remember about you? What would you want your epitaph to say?

ᘒ *Day 190* ᘓ

TODAY'S PRACTICE

Meditation: "Body"   Read, write, and journal.

INSPIRATION

The Vedic Hymn of Creation (Rigveda 10.129), was composed around 1500 B.C. I have read it numerous times and every time I reread it, I find it astonishingly contemporary. The poet wonders how the universe may have been created and speculates about its origins from different perspectives: wondering, doubting, asking questions, giving answers,

I feel that our creative mind functions on a similar model. Before an idea conjures up in our mind there is neither the fictional world nor the characters or setting. What stirs them? Where do they come from? We create something out of nothing. We breathe life into something new. Deep from the utter darkness, by the force of inner creative heat arises something new and turns into a story, an essay, a book.

Our work in progress is written 60 percent by us and 40 percent rises from the work itself. Most times we don't know what will emerge, who will suddenly appear, or how they will behave. What sort of hurdles and conflict will they face? How will the story end? We begin with trepidation but with the hope that our daily and diligent work will amount to something eventually. At some point, somewhere from within, we hear the work is complete. Then we hear and receive signals from the universe which help us revise the final draft.

Working in the creative zone, even the best among us must intuitively feel their way through a storyline. That inner creative fire is constantly guiding us, sometimes as clear as a good friend sitting next to us, but at other times a feeble voice from a distance. Its tides ebb and flow but are eternally present.

Writing Meditation Practice drives forth creative energy, cultivating the "force of inner heat" which makes the creation of new stories possible.

JOURNAL PROMPT

I get my ideas when I'm away from my writing desk – in meditation, walking, cooking, weeding the garden, painting. Some writers get their best ideas while listening to music, some others in utter silence. What sort of environment or circumstances stir your innovative ideas?

❧ *Day 191* ☙

TODAY'S PRACTICE

Meditation: "Walking Through the Forest" Read, write, and journal.

INSPIRATION

For many, walking is a favorite nonverbal activity. Whether it is a stroll through a garden, a quick sprint in the neighborhood, or a leisurely walk in a foreign country, this form of exercise invites contemplation, exploration, and enjoyment of familiar as well as new places.

Any vigorous physical activity makes your body release endorphins, the feel-good chemicals. Endorphins relieve stress, anxiety, and pain the way opioid drugs do. They are the cause of the post-pleasure you experience after having done the exercise.

Writing and reading are sedentary activities. Some of us sit for more than four hours unless we have to use the bathroom. But movement gets your blood circulating, which helps send more oxygen to your whole body, heart, and brain. The American Physiology Society recommends moving if you have been sitting for three hours. Writers or people working in an office often forget to take a break for movement. Sitting for too long reduces oxygen levels to the brain, increasing the risk for dementia.

So you may sit to write or read for long hours but remember to take a break of doing a nonverbal activity after every one to two hours.

JOURNAL PROMPT

Take frequent breaks to move today if you sit many hours. It will help your cognitive brain function as well as your muscles, heart, lungs, and mood. Physical movement makes you healthier. If you want your body and brain to be in tip-top form, take a walk outdoors or pace in your room. Briefly journal any reflections you might have afterward.

⚘ *Day 192* ⚘

TODAY'S PRACTICE

Meditation: "Walking Through the Forest"   Read, write, and journal.

INSPIRATION

Sauntering in the woods is drastically different from strolling on a beach. Yet both are walks. Both invigorate. Both help you think. Both are good for the body. On the beach the wet sand feels smooth and cool to the soles of your feet, the hot sun massages your shoulders, and the gentle wind ruffles your hair. And if you walk closer to the water, small waves lap over your feet, ankles, and knees. The salty smell of the sea intoxicates you as you hear a flying seagull screech against the clear blue sky.

"You may have taken this walk for weeks on a family holiday, or you may be alone strolling the beach in different weather conditions. Under the sun, sweat slides down your spine. When the wind off the ocean is fierce, you are pelted with grains of sand. Occasionally on stormy days, the sea lunges onto the beach and dark clouds roll in. Flocks of sea birds over the dunes sway on one leg with heads tucked under wings," observes Mindful Writer Martha Swiss.

No matter who you are, or what mood you are in, a walk makes you feel good, purposeful. You have a goal and destination in mind. No matter where you are, a barefoot walk in the neighborhood or park, or around your front or back lawn, is simply a gift. The only thing you must do is to put one foot in front of the other... just the way you do with words. One word after another, and a whole book is written!

JOURNAL PROMPT

When did you first experience walking? Whom did you walk with? Where? When did it become your daily habit?

⚘ *Day 193* ⚘

TODAY'S PRACTICE

Meditation: "Walking Through the Forest"   Read, write, and journal.

INSPIRATION

There are times when your work is intense, concentrated in a few days or ten, when you must be mentally alert and well rested, when you have to get up early and go to bed late at night, and you have no time to exercise or even walk.

But try to steal short intervals when you can walk. Walking helps when your mind is occupied with the intensity and pressure of work. It gives you focused time to think clearly about the problem at hand. It relieves you of stress. Although it doesn't seem possible, after walking, you magically feel restful.

While you walk, not only will the rhythm of your steps clear your mind and bring focus, but you will also do better in meetings and at seminars. You will better solve dilemmas of how to deal with people with whom you have to interact the whole day.

"A walk after lunch will allow you to see how minor skirmishes unknot themselves. You will foster patience to wait and tackle other conflict mindfully. And at the end of the day? Yes, walk again even if it feels like you are at the point of exhaustion. Believe it or not, if you take a short walk, you will be able to sleep better during the night," suggests Mindful Writer Martha Swiss.

JOURNAL PROMPT

Do you walk during workdays? Or only on weekends? In which ways does walking help you: physically, mentally, emotionally?

ꙮ *Day 194* ꙮ

TODAY'S PRACTICE

Meditation: "Walking Through the Forest"   Read, write, and journal.

INSPIRATION

My sister is a great walker. She lives on Mount Washington, just south of downtown Pittsburgh, and walks three to four miles every day. When we visit her, a morning walk is a must on our schedule. She leads us on neighborhood walks and trails on the mount.

She is fortunate to live in a charming, walkable neighborhood. In her company, our tennis shoes slap the pavement and our breath comes faster. Our conversation ranges from work to families and people we know.

By the time we return home, our limbs are loose and our blood flowing. We have solved the great questions of the day, or at least given them a good shake.

Despite cars whizzing by on one side and the contrasting view of Point Park – where the Monongahela and Allegheny Rivers join to form the Ohio River – our view of downtown Pittsburgh and the distant North Pittsburgh gives the site a uniqueness not found elsewhere in the city.

And the evening walk? It is almost always the One-Mile Walk that begins at the bottom of the Trimont building, where she lives. While the sky is dark on one side, the twinkling city lights greet us on the other.

A practicing psychiatrist, my sister believes it is easier for people to explore and articulate their emotions when they are engaged in a physical activity like walking. To make her new patients feel comfortable talking to her, she sometimes encourages them to walk with her.

JOURNAL PROMPT
Describe a regular walking route you take. Journal about the things you see, hear, and smell that you encounter on your walks.

❧ *Day 195* ☙

TODAY'S PRACTICE
Meditation: "Walking Through the Forest"   Read, write, and journal.

INSPIRATION

My husband and I started traveling in our early sixties. We now travel two times in a year. Our goal is to visit one U.S. state (preferably where a National Park is located) and one foreign country each year. We are against "seeing everything" in a state or a culture different than our own because that amounts to experiencing nothing. We do not want to exhaust ourselves either. While my schedule has always been flexible, my husband's job was stressful. His post-retirement is comparatively free of stress with plenty of time at hand. Walking in any new destination always adds to the adventure.

As our feet move, our pace is slow and our senses engaged. Even the mention of pacing reminds me of the mosaic sidewalks in Lisbon, Portugal, streamside sauntering in Kyoto, Japan, and making space through the throngs of people on the footpaths of Delhi, India. Entering little mom-and-pop shops, eating at hole-in-the-wall restaurants, or talking to street vendors gives an opportunity to communicate with local people and get a flavor of what they think and how they live.

Venice is a labyrinth of winding pedestrian pathways and waterways, a walker's dream come true. The exquisite shop windows, vibrant plazas, and ancient buildings are tucked throughout the city. They give a different flavor to the pleasure of walking. We spent a few days in this paradisical city wandering on foot and discovering places and things that weren't mentioned in travel guides. The smell of the sea surrounded everything, and the narrow streets and plazas, made of gray stones, shimmered after a rain shower. What added more sensuousness to the walks was the mouthwatering smells of delicious foods that wafted from restaurants. Exploring a city by walking adds small adventures to any travel.

JOURNAL PROMPT

Is there a city or town you went to for the first time and explored it extensively on foot? What memories does it conjure up? Describe what you saw, smelled, tasted, or touched.

❧ *Day 196* ❧

TODAY'S PRACTICE
Meditation: "Walking Through the Forest" Read, write, and journal.

INSPIRATION

"In every walk with Nature one receives
far more than he seeks." – John Muir

Walking mindfully in wooded spaces is a pleasure and necessity for mental and physical wellbeing. However, you may not find wilderness close to where you live, because it would mean an uncultivated tract of land, deep and dense with majestic trees and undergrowth, uninhabited by humans, inhabited by forest critters but blessed with solitude.

I do not suggest trekking through unfamiliar woods alone. Ask a friend or your spouse to accompany you. My husband and I explore new treks together. The appeal of adventure amidst the grandeur of towering trees and charm of ferny undergrowth is tantalizing. The great variety of flora growing without human intervention energizes me, as do the enlivening colors, sounds, and smells refresh.

At the back of my mind are the benefits of walking in nature – benefits to body, brain, and heart. They can be compared to the effects of meditation on body and heart-mind. Whereas in meditation your focus is on the breath, in walking your mind dwells in the present and takes in sensory data. The interchange is reciprocal. Nature wants you to take pleasure in its beauty as much as you want to bathe in its blessings. This is what Japanese call "forest bathing."

A mindful writer sauntering through unfamiliar woods has a feast of creative ideas and insights waiting to be revealed. Mulling over the work in progress allows your story to clarify further. Delightful scenery revitalizes you.

JOURNAL PROMPT
What is the deepest you've trekked into wilderness? If you've never walked in the forest, what holds you back? Describe what you imagine you may encounter there.

⊷ *Day 197* ⊶

TODAY'S PRACTICE

Meditation: "Walking Through the Forest" Read, write, and journal.

INSPIRATION

Each one of us experiences walking differently. It depends upon where you are, who you are, and your intention. Are you *forest bathing* or *window shopping*? Are you trekking or hurrying to a destination? Different scenarios suggest different images.

Every time you walk you are going somewhere. But the most beneficial walk is when you are going nowhere! Such a walk is truly productive for writers. Moving around the city is to know where you are, with intention and attitude. Nature walks can be more organic and less planned.

However, trekking on unpaved narrow paths in forested terrain or walking on a concrete road in a large city can both incite fear. Walking through the maze of a metropolis can be as worrisome as a lonely walk on a narrow muddy pathway. A densely populated metropolitan city can stir as much trepidation as a lonely walk through dense woods. What seems picturesque to one can be a deep, dark forest to another.

I grew up in New Delhi, a metropolis of high-rise buildings, suburbs, slums and farmhouses. The traffic, the people, the businesses were overwhelming. But I always took them for granted. I enjoyed the textures, smells, sounds, and sights – for a few hours – but then I wanted to be in a space where I could be alone and breathe freely. I prefer the walks around our quiet suburban neighborhood or through the parks in its vicinity. Mindful walking requires being able to walk freely and at leisure for the sake of walking.

JOURNAL PROMPT

How does your walking in the city differ from walks in the country?

✌ *Day 198* ☙

TODAY'S PRACTICE
Meditation: "Walking Through the Forest"   Read, write, and journal.

INSPIRATION

> *"Space, the final frontier. These are the voyages of the Starship Enterprise.*
> *Its five-year mission: to explore strange new worlds, to seek out new life*
> *and new civilizations, to boldly go where no man has gone before."*
> —Captain James T. Kirk

The quotes below are drawn from real astronauts when they walked on the surface no one had walked before. Each one of these resonate with the same exhilaration for exploration.

"That's one small step for man, one giant leap for mankind," declared American astronaut Neil Armstrong on July 20, 1969, when he put his left foot on the lunar surface. Stepping out of the Spaceship Apollo 11, he said, "(A) real moon's surface outside our window... 200 degrees Fahrenheit. The landing was a very high risk. Walking, far less risky. Genuine exploration at a place where no other human had ever stepped before."

Gene Cernan, on Apollo 17 in 1972 said, "Once I finally stepped on the moon, no matter what was to come of the next three days – or the rest of my life – nobody could take those steps from me. They will be there forever, however long forever is. The more nostalgic, perhaps, were the final steps. As I stepped on the ladder, I looked back at Earth in all its splendor – I call it sitting on God's front porch, looking home – then down at my last footprint and realized, 'Hey, I'm not coming this way again.' It's not like going to Grandma's farm, like I did as a kid, and coming back next summer..."

Don't these declarations give you goosebumps? They all had stepped out of their spaceships and just walked like we walk. But what was different was the place, the space, the ground on which they stepped.

You too can travel to a place you have never been before and feel almost the same exhilaration as the astronauts did.

JOURNAL PROMPT

Imagine… what would your words be if you ever stepped on the surface of the moon, another planet, or in an unfamiliar country?

✎ *Day 199* ✎

TODAY'S PRACTICE

Meditation: "Walking Through the Forest"   Read, write, and journal.

INSPIRATION

A walk in silent and natural surroundings is an opportunity to be absolutely outside yourself. Merge with your surroundings, push through your fears and the situations that intimidate you, get closer to your Authentic Self. That is certainly a reward in itself… and you're worth it.

There are times when I am disappointed with a new locale or circumstance, which makes me feel uneasy. Despite that, I make an attempt to push through and when the walk ends, there are always positive takeaways. When my husband was working, I occasionally accompanied him on business trips. I was nervous about leaving the hotel room and walking around in a new city. I'd convince myself to read a book instead or journal on the balcony as the city came alive on the street below. But the thought of adventuring on foot would nibble at the back of my mind. Once I attempted to leave the room and adventure into town on foot, it took me to another level of experience.

In Nice, France, I learned to make my way around on my own for ten days while my husband was in meetings. I found a wonderful art gallery and had the pleasure of meeting vendors at the flower market – a florist, a baker, a craftsman. We communicated mostly in gestures and it was delightful. But the walk from the hotel to the market was the most pleasurable part of the day. The wet paved stones in Saleya Market, the scents wafting from variegated bundles of flowers, vendors hawking their wares, observing the sunshine breaking through the canopy of the makeshift stalls, watching a man pick a flower and give it to his beloved, tasting homemade chocolate... all left unforgettable impressions, nurturing my previous memories and sprouting new ones.

On my way back, I spotted my husband returning to the hotel early. What a delightful surprise it was for me to encounter him as it was for him, especially when I offered him the flower I had picked for him.

JOURNAL PROMPT

Take a mindful walk. Bring a small notebook with you, and write down what you observe around you.

ꙮ *Day 200* ꙮ

TODAY'S PRACTICE

Meditation: "Walking Through the Forest"   Read, write, and journal.

INSPIRATION

Hiking a long trail can lead to self-understanding. You begin the trail with an intention to leave behind the worries and stress of your regular life, your continual social and familial involvement, and ordinary communication with others.

Even though most of the time you know where you're headed on a trail, you never quite know where it will end. You may walk a loop trail so you return to your starting point or hike a designated number of miles and then retrace your steps. You'll notice how things look different on the way back. You may see sights you missed going out. Somehow the same trees assume different shapes. No hike is ever the same!

A trail takes you over the hills, under trees, over rocky paths, alongside a bubbling stream or shore of a lake. Focus entirely on what surrounds you. Immerse yourself in the natural beauty. Sometimes, when you run into an obstacle – a flooded trail overrun by a stream, muck after rains, or a rocky path – with your boots soaked up to your ankles, the trail may not feel pleasurable at the moment. You may take a detour to finally reach your destination. After the hike is over, you will return home with a feeling of triumph.

"Getting lost on a long trail is common. You hope for the best and keep walking, at times to exhaustion. But doesn't such an experience remind you of the ups and downs and trials and tribulations of your daily life? How many stressful moments and anxiety-inducing events have you tackled... and when life returns to normalcy, you sigh and thank God for regular days!" observes Mindful Writer Alicia Stankay.

JOURNAL PROMPT

Write about something unusual that happened when you trekked on a trail but got lost or came across unexpected obstacles.

❧ *Day 201* ☙

TODAY'S PRACTICE

Meditation: "Heartful"   Read, write, and journal.

INSPIRATION

What happens after the first few minutes of your walking time? Thoughts settle. You are mentally relaxed. Your senses sharpen. You may see the landscape blanketed with white. You hear nothing. Smell nothing. Or you may see green everywhere with variegated bushes and myriad scents. Birds in the trees call your attention, and you notice rotting fungus protruding from the base of a tree trunk. You are enraptured by such contrasting lifeforms: plants, insects, birds, humans.

Do you walk in deep winter months when snow has fallen and your neighborhood looks like a fairytale setting? When the leafless trees lining the roadside are frozen with transparent covering and reach through the blue air toward the brilliant sunlit sky?

It's absolutely quiet then. You can hear yourself breathe. But when you walk, the snow crunches under your boots. The chilled air tingles your nose and courses through your body, expanding your heart and lungs. A car rumbles in the distance. No birds chirp. No leaves swish. You walk with your focus on the inhalation and exhalation and see little diamonds shimmering on the ground. You don't want to look up or sideways as your concentration is on the feet that may sense a slippery spot over the deceptive fluffy snow drifts.

"Experiencing different seasons as you walk cultivates a craving for this short respite from your daily routine. Physical movement reenergizes and provides precious time for contemplation. Your toes and fingers may tingle with a chill or you may sweat. But when you head toward home, you can't wait to sip that hot sweet tea or frothy hot chocolate," writes Mindful Writer Alicia Stankay.

JOURNAL PROMPT

Which season is your favorite and why? Is there a season you don't like? Why? Could you find a way to resolve your issue and enjoy that season again?

⋙ *Day 202* ⋘

TODAY'S PRACTICE

Meditation: "Heartful"   Read, write, and journal.

INSPIRATION

Walking not only gives the precious time to settle your thoughts, invigorate your body, and open your heart, but time to absorb the new feelings that awaken. Your writer's mind translates them into raw, undeveloped, unripe words that may later become part of a story, essay, or poem.

For Mary Oliver, a Pulitzer-prize winning American poet, "the door to the woods is the door to the temple." It is up to you to use it to understand yourself, contemplate your life, or improve yourself in one way or another. A moment on your mindful walk may turn into a portal to a creative project. You just need to pay attention to things you normally ignore or are not interested in.

Original ideas flow in when your body is busy moving. When you are quietly moving your body, you may get lost in thought. Bring your attention back to your breath and ask why, how, what, and when about your work in progress. Be mindful of your breath and watch new ideas float in to further stir your imagination – all fodder for your stories.

If you sit with the blank screen or an empty page waiting for an idea to develop, you would be wasting your time. But as you walk, ideas come out of nowhere. Upon your return to your desk, the words related to your project or a new idea flow uninhibited. The first outpouring of words is raw. You can rewrite and revise the underdeveloped piece until the draft satisfies the strong emotional flow you felt as you walked. Then let it sit for a few days to be revisited and reread aloud on the way to becoming a final draft.

JOURNAL PROMPT

Try 20-30 minutes of walking today to heighten your awareness, giving way to uninhibited feelings and thoughts. It may lead to writing a few lines, a stanza, a page or more. Try it!

ﻬ *Day 203* ﻬ

TODAY'S PRACTICE

Meditation: "Heartful"   Read, write, and journal.

INSPIRATION

From walking outdoors to cooking in an indoor kitchen... let's explore some Indian recipes!

During summer months, I rotate menus between grilled or baked fish with vegetables and rice pilaf, to pasta with scallops or shrimps in tomato sauce, perhaps order out for Chinese, or make goat or lamb with plain rice and greens that taste a bit like collards but are sweeter. My husband, Manoj, grills tandoori chicken and vegetables, or on rare occasions fish, or broils steaks in the oven which he serves with mushroom sauce, baked potatoes, and green beans, broccoli, or asparagus.

But from late fall to early spring, I often cook the dishes featured in this final week of our encounter with nonverbal activities. They are delicious! In selecting these recipes I considered two things. First, the recipes should suit the taste of a wide population, and second, the preparation must be easy. If you follow the recipes, the cooking should be simple.

Basmati Rice and Mixed Vegetable Pulao (Pilaf)

1 cup basmati rice
½ lb. store bought paneer (optional)
½ lb. mixed frozen vegetables
2-3 Tbsp ghee or butter
1 tsp whole cumin seeds

¼ tsp ground cinnamon
⅛ tsp ground nutmeg
1½-2 cups water
salt to taste

Wash 1 cup Basmati rice two or three times until the water is clear. Cut slab of paneer (Indian cooking cheese) into small cubes. Fry in vegetable oil until golden brown. Defrost mixed vegetables of your choice. Melt butter or ghee in a medium pot. Lower heat and add half teaspoon of black and white cumin. Let sizzle and brown for 5-10 seconds. Add rinsed rice. Mix until grains are coated with butter or ghee. Add vegetables and fried paneer and mix well. Add 1½ cup water. Mix and add ¼ teaspoon of cinnamon, 1/8 teaspoon nutmeg and salt to taste. Mix and let mixture boil for 10-12 minutes. Stir well. Simmer covered for 15 minutes. Check a few grains to see if they are soft and fluffy. If not, cover and let simmer 5-8 more minutes.

Serve steaming hot with cucumber and tomato salad.

Later when you have learned how to make all the seven dishes, you can serve cucumber raita or mint and walnut chutney with this dish.

ᘓ *Day 204* ᘗ

TODAY'S PRACTICE
Meditation: "Heartful"   Read, write, and journal.

INSPIRATION

I cook plain rice at least two times a week and rice with green peas once a month. I make extra servings to save for the days when I cook a dish that goes well with rice.

Plain Basmati Rice

1 cup rice
2-3 cups water
2-3 tsp butter or ghee

Wash and rinse the rice. Let soak in water for 30-60 minutes. Drain in a colander. Heat ghee or butter in a medium pot. When it sizzles, add rice and fry 2-4 minutes. Add water. Stir and let boil on medium-high heat for 10 minutes. Stir, cover, and let simmer for 20 minutes. Serve with any of the vegetarian or nonvegetarian dishes we are going to learn to cook this week.

OR

Rice with Green Peas

1 cup rice
½ cup frozen green peas
2-3 cups water

2-3 tsp butter or ghee
salt to taste

Wash and rinse the rice. Let rice soak in water for 30-60 minutes. Drain in a colander. Heat the ghee or butter in a medium pot. Add whole cumin seeds. When they sizzle, add rice and mix for 3 minutes until the grains glisten. Add green peas and mix for 2 minutes. Add water, cover and bring to a boil for 10 minutes. Stir, cover, and let simmer for 15-20 additional minutes.

AND

Cucumber Raita

1 English cucumber
1 green chili

8-12 oz yogurt
salt and cayenne pepper to taste

Peel seedless cucumber. Grate it and squeeze. Chop green chili. Combine in a bowl. Add beaten yogurt, salt, and cayenne pepper to taste. Mix well and let the flavors combine. Serve as a side dish.

✌ *Day 205* ✍

TODAY'S PRACTICE	
Meditation: "Heartful"	Read, write, and journal.

INSPIRATION

Fluffy and Fun Indian Bread: Puri

4 oz whole wheat floor
4 oz all-purpose flour
pinch of salt

¼ pint water
1 tsp melted ghee or ½ tsp vegetable oil

Mix the whole wheat flour (*atta*) and all-purpose flour and a pinch of salt. Make a stiff but pliable dough using water. Knead with melted ghee for 8-10 minutes. Leave covered under a wet cloth or paper towel for 20-30 minutes. Divide the dough into 16 equal pieces. Shape into rounds. You may use olive or vegetable oil to shape them. With a rolling pin, roll out each sphere into thin puris. Heat vegetable oil or ghee in a wok. Let it come to smoking point and gently drop in the rolled puri. Turn immediately and press with perforated wire, frying each slice till it swells and acquires a light brown color. Remove and drain on a paper towel. Serve hot with any Indian pickle, mint, and walnut chutney or cucumber raita.

AND

Mint, Cilantro, and Walnut Chutney

Chutney, pickles, or yogurt raita taste delicious with any rice dish. Today we'll make green chutney that I hope will become your regular side dish with basmati. You may buy delicious mango, hot lemon, sweet lemon, or carrot pickles at any Indian grocery store.

4 oz mint leaves
4 oz cilantro or flat parsley leaves
½ lemon
¼ c yogurt
⅓ cup walnuts

1 small onion
1 green chili, seeded
½ tsp salt
½ tsp sugar

Wash mint and cilantro leaves and separate mint leaves from their twigs. If you don't like the taste of cilantro, you may replace with flat leaf parsley. Add leaves to the blender with juice of one-half lemon and blend. Then add yogurt, walnuts, onion, chili, salt, and sugar to taste. Blend until the mixture is pureed.

Chutney can be refrigerated up to 2 weeks in an airtight container.

ꙮ *Day 206* ꙮ

TODAY'S PRACTICE

Meditation: "Heartful"   Read, write, and journal.

INSPIRATION

When I'm cooking mindfully, completely absorbed in all my senses, my thoughts settle down and I receive great ideas either about my writing work in progress or a pressing family matter. Similar to drawing and painting (once you have learned the basic skills), preparing dinner can be productive in more than one way.

Cooking is one of the few nonverbal hobbies that incorporates all the five senses. The sense of sight is involved as you prepare the dish – see the colors of the vegetables and meats; smell the freshly cut vegetables and spices being ground, roasted and fried; hear the food sizzle and bubble; touch as you peel, slice, wash the ingredients, and use your fingers to eat; and finally taste... of course, taste!

In my experience, not only the senses but also your feelings affect the taste of the dish. For instance, if you are upset (tired, angry, jealous, sad, frustrated) and not ready to enjoy cooking, your food will not taste its best. Honestly, when I'm not feeling my normal self, I prefer ordering out.

But the good news is there are always leftovers. Homemade Indian food tastes better the next day, or the next! What do you think?

Chickpeas with Tomato and Lemon

4 Tbsp vegetable oil
1 tsp whole cumin seeds
1 medium onion, peeled and chopped
½ tsp ground cinnamon
½ tsp ground nutmeg
½ tsp ground cloves
3 cloves garlic, peeled and minced

1-inch piece of ginger, peeled and grated
2 Tbsp tomato paste
2 cans chickpeas (garbanzo)
salt to taste
juice of ½ lemon

Heat oil in a large heavy skillet. When hot, add whole cumin seeds. As soon as they begin to darken, add chopped onions. Stir and fry for 7 minutes. Turn heat to low and add cinnamon, nutmeg, cloves, and coriander. Mix and add garlic and ginger, stirring for 3 minutes. Add tomato paste. Drain the chickpeas, retaining a couple tablespoons of the liquid. Pour this and the chickpeas into the skillet. Add salt and lemon juice. Mix, cover, and let the flavors combine for 10 minutes. Stir gently now and then. Serve with basmati rice and quartered tomatoes, sweet onion slivers, and green chilies.

⊱ *Day 207* ⊰

TODAY'S PRACTICE

Meditation: "Heartful"   Read, write, and journal.

INSPIRATION

Chickpeas with tomato and lemon is one of the yummiest vegetarian dishes I cook. It is zesty, savory, and ample with any Indian breads especially *puri*, fried bread which you have already learned to make.

Chicken Drumstick and Thighs with Ginger

chicken drumsticks and thighs	1 tsp ground ginger powder
1 whole cauliflower head	1½ tsp turmeric powder
2 large red potatoes	½ tsp cayenne pepper
1 medium onion	½ tsp garam masala
1 green chili	½ cup yogurt
1" fresh ginger	salt to taste

Heat oil in a large heavy skillet. When hot, add whole cumin seeds, and as soon as they begin to darken, add one teaspoon sugar. Let the sugar caramelize first on medium and then low heat. Add the rest of the spices and stir for a few seconds then add 2-3 tablespoons water. Add cut chicken drumsticks and thighs to the spice mixture. Mix well, cover, and cook on medium heat for 10 minutes. Let the flavors combine. Add ½ cup of beaten yogurt. Mix well and cook for 10 more minutes. Sprinkle with garam masala, stir well, and let most of the water absorb on low heat.

✎ *Day 208* ✎

INSPIRATION

At our family get-togethers, cauliflower with potatoes is a must. Manoj, our daughters, their husbands, and our grandchildren relish it with rice or other Indian breads such as roti, nan, or puree. Hopefully it will please your family as well. Enjoy!

Cauliflower and Potatoes

1 whole cauliflower head
2 large red potatoes
1 medium onion
1 green chili
1" fresh ginger
1 tsp ginger powder

1½ tsp turmeric powder
½ tsp cayenne pepper
½ tsp garam masala
mango powder (or juice of ½ lemon)
salt to taste

Cut cauliflower into one-inch florets. Slice two red potatoes into same-size pieces. Chop one medium onion and one-inch-long fresh ginger. Seed one green chili. Heat three tablespoons vegetable oil in a large skillet or pot. Add one level teaspoon of whole white cumin seeds to hot oil. Lower heat and let sizzle for 30 seconds. Add chopped onion. Over medium heat, stir until onions are translucent. Add potato pieces and seeded chili. Add all the remaining spices. Finally, add mango powder (or juice of one-half lemon). Otherwise, add a couple of tablespoons of water. Add the cauliflower florets and mix everything until all the pieces are covered with spices. Lower the heat and cover the vegetables. Let the mixture cook for 10 minutes. Then stir well and cover again, but leave a little slit for steam to escape. Let simmer over medium heat 10-15 more minutes. Check for tenderness and taste. Leave on high heat for 4-5 minutes. The last few minutes will brown the vegetables at the bottom. Let cool, then mix well and serve warm.

✍ Day 209 ✍

TODAY'S PRACTICE	
Meditation: "Heartful"	Read, write, and journal.

INSPIRATION

Sweet Milk Vermicelli

6 oz vermicelli
½ pint hot milk
4 Tbsp sugar or brown sugar
¼ tsp cardamom powder
¼ tsp cinnamon powder

⅛ tsp nutmeg powder
saffron (opt.)
3 Tbsp golden raisins
¼ cup halved almonds

To speed up cooking time, heat 3 cups of milk in the microwave. Pour the heated milk into a medium size pot with vermicelli. Add four tablespoons of white or brown sugar. Add cardamom, cinnamon, nutmeg, and two pinches of saffron (optional). Stir until vermicelli is soft and sugar melted. Add raisins and almonds. Serve warm or cold.

OR

Brown Sweet Vermicelli (Sewian)

3 oz ghee
6 whole green cardamoms
6 cloves
6 oz vermicelli
¼ pt hot milk
12 oz sugar

⅛ tsp saffron threads
4 drops vanilla extract or kewra
    essence
1 oz chopped almonds
1 oz chopped pistachios

Heat ghee in a medium pan over medium heat, then add crushed cardamoms and cloves and stir for 1 minute. Add vermicelli and fry until rich brown in color. Add hot milk, mix thoroughly, and cover the pan. Cook 5-7 minutes, stirring occasionally to avoid sticking. When the milk dries up, remove from heat. Add sugar and mix. Simmer until mixture is dry. Dissolve a few saffron threads in vanilla extract and 1 teaspoon water, then sprinkle over the sewian. Stir with a fork. Decorate with chopped almonds and pistachios. Serve warm.

⤳ *Day 210* ⤸

TODAY'S PRACTICE

Meditation: "Heartful"   Read, write, and journal.

INSPIRATION

How many dishes out of the seven above did you cook this month? Was it fun for you? Did your family relish the spicy and unfamiliar smells and tastes? Did you?

If not, what about cooking comfort food that you missed while you were courageously experimenting with my recipes?

END OF MONTH PROMPT

Journal about your own hobbies and nonverbal activities you regularly participate in. Then write what inspired you to add one more wordless activity to your day. Was it walking, cooking, gardening, or any other hobby?

Month 8

Mindfulness and Travel

Suggested Readings

Wild: From Lost to Found on the Pacific Crest Trail
Cheryl Strayed, 2012.

Travels with Charley: In Search of America
John Steinbeck, 1962.

The Art of Pilgrimage:
The Seeker's Guide to Making Travel Sacred
Phil Cousineau, 1998.

Eat, Pray, Love: One Woman's Search for Everything
Across Italy, India, and Indonesia
Elizabeth Gilbert, 2006.

Around India in 80 Trains
Monisha Rajesh, 2012.

༄ *Day 211* ༄

TODAY'S PRACTICE

Go for a walk, cook, garden, make art or craft, or engage in a nonverbal activity of your choice once or twice a year travel to an unknown destination either within the country or to a foreign land.

Standing Meditation: "Spaciousness"   Read, write, and journal.

INSPIRATION

I believe travel is like deep reading in 3D. Travel leads the way to self-exploration. Attentive observation at new places leads to inner scrutiny and understanding. Looking at a new world is a sheer delight.

A trip with my husband, Manoj, tracing the last leg of Lewis and Clark's Expedition from the east to the west coast was an adventure of a lifetime. After reading *Undaunted Courage* and *Journals of Lewis and Clark* (National Geographic Edition) we took a flight to Portland, Oregon, then embarked on a boat that sailed upon the waters of the Columbia and Snake Rivers.

President Thomas Jefferson had envisioned an expedition that would boldly navigate the heart of our country, mapping rivers, land, and mountains; gathering information about agricultural potential; collecting vocabularies of various Indian languages and the culture; and bringing back specimens and scientific descriptions of unknown animals and plants.

Jefferson's vision became a reality when 30-year-old Captain Meriwether Lewis sailed on a keelboat and two pirogues from the Ohio River on May 1803. His crew consisted of 29 young volunteers, along with his co-captain William Clark, and one Shoshone Indian woman with her baby, plus Lewis's Newfoundland dog, Seaman.

From Ohio they sailed on to the Missouri River to discover the passage west was not solely via waterways. They had to cross treacherous mountains. After crossing the Bitterroot range, they sailed the Columbia

River, finally reaching their destination near the town now called Astoria in Oregon.

They suffered attacks from maddening mosquitoes, slept in drenched clothes, and treaded wild prairies in elk leather moccasins that provided their feet and ankles little protection from the slashing of prickly pear hidden in the tall grass. Extreme hunger even forced them to slaughter dogs and colts for food (luckily not Seaman).

The crew demonstrated what could be accomplished with an audacious vision, focused intention, meticulous planning, and physical strength. Their journey took two years, four months, and nine days. Why did reading about Lewis and Clark's journey affect me deeply? Why did I feel the need to follow their path, albeit only partly? What was the cause of my quest?

JOURNAL PROMPT

Journal about a time when reading a book or watching a movie galvanized you into action. What action did you take and how did the experience make you feel?

✍ *Day 212* ✌

TODAY'S PRACTICE

Standing Meditation: "Spaciousness"   Read, write, and journal.

INSPIRATION

From the Portland airport we took a cab to Red Lion Hotel on Jantzen Beach in Hayden Island, Oregon. The eastern sky threatened with thunderclouds, pouring down with a vengeance, while the western sky welcomed us with dazzling sunlight. Our hotel balcony overlooked the Columbia River, partly hidden behind pine trees. Was it the same river upon which sailed the Corps of Discovery? I couldn't believe my fortune. The next morning I saw our boat, "American Harmony," docked right next to the pines!

Brilliant orange sun greeted us. We had time for a walk on the trail that ran parallel to the river. Through the pure air the cumulus clouds announced themselves with such confidence that I straightened my shoulders. One side of the trail was studded with California poppies, yellow daisies, and wild grasses. Did Lewis and Clark admire these blossoms as they passed by? The other side was lined in picturesque cottages with well-manicured gardens.

I couldn't help wondering whether Lewis and Clark had passed these banks. How many centuries of historic secrets was the primeval river concealing? The Columbia shimmered silently.

"Lovely view!" said a woman hugging a teacup with both her hands as she gazed at the river.

"Isn't it!" I responded with a smile. Casual conversation revealed the flowers were a recent planting. I felt silly for being disappointed.

We embarked the boat, settled in our room, and walked up to soak in the January sun. Another couple had the same idea. Our talk inevitably moved to Lewis and Clark. "Did you get to read their journals?" I asked. The woman had not gotten past "today it rained... today sun showed itself... we were soaked to the bone... it was cloudy again..." They both laughed and the man confessed, "To be honest, I read Cliff Notes on the expedition." My husband Manoj chuckled. "I think I'll do the same."

In that case you'd never know, I said to myself, *how "mortified" the members of the Corps of Discovery were when their clothes were soaking wet and how chill ran through their bones, or when Lewis discovered a new bird species and drew it meticulously in his journal. Or how after their fatigue and hunger pains they enjoyed a meal of elk meat, roasted tubers, and whiskey.*

"Mortified" was Lewis's favorite word. When discomforted, horrified, appalled, annoyed, or ashamed, he always expressed the sentiment as, "I was mortified." A further aside, Clark's favorite phrase was "etc., etc., etc.," written so many times I wondered if it wouldn't be better to use the actual words to save the word count.

As our boat sailed from Portland toward Astoria, one thought surfaced: Born in India as I was, molded from the clay of a distant motherland, was it possible for my dust to merge with the dust of the land I had chosen to spend the rest of my life in?

Journal about the difference between what you imagined about a new place while reading a book and the actual experience of being there.

❧ Day 213 ↩

TODAY'S PRACTICE
Standing Meditation: "Spaciousness"   Read, write, and journal.

INSPIRATION

In early November 1805, Lewis and Clark glided into the northern side of the mouth of the Columbia River in dugout canoes. With starved looks, tattered clothes rotting on their bodies, and disheveled hair, they neither had the energy nor wherewithal to moor. Clark named the spot Dismal Nitch.

A group of local Indians arrived in elegantly carved and painted canoes, communicating with a few words of English they had learned from fur traders.

The captains had intended to meet the last trading ship of the season to obtain badly needed supplies and send back journals and specimens of plants and animals to President Jefferson. But a severe winter storm prevented this. This is "the most disagreeable time I have ever experienced," Clark wrote.

Finally on November 15 the weather calmed, and they were able to view the Pacific Ocean from the cliffs above the pounding surf. They had arrived at the western end of their voyage – Cape Disappointment, named some 17 years earlier when another captain had failed to cross the bar in search of an entrance to the Columbia.

At the end of their westward journey Clark wrote, "O! the joy!" They camped for a week, but no food was to be found. The Indians informed them that if they relocated, they would find plenty of elk to hunt on the southern side of the river. They moved their camp and in less than 20 days they built a seven-room log cabin, Fort Clatsop, where they spent the winter, eating elk for breakfast, lunch, and dinner, supplementing it with whale blubber, roots, fish, duck, beaver. They made salt from the waters of the Pacific Ocean to season their food, and fashioned clothes and moccasins from durable elk leather. Using the slow-burning method Indians taught them, they built six dugout canoes from ponderosa pine and on March 23, 1806, they departed eastward for home.

Manoj and I visited Dismal Nitch and the cliffs of Cape Disappointment where a lighthouse is now located. I imagined seeing the land, the water, and the wilderness the way it was long before the country became the United States of America. Pride and tenderness spread through my body to experience the pristine unexploited open spaces and feel closer to the land of my adopted country.

The cause of my quest slowly revealed itself: an unease about dying.

JOURNAL PROMPT

In the middle of writing something from your heart, do you sometimes feel that it may bore the readers and they might stop reading? Do you go ahead and write it anyway?

✎ *Day 214* ✎

TODAY'S PRACTICE

Standing Meditation: "Spaciousness"   Read, write, and journal.

INSPIRATION

Small historic towns, nestled in beautiful landscapes, reflect the persona of the American people – friendly and kind, proud of themselves and their home. Before taking this cruise, we had visited cosmopolitan cities in the United States – New York, Washington, Chicago, Boston, and Los Angeles – and capital cities of the world – Cape Town, Beijing, Tokyo, New Delhi, London, and Lhasa. We had gazed at great monuments and sailed long rivers. But this time we walked through small American towns we had not even heard about.

Had they not been on the path of the Lewis and Clark voyage, they would never have been on my itinerary.

Dalles, Oregon, was the first such town. Settled in 1840, its population is 16,000. Lewis and Clark camped there for three days at Rockfort Campsite on October 25-27, 1805, on their way to the Pacific Ocean, and then on April 15-18, 1806, on their way back home. A rocky high point allowed them to make celestial observations, hunt for food, repair canoes, and negotiate to buy horses from local Indians.

For me, Dalles became exemplary of small-town America, bringing me closer to the land I have chosen to call home.

JOURNAL PROMPT

Do you remember having an epiphany during travel, but only after returning home? Or only becoming aware of it when you reminisce later or look at photos?

❧ *Day 215* ❧

TODAY'S PRACTICE

Standing Meditation: "Spaciousness"   Read, write, and journal.

INSPIRATION

Three other small Oregon towns we visited were Cascade Locks, Umatilla, and Pendleton. "Columbia is too powerful to navigate," wrote Clark. In Umatilla, they purchased horses from the local Walla Walla tribe, then kept two canoes to ferry their supplies and proceeded upriver on foot. With "most excellent young horses" they feasted on beaver and otter and "experienced the best traveling on the western side of the Rockies."

The town of Cascade Locks takes its name from eight locks that were built in the 1870s to improve navigation over the cascades of the Columbia River, which no doubt Lewis and Clark would have appreciated. These locks were eventually submerged and replaced by Bonneville Lock and Dam. The Bridge of the Gods spans Columbia.

The town of Pendleton used to be a booming mini city of saloons, card rooms, working girls, Chinese laundries, and opium dens. Chinese laborers were brought here when railroads expanded westward. We toured the seedy underbelly of Pendleton that connects narrow passages hidden below the streets of what used to be a bustling market above. The regular and the nefarious coexisted.

After a day's hard work, men entertained themselves in brothels, gambling and drinking alcohol. Regular businesses, such as candy stores and butchers, shared the secret underground world with bars and bordellos. Some of the former bordellos are still active but the prohibition years are now staged with mannequins, furniture, and props, trying to recapture the spirit of the period.

JOURNAL PROMPT

Are you from a small town or have you visited one? What are your feelings about a place like that?

ꙮ *Day 216* ꙮ

TODAY'S PRACTICE

Standing Meditation: "Spaciousness"   Read, write, and journal.

INSPIRATION

On September 23, 1806, the Corps of Discovery returned to St. Louis. An excerpt from Lewis's letter to President Jefferson reads: "Sir, it is with pleasure that I announce to you the safe arrival of myself and party with our papers and baggage. No accident has deprived us of a single member of our party since I last wrote you from the Mandan in April 1804."

In reply the President wrote: "I received, my dear Sir, with unspeakable joy your letter of September 23 announcing the return of yourself, Captain Clarke & your party in good health to St. Louis... The length of time without hearing from you had begun to be felt awfully..."

The journals of Lewis and Clark include drawings and descriptions of animals, birds, and plants unknown to the western world, vocabularies of dozens of Indian languages, and maps for thousands of miles of rivers and mountains. They achieved what they had set out to do, focused on an impossible mission, and returning home triumphant.

The twin towns of Lewiston, Idaho, and Clarkston, Washington, our last stops, commemorate the two captains and are located on opposite banks of the Columbia. Here we rode a speed boat through Hells Canyon, North America's deepest river gorge, nearly 2,000 feet deeper than the Grand Canyon. The ride felt so ordinary as compared to what the two captains had experienced that I kept marveling at their audacity and endurance.

JOURNAL PROMPT
Does traveling provide a break from your regular routine to help you see deeper into yourself or solve some of life's serious questions?

ꙮ *Day 217* ꙮ

TODAY'S PRACTICE
Standing Meditation: "Spaciousness"   Read, write, and journal.

INSPIRATION
Experiencing just a fraction of the Lewis and Clark Expedition showered me with gold dust of America's past. I'm a world citizen, yet after the journey that followed Lewis and Clark expedition, the trunk of my life's tree felt rooted in American soil. Its branches that have spread out to the world will continue to grow and flourish. I truly believe that America is beautiful! And I'm proud that it is home.

JOURNAL PROMPT
If you could choose one place in your country to visit, where would it be? If you could visit one foreign country in the world, where would it be?

ᘺ *Day 218* ᘫ

TODAY'S PRACTICE

Standing Meditation: "Spaciousness"   Read, write, and journal.

INSPIRATION

While trekking near Sedona, fleeting thoughts subsided amidst the beauty of the nature. I breathed in the sage-scented mesas and walked on orange-dusted pathways. The sun scorched my skin and frequently made me close my eyes. My Authentic Self awakened to coalesce with the Universe. The magnificent Cathedral and Bell Rocks mesmerized... the cliffs, mesas, and fringes of juniper forests set against searing blue sky.

Next morning we rose early. We were at a hotel a few hundred feet from the Grand Canyon. Hot cups of coffee warmed our hands as we took satisfying sips and settled on a viewing bench. Many miles in the distance, at a 180-degree angle, we saw a hundred shades of gray. A sheen of orange in the eastern sky announced the arrival of the sun. Its radiance replaced distant mist over the canyons. Trees became visible. Suddenly, tips of the canyon peaks alit. The earth was reborn!

Sun painted the peaks then lavishly bathed the earth from top to bottom in orange gold. Everything – the canyons and the trees: blue spruce, firs, pines, junipers, and the ones I do not recognize – glistened in shades of viridian. Sun rays penetrated the gorge, making visible the cascading Colorado River below.

I feel at one with the sun and the trees and the river gorge. One with all that exists. The only sound I hear is my exhalation. Everything is luminous. I hear birds, then people. I feel immortal. I'm the earth.

When my ego returns, the thought arrives that this act is repeated every single morning. It makes my heart sing. At that moment, I fall head over heels in love with Mother Earth.

Write an outline about instantly falling in love with a landscape – more specifically with a mountain, a lake, or a tree you can't stop admiring. How would you consummate this relationship?

ꙮ *Day 219* ꙮ

TODAY'S PRACTICE
Standing Meditation: "Spaciousness"   Read, write, and journal.

INSPIRATION

Our stay at Denali National Park in Alaska remained covered with mist and clouds. The guide had promised an unforgettable view of the Denali (The High One) Mountain peak but weather was beyond his control. Disappointed, on our way to the airport, the driver took a detour and stopped the bus in a random parking lot. Our tour guide asked us to follow him to the base of a low hill. We ascended, chatting and laughing, until we arrived at the top.

Behold, Mount Denali!

My feet firm on the ground, I witnessed the sounds of silence. Snow-covered peaks touched the sky, enthralling, summoning. Below, the tundra valley was ornamented with pastures of varied greens. A menagerie of wildlife, no larger than moving dots, grazed the gentle grassy slopes caressed by soft sunlight and a mild breeze. I became drunk on the rugged beauty and utter silence. Time slowed. Surroundings turned luminous. This is how the earth must have looked at its birth.

My breath synchronized with the heaving soil, like a living cell in the body of the universe. *Each and every microscopic speck in this vast universe matters. I matter. Am I not made from the same stuff as the mountain, the glaciers, the fiords, the rivers, and the trees? They all live in me as much as I live in them.*

Rapture enveloped me.

From my study, I have a new appreciation for the blue spruce, hemlocks, and maples that are visible from the windows. My perspective has shifted. I feel connected to the suburban-bred deer, squirrels, and birds, reminding me of the grand beauty and awe-inspiring mystery of the austere and pristine beauty of the Sedona Mountains, Grand Canyon, and Denali.

JOURNAL PROMPT

Journal about the moment when you encountered a natural element such as a rushing river, a waterfall, a natural rock bridge, a tree that seemed almost so alive that you could converse with it.

༄ *Day 220* ༄

TODAY'S PRACTICE

Standing Meditation: "Spaciousness"   Read, write, and journal.

INSPIRATION

On our way to Yellowstone National Park in Wyoming, the bus stopped for a photo break of the spectacular peaks of the Teton mountain range. The driver pointed to a log cabin in the distance, a cottage in the middle of a meadow of swaying yellow flowers and wild grass.

I hurried to the restroom beyond it, but noticed a sign board: "The Episcopal Chapel of the Transfiguration." I wondered, *What exactly does transfiguration mean?* When I returned, people had already seen the chapel and left. Its sparce decoration and plain log walls moved me. A wooden cross flanked two glass vases with fresh-cut flowers. Behind this display was a large glass panel. The space felt cool and comfortable. I chose a corner seat of the front pew. A ray of sunlight through the glass was blinding. I couldn't see what was behind it. I sat in silence and closed my eyes, inhaling and exhaling deeply. A picturesque image of the Tetons floated to mind. How blessed I was to view this glorious site in person! Peace enveloped me.

When I opened my eyes, the glare was gone. The glass panel was framing the glorious Teton peaks. It so mesmerized me that I couldn't move. The Divine within the chapel had exploded beyond boundaries. Finite had transformed into boundless infinite. *That without is within you!* The wooden cross had transfigured into my supreme Guru – dispeller of darkness, spiritual guide enlightening me about the nature of my existence. This is God!

"Let's go! People are waiting," my husband called from the door. I staggered to the door but was totally grounded within.

Our next stop was Yellowstone, America's first national park. The power of the Great Falls and the force with which Old Faithful erupted seemed a manifestation of the same Divine Intelligence I had experienced in the chapel.

Later I looked up the word transfiguration – a form that completely changes into a grander beauty and greater spiritual majesty. Isn't transfiguration what you and I are doing here on our journey together? Finding direction toward our limitless selves? Empowering our creative and spiritual Self, and learning to come down the mountain to live with majestic joy, the likes of which we have never felt before?

JOURNAL PROMPT
Similar to getting absorbed in a spiritual experience, have you had a feeling like this when listening to music you love or watching a movie? Journal about that experience.

১৩ *Day 221* ৫৬

TODAY'S PRACTICE
Standing Meditation: "Spaciousness"   Read, write, and journal.

INSPIRATION
Nature is imbued with *numen* (spirit). Rudolf Otto, the German phenomenologist of religions, qualified the numinous (spiritual) as being *mysterium, fascinans et tremendum.* In other words: mysterious, awe-inspiring, and filled with terror. Until February 2020, my

numinous experiences had been awe-inspiring and filled with deep mystery... but never terrifying. I connected terror with nature's wrath in the form of storms, cyclones, hurricanes, fires, famine, and such. Not until we sailed through the bayous and marshlands in Slidell, Louisiana, did I experience Otto's *tremendum*.

The sky was overcast on the morning of our tour on the Pearl River. We stepped into the boat ignoring the ominous dark clouds. As soon as we sat on the bench the big raindrops pitter-pattered on the canvas roof. The guide described how the marshland would look if it was a sunny day. Gray days, he claimed discouraged the appearance of pelicans, egrets, blue herons, woodpeckers, otters and racoons; in the bayous hid fish, shrimp, poisonous snakes, crocodiles, and black bear.

How we wished it was not such a miserable, dark, and cold day!

Heavy fog rose from the murky water. Drizzle turned to rain and thundershowers, drenching the stately bald cypress and tupelo trees where Spanish moss hung from their branches. Shades of green slowly turned gray. The knowledgeable guide pointed to floating moss and duckweed, wiregrass, and water celery, and the water-covered islets.

In the moving boat, sitting or standing still was not possible. Shivering under my raincoat, the landscape that intrigued thirty minutes earlier suddenly terrified me. The atmosphere was dangerous, even deadly. Black bears, snakes, and alligators lurked in my mind. What if the boat toppled over? Which animal would gobble me from the bottom of this muddy swamp? Cold, wet, and terrified, I did not yet realize that the experience had an element of the spiritual.

JOURNAL PROMPT

Have you been overtaken by such terrifying emotions? What did "numinous dread" feel like?

❧ *Day 222* ❧

TODAY'S PRACTICE
Standing Meditation: "Spaciousness"   Read, write, and journal.

INSPIRATION

What a thrill it is to travel by trains!

Train travel has its own charm. For me, no other means of travel can compete with a long overnight train ride; airplanes may be faster, the bus cheaper, and cars more private, but trains (and ships) make me feel as if I'm a character in a fairytale.

Something about these modes of transportation – their rhythmic movement, the enjoyment of eating or drinking near a window as the landscape passes by, sleeping while the train moves at full speed, piercing through the space. A fantastic feeling. And once I'm back home, the nostalgia of having had the experience is incomparable.

From leaving the railway station at a slow speed to passing the city boundaries, picking up the speed and rushing through barren land and fields, the fairy wand of the train turns the surroundings into a fantasy land, a magical realm.

Once my husband and I traveled by train in Alaska for hours following the Gold Rush route starting from Skagway. In India we traveled by a luxury train for a week through the central states while sleeping in the compartment at night and touring the cities during the day – one of the most hospitable trains and a colorful journey! Finally, in Canada, we rode the Rocky Mountaineer Train – the most luxurious train in the world. Each single travel by train was a sheer thrill.

You will read more about the Canadian Rockies later this month.

JOURNAL PROMPT

What is your favorite mode of transportation? Why does it fascinate you? Journal about a time when you found yourself seated in the vehicle of a most fascinating adventure.

༄ *Day 223* ༄

Standing Meditation: "Spaciousness"   Read, write, and journal.

INSPIRATION

Deepak Chopra defines peak moments of self-realization as having six characteristics:

1. Loss of ego: *"Rapture envelops me. My ego returns."*

2. Time slowing: *"People seem to be cheering in slow motion."*

3. The inability to hear.

4. The feeling of being one with all that exists: *"I am a living cell in the body of the universe."*

5. A heightened sensory perception: *"Everything looks radiant. Surroundings turn luminous."*

6. Connecting with the inner self and being unafraid of mortality. *"The glaciers, the fiords, the rivers and the trees all live in me as much as I live in them. I'm immortal."*

I experienced many of such moments while traveling that I have shared with you so far this month. To Deepak Chopra's characteristics of peak-moments I would add two more:

- Silence: *"A hush falls. The chatter quiets down."*

- Perceiving the Earth anew: *"Is this how the Earth looked at its birth?"*

JOURNAL PROMPT

Have you experienced many of these characteristics together at certain moments, perhaps amidst great works of art and architecture, or when surrounded with natural beauty?

✌ *Day 224* ✌

TODAY'S PRACTICE
Standing Meditation: "Spaciousness"   Read, write, and journal.

INSPIRATION

Lisa Genova, author of *Still Alice*, writes that every time you learn something new, you eliminate brain shrinkage and plaque, replacing high levels of synapses. Extra synapses create backup connections. To keep the brain always active, you can journal, read, and keep learning new things.

Sleep is a "power cleanser," Genova writes. It is during deep sleep that the brain makes new brain cells, and renews and refreshes itself. Good sleep, good diet, and good exercise are the primary pillars of good physical health. But what are the pillars of mental health? Exercise your brain! When you learn something, you build new synapses that help keep your cognitive reserve at its best.

When I read Genova's article, I breathed a big sigh of relief. I can't change my age or my DNA, but I can learn new things. Travel is an activity whereby all my senses receive input every single moment of the day.

As a traveler, you follow the best possible regimen for brain health without even intending to, exposing yourself to a constant stream of novel things to learn. From the tiniest details to the most monumental sights, most everything you encounter is new. The thrill of meeting new people, seeing unfamiliar sights, and tasting new foods is simply invigorating.

Travel is one of the most concentrated kinds of learning experiences. Feeling good and having positive vibes also energizes you. It makes you happy. Happiness is at the core of good health. Good travel fills you with a kind of euphoria that you don't experience in any other way.

JOURNAL PROMPT

Write about how you feel when you visit a new town, unfamiliar state, or a foreign country. What sort of physical sensations do you have, and what thoughts do you ponder?

❧ *Day 225* ❧

Standing Meditation: "Spaciousness"   Read, write, and journal.

INSPIRATION

It is said that one way to feel happy is to plan a trip with someone you love. I feel blessed to be able to travel with my husband. As I mentioned earlier, we plan two trips every year – one within the U.S., and another in a land we have not visited before.

We believe the world is an exceptionally exciting book, populated with the most interesting characters. If we don't travel, we won't meet these wonderful people. It would be like getting stuck on the opening paragraph of a page turner. What a torment that would be! So we make sure to keep "reading."

Travel is addictive and fully immersive. Each time I am amidst new surroundings, I don't mind letting go of my daily routine. Moreover, I prepare myself physically, intellectually, and emotionally to experience awe and wonder that natural surroundings never fail to offer. I sense and feel something "more than myself," something sublime without, and soul touching within. Natural surroundings make me realize how tiny my day-to-day "problems" that cause stresses and anxieties are, fleeting, and for that reason meaningless.

Only during my travels have I experienced my miniscule self as compared to mammoth mountains and vast bodies of waters. They have made me realize I may be similar to a microscopic cell. But what the cell is to the body, I am to the cosmos, integral to it and significant. The moment I realized this, it was one of those peak moments that Deepak Chopra talks about.

Total immersion in nature is an amazing experience, and you deserve to have it. Every single time, a shift away from familiar surroundings to an alien land is an insightful and wonderous experience. Our travels to

Egypt, Greece, Italy, Spain, Portugal, India, China, Japan, and other countries have never ever disappointed us. Don't be the person who is too busy to travel when young and too tired to do so when old. Go travel!

JOURNAL PROMPT
Which places have you loved traveling? Where are you dreaming of going next?

༄ *Day 226* ༄

TODAY'S PRACTICE
Standing Meditation: "Spaciousness"   Read, write, and journal.

INSPIRATION

In Vancouver we rode a gondola to the summit of Grouse Mountain, then a ski-lift took us farther up. From there, we walked to an enclosed habitat where two 21-year-old bears had been rescued as cubs and nursed by the Forest Rangers. A window of the Grill Restaurant provided a picturesque bird's eye view of the city below.

Our next stop was the Suspension Bridge, made of rope, over Capilano, the name derived from the Indian word *Kia'Palano,* "beautiful river." Shaking and swaying at the height of 230 feet over the raging waters, the bridge is 450 feet long. Our guide told us to remember that if we walked across it, we would have to walk it again to return.

We began with trepidation. In the middle of the bridge, a terrified man held the rail. As we passed, his companions were trying to persuade him to move. At the end of the bridge, a woman stood crying because she was too afraid to walk back. Still many others were walking at a snail's pace, anxiously clutching the railing. But the children... oh, the children! Most were having the time of their lives, balancing themselves with their arms extended and hands free. They were letting their bodies sway with the undulating motions of the bridge.

Another adventure awaited. Five minutes away from the bridge was the Cliff Walk – an engineering feat against the precipice. A series of narrow cantilevered bridges, stairs, and platforms jut out of the granite cliff above the Capilano River. Not for the faint of heart! Only this open walkway separated us from the canyon far below.

At dinnertime, I recalled the anxiety and fear some encountered that day. Instead of having fun, instead of letting go, they were focused on their fear. Such behavior engulfed them in not having any fun at all. Instead of focusing on the fear, focus on the physical self, on others, and trusting that if this was an accident-prone place no tourists would visit.

One of the benefits of mindfulness is to become aware of your body when under anxiety attack. Become conscious of your physical feelings, of the sensations in your hands, arms, torso, and legs. This exercise reduces anxiety... though we tend to forget it precisely at the moment when we must remember!

JOURNAL PROMPT

Have you suffered a mild state of anxiety when at a place where you felt out of control? How do you manage to return to normalcy?

↳ *Day 227* ↲

TODAY'S PRACTICE

Standing Meditation: "Spaciousness"   Read, write, and journal.

INSPIRATION

From Vancouver we traveled by train to Kamloops, the heart of British Columbia, and the major hub for those headed toward the Canadian Rockies. I've traveled by luxury trains in many countries, but the Rocky Mountaineer rail was something special. A state-of-the-art railroad car with temperature-controlled seats and ample leg space, the ceiling and sides of the cabin were transparent. Throughout the journey the open view of the sky, clouds, mountains, rivers, fields, and pastures accompanied us.

At the outer boundaries of Vancouver, we passed industrial clutter, debris, graffiti, and other refuse. Soon the scene changed to open land

and then dramatically to green fields of the Fraser Valley, lush forests and winding river canyons. The height of the Cascade Mountains kept rising. While the Fraser River descended and flowed to the Pacific Ocean, we moved in the opposite direction.

A sumptuous breakfast and elaborate lunch were served in the dining car. Before our taste buds relished various flavors, we admired the artistically arranged food plates. Slow and luxurious mealtimes were accompanied by the meandering Fraser River that appeared sometimes on our left, other times at our right with breathtaking views! We passed a bridge painted red named Hell's Gate. It was on the way to the route well-traveled by the adventure seekers during the era of the Gold Rush.

Within an hour, the landscape changed from forested mountains to rocky and grassy surfaces. As the day ended, our train rushed through the shores of Kamloops Lake. Formed by the waters of the Fraser and Thompson Rivers, Kamloops means "meeting of the waters."

JOURNAL PROMPT
Have you traveled by train? How was your experience?

⸰ Day 228 ⸰

TODAY'S PRACTICE
Standing Meditation: "Spaciousness"   Read, write, and journal.

INSPIRATION
There were days in our travels that I felt utterly exhausted. The reasons included jet lag and long hours of travel. This time it was the fourteen hours of sitting on our seats, though comfortable, from Vancouver, British Columbia, to Banff, Alberta. Besides, we were no longer young. Usually I journal either first thing in the morning after meditation or at the end of the day. I am disciplined at recording what sights we see, especially if a place, a person, or an event strikes me emotionally. But this particular day, by the time we got our room key it was 10:00 P.M.

Exhaustion blinded me, and as soon as I lay my head on the pillow, I was transported to the land of deep sleep.

When I awoke, I walked to the window of our grand room at the Fairmont Banff Springs Hotel in the heart of Banff National Park, where the sheer beauty of the glacial mountain ranges kisses the sky.

No wonder it is nicknamed Canada's "Castle in the Rockies." The hotel is 125 years old and looks like a chateau. Its architectural details and intricate woodwork, chandeliers, paintings, and marble floors were a fairytale come to life. In the coffee shop, I sat with a flavorful brew and journaled. I couldn't believe that just the previous night I had been incapable of even scribbling a few readable sentences.

JOURNAL PROMPT

Are there days of travel when you discover marvelous things you want to journal about, but by the evening you are too tired to write?

✎ *Day 229* ✎

TODAY'S PRACTICE

Standing Meditation: "Spaciousness"   Read, write, and journal.

INSPIRATION

Banff National Park is Canada's first national park and the world's third (the first being the Yellowstone National Park in the U.S.). Even though partly cloudy, the turquoise glacial lakes and deep woods looked stunning. While driving in a motor coach, I realized that the "mountains" we had seen from the train were more like hills. In Banff, the peaks seemed to have gained access into the blue firmament while the sun kissed the ranges. I was awestruck.

And this awe and wonder at the divine creation continued when we were in an eight-minute gondola ride to the peak of Sulphur Mountain with spectacular scenery! The state-of-the-art alpine transport seated four, but they let just two of us occupy it so that we could view six directions.

Then at one point in an hour boat ride on Lake Minnewanka, when we were in the middle of the lake, our guide asked the captain to stop the engine, then requested all of us to keep quiet for a minute for "peace and tranquility." The short meditation transformed that blissful moment into such a powerful experience that even now when I think of it, it brings me calm.

JOURNAL PROMPT

What is it about majestic mountains, flowing waters, and green wilderness that grows on us, helping us become better than who we are in the humdrum of our hurried and busy daily life?

✍ *Day 230* ✍

TODAY'S PRACTICE

Standing Meditation: "Spaciousness"   Read, write, and journal.

INSPIRATION

Emerald, turquoise, lapis blue, snow white... oh the colors! And this was just water! Sunrays helped. Out of the four Canadian Rocky National Parks – Banff, Yoho, Jasper, and Kootenay – we had visited the first three. I would say nothing in the world could compete with them. They have a league of their own.

Our motorcoach guide drove us to the Fairmont Chateau Lake Louise Hotel, located in the Yoho National Park. In Cree, the word "Yoho" means amazement or awe, an apt name. Sun stayed with us through the day despite forecasted thunderstorms. The massive ice glaciers and dizzying mountain peaks, vertical rock walls and gushing waterfalls were paradisical.

Mesmerized by the beauty of the green shimmering surface of the Emerald Lake, I felt tranquil and calm. The guide informed us that the color was due to glacier flow which grates against the sediment under it called "rock flour." These deposits remain suspended in the frozen glacier but when the ice melts and flows into the lake, sunlight reflects the emerald green from the spectrum.

Driving alongside Kicking Horse River, we saw the natural rock formations upon which the water flats have been descending through centuries. Gushing water had sculpted the rock in formations that look man-made. At one place, the rock has morphed into a natural bridge. What other fantastic things take place in nature that we do not see?

Another colorful magic was at the turquoise Lake Louise. Fed by Victoria Glacier, both are aptly named after Queen Victoria and her daughter Louise – the ice of the "mother" feeding the "daughter." An exquisite lifetime's worth of jaw-dropping sights.

I had experienced silence being blotted out by noise but never before had I experienced silence absorbing the babble. I gazed at the horizon where the glacier ends and the lake begins. An unfathomable tranquility overtook me that absorbed the mental static and settled in the lotus of my heart.

JOURNAL PROMPT
Journal about your experience with silence. How does it impact you?

☙ *Day 231* ❧

TODAY'S PRACTICE
Standing Meditation: "Spaciousness"   Read, write, and journal.

INSPIRATION
Our final destination of the Canadian Rockies trip brought us to a cabin at Fairmont Jasper Park Lodge inside Jasper National Park, the largest park of the Canadian Rockies. The cedar chalets of the lodge were connected by picturesque paths that offered unique access to explore the nature surrounding the resort.

On our way to the lodge, we stopped at three different glaciers. The mountains kept getting higher and higher and the lakes turning bluer and bluer in various shades. At Peyote Lake we bore witness to glacier flow drifting down first as ice, then as a braided river, finally reaching the basin to form a lake – a hair-raising experience.

A ride in an Ice Explorer Bus, with tires taller than me, took us to the middle of a glacier. The ice surface was slippery. We took short steps walking like penguins. The temperature was 15-20 degrees lower than the place where we had boarded, just fifteen minutes away!

Glacier Glass Skywalk is a circular bridge constructed of glass. Standing on it we looked down a thousand feet below at Sunwapta Valley. Even a quick glance made me feel giddy. It was as if I was suspended from the sky. I couldn't have had such memorable adventures if we didn't travel.

JOURNAL PROMPT

What unforgettable travel adventures have you experienced that still give you chills? Or a thrill?

⤷ *Day 232* ⤶

TODAY'S PRACTICE

Standing Meditation: "Spaciousness"   Read, write, and journal.

INSPIRATION

At the Jasper Lodge, our cabin was situated facing Lac Beauvert, "beautiful green." By this time we had seen, smelled, touched, and listened to so much natural beauty that we were emotionally and spiritually fulfilled and physically squeezed of stamina.

But the mesmerizing outdoor landscape called. We decided to walk the trail that circled the lake that our cabin overlooked. After ten minutes of walking, the view stopped my heart. The crystal-clear turquoise water shimmered silver. Small shiny waves waltzed over large white pebbles. The upside-down reflections of the mountains, some places green, others blue, gave way to a majestic flock of Canadian geese that floated on its surface while white fish splashed nearby. I didn't want to leave.

Heart wrenching, a good sort of hurt, like when a lover says goodbye to her beloved, there was a promise of meeting again someday.

The beauty that saddened me was stirred by heavenly perfection. I did not know how to respond. Overcome, the moment absorbed all my emotions... including the heartache. Whereas the lover and beloved consummate their love by joining physically, the commune of nature lover and natural beauty takes place in the mind and heart. This union of individual with spirit, artist with art, devotee with God, self with soul is a spiritual sublimation.

When viewing such beauty, you may want to possess it in a photo or painting, but of course you realize none of those reproductions would give as much pleasure as when your inner Self first awakened to that view. You feel animated, all your senses stimulated. The beauty of the moment wells up your eyes, your heart aches, the tenderness and fragility of the moment stings.

Whereas physical desire craves union, nature's beauty desires merging. The latter, the union of Self with the soul, takes place in your heart-mind. The impulse is not external union but internal joining, resulting in the birth of sheer delight or a work of art!

JOURNAL PROMPT
What was it about a scenery that touched you so as to cause your eyes to well up?

ᘒ *Day 233* ᕽ

TODAY'S PRACTICE
Standing Meditation: "Spaciousness"   Read, write, and journal.

INSPIRATION
I gave Jasper National Park a new name: "The Land of Crystal Blue Lakes." Why not? It has 1,762 large and small lakes, of which only 107 are named. I viewed 11 of them: Athabasca, Peyto, Louise, Minnewanka, Medicine, Maligne, Pyramid, Edith, Annette, Jasper, and Lac Beauvert.

Due to its tranquility, serene surface, and water depth, a lake is the perfect metaphor for the mind of the practitioner of meditation. In Buddhism, whereas a novice meditator's mind is compared to a waterfall, an intermediate meditator's mind is a river, and an advanced meditator's a lake.

Novice Meditator

Like a waterfall, the thoughts of the novice practitioner surge, clashing into each other with no pause between. The method to reduce their speed has not yet been cultivated. Several months or a year of daily practice helps the thought process gradually slow down.

Intermediate Meditator

The mind of an intermediate meditator is like a river. Instead of surging and clashing, the thoughts flow one after another like a gushing river. Some turn into eddies, some circle around boulders, while others keep moving. The situation is not as bad as the waterfall because the thinking has slowed. The thoughts do not jumble; one completes before the next flows in. Slowly the river of thoughts widens and becomes devoid of eddies and boulders.

Advanced Meditator

Years of meditation practice further slows the flow of thoughts. Sediments and sandy grains of petty and unimportant thoughts settle down. More importantly, pauses are created between thoughts, giving the practitioner time to decide about the thought and if it is worth thinking about. They let go of petty thoughts and mull over important ones. This results in making sensible decisions such as thinking before speaking or acting.

Our thoughts shape the quality of our life. Experienced meditators accept thoughts that are sensible and kind, positive and productive, and worthy of acting upon. Once the sediments settle at the bottom, the water is clear and the little golden and silver fish of insights and ideas become visible under the turquoise surface. Advanced practitioners of meditation have clarity and peace of mind that reflect in their calm demeanor and serene mien.

JOURNAL PROMPT

Journal about how you see your flow of thoughts – a waterfall, a river, or a lake.

℘ *Day 234* ℘

TODAY'S PRACTICE	
Standing Meditation: "Spaciousness"	Read, write, and journal.

INSPIRATION

No matter which direction I turned, the Canadian Rockies reminded me of a Hindu adage: *"Gods dwell where the mountain peaks are."*

Imagine living in the ancient world when the wonder and awe of nature was believed to be located in high mountains, gushing waterfalls and rivers, and most dramatically displayed in the firmament... the daily rising and setting of the sun, thunder and lightning, clouds and rains, the waxing and waning of the moon, the starlit sky. The wonder of wonder was that these tremendously powerful bodies were consistently steady.

Early humans knew the effect of the celestial bodies upon earth – vegetation, birds, animals, and humans nourished and flourished because of the sun and the rain. They personified the powers of the celestial bodies as they wondered whether these "gods" would ever descend to earth. And if so, where would they dwell?

They surmised that the gods would make the mountain peaks their abode. The high peaks were the most beautiful places upon earth. How could their sheer beauty not magnetize the divine! So the ancients built temples on the top of the mountains and hills which developed into pilgrimage centers, the divine dwellings on earth.

While writing the book *Images of Indian Goddesses*, I traveled to several pilgrimage centers dedicated to local divinities. What places of serenity, peace, and calm! I don't know whether it was the vibes, the mountainous terrain, or the goddess spirits dwelling there.

JOURNAL PROMPT

Have you traveled to a pilgrimage center? Was it located on a mountain peak? What did you experience there?

ᨖ *Day 235* ᨖ

TODAY'S PRACTICE

Standing Meditation: "Spaciousness" Read, write, and journal.

INSPIRATION

Traveling is as unpredictable as our future. There are many reasons for this. A flight may get delayed or cancelled. Worse is when no flight is available for one or more days. It is frustrating but you have to persevere. Oh, what sacrifices we make for the goddess of world travel! We had such an experience on our return trip from Vancouver to Pittsburgh. Our flight was canceled and no other flight was available for fourteen hours. People groaned and cursed.

We were frustrated. But these are the times when Writing Meditation Practice comes to the rescue. We found a quieter corner. I plugged my ears with earplugs, closed my eyes, and settled comfortably to meditate. After 20 minutes I had regained my calm. I continued my contemplative mood by writing in my journal about what I had experienced. Then I read my book followed by walking the airport walkways. We had a leisurely lunch and took a snooze. The few remaining hours before boarding were stretched, but Writing Meditation Practice kept me from feeling infuriated, exasperated, or impatient. Actually, it felt good when we boarded and settled in our seats. Soon a hot meal hit the spot.

At baggage claim at Pittsburgh International Airport, our luggage never arrived. Before my blood pressure could go up, once again I practiced a short meditation, filled in paperwork, then drove home. It took a week for Canadian Airlines to deliver our suitcases.

The late morning when our baggage was delivered, I pulled mine in and kissed it. Without it I had felt as if one of my limbs was missing. You see I had foolishly packed my computer with all my notes in it.

JOURNAL PROMPT

Journal about a time when you accidentally deleted several pages of a final version of your work-in-progress, or the computer ate a story never to be retrieved again!

∾ *Day 236* ∾

TODAY'S PRACTICE

Standing Meditation: "Spaciousness"   Read, write, and journal.

INSPIRATION

The day after we returned home was my 75th birthday, August 29, 2022. From that day on, each moment, each day, each week, each month feels like a gift. Even now I feel blessed to be in good physical, emotional, and intellectual health, as well as spiritual well-being. I plan to live to be a hundred. Yet, "woman (or man) proposes, God disposes."

The thought of death, at the back of my mind, keeps me animated. I wake up to look forward to a routine that has taken me a lifetime to build and hone. I'm as excited about each day at home as I am about each day I travel. Life itself is an adventure. I no longer have as much stamina, but the pleasure of living purposefully makes up for the swiftness and zing of youth.

Your birthday is a great day to express gratitude to your loved ones, extended family, friends, and people who help make your life comfortable and easy – the doctor, dentist, gardener, grocer, postman, cleaning person, and so on. Thank heavens for their love and attention, their genuine friendship and camaraderie, delightful reciprocity and the services they provide.

Also good to remember, no two journeys are alike. Each instance of travel has its own personality. You go deep into a trip as much as the trip penetrates deep within you.

ꙮ Day 237 ꙮ

TODAY'S PRACTICE
Standing Meditation: "Spaciousness"   Read, write, and journal.

INSPIRATION

Winding down from travel, let's have a cup of tea together! It's all right if you are alone. Once you have a cup of tea in front of you, here's a five-step process you may follow. (This ritual is inspired by Thich Nhat Hanh's "Drinking Tea Meditation.")

Pause

Take a few moments to sit with your cup of tea.

Gratitude for Those Who Make It Possible

Imagine the soil, sun, and rain that went to create the drink, and the women and men whose hands harvested, prepared, packed, shipped, and sold the tea. This vision is rewarding in itself as it trains you to see everything with the same eyes, including the person with whom you may be having the tea.

Become Aware of Yourself

Let go of your opinions and attitudes. Feel your stress dissolve. Feel it float away. Feel it get absorbed in the ground.

Enjoy the First Few Sips

Let the taste of the tea nourish your taste buds. Let the aroma satisfy your sense of smell. Let the space of your mind fill up with the taste and aroma of the tea until there is no room for thoughts. Let the thinking mind become the tea-enjoying mind.

Be Here and Now

Silently drink the tea. Notice how your momentary concerns and problems feel small. Feel completely relaxed. See possibilities in the situation. You will feel more creative and return to your next task with a fresh mind.

Such tea breaks twice a day act as pressure valves. They free your mind and help you find solutions to whatever problem you may be having.

JOURNAL PROMPT

Have a cup of tea with yourself or a friend. Then journal about your experience with the ritual of "Drinking Tea Meditation."

ꙮ *Day 238* ꙮ

TODAY'S PRACTICE

Standing Meditation: "Spaciousness"   Read, write, and journal.

INSPIRATION

Last month we focused on nonverbal activities; this month we experienced travel. Observing with senses fully awakened is what we do when we journey to distant places. At the core of travel are awareness, silence, and interaction – the obverse of the writing coin – providing an essential respite from the hours of writing, reading, and editing.

Once home, I restart my routine. When the sun has not yet risen but nature is waking up, I sit in the solitude and silence of my Creative Power Spot. I hear myself breathe and observe my own mind bouncing from one thought to the next. Continually, I bring it back to center. Insightful thoughts may or may not emerge. Slowly the mind quiets; there is peace. This may not happen each morning, but when it does, it is blissful and filled with love and understanding.

The quiet morning is reverential time because of how I feel within me and around me. This segment of the day helps me experience the sacred. I've needed it since I turned 60. I've observed people between the ages of 55-75 waging war against their wrinkles and sagging bodies. Why not accept the body as it is, despite aches and pains, becoming aware of the sensations and feelings, not being afraid of them? Acceptance of your physical self as it matures, and pride in who you have become, alleviate minor discomforts and energize the body.

As your body turns less robust and less stable, it requires your attention and care. If you give heed to the multitudes of sensory signals the body gives, you gain a greater sense of well-being and feel more grounded. Make friends with your maturing body by going within in the quiet of each morning and feel the difference!

JOURNAL PROMPT

Write about one thing happening to your body that's beyond your control. Journal and discover the best possible response and solution to the problem.

✤ *Day 239* ✤

TODAY'S PRACTICE

Standing Meditation: "Spaciousness"   Read, write, and journal.

INSPIRATION

Travel provides useful material that you can weave into your writing. Such a fortuitous incident filled me with awe in Asheville, North Carolina. The launch site for our hot air balloon ride was a vast flat land surrounded by trees. The sky was still dark. The air balloon lay folded on the ground. The passengers included me and my husband along with two college girls and the pilot. We helped the pilot unfold the huge balloon, straightening the edges as he filled it with hot air. It puffed and puffed and rose slowly like a snake from the tune of a snake charmer. Finally the balloon was up with the huge basket ready to take us on the ride. Weighted down with heavy rocks, it swayed gently as the gas flame burnt bright.

We hopped into the basket with the help of the pilot. Once safely aboard, he explained how we were at the mercy of the winds. A brilliant sunrise greeted us. The balloon glided over a golf course, open fields, forested area, and the town of Asheville. We continued to float under the blue sky, relishing a mild wind on our faces. Forty-five minutes seemed to pass in a few moments.

At the horizon I noticed a black cloud coming toward us. It seemed strange because the rest of the sky was sheer blue. Where had this cloud come from? I drew the pilot's attention to it. But he ignored it and continued to talk about the history of hot air balloons. By then the cloud had become thinner and wider and it was headed in our direction. What could it be?

The "cloud" which was now upon us was made out of small fluttering things. And then... at once I found myself surrounded by hundreds of monarch butterflies. We were in the middle of a cloud of monarch butterflies traveling south! They flapped, flipped, or hovered on our heads, shoulders, arms, bodies, basket, ropes, even the balloon for a few moments. No sooner had they arrived than they were gone. We had crossed one another's paths for not more than a minute. The pilot grinned at me with a knowing smile. "It has happened before," he said. "I didn't want to spoil the surprise."

JOURNAL PROMPT
What incredulous experiences have you had on your travels?

✌ *Day 240* ✌

TODAY'S PRACTICE
Standing Meditation: "Spaciousness"   Read, write, and journal.

INSPIRATION
Travelers love adventure in unfamiliar places, meeting new faces and surprises that are part of journeying. But some travelers mock those who travel with tour companies. They complain that a guide takes you to touristy places. "Besides," they argue, "you don't get to encounter things serendipitously."

For my husband and I, touring companies are a blessing. Their guides take us to historic monuments and world-renowned tourist sites and circuits. For older people, adventuring alone in foreign lands is neither safe nor time-saving. When we were younger, we'd rent a car and drive, stopping several times to ask locals for directions. Rarely did we find unknown wonders. We did however get stuck due to a landslide while on our way to a Kali Temple in Himachal Pradesh, and got lost for hours in fields of corn in Rajasthan, India.

Now wiser, we spend our precious vacation time visiting UNESCO landmarks, world famous monuments, and scenic landscapes with the help of a knowledgeable guide. It makes no sense to "adventure" when our time is limited. Famous bazaars and cultural monuments reflect the geographic particularities and peculiarities of a country. Knowledgeable guides inform about people and how and why they achieved such magnificent cultural feats. We couldn't have taken full pleasure in looking at the pyramids in Cairo, the Parthenon in Athens, the Cordoba Mosque in Spain, or Notre Dame in France – all touristy spots – without the help of a guide.

Tour companies are efficient with their time planning. Their guides know the history and have a good grasp of the culture. They are well acquainted with eateries where locals frequent. They have the wherewithal to deal with medical emergencies and find pharmacies for small health hiccups. One can never become a native in a new place. Besides, it is not where you go – popular or unknown – it is what you experience that makes you a traveler.

JOURNAL PROMPT

As you travel, are your senses alert? Do you see, hear, interact, and savor things mindfully, or get lost and waste time? Does your travel change or improve your habitual thinking? Are you the same person you were before you left home, or did the travel to a new place jolt you?

END OF MONTH PROMPT

Walking in nature, far from civilization, is a spiritual activity. In such a contemplative setting, we reconnect with our Authentic Self. This inner connection repairs, heals, and makes us whole (and holy).

Such contentment depends on going deep within, on self-reflection. If you seek contentment in outward satisfactions, however, you remain thirsty, empty, unhappy.

The essence of your journey does not depend upon where or how far you go, but rather upon how deeply you excavate within.

When you experience rapture in nature, joy in music, or pleasure in art... when you feel ecstasy, awe, and wonderment... you get an inkling of who you truly are and why you are here on this earth.

MONTH 9

MINDFULNESS AND STILLNESS, SILENCE, AND SOLITUDE

Suggested Readings

Stillness Speaks
Eckhart Tolle, 2003.

The Art of Stillness: Adventures in Going Nowhere
Pico Iyer, 2014.

Journal of a Solitude
May Sarton, 1973.

Thoughts in Solitude
Thomas Merton, 1958.

Invitation to Solitude and Silence:
Experiencing God's Transforming Presence
Ruth Haley Barton, 2004.

ꙮ *Day 241* ꙮ

TODAY'S PRACTICE

Your daily Writing Meditation Practice schedule is set! You meditate, reflect on the day's inspiration and prompt, journal, read, walk, and are thinking of planning a trip to somewhere. Fantastic!

This month we'll focus on stillness, silence, and solitude. You've already experienced this during the month of breathing exercises. Now your understanding of tranquility and level-headedness will grow. Writing Meditation Practice motivates you, setting your mood so the muses are waiting for you.

Meditation: "Mindful"   Read, reflect, and journal.

INSPIRATION

In this age of speed and constant movement, nothing is more restful than slowing down, going within, and sitting still in solitude. Peace arises when you sit still. In the aura of this calm lies profound wisdom. When you are walking outdoors, sit for 5 minutes and feel entertained listening to birds or crickets or rushing water. Nature's sounds add depth to any time of the day or night.

Last month you discovered how much pleasure and insights travel brings. If it was practical I could take a short trip each month in addition to two longer trips a year. Yet, sitting at home in the silence of my Creative Power Spot settles my mind and opens my heart. At such moments I genuinely feel going nowhere is as fulfilling as going places.

Each day before or after your meditation session, make it a habit to sit quietly for a few minutes to focus on your breath. Let whatever moves you rise to the surface. This will balance the habitual movement and speed.

Doing nothing, and going nowhere, is vital to our very survival. These days we are addicted to speed and movement. If we are not moving physically we are surfing online. The mind keeps count. It doesn't know the difference. For a while each day, take time off from the world of information and constant entertainment to take pleasure in stillness. Do this often and see what happens this month.

JOURNAL PROMPT

The practice of sitting still in silence is easier to begin if you add it at the opening or end of your usual meditation session.

‿ *Day 242* ‿

TODAY'S PRACTICE

Meditation: "Mindful"   Read, reflect, and journal.

INSPIRATION

The point of whatever profession you are practicing, or whichever career you are preparing for, is to go somewhere. If you want to ascend the corporate ladder, you take a business flight within the country or somewhere around the world. Not a single institution encourages you not to travel unless you have a lowly desk job. The idea is if you don't move, you won't grow.

But remember what I have been saying all along? Most of your problems and their solutions lie within you; peace of mind comes from inside yourself. It is not the movement but your response to situations and events that you make with your body and mind that unsettle you.

Sitting quietly and mulling things over, going within, things are revealed the way they should be, and not otherwise. Sit still and discover this truth.

World travel has taught me that a pleasurable trip acquires meaning only after I return home. My experiences grow deeper when I sit back and look at the photos I have shot. With attention, I absorb the experiences and relive the journey as *sights* turn into *insights* for life.

It may seem contradictory that writing about travel is included in a chapter about sitting still. But it is not. I believe setting travel within the framework of solitude of your serene home makes perfect sense. The sensory pleasures of travel gain richness when revisited in the quiet. The reminiscence of pleasurable moments makes life exciting and precious.

JOURNAL PROMPT

Reminisce an unforgettable day that you spent away from home. How does reliving the day in your journal feel?

⤷ *Day 243* ⤶

TODAY'S PRACTICE

Meditation: "Mindful"   Read, reflect, and journal.

INSPIRATION

For some, not going anywhere or not doing anything sounds boring. But you cannot equate *stillness* with *inactivity*. Stillness is to sit and relax your mind. It is to let fresh thoughts come without conscious effort on your part. Let original thoughts surface without you consciously imagining them.

If you are a contemplative person, sitting still comes easily to you. Think about this: your three-pound brain has the ability to contain the whole universe. How awesome would it be if you could train yourself to travel within and get charged with ecstatic moments of your inner journey? The American poet Emily Dickinson seldom left her room. She wrote 1700 poems by traveling within her braincase.

The French philosopher Blaise Pascal noted, "All the unhappiness of men arises from one simple fact: that they can't sit quietly in their chamber." This practice of sitting quietly by yourself trains your mind the way exercise trains your body. It strips you of your masks and garbs, leads you deep into yourself where you become one with your Authentic Self, wiser and kinder.

Sitting for 5-15 minutes in stillness is like building a sacred halo around yourself. You help establish something beautiful to take with you for the rest of the day. You don't have to go to the temple or church to meet the divine. You can meet your divine Self in the stillness of your body.

JOURNAL PROMPT

Have you added 5 minutes of silent sitting before or after your meditation? Journal about how adding this quiet sitting to your meditation practice feels. Slowly increase the time for silent sitting and notice the "progress" you make.

ꙮ *Day 244* ꙮ

TODAY'S PRACTICE

Meditation: "Mindful"   Read, reflect, and journal.

INSPIRATION

If you want to enrich your writing and spiritual life, pay attention to every moment. Embrace all of life, each stage, even when you fumble and stumble. Be aware that you have fallen, because only those who are creatively and spiritually unconscious don't know that they have fallen. Those who intentionally sit in silence and solitude elevate their whole self by loving their successful as well as unsuccessful Self and gaining perspective and calm.

Intellectual knowledge and emotional experiences are both necessary to create and live. You don't live by merely thinking all the time. Feeling is integral to thinking. Being attentive and aware means to know, to create, and to grow.

The mindful life results in concentration, compassion, kindness, and wisdom because the practice keeps you awake. Inner whispers respond to the slightest warnings when dormant instincts awaken. In the depths of your being, the mindfulness is alive. Meditation opens the "third" eye, so to speak, at the very depth of your spiritual nature.

JOURNAL PROMPT

Journal about how creativity and your writing are connected with your spiritual living.

∾ *Day 245* ⌇

TODAY'S PRACTICE
Meditation: "Mindful"   Read, reflect, and journal.

INSPIRATION

What is a life of contemplation? It is to realize that we come to the world alone and we leave alone, that our solitude is absolute. To be an authentic individual is to be responsible for our thoughts, deeds, and words, and to be free. Both responsibility and freedom convey an interior solitude.

Those who neither know solitude nor freedom of choice suffer from superficiality, resentment, anger, and hate. But those who practice interior solitude and silence experience self-contentment, kindness, and creativity.

The sky, the sea, the mountains, the rivers, the forests are what they are in their silence. In the same way, we need to be ourselves in inner solitude. Whether poor or wealthy, having good times or going through difficult times, inner stillness is always present deep within ourselves, to elevate us above our condition and its passing phases.

You are made of what you desire. Your life is shaped by your quiet intentions, goals you make, the purpose of the life you envision. The clarity of your mind and your focus make you true to who you are.

You have decided to lead an authentic life, a creative and contemplative life, and this year you are doing something about it – you are walking on this path of creativity and spirituality. You have shown yourself that you are determined to hone your artistic mind. Because you see, you are either a creative mind or you are not. There is no gray area.

JOURNAL PROMPT
How does your creativity connect you to your authenticity? Journal about it.

❧ *Day 246* ❧

TODAY'S PRACTICE	
Meditation: "Mindful"	Read, reflect, and journal.

INSPIRATION

Solitude is real, not just potential or imaginary. You are born alone and you die alone. Most of your fears are rooted in facing this truth. There are certain moments when you become aware that you are a solitary being. You are not certain where you are going. You become anxious. How do you solve this problem? You face it by confronting it so that you may rise above it in silence, witnessing it objectively. In the light of the values you have developed so far, it is trivial.

You have chosen to take this journey that balances your sense of outer solitude, your relationship with your inner solitude, and your warm relationships with family members and family.

However, it is only in solitude that you find the divine within. In silence you clear away the cobwebs of words that you yourself lay down between the clear mind and thinking. Silence respects authenticity; thinking defiles it. Silence is believed to be the mother of authenticity and truth. Mere words do not contain truth and reality. Truth rises from the inner silence.

Stop thinking about how to live. Simply live. Spend some time in silence each day and start living peacefully for the rest of your life. Do what is meaningful to you, and watch your thought process and your life merge. You have attained peace.

JOURNAL PROMPT

Journal about how you may incorporate 10 minutes of quiet time in your day. Which time is most convenient for you?

℘ *Day 247* ℘

TODAY'S PRACTICE

Meditation: "Mindful" Read, reflect, and journal.

INSPIRATION

Having discovered the divine silence within yourself, watch as it slowly overflows and seeps into the rest of your day. When you become aware of it within yourself, you find this silence in the people you know. In doing so, your own silence comes vividly alive.

A point to keep in mind is that speaking does not necessarily break your meditative silence. It will become part of your mindful nature. It is broken only when you want people to listen to you, only when you want them to pay attention to what you have to say. Listen to them and watch how you are using the inner power that silence produces.

Conceited speech wants everyone to be quiet and listen. When you speak with that attitude, you impose silence on others. But as a mindful person you speak gently and listen attentively. You only speak when and if it is necessary.

Wherever you go, your inner silence goes with you. You can lead a contemplative life as much in the city as in the woods, on a sea beach, or in the desert. Simply sit still and close your eyes, using earplugs if necessary. Sit for 10 minutes each day to keep your sanity and attract spiritual demeanor. Letting silence and solitude envelope you for some time each day is equivalent to praying.

JOURNAL PROMPT

Journal about the time when you pray. How is it similar to sitting with humility in silence?

✤ *Day 248* ✤

TODAY'S PRACTICE
Meditation: "Mindful"   Read, reflect, and journal.

INSPIRATION

You say your work, family, and community do not leave time for you to spend in silence. This is no excuse as 5-10 minutes can be found each day if you are determined to lead a life of contemplation.

Being a writer, you deal with language and word choice all the time. You know how important pauses are between words. In your sentences and paragraphs, you know how to balance words and spaces. You understand the true value of silence because you know the significance of words. So how would you not recognize the appreciation for inner quiet?

The sediments in your mental jar only settle when you find time to sit and observe to the best of your ability this moment, the present moment. You intuitively know how much time you must spend by yourself each day in order to stay grounded. You know about it as much as you know about working out 4-5 times a week or eating 3-4 times a day.

Explore your rhythms for sitting alone in silence and enjoy the presence of the one who is always present in you. Being in solitude is a golden opportunity to be with your Authentic Self.

JOURNAL PROMPT

Have you yet designated 10 minutes from your day to sit still doing *nothing?* If not, then journal about the reasons that are keeping you from doing so. What does your journal say?

✤ *Day 249* ✤

TODAY'S PRACTICE
Meditation: "Mindful"   Read, reflect, and journal.

INSPIRATION

You know your creative life would be bone dry if you did not pause for quiet time as you walk or are engaged with a nonverbal activity. This is not different from the balance between time with family and friends versus regular time with yourself. Time with others loses its energy and meaning without the quiet time with self.

Your time spent during cooking, gardening, painting, and other unhurried activities creates healthy intervals in the otherwise hurried and noisy day. Such short duration of creative periods is essential. They help you resettle and recharge. If you practice this, joy erupts and surprises you.

It is important for you to continue to remain creative until the end of your long life. Never be satisfied with a superficial living; such a life invites discontent. For you, the tension of seeing things in noisy surroundings that are not right is a source of unease. Not satisfied in the company of inauthentic people and their small talk, you don't waste time with those who have only a social face to show.

JOURNAL PROMPT

When physical or psychic pain makes you suffer, sit silently and focus on your inhaling and exhaling. Keep sitting until it passes. In the silence of your Creative and Spiritual Power Spot, pour your free thinking and new thoughts that emerge onto the pages of your notebook.

᭰ *Day 250* ᭰

TODAY'S PRACTICE

Meditation: "Mindful"   Read, reflect, and journal.

INSPIRATION

No routine is imposed upon a writer in older years when children have graduated, married, and gone. Your understanding spouse may be retired, passed away, or you may be divorced. Surrounded by silence, you have the whole day that you can design as it suits you.

Mornings are perfect for practicing meditation, journaling, reading, walking, or a nonverbal activity of your choice. You practice your craft as you write your story, essay, or poem. You concentrate with your whole self – mind, body, spirit – toward the one single end of what you are writing. Absolute silence is crucial.

Try this: One day as you are walking outside, pay attention to the incessant noise of lawn mowers, garbage trucks, grinding of car brakes, and pounding of traffic. In other words, pay heed to all sorts of noises.

When you return home, sit comfortably at your writing spot and listen to your breathing. It is time to be silent. Listen to the quiet. Let it reveal the richness of being enveloped in this thick blanket of silence. Get back to the uncertainty, anxiety, and great effort of writing the work-in-progress and feel energized and let the eternal hope return.

JOURNAL PROMPT
How does being enveloped in your own personal blanket of quiet feel?

✷ *Day 251* ✷

TODAY'S PRACTICE
Meditation: "Walking Through the Forest"   Read, reflect, and journal.

INSPIRATION
When my daughters were young and I worked at the university, the food still needed to be cooked, clothes washed, the house cleaned, the shopping done, and just when things were feeling caught up, the kids would get sick. I'd long for a stretch of days to be alone with myself. As much as I loved my family, I craved my time in silence and solitude.

I couldn't have it then, but now I have it in plenty. It feels like a gift from the gods.

There are people, especially women, who never get to be with themselves and cultivate an inner life. With four or five children and a job (or two, because bills must be paid) they give up an essential part of themselves. They have no rest, no quiet time, no stillness. They do not know they have valuable powers hidden within them. With no personal space or time, they undervalue or devalue this power.

When I feel blessed and grateful, I think about such women. I'm grateful for my family life: my husband, our daughters, their spouses, our grandchildren, and the bonus of my solitude. My life is as good as it can get. I am thankful for slowing down, to being attentive and aware, to being able to write and read, all because I have experienced the joy and blessings of silence and solitude. So I share with you what I have gained, learned, and experienced from being a practitioner of Writing Meditation Practice.

I commune with myself at the Sacred Power Spot, my space of silence and time of solitude. In communing with myself, I commune with others. Here I feel the presence of authentic power within.

JOURNAL PROMPT

How do you feel when you spend time with yourself? Bored? Lonely? Introspective? Insightful?

ꕥ *Day 252* ꕥ

TODAY'S PRACTICE

Meditation: "Walking Through the Forest"　　　　　　　Read, reflect, and journal.

INSPIRATION

Loneliness and boredom are protean in nature, neither good nor bad. Yet through practice I have learned to turn these two conditions into solitude. I focus on myself – breath and body. When I thus intensely become aware of myself, new sensitivities surface which bring me in touch with my existence, the thrilling thought of being alive. It reminds me of the existence of those I deeply love.

I have learned to change the negative into positive by practicing meditation, journaling, sitting by myself for 5-10 minutes as sunlight warms my back, or shines on water or on summer blossoms. The habit of spending a little time with myself turns the time I spend with others more pleasurable and playful. For me, solitude is one of the basic necessities, like nourishment, shelter, and clothing.

If I have a negative encounter, I ask myself if I did anything wrong, even when I think I'm not to be blamed. I'm pretty sure she teased me or he provoked me or she wronged me. Self-reflection comes to the rescue. I mull over the incident in silence, realizing whatever wrong happened had not much to do with her, him, or them. All the negativity I'm feeling is a reflection of my own inner landscape. The thought settles and I'm back to my normal self. But again, I can mull things over only in silence.

When you sit still quietly, pondering what you have encountered, how it affected you, and how you have affected others as the consequence of your interaction, it lends self-understanding and continual self-improvement. This can be done only when you are alone, self-reflecting, sitting in the silence of solitude.

JOURNAL PROMPT

Journal about a recent argument you had with someone, or a feeling of resentment. After filling 2-3 pages in your notebook, what do you discover?

ᘛᕐ *Day 253* ᕐᘘ

TODAY'S PRACTICE

Meditation: "Walking Through the Forest"   Read, reflect, and journal.

INSPIRATION

It is said that a new concept takes a hundred repetitions before you can fully comprehend it. Pause, become still, and reflect in silence on what is being said. Ponder the material.

Let this month's entries awaken you from conditional thinking. Great thoughts grow out of silence. They have the power to take you back to the silence, to inner stillness.

What is this stillness I talk about? It is the peace and contentment within, the calm you have gained by spending time with yourself. It is the inner awareness that makes sense of the words on this page to be perceived as thoughts. Without that awareness these words would have no meaning. The stillness, silence, and solitude make you conscious of that inner awareness that gives rise to thought.

The words you write to create worlds on paper are rooted in an amorphous dimension. What you are reading this month is infinitely deeper and vaster than language. In fact, the source of language is silence.

Silence outside you becomes the stillness within you. When you are in the presence of silence, pay attention to it. Then turn your attention within; notice the stillness. The calm within also enables you to experience silence without.

Look at the trunk of a tree, firm and still. Look at a flower, a fruit, a plant. Its beauty lays in not pretending to be something else. It lays in its stillness and silence. Learn from nature to be yourself and be still.

JOURNAL PROMPT

Are you different when you are by yourself than when you are with others? How free do you feel to be yourself when you are with loved ones or your friends? Do you feel you wear different masks around other people? Why is that? Journal without inhibitions about why you wear a mask. What is it about you that you don't want others to see?

⟆ *Day 254* ⟅

TODAY'S PRACTICE

Meditation: "Walking Through the Forest"   Read, reflect, and journal.

INSPIRATION

When I write, read, paint, or attempt to find a solution to a problem, I sit in silence. Universal Intelligence and stillness operate together – authentic human intelligence that dwells in silence and stillness.

For a week, conduct an experiment with yourself. Practice sitting still in silence and watch what is born out of it. For the first couple of days, as in your early days of breathing exercises and meditation practice, thinking will interrupt you, but the more you practice, the more days pass, the more you will notice true wisdom emerge. This will direct your writing and actions.

How is this possible? Remember, deep in your heart dwells your Authentic Self. This Self is the Universal Intelligence at the microlevel within you – discerning, warmhearted, unperturbed. Hidden behind ten thousand passing clouds of thoughts there is stillness of brilliant sky.

When you rise above your thinking mind, you become one with a deeper intelligence that is silently communicated through your Authentic Self. In silence you are that Self. When you are writing, your thinking mind is pushed to the background. Your wiser self takes over, you are not your restricting ego self. The words pour out spontaneously, not from your mind but the whole body. You are not in control, but unconstrained, unbidden, truly free.

JOURNAL PROMPT

Have there been journaling sessions when you could not stop writing, when original thoughts kept pouring out on the pages of your notebook? What triggered that output?

ꙮ *Day 255* ꙮ

TODAY'S PRACTICE

Meditation: "Walking Through the Forest"   Read, reflect, and journal.

INSPIRATION

Someone new to the practice might confuse the whispers of the Authentic Self with a voice in your head. That voice is loud, pessimistic, and never stops speaking. That voice is critical, unproductive, harsh. The whispers of your AS feel right, sagacious and unexpected. If you can't separate yourself from the chain of thoughts, if you unconsciously identify with that voice in your head, become more attentive. Learn to differentiate between inner whispers and the critical voice in your head. When you are aware, you will know the difference.

The whispers of your AS are not driven by the voice in your head. Rather, they are from the one who is witnessing your ego self and knows all about you and is the wisdom within. Meditation has taught you to become aware of the thinker within you, who witnesses everything. Knowing yourself as the awareness behind the voice in the head gives you freedom from your egoistic self. You will be in control, not your ego.

When you know how to recognize the whispers of your Authentic Self you begin to live in the present moment. Welcome to here-now where you finally realize the significance of sitting still in silence and solitude.

Wherever you go, the present moment is with you. In that moment everything feels connected, as if whatever has happened, good or bad, has happened due to a reason. You only know a fraction of the whole story. You realize you cannot know the whole story. Your thinking mind moves in sequence but the whole story is circular, whole like your AS.

JOURNAL PROMPT
Journal about the difference between the voice in your head and the whispers of your inner guide, your Authentic Self.

ꕥ *Day 256* ꕥ

TODAY'S PRACTICE
Meditation: "Walking Through the Forest"   Read, reflect, and journal.

INSPIRATION
When you sit still and pay attention to various sensations in the space around you – what you can touch, taste, smell, see, hear – you get deeper into the present moment. This is not just what is happening but also what you are sensing in that moment.

The present moment is circular and you are its sacred center. The happenings and thinking move horizontally in a straight line. When you pay attention to *here-now,* you bring your awareness to the body and breath. This helps you ground yourself in the *now.* You are no longer lost in the content of your mind but become settled in your inner sacred center. Stillness makes you realize how much deeper you are than your floating thoughts.

To your amazement, you will have the realization that you are detached from the happening events and actions. Your Authentic Self, your "I Am," is not attached to passing moments. Your AS is always living in the present moment. Equanimity and peace are constant within. You feel it because you are paying attention and you are aware of the here and now. Your concentrated focus is on physical sensations. The present moment is integral with your true Self. It is right here, always alive, and forever present at the core of your being.

Practice living in the present moment and be at peace. Peace comes when you are grounded at your deepest center. Peace does not come by trying to make sense out of the circumstances of your life. Be present here-now.

JOURNAL PROMPT
Journal about what living in the present means? What does Authentic Self means to you?

ᥭ *Day 257* ᥰ

TODAY'S PRACTICE
Meditation: "Walking Through the Forest"   Read, reflect, and journal.

INSPIRATION
If there is one thing you can do to make your life happier, what would it be? Self-awakening. This is the only thing that matters if you want to lead a creative and spiritual life, because such a life is guaranteed to make you happier.

How does one awaken oneself? With years of practice of living in the present moment. You are on the right path. Follow the disciplines of meditation, journaling, walking in wilderness, reading, and sitting in silence by yourself. You may do that anywhere but your Personal Power Spot works best when you are starting something new.

It'll take 5-10 minutes. Time yourself. Sit at your writing desk and bring your body, mind, and heart home. Focus only on inhaling and exhaling. Find your inner power spot in the present moment. When the time is up you'll feel centered.

Begin writing and watch playfulness emerge. Things lose their materiality, their heaviness. Characters begin to act in their settings. The sentences flow one after the other. You don't know where they are coming from but you can't stop writing. What was previously frozen in your mind has liquified and is now becoming visible on your pages. Your consciousness is manifesting into a story. And this draft is purely your own because it is seeing the world through your eyes.

It gets more pleasurable with each version. You work hard at each draft. When you finalize the manuscript that manifested from your consciousness, the feeling showers you with unparalleled pleasure. It is in your style, in your voice, and it is fully yours.

JOURNAL PROMPT

What has your experience been about writing the first and final drafts, and the difference? What emotions do you go through between the first rough draft and the final one?

ꙶ *Day 258* ꙶ

TODAY'S PRACTICE

Meditation: "Walking Through the Forest"   Read, reflect, and journal.

INSPIRATION

Do one thing at a time. Immerse completely in the world you have created through language. Surrender to the work in progress.

Concentration empowers you. Only in silence can you truly focus on something.

Try this. When you are completely engrossed in writing for an hour or two and you have the need to go to the bathroom, as you walk away from your writing space, become aware of how focused you were a few moments ago, and still are to some extent. Sense the spaciousness around you and peace within. This is the leftover feeling that you were not aware of a minute ago. You were in total awareness of the present moment via your work.

Your chapter may be about happiness or unhappiness, about a tragic event or a comic event, about anything whatsoever... but the source from which all that was pouring out was the eternal stillness within. Words rippled on the surface of your mind and you poured them on blank space. Your Authentic Self, the source of your creativity, remains undisturbed.

The scene, the characters, the setting, or the events you are making up satisfy you immensely. They energize you, make you feel pure and real because you experience everything that is beyond the wants and fears of your ego self. When you create the flow of your inner intelligence, your non-resisting consciousness makes the making of it possible.

In real life you complicate things by resisting. In creative life you let the characters do everything they desire. You surrender to your creative flow when you are completely focused on creating. By fully surrendering to your Authentic Self, you accept whatever comes to your mind or wherever it takes you to make that story. You are not struggling, but following the path your creative mind is blazing. You accept happy accidents. A greater intelligence operates through you.

JOURNAL PROMPT
How do you differentiate your attitude when creating versus dealing with your day-to-day life? Do you resist or surrender?

⚘ *Day 259* ⚘

Today's Practice

Meditation: "Walking Through the Forest"   Read, reflect, and journal.

Inspiration

When walking in a forested area, pick up a leaf, a stone, a piece of bark. Observe how still it is. No pretense. Hold its stillness in your awareness. Sense it being transferred to you. Stillness is what it is. It is being here-now. Gaze at it. Does it echo the peace within you?

Whether it's the morning glory that blooms for half a day or the forest pine that stays evergreen for half a century, all natural things are themselves as they are. No need to hide behind their exterior self as we humans do. There is dignity and serenity in this character. Let their unmasked selves infuse you with authenticity and courage to be who you are, as you are.

Besides sights, pay attention to the sounds of nature. By listening to the wind blowing, leaves fluttering, birds chirping, crows cawing, or water gurgling, you too become aware of your inner energy field. An animating presence will enliven your physical self.

Observe the trunk of a big tree. Let it teach you the stillness. Notice how deeply and firmly it is rooted in earth and reflects stillness into its surroundings. There is enormous dignity, sacredness, and simplicity in its character. Let nature bless you with its attribute of stillness.

Journal Prompt

After breakfast, go to a sunlit or comforting place in your home and just sit for 5-10 minutes. Observe the colors, the forms, or growth of a plant, if in view. Flowering plants and succulents and cacti grow at their own pace and have their own beauty, their own strength. What do they teach you?

✤ *Day 260* ✤

TODAY'S PRACTICE

Meditation: "Walking Through the Forest"   Read, reflect, and journal.

INSPIRATION

You may find this month's topic of "Stillness, Silence, and Solitude" strange as our focus is writing. Inviting stillness into your life is about something that is beyond using words. But this is the part of my life that has been one of the most meaningful aspects of my creativity and spirituality.

When I began the practice of meditation, more than thirty years ago, it was the toughest discipline to follow. It required sitting still in silence, but in time I have found it most rewarding. There is a subtle difference between meditation and sitting still in silence and solitude. Solitude does not mean much without being accompanied by silence. You could be alone listening to music, watching television, or talking to a friend on the phone, yet it will not result in any spiritual upliftment.

In meditation, when thoughts float in, you keep returning to your inhaling and exhaling. In sitting quietly, memories float up, ideas emerge, solutions surface. The pleasure derived from meditation is different in essence than the satisfaction derived from sitting that resembles daydreaming. Both are valuable and indescribable experiences.

When we enter silence and solitude, we choose to do nothing, we stop making demands, we cease complaining, no longer being self-important or busy. If we want, we can carry this sensation with us wherever we go.

JOURNAL PROMPT

What has your experience of silence and solitude been like? How does it differ from your meditation sessions?

❧ *Day 261* ❧

TODAY'S PRACTICE

Meditation: "Gratitude"   Read, reflect, and journal.

INSPIRATION

For a writer, to move beyond words into silence is a daunting task, even laughable. But in the long run it pays to follow this path. Learn to trust and honor silence as a way of opening yourself to the vaster outer world as well as deeper inner world.

When you choose the path of silence, your words become more meaningful. Outside, the life of noise, busyness, and speed can wait. You can only communicate and commune with your Authentic Self through silence.

You must leave the familiar places to find solitude in spaces you may not yet envision. This journey demands that you say goodbye to life as you know it because at the core of your heart you are longing for something deeper, something more meaningful, something authentic. And silence takes you there.

An inner journey like this that you have chosen to walk upon demands commitment. Any such journey is replete with unspeakable beauty and terrible danger. You may find yourself utterly alone. At times you will feel you are walking in the right direction; at other times you are not so sure. You may get lost and have to take a U-turn. You will face challenges and have unexpected encounters that will stretch you to your limits and change you for the better.

But finally when you reach the end, you may not recognize yourself. Your body, mind, and soul will bear marks of your sacred journey. You'll have arrived at the center of yourself where you merge with your Authentic Self, your muse, your spirit, and with the universal soul.

JOURNAL PROMPT

What does it mean to "communicate" with your Authentic Self, your muse, your spirit? Have you experienced it by now? What about wording the experience on the pages of your notebook?

❧ *Day 262* ❧

TODAY'S PRACTICE
Meditation: "Gratitude"   Read, reflect, and journal.

INSPIRATION

Being with yourself in silence is the most needed discipline in this busy and speedy world, and unfortunately the least experienced one. It is easier to talk and read about than it is to experience it. (For me, it has been the most difficult subject to write about. How does one compose in words what is beyond words?)

If you want to experience sacred presence within the core of your being, if you desire to feel intimate with something that is more than you, if you want to "know God" and feel it in each pore of your body, then try to listen to the sound of silence.

When I began this journey, I knew only intellectually what I was doing. I did not know where I would arrive emotionally. Yet, I was willing to walk on the path to the unknown. In the midst of running a busy but happy household with two daughters and a husband, struggling first as an artist and then a writer, I was searching for something beyond being the mother, the wife, the artist. "Is this all there is?" loomed at the back of my mind. Was there anything else beyond doing everything better and worrying about how others assessed my roles and responsibilities?

Something was missing. But what was it? I felt undercurrents of loneliness and longing. I was unable to articulate what this "something more" was. For a long time I tried to ignore or avoid these feelings. I read voraciously. I wrote. I painted. I joined a doctoral program. As I taught at various universities, that longing for something deeper kept tugging at my heart. These interior jabs were real. These groanings needed my attention.

JOURNAL PROMPT

What undercurrents of loneliness and longing tug at your heart? How have you tried to address them in the past?

ॐ *Day 263* ॐ

TODAY'S PRACTICE

Meditation: "Gratitude"   Read, reflect, and journal.

INSPIRATION

While learning meditation, I learned that the reason you sit still in silence is because the novice practitioner is like a jar of river water, all shaken up. The requirement of sitting for a long period of time allows the sediments to settle and the water to become clear. Such advice felt unreal if not ridiculous. I had been taught to work hard, not to simply sit there and do nothing.

From the first year of my meditation practice, the sediments were my floating thoughts, busy schedule, unwanted emotions, and all amorphous inner workings that I was unable to control.

By now you know how I tamed my inner agitated self with the disciplines of meditation, journaling, reading, and walking. While practicing these disciplines I had many moments of self-reflection leading to self-discovery. Many more were to follow, tributaries leading to the main river of my spiritual journey.

After years of meditation practice and learning to love and carve time with myself, the water has cleared. I see whatever it is that needs to be seen, that needs my attention. I pay heed. I have begun to write full-time. Out of the silence, my books have sprouted, the Mindful Writers groups, and this guidebook you are reading.

What I had felt to be unproductive time listening to inner whispers while being present turned out to be incredibly productive. The inner dynamics that, up until then, were hidden behind the common noise and busyness made the potentialities visible. Silence made my doubts, fears, and unfulfilled longings float to the surface. And then emerged the original works that I could not have fathomed in the busyness of life.

JOURNAL PROMPT

Skills like typing, playing a musical instrument, and learning a foreign language take a great deal of time investment, but later yield a profound facility and ease. What practice have you undertaken that felt like wasted time at first, but once mastered, led to greater revelations?

✌ *Day 264* ✌

TODAY'S PRACTICE

Meditation: "Gratitude"   Read, reflect, and journal.

INSPIRATION

Showing up at your Sacred Power Spot at the same time every morning trains your body and mind, so much so that the very sight of this space at any time of day will make you feel as if you have entered your own inner sanctuary. This outer place vibrates with joy that echoes in your inner shrine.

In the beginning, even 10-15 minutes of sitting during the guided meditation may have felt challenging. But once your favorite relaxed posture becomes a habit, you let go of whatever agenda is in the mind. Your whole body relaxes in a listening mode. You cease striving and don't expect anything. In time, you receive inner gifts that surprise you.

But when you sit in silence and solitude and enter the inner wilderness, you will face wild beasts. Doubts, fears, and resistance will flare up right at the moment when you'll sense something happening. When you have just begun to understand the necessity of solitude in your day, you'll notice forces, both internal and external, begin to work against you.

At such a time, journaling will come to your rescue. Make a list of all the cares and concerns, doubts and fears, shame and guilt. Jot down the details. Having done so to your heart's content, tear out the pages and make a ritual of burning it in your fireplace or outside in the backyard.

This concrete act will actually help you let go of the baggage of unwanted emotions. They are bound to return. But you keep journaling about them, repeating the ritual every 3-6 months until they recede to the background. Whatever little remains, let it flow out onto the pages of your notebook until all negativity disappears.

JOURNAL PROMPT

Did you perform the "burning of the negativity pages" ritual? How many times? Any thoughts? How did it feel?

---

෨ *Day 265* ෬

TODAY'S PRACTICE

Meditation: "Gratitude"   Read, reflect, and journal.

INSPIRATION

Unceasing determination and tireless effort are great, but spending time in silence and solitude is equally good. To experience it you have to practice.

To enter solitude is to listen to your heart and soul that desire intimacy with your own authenticity and genuineness. Listen to your deep desire! What is it saying? Silence will make its messages clear and concrete. Pay heed.

> *"It is hard to clear 5-10 minutes in my schedule*
> *for sitting in silence and solitude."*

Sit with the sentence in quotes for one minute, internalizing it and understanding how silly it sounds. Do you chat on the telephone, surf the internet, watch television? How long do you spend on any one of these passive diversions? Then why does 10 minutes of sitting thus feel like a waste of time?

Sitting provides time to witness and still the sediments of your mind. You can practice it before or after your meditation session until you are ready to practice it as a separate discipline at any other time of the day.

JOURNAL PROMPT

List one, two, or three passive diversions that take up space in your day-to-day life. From which one can you draw 5-10 minutes today for the more beneficial practice of stillness?

✺ *Day 266* ✺

TODAY'S PRACTICE

Meditation: "Gratitude"   Read, reflect, and journal.

INSPIRATION

Resting the body is as important as resting the mind. You have already listened to and read about the daunting task of quieting the mind. It's time to pay attention to your body. When you are stretching or working out, let go of everything your mind is holding.

Writing Meditation Practice is a journey you take inside your body. Therefore taking good care of your physical body is fundamental for the practice to succeed. If you want to cultivate a healthy connection with your Authentic Self, your body must feel cared for and loved.

So that your body functions at its maximum healthy level, your body demands that you look after it well—giving it nutritious food, physical exercise, sleep, and spending time in solitude. A novice feels unbalanced, abused, full of kinks; breathing is shallow, and muscles are tense and knotted. If you notice such signs, pay attention. Learn your body's sign language. Listen to where it hurts or feels tight. Listen when it wants to rest, to move, to breath, or wants nourishment.

Listening to your body is a special kind of knowing that is neither verbal nor thought. The body communicates in sensations. Get familiar with the sensations of all your physical parts. Your body will talk to you.

JOURNAL PROMPT

Like the balance of movement and stillness, what are some other practices that require both action and inaction? Consider breadmaking where the dough must have time to rise, gardening where seeds must have time to grow, and even writing where creative ideas must have time to develop.

≤ *Day 267* ≥

TODAY'S PRACTICE
Meditation: "Gratitude"   Read, reflect, and journal.

INSPIRATION

You are comfortable with yourself, amicable with others, and leading a harmonious life. You're allowing yourself to be who you are. You have no reason to hide behind masks. You are who you are, at peace with yourself. How did you arrive at this point? For nine months you have been seeking your inner mentor and you feel you have found it. If you had no desire to seek it, no inner quest to seek the Self, it would have escaped you. There is still a long way to go, but so far so good. Congratulations!

Do you realize that your productivity and success cannot be measured by the number of books you have written or the number of awards you have received? You don't measure your success on that scale. While you continue to write, you measure your success by the rhythms of time spent in silence and movement, solitude and community work, and travel to distant places and returning to a much loved daily routine.

Healthy body and strong heart-mind have revealed your never changing and everlasting Authentic Self. Searching for it is the prerequisite for your inner journey, your quest and its reward. Aren't you glad you did not spend your whole life trying to avoid the experience of sitting still in silence?

Don't resist the yet-to-come circle of light and energy that stillness and silence emits around you. For now you may feel it as emptiness. This is because you have not awakened your inner mentor. You are almost there, ready to get linked with the one who knows about you more than you know yourself. It is in this emptiness, this boredom that it awaits you. Soon you will recognize it as the one that fills you with creative ideas, insights, and images.

JOURNAL PROMPT

When you are bored, when you feel lonely or when lethargy comes over you, what do you do? Do you try to understand such feelings by shining the light on them, or do you temporarily distract yourself? In your journal, explain to yourself why these feelings are present in your life and how you can transform them permanently.

⠹ *Day 268* ⠹

TODAY'S PRACTICE

Meditation: "Gratitude"   Read, reflect, and journal.

INSPIRATION

Without a period of solitude in your day, it is impossible to fully live a creative and spiritual life. It is only in silence that you can withdraw from the demands of the outer life. It is only in silence that you allow the noise of your longings and compulsions to settle down. It is only in silence that you can self-introspect. It is only in silence that you hear the voice of your Authentic Self.

In silence, an atmosphere is created in which you can surrender to your higher self. You trust the whispers you hear. Slowly you create space within to listen to your true voice. But it is not as easy to do as it sounds. In practice, sitting still in silence and solitude is difficult. The key is to be patient and persistent as you open the inner spaces and begin to feel its sacred presence.

Practice without expectations of a goal or award. It is about showing up and letting the divinity within do the rest. Simply let your body, heart, and mind expand to their maximum potential so that you may experience your spirit in silent solitude.

JOURNAL PROMPT

"Listen to the sounds of silence." Do these words remind you of a story you read, a song you heard, or movie you watched? What sort of feelings did they leave you with?

ᘡ *Day 269* ᘡ

TODAY'S PRACTICE

Meditation: "Gratitude" Read, reflect, and journal.

INSPIRATION

Between writing projects, you always find yourself passing through a rugged terrain. You may feel alone. But let me share a secret with you. This is a predictable situation on your creative and spiritual journey. Yes, it is unpleasant. The more you practice, the more you will know how to manage it and feel comfortable, even when you are in that phase of between and betwixt.

Having finished one project successfully, you may feel you will never write again. This can be compared to dying to your older self. You feel vulnerable and disoriented. You feel you have no scaffolding around you, no familiar characters and settings to comfort you, just your own small self, stripped to the skin, empty. Use this condition and time to go deeper into knowing your higher Self. Self-knowledge shatters the ego. It gives you an opportunity to understand yourself better. Consider it a gift from the universe.

Sitting in silence helps. It draws you deeper and deeper into solitude. The practice strengthens your concentration, increasing your attentiveness. Attention is the doorway to creativity from what you are feeling. You are left with the blessed feeling that everything is as it should be.

Everything is perfect as it is, and you are perfect as you are. No attempt to control whatever the outcome. No reason to defend what you do or do not do. Seeing the truth of things leads you to personal freedom. You feel a loving presence, a silence that is unlike any other silence, a quiet whisper. Let this joyous presence bless you.

JOURNAL PROMPT

What shifts and changes have taken place since you first started to sit in silence and solitude this month?

∽ *Day 270* ↝

TODAY'S PRACTICE

Meditation: "Gratitude"   Read, reflect, and journal.

INSPIRATION

The inner whispers or wordless communion with your Authentic Self is beyond language, beyond concepts, beyond image. You may ask, "How do I know that the whispers I am sensing are not my petty thoughts masquerading as spirituality? How do I know these are not figments of my imagination?"

I had similar questions when I started on this path. Trust me when I say you will learn to recognize the voice of your Authentic Self the way you recognize the voices of your parents, your spouse, your children. With practice and experience, you learn to recognize the communication that comes from the only source deep within you.

This happens when you have learned to bring the inner quietude right into the present moment. Having practiced sitting in solitude at your Personal Power Spot it has become an inner condition, a familiar feeling. You would be able to respond to its stirrings whether you were focusing within or without.

When this happens, you rid yourself of old habitual patterns of living. Don't be afraid to adapt and adopt your new way of looking, listening, and thinking. External circumstances will not change; *you* will change. You'll discover how generous you have become. Much of what you do and learn for yourself in Writing Meditation Practice will provide for what you end up doing for others.

Self-understanding and self-awareness have enabled you to only say words you mean, think thoughts that matter, and act based on what you believe in and what needs to be done. You begin living with loving heart and trusting mind. Seeds of wisdom have been sown; they will sprout and blossom. How wonderful is that!

END OF MONTH PROMPT

Is there anything you know more clearly about stillness, silence, and solitude now than you did before you began to practice this month?

Have you asked yourself, *Why am I on this journey? Why am I wasting my time doing "nothing"?* If so, go back and read the first few pages of your journal.

You have courageously exposed your tender and vulnerable self to your higher Self. It has unconditionally accepted all of your parts – the good, the bad, the ugly. The inner solitude led you to such a place. Be patient. It takes time to truly feel the sacred space within your heart in the silence and solitude of your Power Spot.

BLOSSOMING

"A candle never loses any of its light
while lighting up another candle."
—Rumi

MONTH 10

MINDFULNESS AND WRITING IN THE COMPANY OF OTHERS

Suggested Readings

Writing Down the Bones: Freeing the Writer Within
Natalie Goldberg, 1986.

Writers Inspiring Writers
Matthew Kelly, 2020.

Process: The Writing Lives of Great Authors
Sarah Stodola, 2015.

Writing Alone and with Others
Pat Schneider, 2003.

Why We Write About Ourselves:
Twenty Memoirists on Why They Expose Themselves
(and Others) in the Name of Literature
Ed. Meredith Maran, 2016.

༄ *Day 271* ༅

TODAY'S PRACTICE

You are at that stage in your journey where your basic practice is set, following the five disciplines of meditation, reading, reflection, journaling, and walking (or a wordless activity of your choice), and of course whatever creative work you do. This forms your intimate circle where you hone your skill and voice. By now your routine has turned into a daily ritual. Good for you! Be proud of yourself!

This month I encourage you to think about practicing your creative work in the company of others, weekly, monthly, or otherwise. Consider retreats whenever you can.

If you are not already a member, I invite you to join the Online Mindful Writers Group (OMWG) to experience firsthand the pleasure and inspiration of writing in a company of like-minded mindful writers. www.facebook.com/groups/706933849506291

Meditation: "Gratitude"   Read, reflect, and journal.

INSPIRATION

Roughly a quarter of a century ago, I devoted my life to writing full-time. I dreamed about writing books that would not only entertain and inform but also educate, inspire, and perhaps even transform my readers. I was determined and wrote with devotion to the craft of writing and dedication to what my readers would want. Most importantly, I was fortunate to have the space and time to devote to my new passion.

As a student and teacher, I had collected hundreds of books – Eastern and Western art history, world religions, philosophy, symbolism in sacred arts, and others. My favorite volumes were illustrated hardcovers about Buddhist and Hindu art in India, China, Japan, and Korea. Those and hundreds more now cover the three walls of my study. The fourth wall has a window with a view of lush maples trees, blue spruce, and hemlocks.

In this room with my door closed, I wrote day in and day out. I wrote, rewrote, and revised, and revised again until my first two books for young adults were finally published by Facts on File. Inc. Ideas about the next book floated in my mind but I was not ready to write its draft yet. I felt lonely. In academia I was used to being with colleagues and students, but now I was alone. I wanted to write with other writers. I had befriended people by attending writers' conferences, so I sent out invitations. Several writers responded and the first Mindful Writers Group was founded in 2011. The rest is history.

The Mindful Writers weekly groups and annual retreats provided an environ where I could write with others. The experience was productive and pleasurable. Even the Online Mindful Writers Group (OMWG, founded in November 2017) where each of us writes alone at home, but the psychological presence of other members also writing, never fails to motivate and inspire.

Writing is a lonely profession, the reason I have dedicated this month to introduce you to various environments where you can write with a partner, write with a group of writers who meet weekly, or with many at a retreat set in awe-inspiring nature. Writing with others can surprise you by affecting your productivity, flow, and skill.

JOURNAL PROMPT

Have you felt pangs of loneliness when you complete one piece of writing but before you begin a new one? Do you crave other like-minded individuals' company when you get stuck in the middle of writing?

ꙮ *Day 272* ꙮ

TODAY'S PRACTICE

Meditation: "Gratitude"   Read, reflect, and journal.

INSPIRATION

Once I made the decision to devote my professional life to writing I wrote after breakfast until lunch when the house was quiet. When both of our daughters left for college I wrote for additional hours until my husband came home. Now as my husband is retired, he creates colored drawings, practices piano, reads, and cooks too. If I wanted to, I could write the whole day. That would be like doing NaNoWriMo (National Novel Writing Month) for the whole year, and pretty exhausting and not so pretty.

I write in 2-3 hour sessions with breaks in between, and never for more than 4-5 hours. Also, I am now accustomed to writing in solitude.

When our daughters were home and my husband was still working, I would go out for lunch dates with friends who were not writers. I wished they were! I needed their company but felt it broke the writing momentum that I had built that morning when I came to meet them. When I told them about it, they didn't understand writer's jargon. *Wouldn't it be great if these friends wrote, too? Then we could write together in the morning, discuss our writings over lunch break, and afterward continue writing until it was time to go home.*

Soon afterward I read Natalie Goldberg's *Writing Down the Bones* and a lightbulb went on. She suggested to invite a writer friend to write together at a café or a coffee shop. It worked like a charm. Why didn't I think about that sooner? Several years later, we started the first Mindful Writers Group. One writer writing alone turned into two writers and then a group of five Mindful Writers writing together.

JOURNAL PROMPT

Which writers have inspired you to plan your writing day in a certain way?

❧ *Day 273* ☙

TODAY'S PRACTICE

Meditation: "Gratitude"   Read, reflect, and journal.

INSPIRATION

The key to cultivating your writer's voice is to read a lot. In the beginning, what you love to read gets all mixed up in your own writing. Before you acquire an original voice that readers can recognize, you have to ride on the backs of those who have come before you. By loving and admiring an author's writing, you develop a student-teacher relationship with their works.

You may highlight and underline sentences, mark paragraphs or make notes at the margins. What you read energizes you, awakens your passions, nudges you to remember, and gives you reasons to write. This connection with authors who have long been gone or are still living inspires and motivates you. They may not be working any longer, yet they continue to teach you.

I strongly feel this way when I write alone in my study. I may be by myself but I'm not cloistered. On the shelves of my study are my companions, the way the members of an online group are when they write. They are my professional ancestors. Their voices are with me cheering, helping, and proud of me for what I am writing.

You may be physically alone, but emotionally great authors – writers you respect and admire, whose books you love to read over and over again – are always with you. And when you do not feel like writing alone, you can celebrate writing with another writer by inviting them to write with you.

JOURNAL PROMPT
Invite a writer friend who lives in your area to write with you for 3-4 hours at a café of their choice. Then journal about the experience.

✒ *Day 274* ✒

TODAY'S PRACTICE
Meditation: "Gratitude"   Read, reflect, and journal.

INSPIRATION
When I started writing with a friend away from my home, I wondered why it improved my concentration. Was it the change of scenery? After several sessions I realized that the background noise – soft conversations, murmurs and laughs – kept my senses busy so that the

deeper thoughts and dormant feelings got a chance to emerge, the same reason many writers I know listen to music as they write. It keeps the writing flow streaming.

In addition, being away from my usual writing spot, first once a month and later once a week, made these outings exciting. I felt I was not only writing but also enjoying the company of others and strengthening our relationships. There is some kind of energy when you write with others that overflows in the space during the duration. Creative energy seems to hover in the environment.

It is interesting to note that when you are deep into your work – body, mind, and heart, writing with others – an authentic halo surrounds you. You are more than yourself. It is as if creative and spiritual energies emit into the space around you.

Writing with another cultivates the feeling of kinship and kindness. Connecting with others in-person is what you are doing. Even when you don't express it verbally, you connect with others through your presence.

JOURNAL PROMPT

When you write in a group, do you feel a nonverbal connection with others? What sort of feelings emerge when a writer friend or a group of writers is writing with you?

ᎣᏃ *Day 275* ᏟᎧ

TODAY'S PRACTICE

Meditation: "Gratitude"   Read, reflect, and journal.

INSPIRATION

Having written alone, with a writing companion, and in a group, I still mostly write alone. Behind the closed door, I'm absorbed in my work. Writing is a journey I have learned to love. No one, not even your most intimate friend or loving spouse, truly knows or understands how intensely you feel or how deeply you think, or what you experience while you are writing a book. Only your inner self, the muse, knows.

You certainly benefit from staying in touch with other writers, but most of the writing and research is done in solitude. If you receive the love of a spouse or friends, be grateful. That lets you not feel lonely. Yet, the essential nature of a writer is writing alone.

At the same time, too much solitude can become a deterrent, as does too much talk. Finding a balance is ideal, as is finding a community of writers that is disciplined, that energizes and encourages, but which spends most of the time writing. It's great to have members of different races and ethnicities, different ages, and various economic and educational levels in the group. This adds spice to your writing.

An ideal writing group should be lively with novice as well as advanced writers. A beginner needs as much consolation and support of the writing community as a successful writer does. Fear of failure blocks creative flow as much as fear of success.

JOURNAL PROMPT

When writing in the company of others, do you each share what you have written? How does this reading aloud affect your draft?

❧ Day 276 ❧

TODAY'S PRACTICE

Meditation: "Gratitude"   Read, reflect, and journal.

INSPIRATION

Journaling, meditating, reflecting, commenting, and writing with others, even if only in cyber space, helps create a literary ecosystem that sustains us. Its benefits extend well beyond the confines of the time spent alone together.

With the Online Mindful Writers Group, each individual sits at their writing space. They can make their own schedule about when to meditate, journal, or comment with the provided post and prompt, and write their work-in-progress. Each decides to enter the inner room of their mind and pour their own voice and words onto the blank screen.

This writing together-alone creates a bond that strengthens as writers interact in-person at weekly group meetings or at annual Mindful Writers Retreat or writing conferences. The focus is on enriching the personal journey and producing new work. It not only allows friendships to begin and grow but also improves skill and creates professional networks. There is time to write together and time to write alone.

JOURNAL PROMPT

Ponder and journal about various ways you are connected with other writers via cyberspace, retreats, conferences, and friendships.

ɤ *Day 277* ʊ

TODAY'S PRACTICE

Meditation: "Gratitude"   Read, reflect, and journal.

INSPIRATION

"Writing Alone Together" embodies the mission of Online Mindful Writers Group (OMWG), in-person weekly Mindful Writers Groups, and Mindful Writers Retreats. Writers are void of connectivity; various Mindful Writers venues fill that void.

While working alone, even serious writers doubt themselves. Unlike other jobs, they don't have colleagues doing similar work, sharing frustrations and favorable outcomes near coffee machines or water fountains. Writing with a group such as OMWG helps assuage self-doubt. Every morning the host welcomes others with a suggested meditation followed by hours of writing. This uplifts the mood and supports the creative process of those who are home alone.

There need not be reservation about saying yes to such a setup. You may or may not "show up" but it is there if you want to have "company." For those who are motivated and self-disciplined, this online writing experience turns out to be revealing. You don't have to be alone to finish an article, to meet a deadline, or to complete a book project by yourself.

You can ask a question, write a comment, and feel part of a community of like-minded individuals with whom you connect each day through words, feelings, and ideas.

The monthly hosts provide you with the mental space you need to clarify thoughts about your work-in-progress or some other idea floating through your mind. Writing requires you to know what you think and how you feel about whatever it is you are writing. But with the support and feedback of other writers, it becomes easier to wade through the process and unravel knots. A daunting task that you might otherwise abandon transforms into something different because of the online give and take.

You use tremendous cognitive power to tell stories. It is a slow, deliberate, and often frustrating process. You may feel you are not making any progress. Your creative potential needs nurturing. But sharing the work on OMWG – and reading other writers' warm, thoughtful responses – makes the process a wonderful and worthwhile experience.

JOURNAL PROMPT

Do you feel inspired when you write in the company of others? What are the benefits of writing with others in-person as compared to writing with them online?

✑ *Day 278* ✑

TODAY'S PRACTICE

Meditation: "Gratitude" Read, reflect, and journal.

INSPIRATION

The guest hosts of Online Mindful Writers Group plan and prepare posts for a week or the whole month. This gives them many opportunities to write about events or incidents they thought they had forgotten. It helps them to dive deep into their memory bank and rediscover experiences worth sharing. The support from others who have similar interests and like minds is priceless.

Host-writers' posts provide new perspectives on subjects that stimulate creativity. Their musings often echo the experiences of other members, which helps you to know that you are not alone. Connection leads to commitment to writing. The suggestions for staying focused, managing time, and planning a daily agenda allow you to reflect on your own habits and make improvements.

An important benefit of connecting with other writers is through suggested books. You get introduced to some titles you may have never heard about. It's wonderful to find new resources that help you achieve your writing goals.

Journaling is an important part of your writing journey, so jotting down your thoughts about the prompts gently coaxes you to explore those areas of life that you may be avoiding or forgetting.

When you read about other writers' events from their life journeys, it often inspires you to write your own. When I've been in a fix in the past and didn't know what to write about, I reviewed my old journals and ended up with many interesting topics. Rewriting and revising previous journal entries made me feel more committed and focused.

JOURNAL PROMPT

Open your journal to a page from earlier this year. Read what you have written and reflect on what you see there.

ꕥ *Day 279* ꕥ

TODAY'S PRACTICE

Meditation: "Gratitude"   Read, reflect, and journal.

INSPIRATION

When you are first invited to host an online writing group, whether for a day, a week, or a month, your reaction may be panic. Self-doubt surfaces. You feel intimidated by what previous hosts have shared and by the caliber of participants. Nervousness can make you forget that your capabilities are as good as anyone else's, if not better.

If you write fiction, you may worry about judgment from nonfiction writers. If you write nonfiction, the talent of the fiction writers may intimidate you. What saves you from such doubt and fear is the commitment you make to the group. It is a good thing that they invited you and trusted you. They consider you to have the standards they have. So stop beating yourself up and simply write in earnest. Write from your heart-mind and the words will flow.

"Having written" is always better than "will write." So write your first post, feel good about it, and words will flow over and over again. Things will emerge when you tap into your values and beliefs. Write about what makes you tick, what brings you joy, what inspires you, and what brings you peace. Give suggestions about making small steps that have helped you progress. In a writing group 99 percent of the members are welcoming, accepting, and gracious. They are grateful for your words of wisdom about being a writer. And they comment, share their ideas, and keep connected.

When your time as host concludes, you realize you have benefitted more than when you were merely a regular participant. You will have gained confidence that you have something worthwhile to share with those who are on the same journey as you at various skill levels. Once you break through the fear, you enjoy the challenge of choosing and focusing on a topic, and matching an image, painting, or photograph to the message you want to impart.

JOURNAL PROMPT
Is there one single change within yourself that you want to make? What would that be? Journal about it.

Day 280

TODAY'S PRACTICE
Meditation: "Gratitude"   Read, reflect, and journal.

INSPIRATION

When I write "to go deep within and get connected to my AS" in meditation, what do I mean? What I mean is that once I am only aware of my inner world, when I have moved beyond thoughts, sensations, feelings, when all sediments have settled down, I feel linked with an inner knowing that is as loving as my mother, as caring as my husband, as close as my daughters who nudge me to choose the right thing, who stir insights, or point me to take the path most may not. It doesn't happen often enough but every time I practice at my Sacred Power Spot I feel its presence within. I don't know what else to say. This knowing is experiential.

I was introduced to "Authentic Self" in Sarah Ban Breathnach's book, *Simple Abundance*. The term clicked for me. Unaffiliated with any religion, it still carries the power of the Hindu "Atman," the Buddhist "Buddhachitta," the Christian "Kingdom of God Within," and Islamic "Ruh." Carl Jung called it "Self" and differentiated it from the ego self. He described it as the totality of our psychic system which you may experience as something that is looking at you, something that you do not see but which sees you.

If you want to live a purposeful life, you must work to awaken your Authentic Self. And when it awakens, life changes for the better. Your impulse to create comes from the Self. It is the organizing center that invents, puts in order, and conjures up images, ideas, and insights for the stories you write. It is your thinking heart, your inner companion, your mentor for life.

The difficult work is to make your ego self listen to the commands of your Authentic Self. The reason so many of us fail to connect, even when we are at its threshold, is because our ego is too big and won't stoop to the Self. It distracts. Ego does not want to do any inner work. Meditation and journaling practices tame it, strengthening your trust in the Authentic Self. Daily practice trains the ego to surface only when you want it. Generosity, sharing, and goodness help you come closer to your Self.

JOURNAL PROMPT

Were you acquainted with the term "Authentic Self" before you started reading this book? Have you connected with it through regular Writing Meditation Practice?

﹋ *Day 281* ﹌

TODAY'S PRACTICE
Meditation: "Arriving Home"   Read, reflect, and journal.

INSPIRATION

You must pay heed to your inner calling. You will feel nervous and afraid. You may say, *I don't have time for this! I can't do this!* But a prerequisite of a higher calling is feeling inadequate to the work.

Creativity is unpredictable. This is so because any original work is a collaboration between yourself and the Authentic Self. You can't know how the next chapter of the book will unroll or how the completed painting will look or what the next stage of your life will be like. You learn as you write, as you paint, as you live. Your work and the nonverbal activities give you glimpses into your higher Self and astonish you at every stage.

It also happens that you may hear the call but cannot take up the challenge because you have conflicting responsibilities, providing your family with the basic necessities of life or what you are being called for may not be financially profitable. You have two choices. Either you take up the call because you are driven and don't care if you partly starve as long as you continue to follow your dream (the way Vincent Van Gogh did, but he had no family), or you postpone your aspirations until a partner or spouse is able to provide enough for the family or until you retire. The universe is watching. And the universe is waiting. It will summon you again and perhaps again for your life's work that you have been dreaming about, and which only you can do.

If you are mindful, you receive little calls every day. They may be little, but they assist your big calling. Look out for *all* the calls, big or small. Keep in mind that once you start, the universe collaborates with your handiwork. When something clicks and feels right to your thinking-heart, give it everything you've got.

The Authentic Self is compassionate, sympathetic, savant. When awakened, it is the most energetic part of your being. Before the year ends, you will discover that you have gifted yourself with a grand opportunity to come closer to this Self. It wants to be discovered as much as we want to connect with it. Strengthen your connection with it through your daily practice.

JOURNAL PROMPT

Today, turn off the logical part of your brain and turn up your mind's free associations in silence for 10 minutes. Connect with something inside you that you have not felt yet. What do you come up with?

✤ Day 282 ✤

TODAY'S PRACTICE

Meditation: "Arriving Home"   Read, reflect, and journal.

INSPIRATION

Once you dedicate yourself to the calling of your higher power, it augments skills required for your project. A good practice is staying in touch with your inner companion and listening to it. Here is an example from my life.

In the spring of 2009, I felt an urge to start a group with whom I would meditate, journal, and write. Yet I hesitated, fearful. What would I say? How would I start the first meeting? Why would other writers want to write with me and return weekly to practice or come to the retreats? Such questions hovered in my mind.

It was during this time that one morning I went to the local library. On the display desk, I noticed a copy of L. Frank Baum's *Wizard of Oz*. The moment I laid eyes on its cover my body felt energized. I spent the rest of the day critically rereading the book. To my surprise, this time I understood its symbolism. The three characters skipping on the yellow brick road along with Dorothy are her fragmented selves – her brain, her heart, and her courage. It is only after she becomes aware of her fragmented self that she integrates and is able to return home as a whole person. At the end of her heroic journey Dorothy finds herself happily surrounded by her loved ones as she "awakens" to her Authentic Self.

Voila! It was as if the introductory topic for my first meeting was handed over to me. The subject was our fragmented selves, how we live disintegrated lives like Dorothy, with our body at one place, our mind at a different place, and our heart somewhere else.

All our lives we have access to our "home," but we don't know it. Hidden under this rubble, the Authentic Self lies dormant. It not only makes us whole but also connects us with the power within.

JOURNAL PROMPT

When you go deeper into a book, it takes you within yourself. You receive insights into human experience, and it may even change you in some ways. Journal about one special book that has strongly affected you.

ᦒ *Day 283* ᦒ

TODAY'S PRACTICE

Meditation: "Arriving Home"   Read, reflect, and journal.

INSPIRATION

Once upon a time the following thought discouraged me from writing for months: *There is nothing original in the world.* Whatever thought you come up with has already been written in some language at some corner of the world. Although I continued to work, what I wrote was mediocre. I had lost trust in my "voice." My writing lost its authenticity because I questioned my validity as a writer. I was not writing as a whole person, with integrated body, heart, and mind. I felt fragmented. There was nothing "new" my voice had to say.

In the middle of the night, a voice whispered, *"You are what's new... your singular way of observing the world, internalizing it, regurgitating it, and then pouring it on paper in words to share with your readers."* For the next several mornings, similar messages repeated themselves in silent sittings. I focused, became more attentive, and once again journaled my reflections about the messages. I was uninhibitedly, fearlessly, and frantically "sketching" in words, accumulating material for future works. What came from my thinking-heart was "original."

When a demand echoes in your heart, it is important to accept the challenge. Through acceptance, the call becomes singularly yours. The secret is in taking full responsibility, trusting the path wherever it leads, and then working dedicatedly as you walk on it. From that point onward it is of no concern to you whether the project succeeds or fails. The only thing necessary is to trust that there is no one else in the world who could or would do the project the way you will. Own your talent humbly, gratefully, and respectfully, and share it with the world.

JOURNAL PROMPT
What is one project you have felt called to work on? How did you heed or not heed the call?

ꙮ *Day 284* ꙮ

TODAY'S PRACTICE
Meditation: "Arriving Home"   Read, reflect, and journal.

INSPIRATION
While you are absorbed in writing your work-in-progress, it is good advice not to discuss business. At the first Mindful Writers group, we decided to leave our egos at the door and not mention how many books a member has published, how many awards have been received, or contracts signed with an agent or editor. Such talk deters the creative flow. Each member must be friendly, supportive, and helpful toward the others and each must have a generous, grateful, and liberal spirit.

Focusing on the writing helps to eliminate competitiveness. The most important part is the love of writing, the craft, and the inspiration and motivation one feels when sitting among like-minded fellows. When writers in a group support each other, there is an aura of comfort and camaraderie. The group fuels innovation for experienced authors and protects novice and vulnerable writers.

JOURNAL PROMPT

Has it ever happened that your emphasis on business over writing ended up hindering your work? How did you find your way back to focusing on the craft?

∽ *Day 285* ᴗ

TODAY'S PRACTICE

Meditation: "Arriving Home"   Read, reflect, and journal.

INSPIRATION

At the Mindful Writers Retreats in Ligonier, Pennsylvania, participants gather, meditate, walk, and write, away from their normal routine. Do you want to recreate a similar atmosphere for your online retreat? Decide on a day, then invite your writer friends and work together. "Alone Together" is an inspiring way to feel motivated.

This retreat has twofold purpose: an opportunity to deepen your practice, and to help you write with others for a longer period of time. Here is a blueprint for a one-day retreat that you may use.

Silence your phone and other distractions. Inform your family members that for a day you'll be engaging in an extended period of writing practice. Keep your journal and pen handy.

Sit at your Sacred Power Spot to practice meditation. Clarify your writing intentions for the day. The sincerity of your intentions and efforts is important. You may talk with the fellow retreaters during meals.

7:00 A.M.	Breathing and Body Scan
7:20 A.M.	Journaling
8:00 A.M.	Walking Meditation

Intentional walking: Depending on the weather, you may walk indoors or outdoors. Start slow. Continue slow. End slow.

Your mind will wander to what you are writing, plot, characters, storyline, what to cook for dinner. Pause. Come back to the breath. When you notice you have gone for a long time with one of your characters or plotlines, pause. Return. It does not matter how long you had gone as long as you return to the breath. This is the walking practice. Give attention to the in-breath and out-breath. Attend to the rhythm of your feet, to nature sounds, to sights, or to the things that surround you. This is an incredible training in presence. You are neither going nor arriving anywhere. Wherever you go, there you are. Nothing to do. Just be.

8:45-9:30 A.M.	Coffee, Tea, Breakfast
9:30 A.M.-12:30 P.M.	Writing Work-in-Progress
12:30-1:00 P.M.	Lunch
1:00-4:00 P.M.	Writing Work-in-Progress

JOURNAL PROMPT

Journal about how you felt at the beginning of the day and at the end. Did you feel energy surface? Are you going to repeat the day?

ꙮ *Day 286* ꙮ

TODAY'S PRACTICE

Meditation: "Arriving Home"   Read, reflect, and journal.

INSPIRATION

As a writer, it is good to write with others but equally good to write surrounded by nature. One of my lifelong habits is never to leave home without a book and a notebook. I may not get the opportunity to read or jot notes, but having these two items gives me comfort.

Sit on your back porch or front lawn. Record your observations. It could be about anything you witness or experience. Repeat this exercise for a week. On the seventh day, make a list of your observations. Pick the one that speaks to you and create a poem or short story incorporating the items on your list.

Making a list of observations while you walk may become a habit. It turns a sensory experience into a piece of writing or a post. Sometimes just one or two things may inspire you, and other days it may include a long list. Save this list for the days when you feel stuck and can't think of anything to write. One topic on the list is sure to serve as a mindful catalyst for a whole story or an essay.

JOURNAL PROMPT

Write about a time when you bonded with nature. Was it intentional or serendipitous? Was it a momentary or a prolonged connection? How did that connection benefit your creative flow?

৬৩ *Day 287* ৬৩

TODAY'S PRACTICE

Meditation: "Arriving Home"   Read, reflect, and journal.

INSPIRATION

After you test out a one-day online retreat with writing friends, consider a three-, four-, or five-day online retreat. Better still, plan an onsite retreat. On such a trip, by the second evening, you will know each other's names and projects. On the last day, you will all feel re-energized, motivated, filled with hope.

At an onsite retreat, you don't have to worry about the food. Simply write and learn more about writing from your colleagues. At home it can feel as if you are the only one writing in the world. But at a retreat, everyone is engaged in writing, experiencing the same fears and insecurities.

The retreat allows you time and focus to write every single day. Talk writing, breathe writing, think writing. Learn what you can during the event, and when you are back home, try all of those things.

You will be surprised to notice that years later, the writers you met on retreats will have become good friends. It's almost impossible not to make connections and a few close friends at writing retreats.

JOURNAL PROMPT

Ponder and write about the fabulous ways you have connected with other writers... through conferences, retreats, and workshops.

---

๑ *Day 288* ๛

TODAY'S PRACTICE

Meditation: "Arriving Home"   Read, reflect, and journal.

INSPIRATION

Reasons to Attend a Retreat

You will write more and talk less! You will leave distractions behind. You will tell friends and family that you are working and don't want to receive texts or calls. Turn your phone on "do not disturb" so you don't get interrupted. You'll be so glad you did. And you'll get a lot more done! Remember, you are retreating from the demands of everyday life with no one to answer to except yourself.

When you meditate and journal and walk during retreat days, you'll be amazed at the level of focus, clarity, and productivity you attain. Once you begin to relax, your mind will settle, allowing your writing to come into focus. In the space created, you will reconnect with the writer you are, the one buried under the demands of daily life back home. At a retreat you are responsible for only one task – your writing. With your mind fully engaged with your work, your creative flow is fluid.

Having new surroundings energizes you. Inspiration abounds. You have run out of inspiration at times. You aren't necessarily blocked, just not inspired. There's nothing like a change of locale to get the juices flowing, and being around a new group of people activates the imagination. Camaraderie flows naturally when writers explore, share their work, and give supportive feedback. Meals, meditations, and walking together further help create an ambiance of fellowship.

JOURNAL PROMPT

How have you made room for writing with others? Have you ever committed the time and resources so that you could retreat to write? If not, why?

ꙮ *Day 289* ꙮ

TODAY'S PRACTICE

Meditation: "Arriving Home"   Read, reflect, and journal.

INSPIRATION

Writing retreats are deeply transformative. They crack us open and awaken us to new possibilities. Nothing is as powerful as walking away from one's daily life to enter a safe environment solely focused on enhancing and supporting your creativity.

At a retreat, notice people's facial expressions on the first day and then also on the last day. Note your observations in your journal. On the first day retreaters are often uncertain, fearful, and defending themselves. On the last day they are candid, connected, and gleaming with love.

When you are free from your to-do lists and the relentless pressure of the "undone," you are free to focus on your heart's desire: connecting with the deep place where your truest writing comes from. You leave behind the excuses, making a conscious choice to commit to your writing for an intensive period of time. The rigor focuses the mind and leads to breakthroughs in your work...and in your life. You clear the decks of routine and obligations that have been weighing you down. Escaping the habitual opens the doors to awakening and creativity.

When you put yourself in a beautiful place where the conditions are designed specifically to support and nurture your writing, you hone your focus toward what you really want. Living, working, and playing with other writers quickly creates an intimate community. When you write intimately with other writers, you become deeply inspired by their stories. When another writer in the group is gifted at dialogue, able to evoke a vivid setting or a memorable character, or is particularly brave about putting themselves on the page, you learn to do the same through osmosis and example.

JOURNAL PROMPT

Place yourself in an unusual surrounding today, with the intention of observing and sensing everything for the purpose of writing. Make notes about dialogue you overhear, body language you observe, and sights and sounds that take place in the space around you.

✌ *Day 290* ✌

TODAY'S PRACTICE

Meditation: "Arriving Home"   Read, reflect, and journal.

INSPIRATION

You know those dreadful days when your muse refuses to visit you? When writing with others, a synergy emerges that nourishes and magnetizes your muse. Your creative genius becomes more reliable. You never lose the potential inside you. Such an atmosphere results in self-confidence as a writer.

Attending a retreat for an extended period of time can not only kickstart a writing project, but also help you complete a significant portion of your first rough draft. When surrounded by writers of different levels, you naturally produce more words. The momentum gained on retreat stays with you even when you transition back into your daily routine.

When you write every day, all day, in the company of others, you create a routine that needs to be protected and cherished after you return home. Whether it's for a weekend or a number of weekdays, everything revolves around writing. You develop characters, you paint scenes, you compose dialogue, you allow yourself to go where you haven't dared or thought to go before. The wheels that turn with full force at the retreat keep turning for a long time back in your study.

Two needs are gratified when you write at home *and* go on retreats: the need for solitude, and the need for companionship. The cherry on the cake is you get to make friends with those who share your passion for writing.

JOURNAL PROMPT

If you have previously written during a group or retreat session, what do you miss the most? If you have not had such an experience before, what do you envision as the most helpful aspect?

❧ *Day 291* ☙

TODAY'S PRACTICE

Meditation: "Self-Forgiveness and Compassion"　　　Read, reflect, and journal.

INSPIRATION

Making Plans Before a Writing Retreat

Figure out exactly what you'll be writing while you're at a retreat. Create a list of scenes or chapters you want to write. Having notes prepared will nudge you and make all the difference in productivity.

Set a goal for how many words you'd like to write. You can make strides every single day toward the target word count. However, set a realistic goal. Make it something you can achieve without discouraging yourself and causing stress.

Make sure to reward yourself when you achieve your daily progress toward the goal. Even if it is just to say, "HOORAH!" there's something about hitting a word count goal that never fails to motivate you! So keep track of your progress along the way until you hit "The End."

JOURNAL PROMPT

What is one measurable and realistic writing goal you can set for yourself to achieve this week?

৬ *Day 292* ৩

TODAY'S PRACTICE

Meditation: "Self-Forgiveness and Compassion"   Read, reflect, and journal.

INSPIRATION

Ligonier Mindful Writers Retreats are organized by Mindful Writers Kathleen Shoop and Larry Schardt. The food served is nutritious and tasty. However, a spread of delicious snacks prepared by other mindful writers are generously served 24/7 and can tempt you to forsake dietary goals.

Make sure your retreat organizers serve healthy food because if you eat fast food during the days you plan to be at your best creative self, you don't want to feel bloated and drained of energy. Junk food can make you tired and easily distracted.

When you eat healthy and nutritious food, your retreats go smoothly, you feel energy the entire time, you have more focus, and you get a lot more words with less effort.

Oh yes, remember to drink plenty of water or liquids of your choice. Say yes to staying hydrated. I tend to stick to high-protein breakfasts, salads for lunch, and grilled or steamed vegetables, fish, and lean meats for dinner.

Try one writing retreat where you only fuel your body with super healthy foods and complete the writing work that you had planned earlier. I promise you will go back again and again.

Experiment by eating a healthy and nutritious meal just before your next writing session. Journal about how your body feels, especially compared to times when you have overindulged.

Day 293

Today's Practice

Meditation: "Self-Forgiveness and Compassion"   Read, reflect, and journal.

Inspiration

Some people neither want to write in a group nor attend a writing retreat, irrespective of the benefits. You can still enjoy the advantage of a change of scenery that's away from the usual daily distractions.

One option is to check into a hotel. Another is to house-sit for a friend. You could also rent an apartment or home on Airbnb. Consider what type of space will feel comfortable. Is the furniture arrangement inspiring? What would help you to be comfortable while you are there? Make sure the writing table is the right size and height. Are the chairs comfortable? If you love to write on the couch, make sure you have one available that suits your needs.

Or perhaps you prefer to consider lower-cost options closer to home. Then look for a café or coffee shop nearby where you can write during the day, free from the typical distractions of home.

Journal Prompt

Journal about the kind of environment that inspires you to feel most creative.

ᘛ *Day 294* ᘚ

TODAY'S PRACTICE

Meditation: "Self-Forgiveness and Compassion"   Read, reflect, and journal.

INSPIRATION

What if, for some reason, you simply can't leave home? Plan a retreat with yourself at home. Set boundaries and time limits, so you don't end up chatting longer than getting your work done. You could write for a set number of hours with short breaks, or you could write in sprints by setting a timer. Remember! Don't stop writing until the timer goes off.

Writing in sprints of 30-60 minutes maximizes productivity. During a sprint you focus on nothing but your word count. Spelling, grammar, and complete sentences do not matter. When the timer goes off, take a break, get up, walk around, think about your next scene, get some water, and do whatever you need to do. When your 5-10 minute break is done, sit back down and run another sprint.

For some writers, sprinting is their single most important productivity tool. They get the most possible words written in the least amount of time. You can do sprints anywhere from 10 minutes to an hour. If you haven't done writing sprints before, try a variety of time lengths and see what works best for you. Once you find a timer length that works for you, stick to it!

JOURNAL PROMPT

Set a word count goal for yourself and start the timer. When you reach the end of your time or the word count goal, reward yourself! It is always motivating to receive a reward for doing a great job.

ᘛ *Day 295* ᘚ

TODAY'S PRACTICE

Meditation: "Self-Forgiveness and Compassion"   Read, reflect, and journal.

INSPIRATION

Why a Writing Retreat Is Good for Your Creative Health

1. Get a break from daily responsibilities, distractions, and the vortex of social media so you can focus on your writing.

2. Sleeping accommodations and food are taken care of.

3. A change of scenery opens new possibilities. A scenic landscape and inspiring people stimulate your creativity.

4. Daily practice hones your skill.

5. Full focus on writing. Total immersion in work boosts the quantity as well as quality of your work.

6. You can write on your own but you don't have to feel lonely.

7. Overcome weaknesses in a supportive atmosphere. Each retreater is harassed by irritating inner critics. Learn how to tame them so they work with your intuitive mind.

8. Learn to solve writing problems from others' experiences: how to find time to write; where and how to submit your work; and how to deal with pesky plots, troublesome scenes, stilted dialogue, and so on.

9. Time to focus on your passion, the opportunity to share your ideas with others, and acquiring new skills and insights that motivate you and boost your confidence.

10. Mealtimes are enjoyable occasions for socializing after the day's work. Meet wonderful colleagues, mentors, and coaches, and make terrific progress on your work.

JOURNAL PROMPT

Which aspects of a writing retreat do you most crave?

‿ *Day 296* ↝

TODAY'S PRACTICE

Meditation: "Self-Forgiveness and Compassion"   Read, reflect, and journal.

INSPIRATION

Guest hosting an online writers' group can be a fulfilling experience. You may ask one or more members to contribute, each choosing a topic that interests you the most, and sharing your posts over the course of a number of days or weeks.

I suggest writing about one of the five disciplines that make up Writing Meditation Practice: meditation, journaling, walking, reading, or writing. Members also enjoy topics such as travel, creativity, art, nature, and beauty.

At the Online Mindful Writers Group, Mindful Writer Eileen Hodgetts posted about her love of books when she was growing up in England. She re-evaluated aspects of those years in the light of memories of what she had read. This prompted other members to comment about memories of their childhood readings.

Eileen said she had felt she was writing into a vacuum but was gratified when many "friends" read her posts and commented. She "met" these writers through their shared memories of their own reading habits. She was the one who stimulated the group conversation, but later suggested she was the one who gained the greatest benefit by learning how our childhood reading later shapes our expectations.

During and since the pandemic of 2020, reading saved us, as did sharing our stories with other writers – people who know and value words. The storyteller beside the fire has never been more important.

JOURNAL PROMPT

What is one thing you as a writer have been unable to do alone? Is there a way that a group writing experience or retreat could help?

෴ *Day 297* ෴

TODAY'S PRACTICE

Meditation: "Self-Forgiveness and Compassion"   Read, reflect, and journal.

INSPIRATION

Before joining Online Mindful Writers Group, Jennifer D. Diamond used to feel reluctant to talk about meditation. She dreamed of becoming a published author but fear blocked her flow. Self-doubt in the disguise of Imposter Syndrome plagued her writing. "Calling myself a writer," she wrote, "felt like stretching the truth, or worse, an outright lie."

Through OMWG, she went from meditating "almost" every day and writing "almost" every day, to a full-fledged daily practice... from "chasing the fleeting glimmers of writing flow, to slipping into that flow every day of the week."

By reading and commenting on the daily posts at OMWG's Facebook page, this writer and others have found a writing community and acceptance, and in the process, a deeper self-understanding. The OMWG space allows for open, enriching daily interactions with other mindful people. Daily journaling, based on prompts, slowly strengthens and transforms your writing voice. Once you discover your unique writing voice, you can overcome any fear of sharing your goals and dreams with the world.

JOURNAL PROMPT

Journal the phrase: "I am a writer." How does seeing these words on your page affect you? Do you believe them? Do you feel a twinge of Imposter Syndrome? Or do you feel affirmation of something you already believe deep inside you?

෴ *Day 298* ෴

TODAY'S PRACTICE

Meditation: "Self-Forgiveness and Compassion"   Read, reflect, and journal.

INSPIRATION

Being a writer means hearing and heeding your inner call to walk a writer's path. What is this walking if not a hero's journey? When you take your first step, you are likely nervous, fearful, and self-doubting. Even though you feel hesitant, keep walking toward the unknown.

On the path of struggle with self-doubt, you fight self-resistance and confront Imposter Syndrome. Over and over again you may stumble or fall, but you get up or are pulled up by a friend, then later by your own strength, until finally you begin to hear your inner writer. With Writing Meditation Practice, slowly your true self is revealed to you.

You feel connected to the Authentic Self. You have found the fountain of an elixir that guides you through the obstacles, the ups and downs, and finally brings you back home. Your true Self grounds you, centers you with the gift of your original voice, new confidence, and courage. You are ready to share your words and works with the world. You know with certainty that you are a writer and writing is the work you were born to do.

JOURNAL PROMPT

Journal about how you see yourself having developed as a writer over time. Were there moments when you felt called to write? Were there moments when words failed to appear? Did you work through any hesitancy, or did it stymy you from continuing? What was it like the first time you shared your writing with others? Has the experience of sharing your drafts and finished content with others changed over time?

ᘛ *Day 299* ᘚ

TODAY'S PRACTICE

Meditation: "Self-Forgiveness and Compassion"   Read, reflect, and journal.

INSPIRATION

To allow you to envision one way in which other writers embrace their calling, here is a sample of the twelve stages of the writer's "hero's journey."

1. You, as a writer, are merrily going on your daily routine. *(Ordinary World)* An invitation arrives to be a guest host at Online Mindful Writers Group. *(Call to adventure)*

2. You don't want to do it. It makes you feel nervous and uncomfortable. You don't trust you have time to do it or are worthy of the task. *(Refusal of the call)*

3. An inner voice *(or an outer mentor)* tugs. You can do it!

4. Hesitatingly you agree. *(Crossing the threshold)*

5. Thoughts race in your mind. *Which topic would I choose?* As you write a rough draft, your hand trembles. *(Tests)*

6. The golden thread of the Writing Meditation Practice guides you. *(Allies)* You walk the labyrinth and approach the demons and dragons *(Enemies)* to penetrate the innermost cave. *(Entrance to the Dragon's Den)*

7. Before you know it, while you are confronting the dragon, half of the month is over. *(The Ordeal)*

8. By the third week, you realize you are enjoying the process. Each morning you see your post, read comments, and interact with other members. You feel motivated, ecstatic, and triumphant. *(Seizing the treasure)*

9. Having almost finished writing the posts, you feel wonderful about yourself. *(Ready to return home)*

10. Something has changed. *(Resurrection)*

11. You have posted without inhibitions, without restrictions. You have shared your feelings and thoughts with other members of the group. You feel fearless, stronger, and an important part of the group. In the process you have enriched your inner self and increased confidence. *(Return with the Boon)*

12. You have sharpened your skills, made good friends, and returned to your regular routine. *(Ordinary World)*

JOURNAL PROMPT

Which of these twelve stages of the writer's hero's journey do you feel you have reached?

∾ *Day 300* ∾

INSPIRATION

Writing with others does not mean becoming a member of a critique group. These are two different kinds of experiences. A good critique group is one in which members read your rough drafts in a safe and nourishing atmosphere, and give useful critiques of what is missing and how your work could be improved.

If you start a critique group, strive for members who are of almost equal merit. Insecure writers do not have the skill set to offer editing assistance and insights. They will try their best to offer some beneficial advice – by pointing out every single flaw they can find. This may not be helpful, depending on the development stage of the piece. Worse, it can certainly shatter confidence. So beware!

Having shared with you the benefits of writing with others and attending retreats, I feel I've come full circle back to where I started as a professional writer – writing alone in the silence and comfort of my study. I now love writing in my study, my Sacred Power Spot. Through years this space has accumulated a presence due to my meditation, journaling, and deep reading practice. It emits a spiritual aura that I sense when I enter the room.

I no longer feel alone. I feel grounded in myself. The walls of the space are lined with books which I know so well. The story of my writing life echoes from the pages of these classics. They know me as well as I know them. I have highlighted, underlined, commented in their margins. My so-called original voice has been hewn by their writing voices and styles. I respect and admire and love the works of the masters.

These mentors are with me each day to motivate, to inspire, and to encourage. They are with me cheering my effort, proud of me for showing up every morning, and leaving a daily word count that I am happy with. Here I joyously reflect the literary richness that has come my way because I have read, chewed, and digested these books. I wrote alone, I wrote with others, and I published books I'm proud of. Now as I write alone in my study, I feel the warmth of the fellowship of writers, past and present.

END OF MONTH PROMPT

Which writers do you admire? Which have influenced your work? Journal about the time when you first realized that you have weaned from their influence and developed your own voice.

MONTH 11

MINDFULNESS, AWE, WONDER, AND DELIGHT

Suggested Readings

Awake in the Wild:
Mindfulness in Nature as a Path of Self-Discovery
Mark Coleman, 2006.

USA National Parks:
Lands of Wonder
DK Eyewitness, 2020.

Another Day Not Wasted:
Meditations on Photography, Art, and Wildness
Guy Tal, 2021.

҉ *Day 301* ҉

INSPIRATION

Awe and wonderment are sacred emotions that kindle spiritual delight, tenderness, and kindness. Ancient Hindu texts teach that within us there is an innate force of joyful wonder, but we have to create outer circumstances for it to sprout and surface. This may happen when you face an adversity or when you watch sunset rays filter through spring foliage.

Wonder is a heightened state of awareness that is triggered when something unexpected happens that disorients yet delights you. It is present in you all the time but remains hidden under mental clouds until something enters your consciousness and parts the clouds.

You have the power to turn each moment into a wondrous one. There is no reason to wait for a stunning natural landscape in search of wonder and awe. It is present in this moment. Pay attention to your vision that is reading the words I wrote with my dexterous fingers. You are reading and comprehending the images from my imaginings that I translated in letters and arranged in sentences that now echo in your mind. If this is not awesome and wonderous, then what is?

In the same way, imagine how you transmute raw ingredients into a fancy dinner dish. This simple marvel has become a jaded action because you perform it repeatedly. But isn't wonder here now? The more aware and attentive you are to your surroundings, the more delight you feel in your daily living. Think about the clothes you are wearing, the house you are living in, the family you have created – and what it was before.

Potent moments of wonder are subtle, fleeting. Your imagination and intuition come together. One moment the feeling is there, the next moment it is gone. But when you are curious and mentally open, when you are bewildered and hold things in high regard, you get connected to your Authentic Self and realize how awe-some the universe truly is.

Journal Prompt

Do an experiment: Pay extra attention to an activity you do every day. Watch your inhaling and exhaling and focus on whatever it is you are doing or saying. Journal about the difference you notice.

∿ *Day 302* ∿

Today's Practice

Meditation: "Body"   Read, reflect, and journal.

Inspiration

Body and Movement

Your body and physical sensations are all you've got. You came to this world in it and you will leave the world in it. (I do realize we are more than our body and senses, but please allow me to focus on the human body for today.)

Unfortunately we do not exploit our body's unlimited potential. We neither pay 100 percent attention to it nor are we aware how many possibilities it has for providing enjoyment. Do you realize that it's only when your tooth hurts or when your foot is broken that you pay any attention to it?

The first step to improve your attitude toward the body is by a 2-minute body scan from the soles of your feet to the top of your head thanking each part for what it does. Pay homage to your physical self thus and watch what happens.

Untrained senses are clumsy, giving way to an insensitive eye that does not find any sight interesting, an unmusical ear that does not hear soothing patterns of sound, a coarse palate that does not taste the difference between delicious and bland food, a rough nose that can't distinguish scents, and unsensitive fingers that don't know texture variations.

When not used to their fullest for the finest things, your senses atrophy. The quality of life is merely adequate, even dismal. But when you make it a point to learn and experience what your body can do, discipline imposes order on sensations, generating a sense of harmony that is highly enjoyable.

Mindful walking and other physical movements offer an unlimited amount of sensual enjoyment. But if you have no interest in moving the body, it will be nothing but flesh. Be assured that no matter how fit you are, there is a possibility to fine tune your body and senses every day. Grow a bit stronger, a bit more sensitive, and surprise yourself at the end of the year.

JOURNAL PROMPT

If you don't walk, begin by walking 15 minutes a day, and add 10-minute increments weekly. No problem if you skip a walk. If you already walk 2-3 miles a day, kudos! Increase your speed or distance at your convenience. And on the way, hear the wind and the birds, observe the color of the sky and the foliage, breathe in scents and aromas, touch the texture of the tree trunk or top of tall grass, then journal about it.

ᘓ *Day 303* ᘔ

TODAY'S PRACTICE
Meditation: "Body" — — — — — — — — — — — — — Read, reflect, and journal.

INSPIRATION

Developing Fine Senses

To develop the subtle and complex emotion of wonderment and awe that delights, you must sharpen the senses. When cultivated to the best of your ability, you are better able to enjoy finer things in life – art, nature, literature, and the divinity in you. Once developed well, they displace the trivial and spiteful.

You may be going through your day-to-day life thinking you are utilizing the five senses, but what you are doing is merely going through the motions of living. What if you are not living as passionately as you could? Mindfulness, attention, and awareness train you to sharpen your senses to their maximum capacity. So much so that you begin to experience physical sensations that you did not know you had the potential to sense.

World literature and art is unfathomably unique and diverse. Even fine arts of a single culture vary immensely. Take interest in the one that touches your heart, that you truly appreciate, and take the first step to develop new subtle senses and feelings. You cannot go wrong. Whatever speaks to your heart-mind is correct.

Appreciating distinctly different arts connects diverse world cultures. The delight you feel when sensing new experiences is exactly the same in the language of the art and heart.

It is therefore up to you to improve the quality of your life, and to grow emotionally and spiritually.

Journal Prompt

Journal about the senses you use the most and the ones you use the least. What can you do to further strengthen the strongest sense and use more often the ones that are neglected?

～ *Day 304* ～

Today's Practice

Meditation: "Body"   Read, reflect, and journal.

INSPIRATION

Seeing

There is sheer joy in seeing. Watch nature through the sun, the moon, the stars, the sky, the clouds, the ocean, the river, the waterfall, the lake, the flames, the crackling sparks. Whether you are a child or a ninety-year-old, you can never see anything better.

How can one learn to use visual skills to the utmost? Start observing nature and art any day, any time. The details in painting, sculpture, architecture, and crafts will surprise you. Take in the sense of composition, color hues, gradations, and visual balance. See artworks *viscerally*. There is no logic to what you learn thus but you will begin to appreciate the world around you with new understanding.

Whatever style or period of art charms you or touches your heart, keep looking at those works. Let them overwhelm you. Digest every nuance and every little thread. Let them hit you in the stomach.

When you encounter a great work of art, it thrills not only your sense of sight but also all your senses, emotionally and intellectually. But it takes time and self-training to be able to derive this level of sensory delight from seeing.

JOURNAL PROMPT

Try living your life with your eyes shut for half an hour. Okay, fifteen minutes? Ten? How does it feel? Spend the same segments of time looking at one natural or art object. What new thing did you discover?

⤳ *Day 305* ⤶

TODAY'S PRACTICE

Meditation: "Body"   Read, reflect, and journal.

INSPIRATION

Hearing

Listening to a favorite piece of music is the highest kind of hearing. Musical compositions are soothing patterns of sound that restore order to your consciousness. Therefore taking in organized and harmonized auditory information helps organize and harmonize the mind. Music restores order and reduces entropy.

For someone who does not intentionally listen to music but does so, it wards off anxiety, a negative mood, or boredom. But a music lover absorbed in listening can feel at one with his higher self, the singer and the world; a feeling of oneness overcomes them. They are not just listening to the music; they are living the music.

As with any arts, to fully enjoy music you must pay attention. Like writing or meditating with a group, by listening to a live performance with an audience you feel the "collective effervescence," an aesthetic energy that throbs in the heart of each listener. The sociologist Emile Durkheim claimed that such an energy is at the roots of all aesthetic pleasure and spiritual experiences.

JOURNAL PROMPT

What kind of music do you like? What happens to your body and mind when you are completely absorbed in listening to a song or musical composition?

❧ *Day 306* ❧

TODAY'S PRACTICE

Meditation: "Body"   Read, reflect, and journal.

INSPIRATION

Taste and Smell

Food is potentially a rich source of enjoyment as it indulges not one but two senses: taste and smell. Appetite is to the stomach what thought is to the mind and love to the heart. A tasty dish can change a frown into a smile.

If the person who cooks in your home makes delicious meals, the quality of your daily life turns pleasurable. You look forward to dining with your family. If not, you can occasionally treat yourself at a favorite restaurant. You wouldn't want to make do with listening to a poorly tuned instrument when you have the option of listening to a great concert. Make the same choice for meals.

In Hindu scriptures, the human body is equated with a temple. With its five senses and the mind, the body tries to obtain as much information as our sensitivity allows. It is through our body that we connect with one another and the rest of the outer and inner world. This connection is quite enjoyable, though it can be painful as well. It does not require special talents or money to improve this quality of life by refining your senses. Find sufficient skills to delight in what your body can do.

Several decades ago it used to be considered decadent to enjoy or make too much fuss over a meal. But now we have gourmet food journals, popular television shows, and "foodies" and wine lovers who take the pleasures of the palate seriously. By doing so they expand their sensuous experience of taste and smell. So can you!

JOURNAL PROMPT
One of the best hobbies to awaken your taste and smell is cooking. Prepare a simple but flavorful dish today and journal about how it makes you feel.

✆ *Day 307* ৼ

TODAY'S PRACTICE
Meditation: "Body"   Read, reflect, and journal.

INSPIRATION
A photograph of a great work of art is the mere memory of the original. In no way can it have the same impact as an in-person encounter. I experienced this when we visited the Galleria dell'Accademia in Florence, Italy. I had seen the reproductions of Michelangelo's marble

statue of David, but was clueless about how I would react to the original masterpiece.

A kilometer from the museum, in the Piazza della Signoria, stands a statue of David that I mistook to be the original. Its resemblance was uncanny. I looked at it from all sides, appreciating the work, but I did not feel its power – the youthful beauty or the vigor written about in essays I had read about the statue. Then I visited the museum and was charmed by other works of Michelangelo.

Suddenly a marble statue, its head almost touching the ceiling came into view. I immediately recognized it as David. I walked briskly, stopping close to it and stretching my neck to look up at the head of the 17-foot-tall young man!

Words such as *magnificence, supreme skill*, and *the work of a genius* lost their meaning. What was this other worldly wonder that I was facing? I circumambulated it three times as if it was the image of the God in sanctum sanctorum.

The male figure carved from white marble seemed to have come from the divine realm. I marveled at its exquisite details – feet, legs, thighs, hips, genitals, left hand holding a sling, chest, back, shoulders, right hand, head, hair. What a depiction of youth and strength! I felt my eyes welling. My heart hurt. My pulse beat faster.

Michelangelo was only 26 years old when he carved David from a discarded marble block. His David seemed to have come to life in that marble body. How could a mere mortal create a thing of such incredible beauty? The divine sculptor had turned matter into spirit.

JOURNAL PROMPT

Journal about an emotional experience you have had at a concert, during a movie, at an art show, or at the theater. What sensations did you have? How did you feel emotionally?

☙ *Day 308* ☜

TODAY'S PRACTICE
Meditation: "Body"   Read, reflect, and journal.

INSPIRATION

Kali in Himachal

While driving in the lower Himalayan Mountains with my husband, we viewed the River Bias as its flow shimmered in the deep valley. The intention of our trip in the state of Himachal Pradesh was to photograph the images of the Indian goddess Kali enshrined in the locally well-known temple.

I had seen goddess photos in art history books, describing such local temples, and this one had attracted my attention. The natural surroundings through which we drove – mountains, forests, river, rivulets – affected the tender positive fine emotions that had surfaced at the edge of my artistic mind. Simultaneously, they were awakening physical sensations throughout my body. I was ready.

I stood facing the Kali image bedecked with shimmering gold ornaments and brocaded silk attire, her face partly covered with fineries. But once I had her *darshan*, the "Hindu looking at" tears overwhelmed me. My body shook. I had to sit down. I wondered why I was feeling the way I did. But I let the eyes shed my emotions.

What happened to me when I mindfully looked at the statues of David and Kali was experiencing joyous pleasure as a culmination of an aesthetic experience.

Like a spiritual awakening, such an intense emotion is either experienced all of a sudden or built up gradually in anticipation. For Kali, I had been imagining it from the hour we left the city and began winding through the mountain peaks. The pleasant summer day, the bright light, the gentle breeze, the glimpses of the shimmering river from the mountain slopes had already put me in a light, happy, and contented mood. Saturated with intellectual knowledge about the symbols and meaning of the goddess, the mere viewing of her stirred within me an artistic sensitivity. Ideally the combination of intellect and emotion is what stirs aesthetic pleasure and triggers deep emotion. That's exactly what had transpired when I couldn't stop my tears.

Journal about a time when you were emotionally affected by artwork or a religious image that surprised you.

✌ *Day 309* ✌

TODAY'S PRACTICE
Meditation: "Body"   Read, reflect, and journal.

INSPIRATION

Natural landscape can absorb you in its majesty, shake you up with its exquisite beauty, and spew you out transformed. This has happened to me over and over again in U.S. National Parks.

Many individuals report feeling connected to the sacred through nature. Were you aware that regions with higher levels of natural amenities have lower rates of adherence to religious organizations? Mountains, hills, lakes, beaches, coastlines, forests, and pleasant weather all contribute to the powerful spiritual effects on people's behavior who live close by.

Spiritual relates to people's thoughts and beliefs rather than their bodies and physical surroundings. Six main spiritual themes emerge from thematic analysis: connection, vibrancy, awe-some presence, joy, gratitude, and compassion. Of these six themes, findings reveal that immersion in nature impacts the human spirit most significantly by providing a sense of connection, vibrancy, and wonderment.

The common characteristics of individuals who love to spend time in nature overlap with those who call themselves spiritual. These traits are kindness, peacefulness, compassion, and being content and happy. These folks stop criticizing others, always have motivating and kind words to share, and operate with an intention of making the world a better place.

✎ *Day 310* ✎

INSPIRATION

I had not heard about national parks until after coming to the United States in 1976. When we visited Yellowstone National Park and Grand Canyon National Park in 2013... *I. Had. No. Idea!* I was enthralled by how awe and delight enraptured me in their presence.

I was born in the lap of the Himalayas, in the valley of Kashmir. I was two years old when we moved to New Delhi, the overcrowded metropolitan capital city. But it was home. My family returned to the valley to get away from scorching summer heat in the capital, to my birthplace about which the Mughal Emperor Jehangir soulfully exclaimed, "If there is paradise on Earth, it is here, it is here, it is here!" Awe-inspiring nature was ingrained in my visual vocabulary. I get affected by the magnificence of nature because my appreciation of nature was cultivated from my childhood.

Shikara rides over Dal Lake, picnics in paradisical manicured Mughal gardens, horse riding in heavenly Gulmarg Valley – at each one of these sites, nature held me in its lap and stood guard as the backdrop. One of the most glorious, most spectacular, and celebrated places on earth... no wonder king Jehangir compared it to paradise.

By now, almost all countries of the world have conserved their most beautiful landscape and natural habitats as national parks for the benefit of their people and future generations. Those who visit them share a kind of reverence for the land, for the environment, and for the feeling it evokes in their hearts.

JOURNAL PROMPT

How do you feel about national parks in all the nations of the world? Have you visited any of them in your country? If so, journal about the feelings the natural surroundings evoke. If not, write about the feeling that stir when you are far away from the city, surrounded by nothing but wilderness.

ᘒ *Day 311* ᘐ

TODAY'S PRACTICE

Meditation: "Gratitude"   Read, reflect, and journal.

INSPIRATION

An astonishingly beautiful place is Zion National Park in Utah. "Zion" means "holy place" or "kingdom of heaven." The park's colossal mountains and steep cliffs and abundant crystal-clear streams are evidence of its majesty. Their beauty transports the traveler to a fantasy world. Temporarily I forgot where I was – in the human world or another planet. I felt the similar current of energy that had passed through my spine that I had sensed at the Kali temple in Himachal Pradesh or when mesmerized by Michelangelo's David in Florence.

Those three different experiences can be grouped as *secular spirituality,* which irrespective of their subject, religious or natural, shook me up by their awesomeness and unearthly beauty. What universal power creates such unfathomable grandeur! Such visions are beyond human understanding.

Like pilgrims on the path to a pilgrimage center, the feeling of camaraderie among travelers in national parks unites them in a shared reverence toward nature. Peoples from different countries and of diverse religions and ethnic backgrounds hold high esteem for natural beauty. It infuses their relationship with each other. They treat strangers as friends. Sharing the aesthetic pleasure and enjoyment of holy nature imbues them with kindness and respect.

National parks have created a new religion, that of secular spirituality; they have created new pilgrimage centers, the national parks; they have created a new breed of parishioners, the travelers.

JOURNAL PROMPT
How does traveling effect you? How does going to a place like Disneyland differ from going to a national park?

❧ *Day 312* ☙

TODAY'S PRACTICE
Meditation: "Gratitude"   Read, reflect, and journal.

INSPIRATION
One morning I watched the sun rise from behind a beautiful cloudy horizon. For a few minutes, I remained mesmerized as the golden yellow orb changed to bright orange, igniting the sky with a fiery otherworldliness. I don't usually go outside first thing in the morning. If I hadn't opened the door to bring in a package, I would not have witnessed those few minutes in which the sun and sky were performing their daily display.

That whole day, the glory of the sunrise stayed with me, connecting me with many spectacular sunrises I had witnessed before. It was like a surprise gift sent along with the parcel I brought inside. Perhaps it was a hint not to ignore the beauty that constantly happens in the world while I'm occupied with my routine.

But my self-created, self-cultivated routine is important to me. I don't feel guilty for missing this or that. Without the self-discipline of practicing meditation, journaling, and reading in the morning, I believe my life wouldn't be what it has unfurled into. Sunsets and sunrises have their time. My creative and spiritual life is enhanced, and rich and complex because I do not wait for inspiration.

Writing Meditation Practice is for a writer the way surgery is for a surgeon. It means practicing whether you feel motivated or not, regardless of whether the muses visit. The more you practice, the more your writing voice strengthens. The words *persistence* and *discipline* land at your feet when you take writing practice seriously.

From my study window, a woodpecker chips away at a tree, his staccato beat consistent. The metaphor isn't lost on me. Writing is about showing up. Every single day.

JOURNAL PROMPT

Find interviews about the writing process of your favorite author. Pay attention to when, how, and where they write and model your writing day based on it.

ᘿ *Day 313* ᘏ

TODAY'S PRACTICE

Meditation: "Gratitude"   Read, reflect, and journal.

INSPIRATION

What has awe, wonder, and delight to do with writing?

Awe is when we experience three emotions at once – fascination, terror, holiness. When an experience stops you in your tracks, blasts you open, awakens you... when the ego collapses, you encounter the land beyond the maps you have visualized. You feel sacralized and one with the infinite universe.

You cannot experience the sacred or have original ideas while living in the daily rut. Something has to shake you up, shatter your unexamined values, question your unanalyzed beliefs. Let the walls of the ego stretch thin. Die to yourself and be reborn in the sacred silence of your being.

Moments of awe can transform you, making you feel like a new person. Afterward you experience an increased feeling of well-being, compassion, insight, creativity, and knowledge of your goals and life's purpose. Jody Foster, portraying the astronomer Ellie Alloway in the movie *Contact,* witnesses a celestial event. Awestruck, she said, "I had no idea. I had.... no... idea. They should have sent a poet." When you experience nature's awe, you are humbled, you are torn apart. Only poetic language can do justice to the experience you feel when we go through the portal that opens up an unfathomable realm.

Which brings me to the point of what awe has to do with writing or writers. *To be continued tomorrow.*

JOURNAL PROMPT

Have you experienced a time in nature in silence and solitude where you found such profound solace and comfort that you couldn't move, so poignant that a poem emerged in your mind, or a whole story line?

ꙮ *Day 314* ꙮ

TODAY'S PRACTICE

Meditation: "Gratitude"   Read, reflect, and journal.

INSPIRATION

As a writer or a reader, you go through the portal that carries you to the world of words and books. This world has the power to obliterate your worldview, crack you open, transform you, and then revive you, changed. There have been times when I have finished reading a book, closed its covers and uttered, "I can see now. I found myself. Wow!"

All my life I have searched for purpose and meaning. What I have discovered with each "wow" is to keep changing and wondering. The meaning of life depends on your purpose, what is your calling. Take the call to your heart, don't do it for the fruit, for the award, leave everything for the universe to complete. And watch how utterly mesmerized you will be by nature, by art, by literature.

There is nothing but awe and wonder in everything. In simple things such as the smell of freshly cut grass, soil after rain, the sight of fish in the waters of a crystal-clear lake, tree branches turned into icicles reflecting sunrays. And it is found in the most sophisticated and masterfully skilled artworks such as Michelangelo's David or the image of Kali. They make my heart ache; they make me shed tears.

Which moments of wonderment have shaken your grounding, changed your habits? Has an experience filled you with such awe? What wonderous sight dared you to disrupt a default pattern and transform yourself?

JOURNAL PROMPT

Have you experienced awe? Where were you? What senses were activated? What changed?

๛ *Day 315* ๛

TODAY'S PRACTICE

Meditation: "Gratitude"   Read, reflect, and journal.

INSPIRATION

Love – whether it be romantic, maternal, or friendship – works as a soothing balm on the deep fear caused by the awareness of death. In the snug bosom of my parents' love, I was unaware of my own mortality. With the caring of my family and comfort of my home, I was clueless about life's temporariness.

By the time I got married to the love of my life, I was conscious of my own demise but could easily put that thought at the back of my mind. Death was something that happened to others – old and sick people.

My husband's love made me forget the ephemerality of life, and in his company, I keep my death at bay. Through the love of our daughters and grandchildren, I feel that I will continue to live through them. A good band-aid for the fear of death.

Love of my close family members and good friendships helps me bring the present moment alive. Just to think that I'm alive experiencing life fills me with awe. Doesn't death have a redemptive quality? One comes to mind. Without the knowledge of my own death, I may not seek deeper meaning. I may live a shallow life. Earnest Becker said that death forces us to respond to life better. What do you think?

JOURNAL PROMPT

Do you push the thought of death to the back of your mind or do you confront it? Write a dialogue between death and yourself in which you freely ask all the questions you have and allow death to respond sincerely.

↳ *Day 316* ↰

TODAY'S PRACTICE

Meditation: "Gratitude"   Read, reflect, and journal.

INSPIRATION

I'm grateful to my body and mind for my life.
I'm grateful to my parents for my childhood.
I'm grateful to my husband for a lifetime of love and companionship.
I'm grateful to my children for maternal love they birth and flower in my heart.
I'm grateful to my friends and all the Mindful Writers for their gracious presence
for strengthening and spreading my calling in expanding eccentric circles.
In my seventh decade of life, I certainly think of my death. But I can't emphasize
enough the awe I feel for getting an opportunity to live this wonderful life.
I know and hear all kinds of people within the country and all around the world
who have suffered and are suffering. I may not have experienced pain and suffering
at that level. Suffering is as much a fact as my life. But I can't help but be awestruck
and filled with gratitude as I look back at my life
from the vantage point of 75.
I have been fortunate to have been given much more than I have given in return.
I have been fortunate to have painted pictures, read and reflected, written books,
traveled the world and shared what I thought would be beneficial to those who
listened. But most of all I am fortunate to have been born a human being, a woman,
born to my parents, married to my husband, having two daughters, two
granddaughters, and two grandsons. How can I not call such a journey of enormous
privileges an awesome, wonderous, and delightful adventure!

JOURNAL PROMPT

What impression do you have of your life lived so far? If you could, what would you change? What would you strengthen? Write about it.

❧ Day 317 ❧

TODAY'S PRACTICE

Meditation: "Gratitude"   Read, reflect, and journal.

INSPIRATION

Approach your life as if you were watching an autobiographical movie. Live in the present. Make each day count. Fear of one thing or another will show its head, but when you are present *here-now* you realize there is no immediate danger. Yes, there is so much not under your control. But there is so much that is. So learn to live courageously. One of the major benefits of creative practices is that they disclose secrets of eternity, universality, and a higher self within you. The sense of "I Am. I'm more than my physical body" infuses fearlessness in you.

A creative life allows you to experience "flow." When in the middle of that flow, you feel your best and do your best. You chattering ego goes quiet. Clock time falls away. You have no self-doubt. Complete trust. You feel selfless. Timeless. Effortless. Enriched.

The best news is you can recreate moments of flow. Surrender yourself to a creative act, to an activity for its own sake. Let go of controlled discipline. Carve out time for flow 4-5 times a week.

- Notice how things around you affect you
- See yourself as part of a larger whole
- Walk in the woods, becoming one with the surroundings
- Watch a movie
- Read a book
- Paint a picture
- Surrender into a foreign environment in an unfamiliar culture

Anything around you can turn into a prop. Take yourself to places that are majestic, overpowering with their nobility, grandness, mystery, and awe. Imbibe their qualities.

JOURNAL PROMPT

Make a list of things you do which you either do not have to do or are not useful to do, and things you would love to do but have no time for.

↬ *Day 318* ↫

TODAY'S PRACTICE

Meditation: "Gratitude"   Read, reflect, and journal.

INSPIRATION

Negatives in life seem to go on forever, but joyous feelings last only for moments. You may have met your basic needs of food, water, shelter, and clothing. And you may have achieved self-esteem, love, and respect... yet the feeling of mortality still hovers at the back of your mind.

Always remember the way your inner mentor is present within you at each and every moment; so are the experiences of awe, wonder, and pleasure present without you. Become aware of them with your mindfulness. They give meaning to your life. When you feel at one with everyone and everything around you, you have a sense of immortality.

You have intellectual knowledge. And you have emotional intelligence. But deep understanding does not come from one or the other. Understanding requires both intellect and feelings. It's when these both join together, when visceral experience meets cognition, when the heart thinks and the mind feels, that you come full circle and experience awe and wonderous delight.

Wisdom emerges when there is deep knowledge as well as passionate whirls of intoxication as well as cognitive ecstasy.

JOURNAL PROMPT

Write about someone for whom you are eternally grateful or something which has given you feelings of awe and wonder.

ꙮ *Day 319* ꙮ

TODAY'S PRACTICE
Meditation: "Gratitude"   Read, reflect, and journal.

INSPIRATION

If you haven't experienced the depth of awestruck moments, you are a breathing body merely pumping blood. Your mind goes everywhere you don't want to go. But making or appreciating art, reading, writing, and travel make you realize you are more than your body. You realize you are capable of experiencing aesthetic delight and peak moments of spirituality. These may be transient but they deepen and heighten the quality of your life. You know how you can glimpse divinity within you. You also know your imagination has no limits.

What I'm saying may inspire you, even magnetize you to the practice, but at the back of your mind remain the questions of how to pay the rent, buy food, or perhaps attend to an ailing family member. You are tethered to your daily life. Yet I'd say without linking to something creative and spiritual, there is no hope. When you make space for the artistic and the sacred, this good inner stuff seeps in until it simply flows into your outer life.

Be always grateful. And be always generous. Then find time and space for your practice. Crave what is meaningful to you. Longing is good. When grief visits you, go through its sadness. It will cleanse you. It may even inspire you. But don't get stuck in it. Come back to the practice; it will make you feel good. Look around. What goodness surrounds you – within your family, your community, your culture, your books? Imbibe good from these people and places, the lack and sadness will evaporate.

Nature, good books, and master artworks are all potent with enchantments. These magical things wait patiently for you to come to them. Cross the threshold fearlessly. You can't encounter flowerbeds unless you take a stroll through the garden.

JOURNAL PROMPT

Have you ever been frustrated, trying to learn something new? How did you handle the situation? Did you overcome or succumb?

১৩ *Day 320* ৩৶

TODAY'S PRACTICE

Meditation: "Gratitude"   Read, reflect, and journal.

INSPIRATION

What you intend to work toward are the contents of your mind. However, "monkey-mind" replaces that content with whatever you pay attention to. Some things are transient, such as the movie you just watched, the book you are reading, or the song you are listening to. But if there are trials or tribulations, problems or struggles that are constantly circling your mind, please replace those with your basic intentions that lead to a meaningful goal.

If you don't have an immediate goal, then think of your mantra, a favorite song, or an inspiring saying, and make that the content of your mind. Your brain will no longer constrict with the burden of your problem. It is not to say to avoid the problem but rather to not make it a broken record in your mind.

Think and say what you feel passionate, excited, inspired about. Thinking and saying galvanizes you to action. But don't be in a state of exhalation all the time. Continue to practice silence and solitude, take a nap, read a book, go for a walk and observe nature.

Too much of creativity and spirituality may blaze you. But being too much in the world may crush you. Follow the Buddha's Golden Path practice and live wholeheartedly. With a balanced day of practice and daily life you are bound to experience more awe-filled moments.

JOURNAL PROMPT

Journal a list of worries and woes that have been troubling your mind. Now add a list of positive replacement thoughts, or reframe the negative into a less limiting context, so you can move forward today with a brighter outlook.

❧ *Day 321* ❧

TODAY'S PRACTICE
Meditation: "Arriving Home"   Read, reflect, and journal.

INSPIRATION

Rationalizing a sad situation does not make it better, but walking through an art museum, watching a movie, listening to music, or going to creative dance or theatre heals. Arts have power to make changes at a cellular level. They touch the same roots from which sadness grows. Fine arts and literature have the power to change you from the inside out. The more positive content you place in your mind, the more the pain is pushed away. What felt unsurmountable yesterday no longer feels so problematic.

Be aware of the world around you at the present moment. Attend to life. The experience of awe and wonder does not just happen. It requires action on your part. Like any mind training, you need to practice it. At the moment when something deeply touches you, think: *Why did this feel so good?* Analyze and remember. Next time you are at a similar space or in a similar situation, recreate what happened the last time you experienced unfathomable pleasure. Next time you get an opportunity to experience inner joy, remind yourself the steps and repeat.

The moments of awe and wonder are sensed in natural beauty, when you are in the "zone," with the "flow," when you and your creation are one. After such creative experience you have an afterglow, and the world around you glistens. This is so because art changes you where your Authentic Self dwells, in your cellular system, the reason it shows in your eyes and face. In time, that sensibility becomes the needle of your inner compass, and you carry your radiance everywhere you go.

JOURNAL PROMPT

Write all the reasons you are proud of yourself. When do you feel in the "zone"?' Which two practices make you feel that they can help you with the inner transition at a cellular level?

✒ *Day 322* ✒

TODAY'S PRACTICE

Meditation: "Arriving Home"   Read, reflect, and journal.

INSPIRATION

How do you know what you are passionate about? How do you know what a "fire in the belly" feels like? For me it was attempting to answer the primordial human questions: *Where did I come from, What is the purpose of my life,* and *Where will I go after I die?* It was sheer curiosity and a fear of death. I discovered some answers in making art, getting deeper into writing, finding my mentor friend within me, and traveling around the country and the world. Those experiences settled my mind, expanded my heart, thinned my ego. I was wholeheartedly devoted to them, and they turned into my passions, my ecstasy, my life.

When the feeling of wonder and awe passed through me, it was as if dopamine coursed through my nerves. It encouraged me to be bold and courageous. In the beginning I was intimidated but I took baby steps. My attention was focused and my intention sure-footed. I did not rush toward the future but patiently walked in the present. Curiosity has been my constant companion.

My practice did not develop quickly. But it grew surely as I worked hard to cultivate each discipline. When the disciplines came together, it was like a lightning strike. Ideas from the aesthetics, philosophy, and world religions took me beyond myself. I became aware that my daily routine benefitted me in more than one way. One of my purposes of life became to share the practice with others. My cup now overflows as it serves other writers and creative minds. Being fully alive pushes away the fear of death.

JOURNAL PROMPT

How has Writing Meditation Practice helped you live several notches "finer" or "better" than your ordinary life? Reflect upon this thought.

∾ *Day 323* ∾

TODAY'S PRACTICE

Meditation: "Arriving Home"   Read, reflect, and journal.

INSPIRATION

Each individual writer has a unique voice. What does yours sound like when you write or speak at a gathering? It involves not only what you say but also how you say it. When you share your thoughtful opinions about the topics of your interest, what do you think your readers gather about you?

Are your intentions clear and authentic? Are your body language and facial expressions sincere? Can you speak with words and without words? Do you feel "fire in your belly?" Does its flame light up those who are listening to you?

You may have doubts, but be audacious and trust your voice. Humility hones it. Express yourself passionately but honestly. Let words flow from your heart before opening your mouth. You will come alive as a creative person with a fiery voice. Go with it!

At first, you'll feel nervous and uncomfortable. But this is part of the process until you find your voice. Keep allowing yourself to expand your boundaries. Discomfort is part of the learning process.

When you are confident your voice is clear, heartfelt, and wise... when you lose yourself in what your heart is saying... when you explore and then find yourself... pour out that inner self with complete authenticity. It will reflect on your face as an afterglow. Do it over and over again.

JOURNAL PROMPT

What thoughts have you contemplated? What words have you spoken and what actions have you done that reflect as an afterglow on your face?

✍ *Day 324* ✌

TODAY'S PRACTICE

Meditation: "Arriving Home"   Read, reflect, and journal.

INSPIRATION

Everyone can and must experience awe and wonder. Why? Because awe heals, sensitizes you to the finer things in life, breaks your heart open, showers you with goodness.

Begin by knowing something new about yourself every day. What is unique about what you think and what you say? What original things do you do? How differently do you process life from run-of-the-mill thinking? When you take responsibility for what you think, say, and do, new pathways open for you to tread upon.

One characteristic of awe is encountering the unknown. It begins with little things – talking to strangers when you travel, getting to know a bit more about the people who come to clean your house, mow your lawn, serve you at restaurants, or meet you as tour guides or drivers. In them, you experience "other."

The ordinary rises to this higher nuance. Awareness about the people surrounding you elevates. Encountering the unknown makes you come alive. This is why travel is one of the ways to experience awe.

"We don't travel to move around... we travel to *be moved*," writes Pico Iyer. "Travel puts blood back into your veins," claims National Geographic documentary host Jason Silva. "It jolts you back into being awake."

JOURNAL PROMPT

What or who is the "other" for you? How has travel changed you for the better? If you have not traveled within the country or around the world, what would have you missed?

◦ *Day 325* ◦

TODAY'S PRACTICE

Meditation: "Arriving Home"   Read, reflect, and journal.

INSPIRATION

It is said that routine can jade you, even make you lethargic, but for me it is precisely the disciplined practice that keeps me awake and energized. However, I balance my daily practice with going out for walks and excursions and going away for travel.

When I walk in nature, the smell of freshly cut grass, mild scent of pine, a bunch of jasmine blossoms, the autumn leaves on tall grass, or the lilies floating on water, wake me from my slumber. I become silvery gems shimmering on the surface of a lake that I attentively behold.

You don't need to be rich to be awestruck. Recite poetry while you are taking a tub bath, or light a candle or listen to music while taking a long shower – these are magnificent stimuli for feeling awe-some.

After having had rich experiences at an art museum, aviary, or conservatory, after you have danced with the external world, you'll find you have begun to spill your own awe onto others. How does that happen? Having had so many awe-some experiences yourself, the fine feeling has entered you at a cellular level and has become an integral part of your physiology.

Don't be afraid of designing your own experiences of awe and wonder. I know unsettling things happen to us all the time. You can try to protect yourself from feeling bad, from pain, from hurt and suffering. You will feel down when it happens. At times like those, go through whatever you are experiencing, but keep in mind that you have the power and capacity to feel joy and delight with equal intensity.

The playfulness of a child resides within us all. Let it out. Surrender to the fun it can provide. Laugh whenever you can. As it is famously said, a fit of laughter is good medicine. Don't live on autopilot.

JOURNAL PROMPT

If you had to imagine an awesome and wonder-filled experience, what would it be?

ꙮ *Day 326* ꙮ

TODAY'S PRACTICE

Meditation: "Arriving Home"   Read, reflect, and journal.

INSPIRATION

It is important to cultivate disciplines that lead to a mindful life. And it is equally important to adopt habits that reveal awe and wonder. You can design such a world for yourself. The first step is getting acquainted with creative arts. What style of music attracts you? Which visual art magnetizes you? Can you get lost in a book for hours? Do you love dancing? Which country would you like to travel to?

Whichever of your five senses is most sensitive, cultivate it further. Use it repeatedly or you'll lose it. Once you know, practice to see or hear or do to hone it every day. Let your heart-mind drench in the aesthetic pleasure of your choosing.

Once your inner self is set on experiencing awe, begin preparing your outer world to be equally pleasurable. The people and places you encounter each day influence your path to awe. Be attentive. What is beneficial to you and what is not? Which individuals and spaces and events will help increase your sense of wonder and which won't?

Be clear of your intentions and theirs. Remember, life is made of present moments. You make them happen. Whatever you pay attention to becomes your life. So, determine to do what you intend to do. When you respect your daily practice, you empower yourself to arrange your inner life, and with mindful living your outer life is shaped as well.

Tell yourself: "I want creativity and spirituality in my life. I will surrender to everything that feels right to my authentic self. When I see, hear, touch, taste, and smell things that matter to me, they become my inner reality. I can choose how I respond to things and people. My attitude matters! I will act upon my intention and live my life authentically. People I socialize with, books I read, arts I look at, music I listen to, places I visit matter. Whatever I put in my mind becomes my reality."

JOURNAL PROMPT

What sort of changes are you going to make? What finer art would you add into your day that would make a difference?

Day 327

TODAY'S PRACTICE

Meditation: "Arriving Home"   Read, reflect, and journal.

INSPIRATION

A fine balance of intellectual knowledge and emotional experiences has the power to change you physically and spiritually. When you honor your traumatic experiences, your pain, your hurt through creativity – journaling, meditation, reading, writing, painting, singing, dancing – your body changes, as does your posture, gestures, and facial expressions.

Let your body make friends with your mind by working intimately. When you are absorbed in creativity, the body, mind, and heart work in unison. A mixed feeling of pleasure and peace circulates through your whole self, so much so that a person working beside you can feel the current of your creative aura.

Not in a mood to create? Then integrate the scattered attention, emotions, and sensations by taking a long warm shower. Or send loving attention to a family member, whether they are physically present or far away, go for a walk in the park, or drive through a scenic route you love.

Stop the flow of thoughts by not letting disturbing sights and sounds circle your mind. See and hear more with your heart than with your eyes and ears.

JOURNAL PROMPT

Write about an incident that changed the trajectory of your life when you were suffering. Was it an intellectual, physical, or emotional occurrence?

ೂ *Day 328* ಌ

TODAY'S PRACTICE

Meditation: "Arriving Home"   Read, reflect, and journal.

INSPIRATION

Do you remember seeing, discovering, or hearing something for the first time? Is it possible to see something *again* for the first time? Is there a way to notice something in the same fashion a child does with a beginner's mind?

Deeply focused moments have the power to jolt oneself into awakening. Your brain becomes saturated with media, especially daily news focused on the chaos caused by wars, natural disasters, or early and meaningless deaths. Gloom and doom seem to be everywhere. This is what you feed your consciousness. Why wouldn't you feel mentally withered?

Venezuelan-American thinker Jason Silva suggests you stand in front of your bookshelf and say, "I read this one, I read this one twice, and I read that one three times." He goes on to say, "But look again! Each book on that shelf could turn into an aha moment. Select any book. Recall the moment you first acquired that book. Didn't its pages make you feel alive? The author was stating something you believed in. How thrilled you were to read that paragraph! You underlined, highlighted, earmarked the edges! Go ahead, reread it the fourth time. Reading, visual arts, spirituality have the power to reverse your parched minds."

Pull out a random book from your favorite bookshelf, open a random page, and read a random paragraph. Imagine as if you were reading it for the first time. You have forgotten the pleasure this book gave you. Yet there are hundreds of books you have collected. The pleasure is hidden between the covers, only if you have a moment to pay attention and contemplate it.

JOURNAL PROMPT

Pull out a book from one of your bookshelves. Read a page or two as if you are reading it for the first time. How does it feel?

✖ *Day 329* ✖

TODAY'S PRACTICE

Meditation: "Arriving Home"   Read, reflect, and journal.

INSPIRATION

Today, think about a flower growing in your garden, or a bright orange and yellow and bronze leaf that is falling to the ground, or a painting in a museum. As you did yesterday with a favorite book, today consider this item you may have seen ten or a hundred times, but approach it with a beginner's mind. What do you notice first? What makes you smile? When you are free, when you are listening and seeing with your heart, when you are not restricted, you enjoy looking or listening differently.

Know the difference between analytical learning and aesthetic delight. The former is knowledge, the latter insight. Awe and wonder can lead you on a new path, but the trail will become visible if you allow yourself the freedom to walk. Give yourself permission today to walk on a path that is not yet visible.

You just planted a seed. From now on, your job is to water and nurture it.

JOURNAL PROMPT

Can you make it a habit to take one single thing and "see it for the first time"? The next morning, journal about how you felt doing it.

Day 330

TODAY'S PRACTICE	
Meditation: "Arriving Home"	Read, reflect, and journal.

INSPIRATION

Awe and wonder give rise to love, generosity, compassion, and ultimately to loving relationships. Here are three things you can do to invite wonderment into your life.

In the morning before you meditate or journal, ask yourself, *What wonderful things do I intend to do today?* Your intention should be related to one of the goals you have made for yourself and which has a positive element to it.

During the day think, *What could I say to someone or do for someone that would surprise or delight them?* This could be anyone – preferably a person you meet once in a while or a total stranger. If you are going to be home all day, say it to the person you live with, or do something for them that eases their work. Or call someone you know who needs your support.

When in bed, ask yourself, *Did I do what I intended? And what were the three most memorable moments of my day?* You could quietly tell yourself about your "good works" or jot them down in your journal. However, make sure to savor the pleasant feeling that stimulates you for a few moments.

END OF MONTH PROMPT

Jot down your one or two default habits, the ones you revert to whenever you are tired. How will you replace the not-so-nice nature of your habits? What will you do to introduce the experience of awe and wonder into your life?

MONTH 12

WRITER'S JOURNEY TO SELF

Suggested Readings

The Essential Rumi
Trans. by Coleman Barks, 2010.

The Dance of the Dissident Daughter
Sue Monk Kidd, 1996.

30 Days:
Change Your Habits, Change Your Life
Marc Reklau, 2014.

A New Earth: Awakening to Your Life's Purpose
Eckhart Tolle, 2005.

✒ *Day 331* ✒

TODAY'S PRACTICE

Meditation: "Awakening the Senses"   Read, reflect, and journal.

INSPIRATION

What sort of relationship do you have with your work? Is it that of a lover and beloved, parent and child, or an intimate friend?

A spark of an idea flashes through your mind. A concept is conceived. A current of energy passes through your body. It lures you to pay attention. You mull it over, reflect upon it, and you are eager to put it into words. But you're also somewhat anxious. Not sure how to begin, finally you write it down in a notebook or on your laptop. This is the beginning of a new relationship between you and your new work-in-progress.

The formless idea is taking form. You feel galvanized to write the first draft. Your body, senses, mind, and heart are absorbed in writing. You are in the zone and oblivious to everything else. You give the work everything you think it requires and demands. You are determined to bring your passion to fruition. The original spark of an idea is flaring, expanding, turning into a bonfire. Slowly, from "nothing," something has emerged.

You continue to think about it when you are engaged in a nonverbal activity or journaling. You research and read related material. The urge to create is forceful. It demands self-discipline and hours of daily work. A writing project may last for months, a year, or several years. It took Henry David Thoreau eleven drafts and ten years before *Waldon* was completed. *To be continued...*

JOURNAL PROMPT

How does your writing piece develop from a creative spark to the first rough draft? What sort of struggles and challenges do you face during the creative process? Have you designed special methods to resolve problems that you come across in writing?

✒ *Day 332* ✒

TODAY'S PRACTICE
Meditation: "Awakening the Senses"   Read, reflect, and journal.

INSPIRATION

Even when you struggle with a dialogue, a character, a scene... even when you get stuck, puzzle over the project, or doubt it... you continue to write. Slowly the idea morphs into a story, an essay, or possibly a novel. The idea, along with your reading and research material have merged. Mild ecstasy emerges and envelops you. Your passion is your pleasure.

Then comes the moment, the dreaded moment when you are unable to continue. Where to take the story next? You divert your attention to something else. You may go for a walk, fold clothes, cook dinner, make a drawing. Get busy with any of these activities that does not use words.

Then at some point, you hear the work call to you. It silently speaks, telling you where you may take it. It murmurs to rewrite that sunny day into the horrid afternoon of torrential rain; it says, *Let her break the expensive teakettle in frustration*; it suggests, *Instead of killing that character, let him grow into a good citizen*; or it whispers, *Change the setting from a U.S. metropolitan city to a small town in Italy, the birthplace of the protagonist.*

The idea of a new writing often sparks from a real-life emotion or a current event or a prompt. Once it sticks in your head it swirls in your mind as you go about your regular day. Sometimes it nudges to research or take notes or talk it out. But once you feel ready again, there is an urgency about the process and you write and write and write.

Pausing in the midst of a work in progress is often suggested by the work itself. Then when it is time to "cook" again, it calls you. There is mutual "give and take" between you and the work. It communicates with you and influences the work as much as you direct it.

By the time you are writing the third or fifth or eighth draft, the distinction between you and the work completely blurs. Like a lover and the beloved, you have become one. After what feels like your final draft, your mind-born seems to have a life of its own.

After you write "The End," a feeling of relief passes through your body. You sense a great load being taken off your shoulders. Your step lightens. A sense of joy runs on a level that has nothing to do with whatever mundane task you may be performing. When the manuscript is ready to be mailed to the editor or to a publisher, the ecstasy is touched with sadness.

JOURNAL PROMPT

Journal about a period when you noticed your intuitive ideas and insights sprouting. Did you use those ideas in your work? Did an insight save you? Was there a time when you ignored that feeling in your belly and then later regretted not following it?

ɕ❍ *Day 333* ❑↲

TODAY'S PRACTICE

Meditation: "Awakening the Senses"   Read, reflect, and journal.

INSPIRATION

Writing Meditation Practice has five disciplines. Here are the taglines for each.

Meditation: Align with the universe

Journaling: Lighter mind, kinder heart

Reading: Author as revered teacher

Nonverbal activities: Letting imagination go wild

Writing: Get into the zone

The Writing Meditation Practice is painstakingly slow but measurable. Writing skill and style get better with regular practice, but progress is not a straight line; readers can feel it. However, in meditation and journaling, only the practitioner feels it. You watch yourself changing from mindless to mindful with increased self-understanding. In turn, self-understanding increases self-compassion and kindness toward others.

No outsider could or is keeping score of your inner self. You notice personal insecurities and fears slowly alleviate. You feel the cacophony of thoughts settling down, the physical discomfort changing to a relaxed body, and an indifferent heart turning kind. You stop judging yourself and learn to live as you are.

The goal of the practice is to bring your day-to-day self closer to your Authentic Self, in writing and in life. The more you become aware of your core values and goals, the closer you get to your true Self. The practice of the five disciplines helps in this regard. The struggle to align your outer nonconformity and inner authenticity is what gives your work meaning and depth.

JOURNAL PROMPT

Journal about what you experienced at the beginning of this journey when you sat still to meditate and journaled for the first time. How long did it take you to feel the effects of mindfulness?

∽ *Day 334* ∾

TODAY'S PRACTICE

Meditation: "Awakening the Senses"   Read, reflect, and journal.

INSPIRATION

I invite you to take a deeper interest in any of the nonverbal activities we have been discussing throughout the year. You never know which one may inspire you, stirring you to the marrow of your bones. Learn from the emotional feel of paintings, sway to the rhythm of vocal and instrumental music, embody the movements of dance, get lost in another world at the theater. What you may learn from any of these art forms will surprise you and have a profound effect on your writing.

If you're approaching retirement age, why not make it a time of *refirement* instead? Refire the passion that has lain dormant, which you never got the chance or time to pursue. Losing a job or getting sick or recuperating from surgery may cause you to be away from the workplace for weeks if not months. An unusual circumstance or event may have forced you to stay home.

I recommend a nonverbal activity (besides a solo walk). Even when you have a nine-to-five job, you could become a weekend photographer or musician or potter or painter. Devoting a small amount of time to a hobby when you are younger goes a long way later on, either during your own infirmity, when you may have to be caregiver to a loved one, or after you retire. A skill is never wasted. It is like money in the bank.

JOURNAL PROMPT

What kind of hobby lays dormant within you? Think about your daily routine from the time you rise at dawn to the time you go to sleep for the night. How does your physical workspace affect your productivity?

༄ *Day 335* ༅

TODAY'S PRACTICE

Meditation: "Awakening the Senses"   Read, reflect, and journal.

INSPIRATION

As you focus this month on your journey to self, I would like to emphasize the significance of voracious reading and writing your heart out. In your quest to write one book, you may turn over half a library.

Consider how other authors expose what they feel deep inside, drawing attention to some truth that is important to them, or exposing a secret they want the whole world to know. They know they may not produce a masterpiece, but this thing churning in their belly will not release them until they take the risk. That's how important writing is.

The most effective writers are voracious readers. They allow authors from across the millennia to speak to them clearly and silently. They let them get into their heads. Thus reading and writing bring people together. People from distant epochs, different cultures and races who perhaps would never know each other, who live in different time periods get intimately acquainted via reading. Books have the power to break free the shackles of time and distance.

It is pleasurable as well as painful to write. At first, you basically write for yourself. And you subconsciously write for someone you love, irrespective of whether that person will ever read it. Simply do your best. Challenge yourself. Even though writing makes you happy when it goes well and feels terrible when it doesn't, you can always rekindle that passion through reading.

JOURNAL PROMPT

Do you feel you would be able to write if you were not interested in reading?

‿ *Day 336* ‿

TODAY'S PRACTICE

Meditation: "Awakening the Senses"   Read, reflect, and journal.

INSPIRATION

It's not easy to accept or think that the most successful career, even the most rewarding family relationships, would eventually end. One retires, the loving spouse dies, children grow up and move away, interests shift. You are left with yourself.

The only true companion that stays with you wherever you go is your inner mentor, your Authentic Self. So befriending your Self when you have everything blooming around you seems to me to be the most common-sensical path to follow. Laying the foundation for your future solitude must be cultivated when you feel blessed on all accounts.

It is one thing to wonder about the purpose in life but quite another to accept the fact of impermanence. As long as you have founded and grounded your life, as long as you have a clear mind and open heart, and your goals are in sight, the understanding of impermanence makes you realize the singularity and vibrancy of life. Writing Meditation Practice helps in this regard.

The older I grow, the more I realize how we face new life challenges. Unforeseen obstacles come our way. Things I have no control over happen. During such times, the energy that I have built and accumulated from the practice displays its psychic power. Discouragement and doubt no longer interfere with my purpose. My progress may slow down but it never stops.

JOURNAL PROMPT

Which three activities bring joy into your day? Which two of your goals bring you closer to that abundance? What one thing gives the most meaning to your life?

ꙮ *Day 337* ꙮ

TODAY'S PRACTICE
Meditation: "Awakening the Senses"   Read, reflect, and journal.

INSPIRATION

Writing Meditation Practice helps clarify the difference between your ego self and Authentic Self – what you show to the world (with your mask on) and who you truly are deep in your heart. The more you practice, the closer you'll get to your AS. Your masks will fall off.

Authentic Self remains with you from the time you give heed to your calling to the time you become one with it. It hints at what you have accomplished so far, and where you are going. It knows the truth of your writer's journey, never doubts it, trusts it completely, and motivates and encourages you to keep going. It keeps the naysayers at a distance. As Sarah Ban Breathnach's sister once said to her, "You have got to start owning your talent, or you'll lose it."

Neither position nor power nor possessions mark your success. It's a bad strategy to compare yourself with other writers who may be on a bestseller list or who may have won awards. Just keep writing, owning your talent, and appreciating the progress you have made. Give yourself credit for completing a story or article. Celebrate the success of getting a work published. Your current work is only one piece in the larger body of work that you will be writing. Never downplay any achievement.

As important as trusting your own talent is the appreciation of your fellow writers' work and being generous with others. Be sure to make a call or send an email or a message about their recent success, whatever that may be. As you bring happiness and smiles to their lives, you share in the increased abundance of joy. Do the same thing for your muse. If she doesn't show up automatically, make sure you pay her daily visits. Just sit and begin writing what is on your mind.

JOURNAL PROMPT

Make a list of your writing accomplishments: workshops you have attended or at which you have presented, drafts you have completed, articles or stories or books you have published, awards received. By doing this you are owning your own talent and skills. Doing this exercise will help you realize how much you have already accomplished... but mostly forgotten.

⊱ Day 338 ⊰

TODAY'S PRACTICE

Meditation: "Awakening the Senses"   Read, reflect, and journal.

INSPIRATION

Today, think about how you spend your typical day. You set aside the time for the things that you must do. How many remaining free hours do you have? What do you do with those? Do you talk on the phone, watch television, surf the web, or listen to self-improvement podcasts? Can you shorten the time you spend or schedule them for just 2-3 days a week so you can open up more space for your Writing Meditation Practice?

Make sure you include practices and activities that meet your goals and echo your calling. How much time have you kept aside for writing and revising, reading and researching? Is there an obstacle that is preventing you from doing so? What can you do about it? In meditation and journaling, contemplate what you want to accomplish and how you can make sure to fit time for them into your typical day.

One of the best ways to meet writing goals is to set deadlines. When you don't have a specified date to turn in a manuscript, time seems to get away from you. A work-in-progress that would have taken months may lapse a year or more. Why? Because we humans tend to daydream, procrastinate, or work on several different projects at once. To avoid this nonproductive behavior, create a deadline for each project.

Once a deadline is set, break the work into manageable segments and assign a date for when each part is to be completed. While writing this book you are now holding, I wrote one chapter in two weeks. I should rephrase that. I *revised* one month's posts in two weeks, but its several earlier drafts were also completed based on deadlines. However, during the years I was writing the fourth or fifth draft of this guidebook, I also wrote the second draft of my forthcoming fiction. Doing so gave me a welcome break from this nonfiction writing.

To focus solely on this project would have been overwhelming. Writing in segments made the writing pleasurable while adhering to a strict schedule allowed me to finish.

JOURNAL PROMPT

How do you spend your day currently? How can you make more time for what you hope to achieve as a writer? Journal about the steps you can take to meet that goal.

ꙮ *Day 339* ꙮ

TODAY'S PRACTICE

Meditation: "Awakening the Senses"   Read, reflect, and journal.

INSPIRATION

Keeping deadlines and balancing your physical, familial, social, emotional, intellectual, and creative/spiritual life is important. An unbalanced life leads to stress and discontentment.

It took me half of my life to harmonize my typical day. I scheduled the time for five disciplines, longer time for writing, time with my husband and time with children and grandchildren according to what I was certain to do. Some of these required daily attentions while others monthly or yearly. You can begin this harmonizing your life earlier. If you are in your thirties or forties, know that scheduling keeps changing from one phase of life to the next. Just make sure you do not neglect any important area.

Stay in touch with your disciplines and adjust the time spent on each accordingly. Every second of your life doesn't have to be filled with activity. Your mind enjoys uninterrupted peace as well. Quiet time feeds your creativity. Day dreaming helps you solve writing problems. There are moments when *being* is better than *doing*.

Remember not to overload your schedule. Learn to say no without guilt. Be wise to what is an important and what is an unimportant use of your valuable time. A clutter-free mind, an uncomplicated schedule, and a balanced day bless you with harmony.

Remember one thing: finding the right balance and harmony is not achieved overnight. If you are attentive to your daily doings, if you become aware of all you do, you will learn how to separate the chaff from the grain of your activities and commitments.

JOURNAL PROMPT
Take an inventory of your physical, emotional, intellectual, and creative/spiritual life. Ponder over this question in your journal: *Is my life in balance?*

✢ *Day 340* ✢

TODAY'S PRACTICE
Meditation: "Breathing and Body Scan"   Read, reflect, and journal.

INSPIRATION

When you refine your daily habits, life unfurls peacefully and contentment infuses your day. You also increase productivity and further hone your writing skill.

Remember that a commitment of 21 consecutive days is a strong foundation for making anything a daily habit. Guess what? You have 21 days left in this month's posts, so let's do it. Let's begin practicing whatever discipline you have neglected. Imagine how wonderful you will feel when you have tamed it by the beginning of a new year. Then you will be able to add one or two new goals and live the year you truly wanted!

But wait! No hurry! One baby step at a time. Begin slowly.

If meditation was your challenge, let's see it disappear by the end of this month. From the guided *Meditations for Mindful Writers* collection, choose the "Mountain and Lotus" in which you are asked to visualize yourself as a mountain. Notice how your posture improves your breathing. You feel grounded, balanced, still. As the meditation progresses, the imagery of a lotus blossoming at your heart center expands your chest and makes your heart swell with peace, love, and joy.

Or you could choose, "Walking Through the Forest" or "Gratitude." Try different meditations and see which ones work best for you.

JOURNAL PROMPT

In your journal today, strategize how you would use the rest of the days of this month to work on one of the five disciplines to make it part of your daily schedule.

❧ *Day 341* ☙

TODAY'S PRACTICE

Meditation: "Breathing and Body Scan"   Read, reflect, and journal.

Inspiration

Did you know that being generous with others, through acts of encouragement and goodwill, and even reading an uplifting story to your children – all such angelic actions – boost your immune system? Sometimes it takes the smallest gesture to make the difference in someone's life, and your own.

I was deeply touched when a guest-host at the Online Mindful Writers Group surprised me with words of gratitude. "What an amazing wealth of knowledge, encouragement, and inspiration we've received on this year-long Mindful Writers journey," she wrote. "From Madhu's teaching and advice to all the wonderful guest hosts throughout the year, each with their unique blend of knowledge and experience! Thank you all!!"

She continued, "The other members of this group are encouraging, caring, and motivated me with their daily posts. The public disclosure of their gracious feelings in return gave me pleasure and encouraged me to keep going."

I journaled about that post the day it was written and genuinely felt good about myself. So many people influence us through their work, but we tend to forget how they pulled us toward our goal or nudged us to realize our life's purpose. The influence of these special people never leaves us. When you are faced with a difficult situation, recall the encouraging words, compliments and advice of such gracious people, and imagine how they would handle the situation. They would provide the moral strength you need through your journal or inner whispers.

Pay homage to such people by remembering them if they have passed. If they are still living, call them to say how grateful you feel, send a complimentary email, or write a note of appreciation. In addition to honoring them, pay it forward by inspiring, motivating, and physically helping others.

Journal Prompt

Journal about someone who positively influenced your life. What did this person say or do that made such a difference? Imagine how they might feel if you called them or mailed a note.

⚘ *Day 342* ⚘

TODAY'S PRACTICE

Meditation: "Breathing and Body Scan"   Read, reflect, and journal.

INSPIRATION

I lost my parents, bother, brother-in-law, nephew, and then a grandnephew within the span of ten years. Just when the pain of separation, the crying, the sobbing, the mourning subsided, I began to contemplate my own mortality. Thoughts that I too could die at any moment kept circling my mind. I wondered if death would come quickly, or if I would die of old age.

Through years of journaling and reading about death in religious scriptures, I chewed and digested wisdom about the fragility of human life and its impermanence. My own fiction reflects a keen interest in death and dying. Now, at the back of my mind, I'm finally a lot more comfortable with the thought of my own demise. What surprises me the most about these years is that the contemplation of death has helped me fearlessly face the thought. When the time comes, death won't have to drag me. I'll see to it that I willingly follow whatever it is that happens when I die.

Since befriending the thought of my own death, my mind is clearer, positive and joyous. I get up in the morning with zest for the day, for life. I use this enthusiasm in my writing, in my relationships, in whatever I do.

Remind yourself that you are the only one responsible to make your goals come true. Only you can be responsible for your future hopes and aspirations, and for making your dreams real. Keep treading the writer's path. Believe in yourself and be open to taking advantage when opportunities present themselves.

JOURNAL PROMPT

Journal about your present or future successful self. What do you have to do to reach this juncture in the next three years? Do your best in every opportunity that comes your way. But if you can't do it, let it go. Don't dwell on negativity. Focus on what went right and is going well.

❧ *Day 343* ☙

TODAY'S PRACTICE

Meditation: "Breathing and Body Scan"   Read, reflect, and journal.

INSPIRATION

If you have been practicing Writing Meditation for more than eleven months now, it may have already become an integral part of your day. You may have even developed a specific pattern that you follow to your own satisfaction. Bravo!

However, if out of the five disciplines there are one or two that you have not been able to practice, jot down two reasons explaining to yourself why this is so. For each reason, write ideas for how you can still turn that around and learn to make it a habit. Try silent meditation of 5-10 minutes instead of the guided meditation that runs for about 15 minutes. If you don't have time to journal, what about moving the practice to a time of day that is more convenient? Is it the walking that you don't do? No problem. Any other nonverbal activity that you find satisfying would be equally beneficial.

This leaves us with reading and writing. If you still find yourself hesitant to do either of these, maybe it's time to start learning how to weave baskets or turn pottery...

Before you sit to write, instead of feeling bored I encourage you to feel excited, so excited that your fingertips tingle. A rush of ideas may or may not circle your mind, but the thrill of writing for the sake of writing must be present. As you write one sentence, then the second and the third, before you know it the creative flow will come out in a stream of sentences. The pleasurable flow affects your behavior. You feel so good.

JOURNAL PROMPT

Journal about the daily rhythms that Writing Meditation Practice has helped you develop. Does the pattern of your practice positively affect the rest of your day?

✌ *Day 344* ✍

TODAY'S PRACTICE

Meditation: "Breathing and Body Scan"   Read, reflect, and journal.

INSPIRATION

In his essay, "The Lesson of the Lilac," the beloved spirituality teacher Eknath Easwaran describes how every morning from the window of his dining room he looked at a lilac bush. In spring, the scent of its opulent blossoms brought heady perfume his way. This heavenly experience continued for about three weeks. Then one day he noticed the delicate flowers turning brown. Their fragrance no longer filled the air. The tiny blossoms had taken their time to bloom, then flourish and fade.

On the opposite end, a pine tree grows for thousands of years before it dies but it too takes its own time to grow. "Nature does not hurry," writes Lao Tzu, "yet everything is accomplished."

You have your own pace, your own timing, and your own direction. Honor it. Don't compare your writing speed, productivity, or growth with anyone else's. It may take you one or two or even more years to write a book. Certainly, I know many writers who write two to three books in a year but why compare apples and oranges? Consider yourself to be the pine while other writers are the lilac. You both have particular strengths, unique characteristics, and singular traits.

You are on a writing journey inside and outside. It is not a race. Your aim is to attain your goal. You are heading toward a purpose. Year after year you accumulate the good work you put in each day. Be proud of what you are working toward. And enjoy the progress you are making along the way.

Your practice has been built one day at a time. You are coming out of the fog of what you thought you were and seeing what you have become and could become in the future. You are moving closer to your true self, witnessing yourself in meditation, noticing your strengths, and discovering things you can improve while pouring out your emotions on the page. You have come a long way on your path, dear reader, at your own speed.

JOURNAL PROMPT

Have you been keeping track of your daily activities? What have you noticed? Does your daily routine detract or interfere with coming closer to your true self? Make a list of things you can change to help move closer to your goals.

☙ *Day 345* ☙

TODAY'S PRACTICE

Meditation: "Breathing and Body Scan"   Read, reflect, and journal.

INSPIRATION

Think about the goals you had planned that you have reached this year. Thanks to your Writing Meditation Practice, you are more kind to yourself, compassionate with others, and more forgiving and generous. Look around you, take a few deep inhales and exhales, take in the people in your life and your surroundings, then be thankful for being here now. You have come a long way, pilgrim! You have made sacrifices to be here. You have given up something to make this pilgrimage, to learn new disciplines, and to unlearn old habits. Pat yourself on the back.

How had you imagined the sacred space in which your personal Power Spot is centered? Can you see it more clearly now? Are you glad you traveled all this way? Are there certain things that you're still holding on to that you must let go of? What must you shift in order to journey the rest of this way to arrive at the center of your being?

Fearlessly you communicated to your family members just how important this practice was going to be for you; did it work? Were you courageous enough to say "no" to some requests that did not align with your goals? Rejoice!

On this journey of self-discovery, there are always bumps along the way. But don't let them derail you. Each day has a fresh start. Take long and deep breaths, clear and calm your mind, and fill your heart with kindness and compassion for the slow cultivation of your Sacred Power Spot. It has blossomed in your heart and is visible from afar. Watch it fully bloom as you voyage to the end!

JOURNAL PROMPT

Imagine the pilgrimage center is a cave. Who do you think is dwelling there? When you enter and behold a wiseman or a wisewoman, what will you say or ask? What would they say?

⟳ *Day 346* ⟲

TODAY'S PRACTICE

Meditation: "Breathing and Body Scan"   Read, reflect, and journal.

INSPIRATION

When you have fulfilled the basic necessities of life and are financially comfortable, it is common to wish for "something more." Movies, popular music, and museums can satisfy your cravings, as can dancing, singing, and painting. But perhaps what you'd find most satisfying are stories – writing them, listening to them, reading them. Storytelling around a fire pit was the most ancient kind of entertainment. Stories have quenched the human need for emotional and spiritual sustenance beyond food and shelter. When you listen to them, your worries and concerns temporarily drop off and are replaced with a sense of freedom from worldly fetters.

Reading or listening to a story rewards you with a dose of "feel good hormone," dopamine. Such an impact can be both terrifying and exhilarating at the same time. As writers, we have an opportunity to help readers navigate their outer world and come to terms with myriad emotions. At the same time, this opportunity comes with enormous responsibility. If a single reader comes away with a greater awareness of inner self and feels inspired, then our storytelling has been worthwhile.

We tell stories to nourish hearts and souls. Those stories take readers deep inside themselves and make them understand the feelings and emotions of the characters.

Imagine the times when there were no schools, no libraries, no Google! The only way to educate and inform people was by narrating myths, parables, and legends orally and through visual arts. People were warned about dangers, explained the inexplicable, and shared what was unknown and unexpected. The characters stayed with the readers, narrating universal themes that exist in every culture, in every religion, in every corner of the earth.

JOURNAL PROMPT
Journal about the different ways your story might impact your readers.

☙ Day 347 ❧

TODAY'S PRACTICE
Meditation: "Breathing and Body Scan"   Read, reflect, and journal.

INSPIRATION
In today's world, you're faced with a constant bombardment of information and social media overload. You are pressed for time, hurried, and not even conscious how overwhelmed you are. Writing Meditation Practice trains you to slow down. Being slow does not imply being sluggish. In a time when doing multiple things at once and rushing are considered positives, being unhurried is a good thing to cultivate. A calm and quiet mind is a kind mind. Don't get caught up

in the rat race which society pushes you to join. Do one thing at a time with an undivided mind.

Each thought is a seed that turns into an action and words. In time, those thoughts bear fruit. Remember the hurried seeds you sow today won't result in fruit as sweet or ripe as possible. An unhurried mind opens the door to new ideas. Irrespective of the circumstances you may find yourself in, stay calm. A sound mind is never distracted; it is kind and concentrated.

Knowledge easily available and in abundance distracts. You often don't take the time to marvel at one thing. What would help you to relish the things you have longer? What would inspire you to discover the extraordinary in the ordinary? What would make you more mindful?

Slowing down! Reading slows you down. Stories give you the depth to empathize with the characters. Page after page you come to understand their complex characteristics as you reflect upon their motivations and viewpoints. You gain empathy from fiction and hopefully it seeps into your real life.

JOURNAL PROMPT

Journal about the tasks you do in a hurry that you would love to have more time to indulge in.

---

৩ *Day 348* ৩

TODAY'S PRACTICE

Meditation: "Breathing and Body Scan"   Read, reflect, and journal.

INSPIRATION

Practicing any fine art is good training in mindfulness. Attention and awareness deepen and enhance the senses of sight, hearing, and movement. The regular practice of any of the fine arts does not only hone skill in that particular art but also develops a keen sense of observation and cultivates appreciation of beauty.

You can learn to look at a single object or marvel at the view of a scene from different angles and observe how it changes from moment to moment. While painting a landscape, you might observe how shapes, shadows, light, even colors change. A painting recreates what its maker sees into something new based on mood, atmosphere, and of course the image itself.

An artist shows the onlooker certain details or a perspective the naked eye may not see – the detail and delicacy of a flower, or a butterfly, or a bug that you may otherwise easily pass by. When you paint a person or creature, a fruit or a flower, do you think it studies you the way you study it?

In an artwork, a moment is arrested in time. A photograph "freezes" the moment as an image, a poem or a story in words, while a musical piece recreates it in song. All these I call finer things in life. Art elevates us from the mundane existence to an aesthetic, even spiritual sphere.

JOURNAL PROMPT

Is there a painting, a photo, a song, or a story that inspires you so much that you go back to it repeatedly? What is it about this artwork that intrigues you?

ঌ *Day 349* ৶

TODAY'S PRACTICE

Meditation: "Arriving Home"   Read, reflect, and journal.

INSPIRATION

Most authors draw on some of their own life experiences to fuel the journey of their fictional characters. When a writer transfers personal feelings onto their character, the story comes alive. Readers cry, laugh, or hurt when the characters cry, laugh, or feel pain. The readers physically experience the emotions as they read. Great stories help readers navigate their own lives' obstacles and upheavals.

People of different world cultures and various religions live very differently. Each person's and each family's circumstances are unique.

But reading builds bridges. Stories set in other cultures expand our horizons far beyond the geographical confines of where we live.

While in some cultures the natural world takes center stage, in others family relationships and neighborhoods matter most. And yet in another culture, single-family units are supreme. But each of these peoples have one thing in common – they tell, listen to, or read stories. In the beginning, their history, culture, and belief system were passed down from generation to generation either orally or in drawings, later through written text and advanced dance-drama form.

Reading legends, folklore, and epics from other cultures teaches us that we may look different, live differently, and express ourselves in different manners, but at the core of our being, we have the same primordial questions, the same fears, the same hopes and desires and dreams.

JOURNAL PROMPT

What aspect of your culture or daily life would you most want to tell someone from a future time or different culture?

ঙ *Day 350* ৬৮

TODAY'S PRACTICE

Meditation: "Arriving Home"   Read, reflect, and journal.

INSPIRATION

The spiritual space that we've created here together in this guidebook is as safe and secure as the Sacred Power Spot where you sit at home to practice. This daily practice creates a presence that grounds you for a day in a meaningful way. An energy stirs and comes alive as you practice and becomes relevant to your writing life. In meditation and journaling, freely expressing your thoughts and feelings is like prying open an oyster and discovering a pearl within.

Jot down anything that may be enclosing the pearl like the beauty of your intentions for the New Year. Make sure when you repeat the practice next year, it turns out even better and more energized. Repeat to yourself your intention to practice meditation; the intention to journal; the intention to read, write, walk. The sincerity of your intentions is the key. Implementing it turns into success.

There is power in discovering a genuine practice. There is power in mutual learning and teaching. In meditating, journaling three pages on a writing prompt, or mindfully reading a suggested book, you have safeguarded your adventurous journey toward the unknown. Now you are almost there.

You have walked with humility. You have experienced the thrill of progressing in your practice. You have been willing to learn something new each day. Now is the time to ask bold questions from yourself that you have hesitated to answer before. *How does it feel? Are you closer to your Authentic Self? Has something wonderful happened yet?*

JOURNAL PROMPT

Which dormant passion or emotion have you kept hidden that you hesitate to awaken? Why not identify it on the pages of your notebook today? Even if it tenses you up. You may be surprised to find your heart wide open after you have poured it on the pages.

‿ *Day 351* ↲

TODAY'S PRACTICE

Meditation: "Arriving Home"   Read, reflect, and journal.

INSPIRATION

To write a powerful book you must select a potent theme with a poignant story. No classic and enduring volume has been composed on the ho-hum life of an insect, grass, or mud. But on the other hand, there was a movie made about a housefly that I thoroughly enjoyed which taught a lesson or two. And what is creativity if not an enhanced way of recreating the ordinary activities into impressive artwork! Whatever we do, when we do it with full attention and awareness – in other words, mindfulness – it turns into art.

An artistic mind observes a thing in a special way, expressing it creatively. It begins with an idea. Or it might even end with the idea, such as the artist Duchamp who submitted an artwork to the Society of Independent Artists' salon in New York of an upside-down urinal, signed and dated with the appellation "R. Mutt, 1917," and titled *Fountain*. (You can Google the rest of the story.) A hundred years, later, Mike Bidlo made Fractured Fountain (2015) as an edition of eight works influenced by Duchamp's "original." Such artworks have provided countless artists with something of a starting pistol for the idea of art-as-concept in the twentieth and twenty-first centuries.

What does Duchamp's bold action teach writers? If you have an idea for a story but it sounds rubbish, go ahead and write it anyway. Any first draft is almost always junky.

The first draft is for your eyes only. You can rewrite, revise, and edit that draft but you can't do anything with a blank page. Allow yourself to be bold and crappy. Just write! With each revision, you are bound to get better, possibly breaking literary boundaries for future generations to marvel at. Persistence and fearlessness are the key to maturing from an amateur to a professional writer.

When you write alone at your Power Spot, with all the research you have done and all the books you have read, all that becomes an integral part of your work-in-progress. It is the most intimate part of your writing life. No one needs to see you at the moment. It would be like a magician showing the secrets of their tricks before you watch them perform.

If the artist Duchamp could submit an upside-down urinal, titled *Fountain*, to the Society of Independent Artists' salon in New York in 1917 that still inspires twenty-first century sculptors and painters, why can't you write a piece with a topic you falsely believe is crappy?

JOURNAL PROMPT

What are your demons, your spiritual discontent, that you are too afraid to admit even to yourself? Journal about it freely for as many pages as you need. Don't stop to think. Just write.

⤷ *Day 352* ⤶

TODAY'S PRACTICE
Meditation: "Arriving Home"   Read, reflect, and journal.

INSPIRATION

In your writing, focus on your strengths. As I mentioned elsewhere, I am contemplative by nature. I have an insatiable appetite for knowing human life and its dilemmas. I'm a voracious reader of theology and aesthetics, which is the reason I write about creativity and spirituality. So I encourage you to also play to your strengths. If you feel pathos, then write about the suffering of people. Go deep into their hearts. Let your stories bring solace to them, as well as any sadness you observe. If you have a sense of humor, let yourself be hilarious.

If you are good with dialogue, let your characters talk, downplaying the narrative. If you are great at delineating settings, magnetize readers with details in the landscapes or interiors. Always keep in mind what you are good at and concentrate on that talent. Let your secondary strengths enhance your primary one.

Writing is as hard for a beginner as it is for the best among us. But the only way to overcome initial difficulties is to keep writing. That's the only way to penetrate the process of writing and to enhance your skill. Only through daily writing will your unique voice and style begin to reveal themselves to you.

There are hundreds of writers in your genre who are pathos filled, contemplative, or funny, but don't mind them. You don't have to compete with them. Use them for your research. How do they accomplish what you want to do? Remember you have your own way of expressing things. Think of the nightscapes of Rembrandt. Compare them with Van Gogh's spiraling starry nights. What Rembrandt saw in the night was all his own. Make your night skies as original as the way these painters did; no one had seen such artworks before and no one will paint like that again.

JOURNAL PROMPT
What is your original contribution to writing? Laughter, tears, thoughtfulness, mindfulness, seeing the world, gardening, cooking?

⤳ *Day 353* ⤳

TODAY'S PRACTICE
Meditation: "Arriving Home"   Read, reflect, and journal.

INSPIRATION

In between periods of writing, do you feel anxious that you are not good enough? Do you realize that almost all writers, from the fledgling to award-winning and bestselling authors, battle the same anxiety?

So when you are judging your writing, battling with yourself, you versus you, remember this is part of being a creative person. Only when you are deep into writing does this feeling cease. From the moment you wake up, make coffee, scramble eggs, and pack lunches, let some part of you focus on the moment when you will go to your Power Spot and get back to work. You should be always seeking to improve. Not seeking perfection, however. Perfection is like the horizon no one actually reaches because it keeps moving away from you.

Keep in mind that all your anxiety arises from deep discomfort, an unspecified anxiety about your work-in-progress. You may have an impulse to uncover something that is troubling you, and you want to write about it. The impulse to write is potent. You likely don't know where it will take you. What will it lead to? But you must return to your desk to explain it over and over again.

Publication should be the last thing on your mind. Your body, heart, and mind are writing to explain whatever it is that has taken hold of you. Allow yourself to become fully focused on writing a rip-roaring story that will offer wisdom and entertainment to your readers. Writing stories for providing pleasure to your readers is not easy; it is divine work.

JOURNAL PROMPT

I feel a burden has been taken from my shoulders when I finish writing a short story, an essay, a novel, or a nonfiction book. Journal about how writing "The End" feels to you.

∾ *Day 354* ⌣

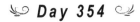

TODAY'S PRACTICE
Meditation: "Arriving Home"   Read, reflect, and journal.

INSPIRATION

The act of writing is intimate. The characters in your head become real to you. Yet it is also isolating. This is not very different from reading. Other instances of aloneness are when you allow or encourage your mind to unplug from the daily monotony. In writing, reading, sleeping, or just daydreaming, you intentionally or unintentionally move into the world of imagination and creativity. Under such circumstances, the muses show up.

New ideas and insights come when you write, read, or dream. When an idea pops up in your mind, mull over it. The more vigilant you are about delaying writing it down, the more it develops into a mature thought. Then surrender it on the page. It will reveal itself most accurately as an emotional movement that you may use in your current work or save for later.

But you must finish the thought by writing it down! The gem will shine on the paper after the cutting is thoroughly done in your mind.

Don't get anxious about one story or one essay that you are not happy with. Understand that you are not writing just that one piece or one book. You are writing a whole body of work. Whenever you feel blocked or are stuck on a small part of your work, remind yourself it is just a passing phase. More ideas will come. You will continue to write and produce a much bigger body of work than what you have now.

JOURNAL PROMPT

Do you get discouraged in the middle of creating an article, a novel, or a nonfiction volume? Does writing day in and day out make you feel lonely? Sit back and think of the writing you have done so far. Journal about the inspirational moments that make it all worthwhile.

ᏬᎾ *Day 355* ᏬᎭ

TODAY'S PRACTICE

Meditation: "Arriving Home"   Read, reflect, and journal.

INSPIRATION

At age forty with a doctoral degree, and at age fifty with a decade of teaching behind me, I still felt I had not yet found my way. More than half of my life had passed, yet I believed that *I had not found my calling!*

The more I read, the more satiated I felt. At the core of world religions was the lesson that to live a contented and joy-filled life was to live simply and fully. The lesson is simple but difficult to cultivate. Eventually, I developed a regimen of the five practices with which you are by now familiar. They guided me on the path to a mindful living and spirited life. Even at the current phase of my life, I see progress and note areas where I can improve.

Reading has made me realize that those primordial questions about the universe only beget more questions. There are no definite answers. I have to learn to be satisfied with the unknown, learn to live with the feeling that some questions can never be answered, feel certain in uncertainty. The closest thought parallel to this is one of Buddha's teachings that the only permanent thing is impermanence.

The practice has helped me to go within and experience the source of vitality and pure joy. That experience has made me stop asking unanswerable questions. Having experienced this joy, I'm able to recognize others who too have experienced it. Such a person exudes serenity, equanimity, and inner bliss. You realize it is possible for each and every one of us to experience this. Perhaps the pleasures of stillness, compassion, and wisdom derived from the Writing Meditation Practice are closest to everlasting joy.

JOURNAL PROMPT

Have you found the pathway you are searching for? What do you intend to do to find your way? What questions or goals do you have which may bring you closer to yourself?

ᯪ *Day 356* ᯪ

TODAY'S PRACTICE

Meditation: "Arriving Home"   Read, reflect, and journal.

INSPIRATION

What is spirituality? It is the most elevated part of your psychic life. In this state of mind, you contemplate things that are beyond your grasp: birth, death, and the unknown. You remain open to everything and anything.

In your daily life, you navigate all that is known, logical, acceptable, and predictable. You do not mind exposing yourself to them. Accepting things that are beyond your control and unknown, however – and yet not running away from them – makes you spiritual.

In spirituality you seriously delve into things that are beyond your grasp. You exert all your effort to understand them. Your goal is nothing but to comprehend what Hindus call *samsara*. Then at a certain point you let it all go. You shed your baggage. By becoming detached, you contemplate how to make sense of contradictions.

Such contemplation requires authenticity and purity of heart. No self-judging, no self-criticism, no interpretation of thoughts. This state leads to stillness in meditation and eventually, at a more mature stage, to the sweetness that rises. This experience transforms you. You no longer want to transform what is around you. You begin to savor your own life more fully. You continue to make choices and pursue your goals. But you no longer cling to victories or defeats. They become merely experiences that have enriched your life.

JOURNAL PROMPT

Journal about what "spirituality" means to you. How does what you believe in enhance your day-to-day life and help you answer the primordial questions?

⤷ *Day 357* ⤶

TODAY'S PRACTICE

Meditation: "Arriving Home"   Read, reflect, and journal.

INSPIRATION

Mountaineers climb insurmountable heights because they hear their call. You too have been called to ascend your inner mountain, to narrate unforgettable stories and to live a contented life. So dig deeper, contemplating what you excavate and create. The challenges and difficulties you face stretch your imagination, expand your thinking, and give you opportunities to grow fearless in expressing your ideas and to grow wiser. On this path of self-understanding, growth, and transformation, pay heed to your authentic voice.

When the body is young, and life's physical challenges and rewards engage our zest for living, the need for meaning and purpose goes unnoticed. Our need to find answers to ultimate questions usually surfaces later. We ask, *Is this all there is?* Starting from age fifty or so, there stirs a deep-seated need for meaning and purpose in life.

Fortunately, there are many paths which guide us toward peace and wisdom. Walking on such a path trains the mind well, protecting the body and allowing it to heal itself. One such path is Writing Meditation Practice. Self-awareness heals mind and body. The Buddha says, "You have no better friend than a well-trained mind – and no worse enemy than an untrained mind." Put all your effort in training the mind with WMP.

Compassion and wisdom involve connection, appreciation, and happiness for oneself and others. With a kind heart and wise mind, emotional balance is easy to acquire. The more we cultivate kindness, the wiser we become.

JOURNAL PROMPT

Are you "following your bliss" yet? If not, ask yourself in your journal, What is it that my heart desires? Why am I not able to begin what I truly desire to do? What is keeping me from taking my turn?

⊱ *Day 358* ⊰

TODAY'S PRACTICE

Meditation: "Breathing and Body Scan"   Read, reflect, and journal.

INSPIRATION

How we spend our days, wrote Annie Dillard, "is how we spend our lives."

No matter what else you do during the day, always remember to practice the disciplines. Together meditation and journaling strengthen your concentration and increase productivity. A nonverbal activity creates space in which to think and receive ideas and insights about your work in progress. Reading introduces you to other writers' voices and styles, which stretches your imagination. Finally, let the writing process flow through your body like blood, making you feel alive and energized.

Whether you follow the complete Writing Meditation Practice, or a few of the five disciplines, or merely simply read the daily inspiration and journaling prompt, I hope this year-long guide is resonating with you. I hope you sit at your Personal Power Spot to practice. Allow the ideas that are attracted by your being and thinking to come to you. And finally, don't just call yourself a writer; *be* a writer. Sit and write as long as you possibly can.

JOURNAL PROMPT

When you started working with this book, what had you planned for your mindful writing journey? Are you surprised at what you have accomplished so far? What did you not yet accomplish? Journal about it. Congratulate yourself for what you have achieved, and be gentle with yourself about what you haven't. We still have two days left for you to create a plan that you can practice for the future.

～ *Day 359* ～

TODAY'S PRACTICE

Meditation: "Awakening the Senses"   Read, reflect, and journal.

INSPIRATION

The daily habit of Writing Meditation Practice has brought me closer to myself. I've discovered joy amid pain and suffering, joy amid sitting, joy amid peace and joy amid creativity. This is the reason I felt a deepening urge to share this practice with whomever would listen. And more importantly, why I felt compelled to share the personalized practice with you, dear reader.

When the joy of practice overflowed and I could no longer contain it, I was ready to shout it from the rooftops. I wanted you to feel one with the "other," to feel aligned with the universe, to see yourself in the eyes of the one you didn't know yet. I wanted you to feel grounded, to harmonize your life, to experience joy and feel blessed whenever you struggle to create.

The more you practice, the closer you come to being your Authentic Self. And in being, and then finally becoming your true self, you understand what it is to know that all human beings have a true self. This realization softens your heart.

One more thing that years of Writing Meditation Practice has made me realize. When the five disciplines harmonize, they stir finer qualities. These qualities seem to emerge as byproducts without your paying deliberate attention to them.

You may have already cultivated them, but perhaps they have not yet come to your sphere of consciousness. Sense them. Feel them. Discover them. Here is the list:

- *Being physically present in the moment*
- *Gratitude*
- *Generosity*

- *Forgiveness*
- *Fearlessness*
- *Patience*
- *Contentment*

These traits have subtly elevated the quality of my familial, social, creative, and spiritual life. My mind uncluttered, my days simplified, these positives keep nourishing my artistic and spiritual growth.

When I became aware of the side benefit of Writing Meditation Practice, I felt a tenderness within myself, also a *tenderness* about everyone and everything in the world around me.

I feel *wonder* and *awe* not only from being in nature but from looking at ordinary things as if seeing them for the first time. Being alive, having the gift of one more day after waking up well rested, enjoying a delicious first meal of the day with the man I adore, writing what is swirling in my heart-mind and so on. You get the picture.

Each time I remind myself that *this* moment is filled with magic and mystery, my appreciation for the universe deepens. I contemplate how imagination and inspiration are rooted in *wonderment*. The feeling I am left with is the *joy of contentment*.

Writing Meditation Practice has brought me closer to you via my Authentic Self. I invite you to keep getting closer to your Authentic Self until you're one with it.

JOURNAL PROMPT
Which of your positive qualities let you penetrate deeper within yourself and touch the finer feelings?

✒ *Day 360* ✒

TODAY'S PRACTICE
Meditation: "Arriving Home"   Read, reflect, and journal.

Inspiration

The final morning of our arduous yet fulfilling, calming, heart-widening year-long journey has arrived. Tomorrow we return to where we started, but with our minds sharpened and hearts wide open. I hope the year provided you perspectives on every significant aspect of your life: physical, emotional, intellectual, creative, and spiritual. It underlined how fundamental regular writing, reading, and spiritual matters are for your well-being, and how important emotional bonds are in familial relations and friendships.

You have finished reading the book. That was the first rough look. Now you may start all over again. From tomorrow, explore the gift of each day as it unfurls, partly as you know and partly in some other way. But one thing is certain – the habits of meditation, journaling, reading, writing, and walking have now become an integral part of your being.

You'll continue to practice these disciplines for the sake of your well-being. You'll take a leap of faith to discover what blessings and rewards a second year reveals. Allow yourself to focus attention on the things that you have learned, things that matter to you, so that by the end of the next twelve months, you are wiser and kinder still and continue to strengthen your intentions, making sure they benefit you and make you feel fulfilled.

Be thankful to your heart-mind (*Buddhacitta*) that nudged you to buy this book of the long journey to grow, learn, and create. As I wrote each day to motivate and encourage you to practice Writing Meditation, I felt myself growing, learning, and creating. My commitment and determination to write for you, dear reader, inspired me to move forward as a writer and deeper inward in my spiritual life. I find your validation for this book to be the reward. It has allowed me to extend the practice in expanding circles. I wish you another fearless, authentic, and productive journey of twelve months.

End of Year Prompt

Ask yourself why you set out on this year-long voyage of self-discovery. What did you gain from this daily adventure? Journal about the fearless, authentic, and productive journey of the next twelve months.

❧ POSTSCRIPT ❧

Three cheers for completing your year-long journey of mindful writing meditation practice! Today is a good day to journal! Let yourself be spontaneous, honest, and focused on journaling in detail what you learned about yourself and your writing life this year. Write until your wrist is tired, until your mind can't think of anything else about the last twelve months of adventure you just completed. Here are a few questions to get you started.

- How do you feel? Overwhelmed? Content? Proud?

- How is your focus on daily tasks now compared to before you began this journey?

- How do you feel, artistically and spiritually? Do you feel more empowered?

- Do you find yourself going deeper into meditating, journaling, creating, and reading than ever before?

- How has your writing skill and productivity benefitted?

- How has your sense of awe and wonder over nature and the simple things in daily life changed?

- Have you started to travel or have you become more mindful during your regular travels?

- Do you enjoy writing with a group or on retreats?

- Do you spend time in solitude?

- What small daily goals have you added?

- What do you now view as your life's purpose?

There are so many questions. If the year has passed by too fast, that is okay. You have cultivated a good daily habit. What about starting again?

UNBLOCK YOUR CREATIVE FLOW

And then again? Remember, the third time is the best time. Three is a magic number. We can sow the seed of going on this journey again and then again and experience where we arrive – back home, wiser, more skilled, stronger. Trust me. I have been doing this since 2011.

Each month you assembled elements of an integrated body, a thinking heart, and a feeling mind. You are less mindless and better at being mindful. This was the sowing stage where you worked at developing attention and awareness. You learned how to practice breathing and reduce the number of passing thoughts. Pouring those thoughts that persisted and emotions that emerged on the pages of your journal has become a habit now. Who can be a better companion than your own notebook, your personal therapist? Save it forever or burn it after three or five years. That is your choice.

In your own practice of reading, what new genre did you add to your reading list? Were the number of books you read more than ever before? Have you become a faster reader? Did you try your hand at poetry? Kudos! The seeds you've sown have sprouted!

Did you carve out time for a walk outdoors or to engage in a nonverbal activity? Have you let yourself daydream, opening the windows of your mind to let ideas fly that inspire new works? Have you experienced the unblocking of your difficulties in regard to your writing or revising?

Walking in nature is one way to let the birds of inspiration twitter in your mind. Another way to get inspired is to travel – to another town, state, or country, or even a new place in your hometown. Did you experience new people, places, cuisines, sights, sounds, and tastes? Did such remarkable moments enrich your creative vocabulary and artistic vision?

Travel delights and thrills. Don't you agree? The world has so much to offer – awe and wonder – but only if we let it. Natural as well as urban places give us opportunities for warm interactions with friendly people we previously imagined as foreigners, even aliens. By traveling you make memories to bring back, so you can enjoy them in the quiet of your home sweet home.

Equally inspiring is returning to the silence and solitude of your Sacred Power Spot. Have you rethought your daily routine? Are there parts of your day that have lost meaning? What could you replace them with? What can you add that would enhance and enrich your day and life? By now you know this simple tweaking of daily goals is what assures your life's purpose and becomes your reality.

By now you are also aware how many other people have a desire to write. They begin a project with gusto, then the initial enthusiasm dissipates – they find it difficult to continue. Were you one of those in the past? Congratulate yourself now. You did not give up, because you are still with me. Something in you assured you that you could do this. You found motivation in practicing Writing Meditation. You have been encouraged, and feel charged and ready to continue, filled with physical vigor and mental vitality to begin another year of Writing Meditation Practice.

Your intention to go on this journey has been actualized. You are now bound to realize your dream of getting fresh ideas, innovative thoughts, and the passion to gather and shape them into more stories, essay ideas, or another novel. Get a book published!

You have learned how to entice the muse to arrive. It may not have been easy in the beginning. But you have learned how to affirm your intention, writing for hours without censoring or curtailing what needed to be said. You have cultivated courage, determination, and patience. Your mindset has grown and changed. You've been introduced to the braided practices of meditation, journaling, writing, reading, and walking in nature. Most importantly you will continue to cultivate mindfulness to live a creative and peaceful life.

You have stirred the divine within, your true and Authentic Self, your inner source of creativity and spirituality. It is always with you. Once you are linked with it, you will never lose it. Has the magic begun yet? I hope Writing Meditation Practice has helped you hone the fluidity of creativity as much as it has refined the logical side of your writing. More importantly, I hope that you now feel your integrated inner self reflects in a more harmonious outer world.

FEAR OF DEATH

Throughout this year, we have made attempts to study ourselves in every way possible. This self-introspection and contemplation has a natural outcome. It makes us conscious of our own death. As it is, we tend to push the thought of death to the back of our minds. Why is this so? It is one of our deepest fears. Like twins, our breath and the thought of death stay beside us all our lives. But ultimately what is more important – the thought of death, or living fully in the present moment?

When you make breath your constant companion, the fear recedes, and for some of us it leaves. Breath brings you to the present moment. It makes you aware of the vibrant and vital present in which you are living. When you lose awareness of the present moment, you hover between thoughts of past and future. Then that fear of death that resides permanently in your mind pushes through and surfaces. In the meantime, the present moment passes you by.

Awareness of the breath brings you gently back to the present, in which you are alive here and now. So often, it happens that the mind pulls you back to the past or pushes you to the future. That is the nature of the mind. But by now you have learned the skill of bringing your attention back to the breath. You only use the powers of remembering and envisioning when you are either planning for the future or need to reference a past experience for a relevant task.

It is not the *fact* of death that scares you, but rather the *fear* of death. Deep in your gut you know what is born must die. You accept this fact, yet you ask when, where, how are you going to die? These incessant questions make you miserable because they are unanswerable. Better to focus on the now. Later, why regret that you did not enjoy the *present moment* when you could? Accept the present as it is. Soon something is bound to change.

The power of language, literature, and the arts raises humans above the rest of the animal kingdom. Emotion and feelings are uniquely human. Each of us has a divine spark; each writer has a unique voice, but this spark, this voice, is dormant under layers of debris, enclosed in a hard shell. Each of us can liberate this voice by excavating layer after layer of muck under which lays a jewel mine – gems of intuitive sense, insights, imagination, and creativity. The tools of excavation are meditation, journaling, reading, walking in nature, and writing or any arts.

When Writing Meditation Practice links you intimately with your Authentic Self, the universe is able to send messages to you in myriad ways as it functions only in the present moment. Communication at the subliminal level is possible only in the now. Imagination and creativity flow only in the eternal now. When you learn to be in the present moment, food tastes yummier, colors are more vibrant, music affects you at a visceral level, and your mind is spacious and boundless. You open to the possibility of synchronicities, insights, and novel ideas. Being one with your Authentic Self makes you fearless. You become unafraid of an unknown future. As your Authentic Self is always present, you gain confidence and feel compassionate for yourself.

HUMANITY AND DIVINITY DWELL WITHIN

Mostly, you tend to forget that you are not only a physical being but a creative and spiritual being as well. This is so because you tend to live outside yourself. But this journey has taught you that humanity and divinity dwell deep within.

Having lived long enough, I no longer identify myself with my constantly changing body. But I used to, as most people do. They live in and for their physical body. They try to look younger and prettier. It's admirable to watch people taking good care of their health, but trying to reach an unreachable ideal is foolish. You can never be eighteen again!

At the core of your being, you are not merely physical. You are one with an inner divinity that inspires you to create. In turn, creativity stirs humanity's wisdom and compassion that lead to spirituality. You are happier and more peaceful when you identify with your Authentic Self.

At some point in your life, when you felt unsatisfied, you may have wondered, *Is this all there is?* Your desires kept increasing. Physical gratification was unable to satisfy emotional and spiritual problems. You began looking elsewhere for the solution. This book has allowed you to discover things within, beyond those physical rewards.

Some also feel they have nonphysical needs but do not know how to satisfy them. They believe youth, power, possessions, and prestige will bring them satisfaction. Yet even when they obtain these things, they remain dissatisfied. Unfortunately most die without ever knowing their inner humanity and spirituality, without realizing their outer creativity links them to their creator, to pure spirit, to the Authentic Self.

The wisdom traditions of the world have a great deal to teach about the true self. They teach that we are much more than our body. As a student of world religions, I was introduced to artistic endeavors, self-contemplation, and self-witnessing. These teachings ingrained in me the value of treating my body as an inner shrine in which the pure spirit dwelled. Practicing thus, I became aware of my divine Self within, which connected me deeper to my creativity, painting, writing, nature, and to the rest of the world. This in turn led me to develop Writing Meditation Practice.

We cannot live like animals do. We cannot live in threat of our lives, ever vigilant, constantly feeling insecure. At the same time, we cannot live purely to satisfy personal desires. That way never leads to peace, contentment, or joy, though enjoying these is your birthright. As humans, we must take care of our changing bodies in every way we can, but nothing else matters if we do not become aware of our unchanging inner Self.

You can certainly change your attitude toward yourself about how to live your daily life. And now you have the tools, five disciplines to help connect to your pure spirit, your Authentic Self.

Dear reader, your most important task is to affirm your own creative work and originality in the world through your writer's unique voice, and to grow and transform yourself. Every artistic person's task is to elevate their readers, listeners, and onlookers through their writings, music, and works of visual arts. By ignoring the path to the divine spark within, the source of your flow, you not only hide your genuine voice from yourself but also cheat yourself of the vitality of human life.

However small or great your achievement has been, its real value is that you have birthed it with your own effort and in your own way. Each of your creations represents something that never existed before – something original and unique.

What thoughts gratify you? What words bring you solace? What actions matter to you? Be present at whatever is happening so that you may think analytically, speak honestly, and act meaningfully. The universe speaks to you in the present moment. When you learn how not to get carried away with success and self-celebration, when you learn not to beat yourself up about your failure, when you learn not to compare yourself with anyone else, wonderful things begin to happen.

Something much more joyful exists beyond successes and failures. You find yourself at the peak of joy and contentment in the daily give and take with your inner guide and people who surround you. You cannot find peace anywhere in the world if you are not first at peace within your own self. When this occurs, you will be able to make peace with the whole world. Your treasure is hidden in the lotus of your heart. Make a space within to let in the divinity and let out the flow of creativity.

For the first time, all of my work as a writer, artist, and teacher of Asian arts and religions has come together. This book draws from my nonfiction, novels, meditations for writers, and my artwork. It is the culmination of everything I've learned and taught over the past three decades. I'm excited to have been able to weave it into a truly comprehensive book to share with fellow artists and writers and those who might be interested in this subject. I have included insights gleaned from my life experiences, what these insights mean to me, and why I considered them important to share.

My hope is that this guidebook will become an invaluable resource for anyone looking to increase productivity, deepen thought and emotion, and sustain concentration that leads to a completed manuscript and a vital life.

Dear reader, I hope that in this adventuring with me, using the tools and discipline of Writing Meditation Practice, you have found the journey not only pleasurable but also transformative. I hope reading and practicing has conjured up a renewed world for you, making you aware of your innate beauty, your true voice, and your Authentic Self.

I hope you share your thoughts and experiences with me via my webpage, www.MadhuBazazWangu.com.

Warmly,
Madhu Bazaz Wangu
April 2023

༄ GUIDED MEDITATIONS ༅
BY MADHU BAZAZ WANGU

Meditation for Mindful Writers:
Body, Heart, Mind

Body: https://cutt.ly/Mji0Dw5

Mindful: https://cutt.ly/MjbH8xy

Heartful: https://cutt.ly/3j32HRy

Meditation for Mindful Writers II:
Sensations, Feelings, Thoughts

Walking through the Forest: https://cutt.ly/Lj1K9Mk

Awakening the Senses: https://cutt.ly/njmJoSj

Mountain and Lotus: https://cutt.ly/ekuL384

Animating Seven Energy Centers: https://cutt.ly/AjU1GyS

Meditation for Mindful Writers III:
Generosity, Gratitude, Self-Compassion and Trust

Spaciousness: https://cutt.ly/TkwVNch

Gratitude: https://cutt.ly/KjaLYBz

Arriving Home: https://cutt.ly/ajNGMC8

Self-Forgiveness and Compassion: https://cutt.ly/TkgGT8w

Breathing and Body Scan: https://cutt.ly/5jcYgcN

⤳ ACKNOWLEDGMENTS ⤳

This book is very personal to me. My work—as a writer, artist, and teacher of Asian arts and religions—has coalesced here. The volume draws from my writings, meditations, and artwork. It is the culmination of everything I've learned and taught. The text between these covers includes what I have gleaned from life experiences, what these mean to me, and why I considered them important to share with others.

But I couldn't have done this without the unconditional love and immense support of my husband, Manoj, and our daughters, Śrimal Wangu Choi and Zoon Wangu. They read and critiqued rough drafts of the manuscript. Their comments and encouragement were invaluable.

My heartfelt homage to my parents, Prem Nath Bazaz and Badri Bazaz, who taught me self-discipline, self-contemplation, and the significance of learning and arts. And deep tribute to my professors: in India, Ratan Parimoo; and in the United States, Fred W. Clothey, Katheryn M. Linduff, Wing-tsit Chan, Juan Adolfo Vazquez, Edwin Floyd, and Diana Eck. I'm grateful to them for molding my foundations that provided me skills and knowledge to grow into who I have become.

I'm most grateful to my multi-talented editor Demi Stevens (Year of the Book Press) for her insights, thoughtful suggestions, and cheering up during the dark days of editing and rewrites. Thank you for creating the exquisite layout and structure of the book.

Heartfelt thanks to Kathleen Shoop, Wende Dikec, Timons Esaias, and Carol Silvis for proofreading, support, and friendship! You have helped me more than you know.

My deepest gratitude to the Online Mindful Writers Group that begins each morning with a stimulating post that animates the day. From the end of 2017 to 2018, OMWG was a weekly site. In 2019 I started daily postings and invited well-established authors as guest-hosts to post something about the practice we follow. In 2020 and 2021, I extended the invitation to post for a week which was graciously accepted. Then from 2022 many generous authors and budding writers accepted my invitation to write for a whole month. A few have served multiple times in the last five years. That tradition will hopefully continue into the future.

I'm grateful to each and every one of the Mindful Writers mentioned below, for taking time out of their busy schedules and inspiring the group to reflect, journal, meditate, get inspired, and lead a creative, artistic, and emotionally and spiritually fulfilling life. Thanks to:

Sudha Balagopal	Eileen Hodgetts	Fritze Roberts
Amy Baverso	Shahrukh Husain	James Robinson
Lorraine Bonzelet	Larry Ivkovich	Larry Schardt
Gloria Bostic	Lori Jones	Linda Schmitmeyer
Deborah Catanese	Lisa Kastner	Kathleen Shoop
Meredith Cohen	Stephanie Keyes	Carol Silvis
Marjorie DeAngelis	Ramona DeFelice Long	Ellen McGrath Smith
Jennifer D. Diamond	Donna S. Lucas	Audrey Snyder
Wende Dikec	Nancy Martin	Donna Snyder-Lucas
Timons Esaias	Janet McClintock	Nancy Springer
Karen Fatica Geiger	Susan Meier	Alicia Stankay
David George	MaryAlice Meli	Martha Swiss
Kathleen George	Mike Morley	Denise Weaver
Kimberly Kurth Gray	Gail Oare	Michele Zirkle
Hilary Hauck	Rudri Bhatt Patel	
Lisa Hering	Renuka Raghavan	

Finally, thank you for reading and rereading *Unblock Your Creative Flow* and making it part of your precious day. Your thoughts and feelings about this book matter to me. Please share them by posting a review on Amazon, Goodreads, Barnes and Noble, or any one of your favorite book sites.

✌ ABOUT THE AUTHOR ✍

The founder of Mindful Writers Groups and Retreats, **DR. MADHU BAZAZ WANGU** has won awards from *Writer's Digest*, Feather Quill, Readers Favorite, Next Generation Indie Book, Indie Excellence, and TAZ Awards. She inspires novice as well as advanced creative people to become better writers and creators, and authentic human beings by following the practice of Writing Meditation.

Madhu shares time-honored practices using personal anecdotes to teach Writing Meditation Practice. The practice is not only entertaining but also life transforming. Introduced to writers in 2011, it provides daily skills, tools and rituals for making yourself the better versions of you.

Madhu has written about her own struggle, trials and tribulations as well as pleasurable experiences that have come her way and taught her what it means to feel awe, wonder and afterglow of creative flow. Currently she is writing her tenth book, the fifth fiction, tentatively titled, *Meaning of My Life.*

Dr. Wangu is a regular workshop presenter at writing conferences. She was the Featured Author at Beaver County Book Fest in 2017, Inaugural Guest at International Indo-American Literary Festival, 2020. That year she won Pennwriters Meritorious Award.

Visit the website
MadhuBazazWangu.com

Read daily posts at
Online Mindful Writers Group
https://cutt.ly/ejcDWXs